The Shame and the Sorrow

EARLY AMERICAN STUDIES

Daniel K. Richter and Kathleen M. Brown, Series Editors

Exploring neglected aspects of our colonial, revolutionary, and early national history and culture, Early American Studies reinterprets familiar themes and events in fresh ways. Interdisciplinary in character, and with a special emphasis on the period from about 1600 to 1850, the series is published in partnership with the McNeil Center for Early American Studies.

A complete list of books in the series is available from the publisher.

The Shame and the Sorrow

Dutch-Amerindian Encounters in New Netherland

Donna Merwick

PENN

University of Pennsylvania Press
Philadelphia

10 9 8 7 6 5 4 3 2 1

Published by
University of Pennsylvania Press
Philadelphia, Pennsylvania 19104-4112

Library of Congress Cataloging-in-Publication Data

Merwick, Donna.
   The shame and the sorrow : Dutch-Amerindian encounters in New Netherland /
Donna Merwick.
      p. cm. — (Early American studies)
   Includes bibliographical references and index.
   ISBN-13: 978-0-8122-3928-7
   ISBN-10: 0-8122-3928-8 (cloth : alk. paper)
      1. New York (State)—History—Colonial period, ca. 1600–1775. 2. New Netherland—
History. 3. Indians of North America—New Netherland—History. 4. Indians of
North America—Wars—New Netherland. I. Title. II. Series.

F122.1.M53 2006
974.7´02–dc22

                                                                    2005055043

For Douglas,
who is also stirred by the mysteries of the past

Contents

List of Maps

Figure 1. Anon., *Niew Amsterdam ofte nue Nieuw Iorx opt TEylant Man (New Amsterdam now New York on the Island of Man[hattan])*, c. 1664, depicting 1650–53. Nationaal Archief, The Netherlands, coll. Leupe Supplement (4.VELH), inv. nr. 619–14.

Soundings

This is the island (Fig. 1). We view it as the mariner does. We see alongshore scenery: the sea edge, coastal craft, and a wharf. Houses of shore-inhabiting people. The town seems timeless. It is still. Set before us like a coastal marker, it seeks only to resemble a profile view constructed long ago for seventeenth-century sailors. It rests in faint, unsteady light. Faded yellow and washed-out browns. "What belongs alongshore," one author has written, "is always faded, for the coastal realm fades everything, shades everything into glim."[1]

The island hides the land behind it. The continent that we know to be there and to which the island is offshore is given no hint of presence. Perhaps we are to think that enough presence is here, here on the ribbon of land between the wilderness of the sea and that of the continent inshore. Perhaps we are to think that the continent is somehow less valuable than the island. Certainly, the houses have resolutely turned their faces from it. Perhaps alongshore is better than inland.

There is an inland, and it is not as serene as the narcotic beauty of the watercolor would have us think. The town is, after all, not outside time but set in history. We know that the artist sketched it around 1664 to depict the early 1650s. We've come to know something about the houses along the strand, something about the warehouses, the fort, and the windmill. Of this maritime people, we've now written life histories. We can give accounts of their politics and the ways of their daily lives. We know that there were also those whom these alongshore people distinguished from themselves by calling them "inlanders," natives. Here, in this scenery, the artist has given them only an incidental presence. A few paddle in open skiffs toward a vessel that is releasing a volley of fire to signal its departure from the harbor. It flies a Dutch flag. Perhaps the inlanders intend to trade. They appear to proceed without fear.

Fear is, in fact, the last thing this seascape wants to convey. There are no signs of conflict, neither in the tranquil present nor left over from earlier years. No rubble of stone or wood, no older foundation stones tell us that this waterfront land was won from another people, those who called this place "the island of the hills." Nothing says that there is still violence between the islanders and inlanders. Like the harbor, the marginal lands that encompass it are all but empty. Set to the left and right, they peter out into lowlands and beaches, bleached out and uninhabited for miles and miles, as far as the eye is given to see. No one is shown farming beyond the town, neither the alongshore people nor the natives. No one toils in woodlands. There is a term that these shore people like to use for their settlements in such places: quiet possession.[2] Surely this is as quiet as quiet possession comes.

Yet being set in history, time will not let the dreamlike atmospherics of this place go undisturbed. Being the view of a real alongshore town rather than a make-believe one elicits questions about presences and absences. What strange thing is the artist saying, what interpretation is he offering in declining to give any indication of the continent to which this place is only marginal, to which it is, or seems, only an entrepôt? Even if he is following an artistic protocol, why is he satisfied to sketch a town that wants only adjacency—adjacency to the sea before it and to the continent beyond?

Of course, before Europeans first sighted it, this place had been interpreted. But now ordinary sailors were making sense of it as they hazarded closer and closer to shore, terrified of death on hidden rock ledges or shifting sandbars. They explored the edge of the New World with what the Dutch called a *dieplood* and the English a dipsey lead. A sixty- to seventy-pound weight attached to perhaps six hundred feet of line, the *dieplood* let them test the depth of the waters. But even more. Tallow or soap secured in its concave end allowed them to gather traces of bottom sand or blue shells. Before their feet touched shore and before they erected their shore forts, the *dieplood* touched the indigenous Americans' ground.

Our artist has denied us of some of the raw materials we might want for interpretation. He has not, for example, included the forests that covered much of this place, Manhattan Island, in the early 1650s. The Europeans and natives both depended on wood for their survival. They sawed or bent it into shape for dwellings; they burned it for fuel. They twisted and turned it into the ribs of boats and rigging.

Once set ablaze, wood was also the cheapest resource Europeans and natives had for killing one another. They themselves told stories about it. In the mid-1630s, about fifteen years before the scene our artist hoped to catch, a group of natives encountered some Englishmen. They met along another waterside, not far from the island and in the Connecticut country, already claimed by both the Dutch and English who were trading there. Agitated by some presentiment of danger, a native cried out, "What Englishmen, what cheere . . . will you cran us?" "Cran" may have been a corruption of the Dutch word *kwalm*, meaning "dense smoke." In English, it referred to an iron arm built for cooking over an open fire. Here, it meant, Will you kill us by setting our village ablaze and burning us alive?

Untold numbers of Algonquian-speaking men, women, and children died when Europeans set their villages on fire. During the same years, countless New Netherlanders died in fires set by natives. First it happened around Manhattan Island and then along nearby coasts. It was not just that fire was more easily available for killing than musket balls. It was so much more destructive. It could consume and destroy wildly: inhabitants and their houses and barns, stores of supplies, boats, animals, and sometimes all the crops standing in a field. For powerful bands of men—Mohawks over Esopus, Dutch over Raritans—the power to torch a village was an extortioner's tool. Before it leaped from brands and torches, fire fueled their protection rackets: show yourselves to be on our side; otherwise, we cannot ensure your safety against burning, not at the hands of your enemies or our own. The Europeans had learned these war techniques in their homelands. So had the Mohawks in theirs.

The Netherlanders who first settled here wanted the peaceful encounters that this view suggests. They wanted to feel the New World like the sailor with his pebbles and blue shells, lightly in the hand. They wanted to think that they could have only an anchorage alongside other peoples' lands and cultures and, by that, have the right to only a faded-out sense of responsibility for the people and things around.

But they betrayed the quiet occupancy this picture offers. They betrayed themselves—their ideals and values—and the indigenous people. There were moments when they publicly acknowledged this. For that reason, I have put these reflections under the words "the shame and the sorrow."

Perhaps you will think the words are too wimpy. They are too feeble to comprehend the consequences of the strangers' intrusion into North America. They are too exculpatory. In this, our time of post-colonialism and neocolonials, they are insufficiently accusatory. But if "the shame and the sorrow" are inadequately aggressive, it is because the records tell me of neither an aggressive invasion nor a determination to conquer the native people. Too often, they point to Netherlanders convinced of their rights as traders but unconvinced of the sovereignty that circumstances were increasingly requiring of them.

I would like you to consider each of the chapters in this story as part of a gallery's installation on Dutch-Amerindian encounters in New Netherland. Each picture in the exhibit asks for its own set of reflections. I've framed each of the objects, realizing that I'm defining the conditions of its representation and your contemplation of it. I hope I have done it faithfully.

Drawing a story under the words "the shame and the sorrow" is not entirely original. In 1971, similar words were the title of a film. *The Sorrow and the*

Pity documented the memories of French men and women who had lived through the German occupation during the Second World War.[3] In remembering those years, French citizens were able to locate acts of valor and sacrifice: their own and those of others. But equally, the documentary asked them to rediscover betrayal—betrayal of France's cultural past and humane values, betrayal of one another and themselves.

Their shame and sorrow, they knew, would be the years' ineradicable legacy.

PART I

Alongshore

In the late sixteenth century, Netherlanders stepped onto the stage of what we would later call the Dutch maritime empire. Beginning in 1594, Dutch merchants began reaching the Indies. They returned to the Netherlands with stories of immense riches awaiting further voyages of discovery and exploration. In 1602, the United Provinces granted a charter to the East India Company. Soon it was extending its reach from Java in Indonesia to the Moluccas, the Malabar Coast of India, Ceylon (Sri Lanka), Formosa (Taiwan), and Japan. By mid-century, it had displaced the Portuguese as the dominant European power in the Indies. In the same decades, other Netherlanders began imagining their way into the New World. The West India Company's 1621 charter gave it monopoly status along the coasts of West Africa and Brazil, the Caribbean, and a place in North America later called New Netherland. In 1625, the directors purchased *1626?* Manhattan Island.

The Dutch sailed as alongshore people. And it was as maritime people that they made intelligible to themselves the strangeness of New Netherland and their encounter with native peoples. The stories of their ventures were of voyaging out in pursuit of trading enclaves: Footholds alongside the kingdom of Ceylon, in the harbor of Nagasaki, or on Manhattan Island. Some stories washed ashore at Zuider Zee ports such as Enkhuizen and Hoorn. Those of Jan Huyghen van Linschoten became the foundation of Dutch travel literature. Others became the intellectual property of trading companies as skippers handed over their logs after following directors' orders such as these: locate and settle a central rendezvous for the trading fleets we'll be sending out. If possible, let it be an uninhabited offshore island. Above all, establish amicable relations with the overseas residents. In short, remain alongshore.

Understanding maritime empires is difficult for us. We understand the land stories of territorial imperialism. Tales of European settler societies dispossessing natives of their lands do not read like morality plays. But regrettably, they do make sense to us. We assume that colonial intruders will want to drive inexorably inland, hoping to see power spatialized before them, desiring the assurance that comes of identifying virtue with working the land.

We assume, too, that somewhere behind colonialism is a metropolitan's proud and bellicose sense of nationalism. But in the first half of the seventeenth century—that is, during most of the existence of New Netherland—the aspirations of the Hollanders and the political environment to which they were responding were the opposite of these. In 1644, the directors of the East India Company represented to the home government their notion of colonialism, territorial dominion, and nationalism: the places they'd captured in the Indies were not national conquests but the property of private merchants who were entitled to sell them as they wished, even to the king of Spain or any other enemy of the United Provinces.

The Dutch maritime empire is the name we give to all the incidental theatrical acts that were the condition of its possibility. They were performances played out in Dutch seaside villages, on quarterdecks, and in encounters with indigenous people. They were also writing performances. Taken together, the theatrical acts were the sine qua non of empire.

Chapter 1
Alongshore: Stories to Tell
of the Virginias

The six men waited for a response to a petition laid before the States General of the United Provinces. They were men from North Holland. Dierck and Cornelis Volkertsz, Doctor Verus, and Doctor Carbasius were from the port of Hoorn. Pieter Nannincx lived in Medemblik, a coastal town nearby. He was an accountant. Pieter Dircxzen was a companion of the five men. It was late September 1621.

Their request was minimal enough. But they knew exactly what they wanted. Might they fit out and send a ship to "the Virginias." They would store aboard only permitted merchandise. It would be used for trading in the Virginias and, they assured the committee, they'd make a profit. This done, they would instruct the ship to return with their cargo and clerks.[1] Their request was approved. But a tough caveat was added: make good use of exactly nine months and one week to supply the ship, carry out your trading ventures, make some kind of profit—whatever and wherever that might be—and get back to Holland.

Volkertsz, Verus, Carbasius, and the others were marginal men. They were marginal to the larger purposes of the States and its interests in the Virginias. They were also marginal to other groups of men who were just as eagerly eyeing off the Virginias and promising significant profits by opening markets there. Such venturers were also promising to deliver knowledge about further lucrative discoveries that the States might follow up: coastlines, rivers, islands, places to trade.

But the six hopeful entrepreneurs were also marginal in a now obsolescent meaning of the word "marge." They were from coastal towns in the marginal zone between "what seamen call 'open ocean' and what landsmen might call 'ordinary inland landscape.'"[2] In that sense, they had everything in common with other Dutch men hoping to get rich by sending one—or four or six—permitted voyages to the West and East Indies, even with most of the members of the States.

On the edge of the sea and the edge of land, the marge was a place of residence. It was also a state of mind. This book is about that state of mind. And it is about its consequences for people in another far-distant coastal zone—people who spoke Algonquian, or so their language would come to be called. They lived in the southern waterlands in places such as Rinnegackonck, Kestateuw, Pagganck, and an island that the local Manhates seemed to call the "island of the hills." Soon these would be called (but not by them) New Netherland.

The towns of Hoorn and Medemblik were alongshore to the Zuider Zee, a great bay that held special kinds of terror. The sea bottom shifted constantly and unpredictably. Convulsive storms and the strong tides made it even more perilous than the fierce North Sea. It's much less dangerous to navigate to Spain, said one man, than to try the "passage over the Zudder-Sea."[3]

Hoorn and Medemblik shared about sixty kilometers of the low broken coastline, with Monnickendam and Edam to the south and Enkhuizen midway between them and off to the east. To separate what was seaward and landward, the people of Hoorn, Enkhuizen, and Medemblik had erected a continuous *strandwal*, or coastal dike, between their towns. The *wal* was a thick hedge of wood, probably elder wood. People knew where to collect it (the island of Wiering) and how to set it in place so that the roots faced seaward. They knew it needed close watching and, for parts of it, replacement every five or six years (Fig. 2, Map 1).

Figure 2. Living alongshore. Salomon Jacobsz van Ruysdael's *River Landing* (1643, detail) helps us imagine each of the towns and cities named on Map 1 as riverside- or sea-oriented places. Here sea and shore merge imperceptibly. Other Haarlem artists were painting landscapes consciously inspired by the techniques of marine painters. Statens Museum for Kunst, Copenhagen.

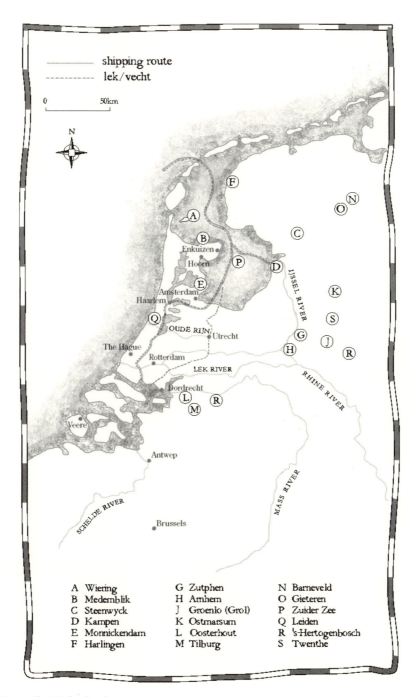

Legend (within map):
- shipping route
- lek/vecht

0   50km

N

JSSEL RIVER
OUDE RIJN
LEK RIVER
RHINE RIVER
MASS RIVER
SCHELDE RIVER

Enkuizen
Hoorn
Amsterdam
Haarlem
Utrecht
The Hague
Rotterdam
Dordrecht
Veere
Antwep
Brussels

A Wiering	G Zutphen	N Barneveld
B Medemblik	H Arnhem	O Gieteren
C Steenwyck	J Groenlo (Grol)	P Zuider Zee
D Kampen	K Ostmarsum	Q Leiden
E Monnickendam	L Oosterhout	R 's-Hertogenbosch
F Harlingen	M Tilburg	S Twenthe

Map 1. The Netherlands, c. 1650.

The coasts taught people to live with essential instability. Sand dunes continually moved and with them the bundles of elder-wood reeds: toppled and crushed overnight, a defensive boundary marker suddenly nowhere to be seen. Only the towns stared down the marge's signs of instability. In a sense, they were networks of walls: encircling city walls; stone embankments reinforcing inner harbors; walls set against eighteen-foot tides that delivered powerful sea surges with the full or new moon. Enkhuizen had an outer groyne and a second row of dikes to protect shipbuilders. Medemblik gave itself the walls of a fortified castle. Hoorn erected a towering *vuurtoren*, today's lighthouse. The whole area was called, simply, Waterlands.

By the time Volkertsz and Carbasius were turning their thoughts to the Virginias, the industries of the Zuider Zee towns were flourishing. The sea fisheries and maritime carrying trade were making some men rich. Ordinary townspeople and coastal villagers were capitalizing on the trades as well. They had learned to make the discriminations and develop the skills that such complex industries required. To work the herring fleets, skippers and sailors had to know when the fish came into Dutch waters (early autumn) and when it was best to start looking for salmon or cod (April to July). They had to be knowledgeable about newfangled changes. The herring could now be salted and barreled at sea—look for the large ships doing this, the keeled and deep drafted *buizen* that could handle 840 barrels of fish and be put to use after the herring season as cargo ships trading around European ports from the Baltic to the Mediterranean. Experienced seamen lifted anchor only after discovering who owned which of the ship's nets or what percentage of a net. Enkhuizen's investors and skippers had to calculate that their vessel would be only one of about a hundred regularly leaving port in the chase for herring.

The townspeople of Hoorn and Enkhuizen also learned how to profit from salt. They collected it in its rawest form from France, Spain, and the Canary Islands and shipped it home to salt pits within the city walls. Once, about sixteen years before the petitioners' request, they were seeking it—and fighting for it—in the New World. They knew how much salt to use in a barrel of fish and how many barrels one of the great *buizen* could fill. They learned how to refine the salt, clear away the stubble, and work it into white table salt. They learned the legalities that governed the packing sheds: salt the herring or cod only in sheds with open doors or on high streets or on the docks. Finally, they knew how to ship salt to markets in the Baltic.[4]

Some townspeople became ships' carpenters. They became members of the guild and mastered a knowledge of wood types and timber markets. They learned to circumvent the watchful wood mongers who would forbid them selling their leftover timber. There were also shipbuilders: some were contractors, some were not. Each would have realized that the larger the seaport, the more they would have to pay for a foreshore property suitable for a slipway and woodshed. They would have expected to build ships for markets discovered by their own seaport and not those—the warships or the stately vessels—that were the specialty of other ports. Each would have known that there were towns only near the bay that, wanting profit from shipbuilding, made themselves alongshore. Edam engineered channels and slips and grew famous for building ships of all burden.

The shipbuilders were only one sort of businessman who needed a sharp eye for the kinds of ships moving around the Zuider Zee. A Hoorn or Enkhuizen merchant trading to Norway for timber had to know that an old vessel would serve for shipping fir home. But logs for masts required *fluijts* with deeper holds and special arrangements for loading. He needed to know that a *buitengewoonschip* was a vessel especially assigned to protect the *retourvloten*, the Indiamen returning from the Far East. He needed to know that *schuiten* or *slabberts* (but certainly not *buizen* or *hoekers*) were best for the inland trade or searching rivers for plaice and shellfish. He didn't need to be told that the Mediterranean trade was astonishingly lucrative but very dangerous.[5]

The stories told in the Zuider Zee seaports were as soaked by the sea as were the local skills and local knowledge. Some stories were sung. On an *Oostindiëvaarder* (Indiaman), each demanding task—hoisting sails, giving orders, weighing anchor—had its special song or chant. Other stories made sense of the mysteries of the sea and the townspeople's relationship to them. About the herring, locals said that God had sent them to Netherlands waters. Why else would they swarm so remarkably close to the seashore and swim toward "any light, fire or humane Creature: as it were saying, 'Come take me.'" People said that the multitudes of herring seen at night resembled lightning striking far off in the distance. Their eyes are "bright like fire." Strange and monstrous creatures fished from the seas gave a sense of veracity to tales of a sea-woman and a sea-man. In one version, a sea-woman is taken up at Haarlem and a sea-man in Friesland. Both live to an old age, unable to speak, and the mermaid, locals say, sought often "to get again into the water." In another account, the sea-woman is seen at the edge of the sea and taken to Edam by some women of Enkhuizen going in a small boat to feed their cattle. Again, legend had it that a statue of Medea once stood at a place along the Zuider Zee. And from its wondrous intervention, Medemblik took its name.[6]

Such stories had a beginning, middle, and end: the sea-woman and sea-man live to old age. Medea's seaport becomes Medemblik. But the event that had a temporal dimension most like a good story, starting out and moving to an end, was the sea voyage.

*   *   *

By 1621, merchants and seamen from the Zuider Zee trading towns had stories to tell of the Virginias. Cornelis Hendricksz, a skipper from Monnickendam, had been there. Seven years earlier, he had made the voyage that Volkertsz and his associates were now hoping to organize. Hendricksz's employers were prosperous investors from the northern seaports and Amsterdam, a city some distance to the south. His backers were ambitious merchants. They were also imaginative. They knew how to structure, finance, and evaluate the results of long-distance voyages of discovery and commercial exploration. One day soon, men like them would imagine their way into a place called New Netherland. They would begin a permanent encounter with the native people.

Hendricksz had sailed for the Virginias in 1614. The report he presented to the States carefully displayed the business acumen and purposefulness of his principals as well as his own. It reminded the committee of the venturers' considerable stake in exploring what they called America between New France and Virginia. Nominating themselves as directors of a New Netherland Company, they had financed an extensive expedition for new overseas markets and were now able to present the States with the commodity it liked best: information. They had details about the latitudes within which their ships had navigated and traded, that is, "from forty to forty and five degrees [north latitude], situate in America between New France and Virginia." More important, they had proof of having explored even more distant seas and coastlines: more southerly, between the thirty-eighth and fortieth degrees of latitude, Hendricksz had discovered some new country, a bay, and three rivers.[7]

Following custom, the company directors presented a map of all this to the assembly. Although Hendricksz had done the surveying and constructed the map, the investors suggested that they, not he, deserved the credit for putting the coasts on paper. Among other things, they'd thought ahead to the most important age-old requirement. They had arranged that he would set out for a place where he would find a small yacht left behind by a skipper sailing for them on a previous voyage. With this, he had been able to explore close to the coastline, farther along another, distant marge.

They had named the small charting vessel *Restless* (*Onrust*).[8] For Dutch navigators and entrepreneurs, *Restless* must have had meanings obscure today. Perhaps it was a metaphor for the restless sea. Perhaps it stood for the restless quest of the ship of life wandering the world's seas and, as a later writer put it, "threatened by monsters and shipwreck . . . [saved] only by the light of God." Onrust was also the name chosen by the East India Company for an island set off the shores of Djakarta in Java. They valued it highly as a place for maintaining the company's ships. An island: valued for facilitating the restless search for profits. Now a coastal yacht: valued for the same restless purposes[9] (Fig. 3).

From all this, the directors thought they had a good case for claiming exclusive rights to trade for four years along the newly discovered coasts. Hendricksz, for his part, had his memories of three years of navigation. He had been paid to have the temperament of his two-masted yacht: to be dissatisfied with anything less than searching out the next bay or headland, to be outbound and inbound, restless.

He also had his stories. The report delivered to the States in summer 1616 was not in his own words. Undoubtedly, the notary who accompanied him and the directors on their first appearance before the committee would have constructed it into proper prose. At their next meeting, he spoke out. He may have seemed the least significant man in the room. But he was not. Only he and his navigating justified what a prominent Dutch jurist was then saying constituted the rightful acquisition of unknown lands. They could be claimed because they'd been "discovered at sea." So a seafarer like Hendricksz was crucial to discoveries—and if he were a careful observer and meticulous recorder, he needn't have bothered to put a foot ashore.[10]

Figure 3. In *Rest Elsewhere*, the artist is suggesting that the restless pursuit of the world's riches is similar to the Christian's quest and enjoyable repose after overcoming life's threatening journey. *Repos Ailleurs*, device of Philip van Marnix van St. Aldegonda in *Album Amicorum* of Abraham Ortelius, 1579 (detail). Permission of the Master and Fellows, Pembroke College, Cambridge.

Hendricksz reported briefly. First, the geography of his discovery: "certain lands, a bay, and three rivers situate between 38 and 40 degrees." Next a list of his trading activities and observations. These he itemized, reducing them to just five sentences. He'd seen a country full of trees; he'd seen deer and turkeys and partridges. He'd experienced a climate as temperate as theirs in Holland.

Flora and fauna and climate—and then: inhabitants. The natives incited no thicker a description in Hendricksz's listing than the inanimate objects. But going on: with the natives, he had traded. The exchange brought him furs, robes, and other things. He had also bargained for three additional commodities that the natives who called themselves Minquaes had put on the market—or, at least Hendricksz put the transaction into the language of commodity exchange. He had, as he said, also "traded for, and bought from the inhabitants" three men whom the company had put ashore from an earlier voyage and who had somehow made themselves employees of the natives. He said nothing more. From the stories of other men, he learned what to offer as the purchase price for furs: kettles, beads, and other merchandise. The same stories now recounted back in Holland—those of a seemingly incidental encounter with native Americans—were, of course, not that at all. Together with his maps, his notarized testimony gave proof of having opened new trading relations with local people, markets, and trade routes. Taken together, these three achievements established that his was a successful voyage of Dutch discovery and possession.[11]

*   *   *

During these early decades of the seventeenth century, sea captains' stories broke again and again against the shore from Medemblik down to Monnickendam. The States and the directors of the East India Company (VOC) and later the West India Company liked to think that they were their intellectual property. Routinely, and theatrically, they would oblige a departing skipper to sign assurances of their rights. And the theater went into additional acts when the voyage ended and the captain delivered his logs and chests, together with an account of everything that had happened to him during the voyage. Usually, the theater was enacted as soon as the vessel announced its arrival home. Representatives of the States or companies would either wait alongshore for their papers and maps or board a lighter and collect them aboard the anchored ship. They could require the skipper and crew to keep their discoveries secret and, above all, prevent them from sharing their maps. After the papers had been thoroughly examined, the skipper received his reward for his "dangers, trouble and knowledge."[12]

But the same officials anticipated that skippers would deceive them—stow away secrets, fail to disclose some profitable information. A captain exploring for the East India Company in the Virginias about five years before Hendricksz's voyaging was made to read the board's distrust of him. To the agreement that detailed accounts needed to be delivered to them, they added, "without keeping anything back." When everything was settled, the pay could go to sailors of many nationalities according to the rules set by skippers. No difficulties there. But the knowledge was theirs.[13]

But the stories that the seamen from the Zuider Zee had to tell were too prodigal and too exciting—or if they were not exciting, they could be made to be—to be somehow trapped like shoals of fish in the nets of profit-driven boards of directors and their documentation projects. The stories from the Virginias were full of their own excitement. Seventeen years from the time of Volkertsz's request, a ship would arrive in Medemblik from a great river they were calling the South River (Delaware River). No one was told why the ship was detained in port for a year. But about other ships and voyages, publicists were eagerly sharing with the public what information they had. Words such as "We learn by the arrival of the ship whereof Cornelisse Jacobsz May of Hoorn was skipper" promised a tale of adventure. Or listen, they said: "a ship belonging to Monnickendam having been wrecked in that [far distant] neighborhood. . . ." The author of a travel book drew readers into vivid action scenes: you can see both islands, he wrote, "from the quarter deck."[14]

These were real and enticing details not to be missed. And the excitement was enhanced by the accounts of seafarers setting sail for other destinations, too, men who plotted a course from the western shores of the Zuider Zee north to Texel and thence to the East Indies or the Ijszee. Texel was a West Frisian island whose harbor served as a rendezvous for convoys of ships—at one time, 210— many of them sailing for the *Companieën van Verre*, the Companies for Far Journeys. A Dutch writer praised it as one of the great gateways to the sea. A popular Dutch playwright of the time assumed that everyone in his audience knew its importance. He could use it as a metaphor for death: everyone who journeyed to another world had to pass through it.[15]

So in the towns and villages along the *strandwal*, stories from the East Indies mingled with those from America or, as it was often called, the West Indies. Soon some were printed for a public that delighted in what one publisher promised as "tales of wondrous occurrences."[16] For that reason, one popular writer criticized sea captains who, when he published his little emblem book in 1614, were now sailing everywhere but still couldn't find any evidence of the exotic "monstrous beasts" reported to have lived in Asia.[17]

Some men were wonderful storytellers. Others, sensing advantage in this, fashioned themselves into being so. David Pietersz de Vries of Hoorn was one of these. So was the mariner who constructed his log into an adventure story, cunningly describing the public festivities arranged in Amsterdam for the home-coming of his ship, the return of each resident seaman to his own house, the search of others for an inn, and then each going "his own way." Still others were scarcely storytellers at all. And some, like Jan Pietersz Coen, who sailed from Hoorn for the East India Company, founded Batavia, served as resident director-general of the Indies, and returned to Hoorn in 1623, were exotic stories in themselves.[18]

Jan Cornelisse May also had stories to tell. He too was a skipper from Hoorn and in 1612 sailed the seacoasts between New France and Virginia. He began his outward voyage of discovery in 1611. Like Hendricksz later, he put his stories in reports laid before the States after inscribing them in his log.

May was a supreme storyteller. He was not an entertainer but, rather, a professional in his trade, a man who knew how to talk the language of com-mercial adventuring. So we haven't accounts of him yarning along the North Holland foreshore in one of its thatched cottages. Like Hendricksz's, the imag-inative world of his voyaging was primarily written down for the States and the admiralty. The stories were retold, however, to a public both inquisitive and, as we'll see, outspoken about the way they wanted their seafarers' exploits reen-acted in print. Read with the least imagination, even fragments of a narrative such as May's were anyone's series of adventure stories.

The journal presented one exploit after another. This was not because May was seeking a popular audience, although he was like other navigators in directing his principals' attention to the many times he endangered his life for the sake of their enterprise (and was therefore deserving of special reward). The perils, escapes, and achievements he logged were not those of the open seas or of going inland. They were perils arising from charting the offshore waters, the shelves and the bottoms where land was its most liminal and contradictory self: both the cause of shipwreck and the promise of safety. His exploits were the feats of seamanship that the trading companies expected, the acts of taking possession from "at sea." So his readers were sharing the dangers that arose from his restlessness in navigating shorelines: finding and ceaselessly recording his global positioning; doggedly moving on, as he wrote, *om coopmanschap te doen*, in order to engage in trade.[19] Or, as other entrepreneurs would say four hundred years from May's time, he sailed in order to satisfy a niche market, this one in furs.

May hoped to discover a northeast passage to the riches of Cathay and the Indies. If it all worked out, the exploration would bring him a salary of over fifteen hundred guilders—and make some investors nothing less than million-aires. He followed instructions that took him north from Texel, then around the northern shores of Scandinavia and to a course set for what they called the Ijszee. He was then to sail east through the straits of Anian and south to the Far East. But the pack ice of the Ijszee defeated him, so he decided to overwinter along the east coast of Nova Francia (Canada), surveying the entire unknown coast from Terra Nova (Newfoundland) to the Virginias. He would also seek out encounters with the natives. He would give his principals for North America what they wanted in the Far East: a clear sense of how future trade might be conducted.[20]

So the accounts he put before his directors were crowded with daily notations. They were observations on his ship's condition ("very white with the snow"), descriptions of bays and inlets, notations rectifying earlier mariners' errors. His log was a record of place names signifying acts of possession. The same names expressed emotions that could not have been lost on other seafarers or the public: "All Saints Bay" and "All Saints Island" because they'd passed them on November 1; "Beautiful Harbor" since it was "as lovely a harbor as there might be in all the world." He named a bay of islands that sheltered him on February 2 "Candlemas," for the religious feast of that day. A harbor featuring two old sloops urged him to name it "Sloops Bay." "Vosje Island" would be a place "after the name of our ship."[21]

The entries also described a theater of commercial exchange. They caught the crew in tableaux bargaining with coastal-dwelling natives. Usually the aborigines were few in number. And always they were encountered in a space that the strangers—and possibly the natives—understood best: the marge between the open ocean and inland. Exchange took place on the land's edge—where a wooded copse, thick scrub, or high dunes could not screen the meeting place from offshore watchfulness—or on the deck of the ship anchored close in. The seamen and the natives both kept these locations in anxious and constant focus. None imagined that the encounters were anything but those of strangers, potentially murderous strangers.

On at least twelve such occasions, May and the others exchanged trading goods for furs. As good merchants did at home, the seamen first examined what they called—and thought the native vendors meant to present as—samples of their merchandise (*monsteren*). Less often, they shared food, drink, and tobacco. Once, a native let two arrows loose against the sailors watching in a launch. They returned fire but with no loss of life. May did not take it as his task to interpret the intentions of this man or of the natives generally. He had no interest in describing them as dirty or clean, lying or truthful, irreligious or religious, primitive or civilized. He wrote them into his log variously, and generally not pejoratively, as *imboorlingen* (natives), *volck* (people), *wilden* (primitive men in nature), *een wilt man* (a savage or wild person). Once a fellow officer on his supply ship wrote that the men and women were nearly naked and always armed. May wrote nothing of this.[22]

The episodes were action bites within a longer account that May's superiors would make sense of by putting it alongside information gathered from other voyages. Meanwhile, the public encountered the story of May's attempt to reach Cathay and his overwintering in Nova Francia. They also learned of the adventures of the *Crane,* his smaller escort vessel. Somewhere along the shores of Nova Francia, natives had killed its senior officer and five crewmen. Whether the reading public found entertainment in the details of the men's deaths—three beheaded, three dying from horrific wounds, all buried on a remote island—we don't know. They were keen to read of dramas at sea: the heroic, the tragic, the romantic. Had they been privy to May's journal, they would have felt the strong emotion he expressed. He named the bay where the killings occurred "Sorrowful Bay." For the island where the bodies were later buried, he chose the same name as that chosen by crewmen of the fleet that had sailed to the Indies in 1595. They had buried many men "on a small island . . . [where] there were so many dead buried that they baptized it '*Hollandtsch Kerckhof,*' the Hollanders' Burying Ground."[23]

Jan Huyghen van Linschoten from Enkhuizen was May's opposite as a storyteller. As against May's weighty professionalism, he wrote with unbounded exuberance. He had more tales to tell than he could control. He published his early stories in 1596, just eighteen years before May undertook his journey. In his *Itinerario, Voyage ofte Schipvaert naer Oost ofte Portugaels Indien,* Huyghen's voice as storyteller urged readers to a sense of his own enchantment. It was the beginning of Netherlands travel literature (Fig. 4).

At the age of seventeen, van Linschoten left Enkhuizen and sailed with the Portuguese to the Indies. With a touch of picaresque contrivance, he told readers why this was so. He wanted to see "strange lands, or to seek some adventures." But there was nothing of contrivance in descriptions of the Indies so buoyant that one editor paraphrased what he saw as *de Indische Wonderwereld* and twice again (at a loss for words) as *het wonderland Indië,* and again as *die wonderlanden.* Van Linschoten gave his readers stories of riches and wonders in abundance: a *toverwereld* (world of magic) would open to them, a place of wondrous races of people (*zonderlinge mensenrassen*) and unimaginable customs: altogether an atmosphere that was *sprookjesachtig,* like a fairy tale. But he also wrote as a merchant. The East offered unequaled possibilities of wealth for commoners like himself. A trader with two or three hundred guilders to invest in trade would easily turn it into seven or eight hundred.[24]

Van Linschoten had nine years of stories to tell about the Indies. The States recognized the value of his experiences. There were unexplored market

Figure 4. Van Linschoten's wonder at the strangeness of the East Indies is palpable in the *Itinerario* (1596). Yet his mark as a merchant is carefully placed in the upper-right-hand corner of this engraving, announcing him as seeking commercial opportunities as well as observing exotica. Engraving/book illustration: Nuces Indica, Magni in India . . . Botanic Illustration from *Itinerario, Voyage ofte Schipvaert . . . Jan Huygen van Linschoten* (detail). Collection Nederlands Maritime Museum, Amsterdam.

opportunities in America, and he could be employed to give advice about opening these to exploration and investment. It was only a matter of time before a company similar to the East India Company would look to the West—and look to them for an exclusive license.

Always pragmatic, the states selected from van Linschoten's Indies experiences those that seemed useful for what they called new navigations. A later Dutch historian, W. J. van Balen, was far more comprehensive in writing about the young man's adventures. He returned his readers to Enkhuizen, to the marge. What, von Balen wondered, was the source of the imaginings that had enticed the young man to the Far East? The nurturing of van Linschoten's fantasies, ideas, and capacity to embrace strangeness needed, van Balen decided, "the dunes that lay along the water's edge." Van Linschoten needed to live alongshore. Had he and his family continued to reside in Haarlem—as they did for the first ten years of Jan's life—he would have been just an inlander, perhaps a city official, or an artisan or a man *te land,* working the land. Alongshore made people different. In the tides of the sea and its surges, their daily lives were dictated more by the moon than the sun. No, being beached produced its own kind of visionaries. The traveler who described Medemblik in 1663 as only a sea town probably meant to be disparaging. But he was unintentionally prescient in continuing: it's fit for seamen and fishermen "but nobody else."[25]

Townspeople of seaports like Hoorn were long-distance visionaries as well. They listened to the stories of the skipper-adventurers who put to sea with the Kermis fleet that sailed in September, or the Christmas fleet that set sail in December or January, or the Easter fleet that left in April or May and then coasted off the shores of other beaches. The townsfolk were part owners of the stories told and retold, even as they were, often the humblest deckhand among them, part owners of the ships and their permitted merchandise, the wharves, the nets, and waterfront sheds.

*   *   *

Nowhere in the stories is the world situated in America between New France and Virginia ever described as a *wonderwereld.* The tales of world voyaging continued, and continued to be published. Maps, too. But the public's appetite was mainly for descriptions of journeys that were wonder voyages, those to the Indies or around the world. Thirty-five years after the voyages of Hendricksz and May, a director of the company governing New Netherland seemed to confirm a comparatively dampened-down excitement about the Virginias. He felt that *"the name of New Netherland was seldom mentioned . . . [before] and* now heaven and earth are, as it seems, moved by it and everyone wishes to be the first to select the best part of it." Seven years later, in 1657, a merchant trying unsuccessfully to make a beginning there cursed the sea captains who still lacked the skill to navigate their way easily to New Netherland. Both men were frustrated and for that reason leaning on exaggeration.[26] Besides, in the beginning, the Virginias were exactly what the Dutch wanted.

They had an island.

Chapter 2

"The Island"

In 1618, the States called it "the island of New Netherland." They referred to it as an island two years later and once again in 1622. We can't be sure where it was. It needn't have been the island that an early skipper named "Manhates," for the natives who lived there. It might have been nearby *Nooten Eylandt* (Nut Island, today's Governor's Island). It might have been a mysterious place called *Prinsen Eylandt* (Prince's Island, near Burlington). That, they said, was a high island in a body of water they called the South River (Delaware River)[1] (Map 2).

Somehow, from a loose string of trading posts, a single island was emerging as a place of rendezvous. In mariners' worlds, such places were essential. No skipper sailed into the open seas without knowing the location of *verwachtplaetsen*, meeting points that skippers sailing in pairs or convoys marked on charts and confirmed with one another before voyaging out. Often, a trading company or private investors chose them. On one occasion, the East India Company foresaw that ships in a fleet sailing from Amsterdam and the islands of Saint Paulo might stray from one another. Establish a rendezvous, they commanded. An island "lying at about 32 degrees is deemed the most suitable." Await one another for ten or twelve days either at anchor or cruising within sight of the land.

Skippers kept lists of such prearranged assembly points. They were something like the *Annotatiën van de verwachtplaetsen* that May kept in 1611–12. The notes were an important document delivered to company officials or investors at the completion of a voyage. Texel was a place of rendezvous. So were the faraway islands of Kildin on the coast of Lapland and the equally exotic 7 Islands off the same coastline. Somehow they were available to Dutch mariners who sought them out, though they were not in their ownership.[2]

An overseas rendezvous of one's own was of great importance. For Jan Pietersz Coen, the most gifted of the resident directors-general sent by the East India Company to the Indies, nothing was of greater urgency than establishing a general rendezvous. Such a location did not come easily. But it was the docking station for a seventeenth-century trading company. It was the terminal of its long-distance voyages, a place of its ships' arrivals and departures, the

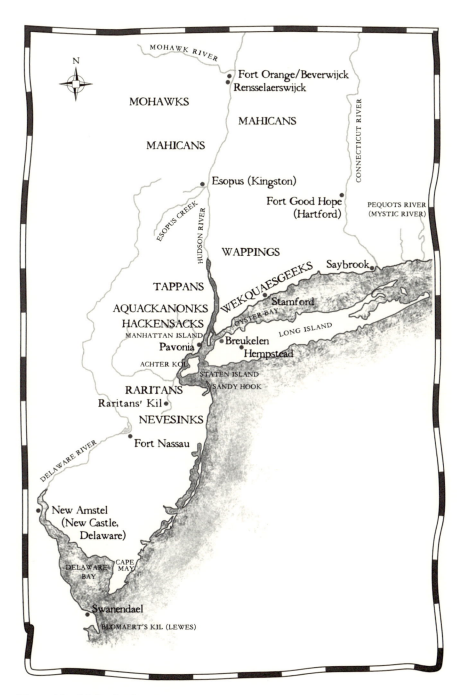

Map 2. New Netherland, c. 1650.

center of cargo collection, storage and dispatch, the residence of the company's personnel.

Dutch general rendezvous were spaces leased or purchased from local people in order to trade and explore farther afield. The States considered them footholds from which to carry forward what they called their experiment in voyages of discovery. By the mid-1590s, Portugal's rendezvous on the island of Goa had evolved into a place of wonderment to a knowing merchant-seaman like Jan Huyghen van Linschoten. Had he been writing of it considerably earlier, he might simply have written that in Goa, "all the [Portuguese] merchants foregather." But in the 1590s, he could record a larger throng of merchants. "All the merchants foregather and all things come in, being sought, bought or sold, even from Arabia, Armenia . . . [and] Persia," from Burma, Siam, and the "*wonderlijke wereld van China.*" The island's doubled geography—its separation from the Indian continent and adjacency to it—intrigued him. He was eager to describe its wall on the east side, and three gates on the banks of the river that separated it from the mainland—and each gate that had a Portuguese captain and a clerk who kept watch. The island, he pointed out, was the center of a loose string of outlying Portuguese trading posts: the *handels kantoren en factorijen* set up by Portuguese merchants truly *handelsdrijven*, market-driven for profits. Such islands, others said later, were "the nursemaids of maritime independence."[3] Offshore, they were your best chance for independence from nearby regents and kings. In a trading world, they were your best chance for what you most wanted: political and religious neutrality.

Following a fleet sent out in the mid-1590s, it took almost twenty-four years for the Companies for Far Journeys and then the East India Company to establish even the rudiments of an equally satisfactory central rendezvous in the Indies. In the earliest years, the company's captain-admiral reported that they had only an office somewhere on the island of Java, probably at Bantam in west Java. In the following years, they had a number of offices at coastal locations such as Djakarta. But officials continued to urge a centrally located rendezvous where the company could establish at least a warehouse.[4] After another five years, in 1610, the directors could be more specific. They thought they knew the kind of place they wanted. Initiate discussions with the king of Djakarta, they ordered. Let him know that "we desire a place to build a fort to our specifications, a place serviceable for a rendezvous for the whole Indies navigation and for our ships." They later advised that it be an uninhabited site, preferably an offshore island. Such a rendezvous would remove local interference. A footing on an inhabited island could be purchased or leased from a local ruler. But such an arrangement would involve anchorage fees and probably exorbitant gifts. "If . . . uninhabited, so much the better, because that would eliminate irksome tolls and other interference."[5]

At about the same time, in 1610, captains sailing for the company located several small islands suitable for repairing the company's ships. The most useful of these islands they named Onrust. Here they erected a two-story warehouse, workshops, and a hospital. Coen, as resident governor-general, was making use of it in 1619 while erecting the fort at Djakarta, and in the late 1620s it was serving as a dockage area for refitting the company's ships. Meanwhile, he designated Djakarta as center of the trade. Against the wishes of the directors for a rendezvous peacefully negotiated, he forced the sultan of Bantam to make the foreshore available. Coen and the others looked upon it not with the eyes of landsmen looking for territory but with the eyes of seamen. They saw a place oriented to the sea and sea channels "in the region of the Straits of Malacca or the Straits of Sunda, where the trade routes and the monsoon winds converged."[6] Soon they began to transfer their ships, cargoes, and building materials to the right bank of a river just inland from the shore. In 1619, Coen named it Batavia. He had wanted to call it New Hoorn.

In 1619, the island of New Netherland was years away from being anything like the magical world of Goa or even the promising rendezvous at Batavia. Ten years earlier, Henry Hudson could see nothing more in the harbor of New Netherland than drowned land resembling islands, maybe islands in a lake, perhaps in a bay. The land, he did say, was "very favorable to call into." Dutch voyagers were now coming to its coasts: the edges, margins, and riverine foreshores of this place a later visitor called "the New Low Countries" (Map 2). These were men resembling the tramp traders who had voyaged to the Indies in the decade before the East India Company received its monopoly in 1602. Sometimes they commanded unruly, not to say mutinous, crews. But they were skilled venturers, often renowned navigators, and some were partners in costly ventures chartered for discovery and trade. One skipper had made eleven voyages to the island. Nevertheless, they had to identify themselves as simply various traders. They were transients permitted to frequent the newly discovered seacoasts as short-term competitors in the game of discovery to which the sea provinces and the States, looking for a winner, had sent invitations and for which the entrants had been bankrolled by men from Dordrecht, Delft, Amsterdam and Rotterdam, Enkhuizen and Hoorn. They were players who, like their merchant-syndicate backers, knew when to close and walk away from the game of trade and who expected it would happen as soon as a winner was decided upon and given a monopoly.[7]

That was now in the offing. The West India Company would carry forward in a long-term way the exploitation of New Netherland that adventurers such as Volkertsz and his associates had been permitted to try their hand at under short-term contracts. So commercial agents and perhaps a crewman who might have been left behind were being fetched home to Holland. From a trading station probably consisting of little more than a store, a few primitive dwellings, and a yacht built for trading and surveying, traders, ships' carpenters, and their cargo were being brought home.[8]

But not, of course, from a place called a colony. All the men engaged in the chase for discoveries in North America spoke of possession but not of colonies. In December 1621, just five months before four investors had received permission to send two ships to New Netherland in order to trade away and dispose of old stock they had there, the English ambassador to the United Provinces, Sir Dudley Carleton, had tried to answer the worries of the Privy Council about a colony of the Hollanders in the "North of Virginia" within (as alleged) His Majesty's dominions. He'd made some inquiries and, he assured them, called upon the most reliable informants: Amsterdam merchants and Prince Mauritz of Nassau himself. "I cannot," he wrote, "learn of any Colony, either already planted by these people or so much as intended."[9]

He offered further proof. Sixty Walloon families have asked me to "procure them a place among His Majesty's subjects of those parts." If there were a Dutch colony, they would not be asking, as Dutch men, to mingle with strangers and to be subject to our government. He did, however, communicate with the States regarding matters concerning what he too called the island, or, as he carefully worded it, "the Island of Virginia."[10]

Carleton had seemingly reassured himself and the Privy Council that their plantations needn't fear competition from the Hollanders. The Dutch could make no future claim to possessions because they had—even as they had admitted—established no colonies. But in equating claims to possession with colonies, he had misunderstood the Netherlanders' way of claiming overseas possessions.

His own words denying the existence of a colony and setting out what the Dutch were engaged in on the island described almost perfectly the practices that *constituted* a Dutch way of taking possession. He had, he wrote with confidence, discovered "only" this kind of activity: in 1616 or 1617, two companies of Amsterdam merchants "began to trade into those parts, between 40 and 45 degrees [north] to which, after their manner, they gave their own name of New Netherlands; a South, and a North Sea; a Texel; a Vlieland; and the like." To these places, they have continued to send ships "to fetch furs; which is all their trade: for the providing of which they have certain Factors there, *continually resident,* trading with the savages."[11]

But for the Dutch, discovery established by first navigations recorded in place names and latitudes laid on charts and in logbooks, together with evidence of continual residence and continual trading, in fact established legal possession. Hendricksz and May had made their contributions to this—and it is certain that the Leiden scholar Joannes de Laet knew exactly what he was claiming for his countrymen in citing among the sources for his magisterial *New World* (1624) "divers manuscript journals of divers captains and navigators, whose names we have printed here and there in our *Description.*" He knew how to use a phrase such as *nadere outdekking*, that is, discovery based on a detailed scrutiny of coastlines, latitudes, and harbors. Therefore, he could go on, our countrymen call this portion of the West Indies New Netherland "because it was *at first more fully discovered* at the charge of our Netherlanders, and *for some years in succession was visited* and provided with a fort and habitations, by the Netherlanders, acting with a special charter from . . . the States General of these United Provinces."[12]

So while a number of entrepreneurs—sixteen by name and numerous associates and fellow shipowners—were busily and angrily winding down their operations in New Netherland pending the establishment of the West India Company, the ships of one company had been ordered to remain there the whole year. In little over a decade—and then repeatedly—the Netherlanders would take care to describe their regular trade with the indigenous people as grounds for possession of New Netherland. "For a long time," a high-ranking official then argued, the people there have "traded in the river Manathans . . . having purchased from the native inhabitants and paid for a certain island also called Manathans, where they remain surrounded on all sides by the natives of the country."[13]

Encirclement by natives was not a point stressed because it acknowledged the perseverance of the company's people in the face of adversity from every direction. Nor was it a warning of some sort of impending conflict and therefore the termination of the company's hitherto successful operations. Rather, it was an announcement that trading had gone on "for a long time" and from a location duly purchased from the owners. Moreover, the company was still advantaged by the presence of a great number of native customers ready to trade, in fact, clients on all sides. Possession of the island was an ongoing and indisputable fact of life. It had nothing to do with planting and fencing in, agricultural fertility rites, places for husbandmen, or perambulated boundaries—in short, with the distribution of lands.[14] Instead, from a pied-à-terre contracted with the rightful local owners, it was an ambit claim to further exploration and monopolistic opportunities for trade.

Not that the members of the States were unaware of the possibility of peopling the island of New Netherland. At the same time as the tramp traders were abandoning their profit-taking and making way for the West India Company, one of them, the New Netherland Company, put to the States, the admiralty, and the Prince of Orange an offer it had received. It must have looked too good to refuse. An English preacher residing in Leiden was offering to lead

four hundred families from Leiden and England to the "island" of New Netherland. Their numbers were impressive, and they would, they said, also make
themselves useful at shipbuilding and whatever else seemed necessary. More
important, they would work to propagate the "true, pure Christian religion" to
the natives and "plant there a new Commonwealth."

The petition was rejected at least twice. Perhaps this was because of an
accompanying request that projected a geography of colonization beyond the
island. The petitioners foresaw rival territorial claims and consequent incidents
of violence in and around New Netherland. Initially, they were not specific
about the identity of the potential enemies. They warned vaguely that all forms
of violence initiated by unnamed "potentates" needed to be guarded against.
Two ships of war would have to be dispatched for the families' protection.

Continuing, they imagined the English king using force against the Dutch.
Together they would be the objects of attack from Englishmen sent to support
the king's design of dispossessing the Netherlanders and drawing strength
from their more extensive territorial occupation and population. Territories,
not spheres of commercial influence, would be in conflict. As for the island
itself, the request called for the rudiments of what would one day be called
"governmentality." Through an enlarged company bureaucracy, the Dutch state
would take on the function of providing military defense for the colonists. It
would also introduce laws and codes regulating the religious instruction and
conversion of the natives and make itself accountable for administering the
plantations of an enlightened Commonwealth. All this would be under the command of a government of the United Provinces that would surely recognize
in this little Commonwealth a reflection of and valuable contribution to "its
glory." Weren't the triple purposes of emigration and settlement right before
their eyes? Though they did not cite his words, an English minister had laid
them out during these same months: "to plant a rude wilderness; to enlarge
the honour and fame of our dread Sovereign; . . . to display the efficacy and
power of the Gospel."[15]

Who could knock back four hundred zealous and loyal colonists? But the
request was—English. The Dutch state that the petitioners invoked not only
didn't exist, but becoming a nation was something the northern Netherlanders
had determined to avoid. And stating that the republic had fought for glory
during the revolt was something an average burgher would probably not quite
understand or feel the need to confirm or refute.[16] But perhaps the mispercep-
tion is best noticed by considering an island the Dutch held twenty-one years
later, in the early 1640s. They valued it greatly. The island was Deshima. It lay
off the Japanese coast of Nagasaki—offshore but near enough to be connected
to the great trading city by a small bridge. The island was no more than the size
of a cricket oval, just 400 feet long and 240 feet wide.

The chief concern of the States at this time was not four hundred English families but the closure of New Netherland to its own free traders. Previously, it had accepted them as participants in an experiment "free and open to all."[17] Now it sought to exclude them. It was ready to establish a place of exploitation subject to the monopolistic practices of the West India Company. The Dutch word for exploitation is *uitbuiting*. It is built up from *buit* and is a frightening term. Readers of contemporary pamphlets and tracts commenting on the wars in northern and central Europe would have found it familiar. It meant "booty" or "loot" and implied the use of force and theft.

But for the moment—and for the future, as they imagined it—the intention of the States and the company was for peaceful exploitation, not force. They would lie alongshore and maintain a fleet of ships that might—just might— resemble the giant *spiegel-schepen* already returning from the Indies. Here were cargo ships painted with bright colors, their sterns trimmed with reflecting mirror and gilt. People called them *zeecasteelen*, floating palaces. They were bulging warehouses carrying home the products that the company directors would soon auction; they floated home the treasures that officials and merchants had collected, and chests of curiosities that sailors and soldiers had surreptitiously accumulated.

By 1626, the company could report to the States that in the previous year it had determined the island that would be its general rendezvous. It had purchased the land. Manhattan Island. Seemingly no shame or sorrow in that.

PART II

Shared Beaches

The Netherlanders' first sustained encounter with the Algonquian-speaking Americans occurred in 1624. They settled trading stations on the Delaware and Connecticut Rivers, as well as north on the Hudson River near present-day Albany and on Manhattan Island. Southern New Netherland became a waterlands onto which were projected distinctively Dutch aspirations and domains of knowledge.

During these decades, the Netherlanders' uprising against Spain (1568–1648) had fixed their attention on the Iberian Peninsula. Now the Indies companies were prepared to challenge Portuguese and Spanish expansion overseas. Following the voyage of Vasco da Gama in 1497, Portuguese merchants had established in the Indies an empire of dispersed trading enclaves that the companies were eager to displace but also imitate. The largest was only a few dozen square miles in area. Their factories—which yielded immense profits, particularly in spices—were founded not on colonization but on the navigational and mercantile skills of transient merchant-entrepreneurs.

Soon the East India Company was also the master of strategically distributed factories. The same pattern was laid down in the early years of New Netherland. The shore fort built in 1626 on Manhattan Island, the distribution of limited personnel, the animus against colonization, and the ambit claim to a far-flung trading monopoly—all were Dutch improvisations on an admired model of economic exploitation.

The West India Company was also looking to Spain. The Spaniards overseas were precisely what the Netherlanders were determined not to be. They were conquistadores; the Dutch would be simply *coopleiden*, traders. The opposition was part of an emerging discourse meant to normalize the Netherlanders' intrusion into North America. Another was the Grotian insistence that while overseas residents' rights to retain lands owned prior to European contact were inviolable, foreign traders might nonetheless legally enter the harbors of other nations if they came without coercion. Correspondents on Manhattan Island were soon offering assurances that the company's presence was legitimate. Coercion had not been necessary. They were carefully purchasing the limited lands needed. The native peoples were wholeheartedly welcoming them.

Dutch responses to the model of Portuguese expansion, the brutality of Spain in the Americas, and the humanism of Grotius folded back into a distinctive culture. I have used "alongshore" as a metaphor for that distinctiveness. A metaphor gives us a way to read. It causes us to notice, draws our attention. We come to recognize that its meaning is in an endless number of instantiations of it we want to mention.

Alongshore, then, is a way—not the only way—of reading the history of Dutch-Amerindian encounters in New Netherland.

Chapter 3
The Quarterdeck and Trading Station

The West India Company took almost two years to make sure that the island of the Manhates was the right place. We are too far offshore to see those years and events clearly. We haven't been given the charts and paperwork to discern anything other than indistinct sightings.

Landmarks are fogged out. Perhaps significant ones. Instead of hearing the sound of many stories and multiple voices, we have mostly the discourse of the company directors. Stories from the boardroom: guarded, coded, in-house. Accounts not particularly concerned to describe the resident people among whom their subordinates were now establishing themselves. We have a lot of stories written with hindsight. But they can be a problem.

During this time, 1624 to 1626, the company's men were doing what the East India Company's officers needed to do years earlier: they were giving consideration to a number of islands and riverside locations as possible rendezvous points. Following the logic of any overseas trading company, they had landed small numbers of personnel in several locations. To make a beginning, the directors had selected a man from the marge of the Zuider Zee. Cornelisse Jacobsz May would locate and equip the places from which the choice of a *middelpunt* might soon be made. One day, the natives would say that they treated him and his companions like the apple of their eye.

May had sailed to the Virginias earlier. He'd explored the coastline for perhaps a full decade and in 1614 was commanding a ship owned by three merchants of Hoorn. Cornelis Volkertsz was one of them. Throughout the summer of 1624, May was examining islands and rivers on the southern coast of lands reaching from today's Delaware River to the entrance to the Connecticut River. He was also eager to establish a trading post (Fort Orange) along Hudson's river and at a distant location where earlier voyagers had traded successfully for furs (Map 2). He was leaving men at four locations, maybe five. Each lay at a great distance from the others and was probably a crude trading compound that an earlier tramp trader had found advantageous and where one or another may still have been living. May hedged his bets, overseeing the building of a rough redoubt at one location and establishing forts at two others.

He named a fortified trading station on Prince's Island "Wilhelmus." The men thought well of it because it had timber and arable land and was twenty-five miles upriver, far enough to attract native traders. Perhaps that would be the place. But then again, Nut Island, where he'd established another trading post just off the island of the Manhates, offered another possibility. It was sheltered by the arms of the harbor and free of the dangers of inundation to which a possible settlement on the island of the Manhates just across the channel to the north might be exposed. Two rivers closed it in, and either could cause the familiar tragedy: buildings washed away and lands drowned as water crashed over uncertain embankments.[1]

So Nut Island could be the site. An impermanent trading post could be set up somewhere along *het noordt rivier* (the Hudson River). The directors referred to this secondary trading post as a *logie*. The term was familiar in the East Indies and polar lands. It signified a dwelling built of wood or animal hides and, if necessary, transportable. Even after the rejection of Nut Island and the choice of the island of the Manhates, the small island's attraction was something like that of Onrust off Batavia. The traders kept it in use, on one occasion landing cattle sent from Holland and then shipping them to the larger island for better pasturage. In a way, the fortified site on Nut Island influenced the thinking of company officials and an engineer when they began the fort on the island of the Manhates in the second year of the company's explorations. They located it on a point opposite Nut Island. That would give the two forts control of a channel estimated to be about seven fathoms deep in the middle and a gunshot wide. The two forts would guard the entrance to the great river running to the north.[2]

As in the Indies, decisions about the best way to put the people and paraphernalia of the trading company ashore were made by those who could not be called landsmen. Where to make a landing and how to erect the first buildings and bring the station into profit as quickly as possible were determinations made by men on ships. The company addressed May as *commandeur*. It was a decades-old and familiar reference to a skipper of the North Sea herring fleets. It had nothing to do with an officer in command of land soldiers. A later writer spoke in awe of men like May, who had difficulty mapping the interior of a country but could chart the five shoals off the coast between the Delaware and Hudson Rivers as accurately as a modern marine cartographer.[3]

Now, like Hendricksz before him, May was on the move in some of the New World's waterlands: cruising and surveying in alongshore places; moving along sounds, estuaries, and bays; setting sails and trading goods. Never stationary for long, May went about setting up his trading posts. Each was a transit stop to the others: Nut Island, Prince's Island, Castle Island, and the island of the Manhates, too. Telling his stories when his ship arrived home, he gave a publicist exciting material to put alongside news of other overseas ventures such as "a fleet . . . [just] arrived from Archangel."[4]

In 1625, Willem Verhulst succeeded May. He was another man in motion, a Zeelander. Contemporaries captured with a single hyphen the essence of men from the province where land and sea became one with the other: he was a Zee-lander.

But Zeeland was not *a* land. It was an archipelago or, as they said, fifteen or sixteen isles. These were small and vulnerable stretches of land, each isolated in its combat with the sea, each forced to shape-shift as the sea, at will, threw at it mountains of sand and water. Once, a man from the island of Schouwe could walk to the shore of the island of North Beveland; later, in 1593, the two islands were (wrote a visitor) "greatly distant." Once, someone estimated that South Beveland was twenty leagues in circuit; by the end of the sixteenth century, that had been halved. But, then again, once Middelburg was an unremarkable town in the middle of the island of Walcheren. But in 1593, it was loading and unloading hundred-ton ships that had sailed up a canal cut through the island from the port of Armuyden. Zeeland was "a countrie of the Sea."[5]

Verhulst lived out this elision of sea and land in a special way. It was a platform for images and behaviors that he carried to the *zee-landen* of New Netherland. In early 1625, the company contracted him to take command of four ships bound for New Netherland. He was to take aboard a number of company employees and perhaps as many as forty-five colonists. Farm animals and equipment would have to clutter the decks and holds as well. All enough to promise a self-sustaining operation. We can read his instructions. He would have known they had a special importance. "Instructions" obliged a man to establish the essentials of the task assigned: the trade and everything (even mercantile law) related to it.[6] So in New Netherland, he was to discharge the personnel at a site he thought most promising and act as provisional director.

So the skipper began a voyage that was to keep him on the island of the Manhates—or, better, moving in and around the island—for about sixteen months. He introduced practices that met the circumstances presented by the network of islands and trading posts where he was now expected to establish some order. But the things he did weren't entirely novel. They were like the earlier steps taken by the East India Company to get it properly set up at Bantam and Batavia. They would give the trading company a significant presence in North America, and that meant achieving adjacency to the peoples who made their homes along its coastal fringes and inland recesses.

In 1925, almost three hundred years after Verhulst left the New World waterlands, a Dutch historian, F. C. Wieder, studied his practices as he began to direct the company's affairs. He thought Verhulst governed New Netherland in part "in the manner of a ship." And so he did. He presumed that he had authority by virtue of maritime law and, closely related to that, commercial law. This was the *handelsrecht* that seafaring men and women knew was practically identical to maritime law. The company directors, as maritime entrepreneurs themselves, made the same presumption. In time, they would introduce Dutch-Roman law. For now, they would establish only the necessary elements of it, keeping its interpretation in their own hands and doling it out in nothing more than provisional orders for one employee or instructions for another such as Verhulst.[7]

Meanwhile no one seemed to think it strange that the commander conducted on land the ceremonies and practices that kept maritime law in existence at sea. In their first set of instructions, the directors had also called upon this elision. Let religious services, they said, be conducted *soo binnen scheepsboort als te land,* as on shipboard so on the land. Let the colonists be obedient to the articles of behavior that govern each ship. Let some of these articles— there were at least thirty-seven—remain in force even after they have landed.[8] That no firm line existed between things of the sea and those of the land was as logical as the sea's own refusal to obey a fixed high-water mark or a dune's refusal to stand still.

So the government of the waterside trading station was, wrote a scholar, a "continuation of the organization on shipboard." It wasn't necessary for Verhulst to invent novel strategies to bring about an amphibiousness of command: it was simply the way it was and should be. To reach decisions at sea—the setting of courses or undertaking of armed engagements—he would have raised a white flag and, by that, assembled a council of the captains of each supporting ship. Similarly now on land. A place on the council belonged to skippers anchored in port. In the Dutch Caribbean trading station at Curaçao, it was the same. Captains longest in the company's service were given precedence in the council's decision making about affairs even on the island. Seven years after the founding of the East India Company, the Indies' governor-general was also living aboard ship and making decisions with a council of skippers located at various stations. And in New Netherland in 1649, captains still had a vote on the council.[9]

In a sense, Verhulst never left the quarterdeck. On shore, he dined with officers who were honored to be called *schipmannen van der tafelen,* his mess in the cabin aboard ship. He had a residence of some kind on the Delaware River. But the only reference to it suggests a beached quarterdeck, a place where he might make decisions by calling together the skippers who were present on the river. The records contain a directive concerning the discovery of precious metals. It gives us a sighting of this strange waterland world and then fogs it out again. Let the discoverer bring them to Verhulst or bring them "on board the ship."[10]

And why would the commander not govern as sure in his authority on land as on a ship's quarterdeck? There were two words for "ceremony" in the Dutch language. Each derived from places where solemn behavior was customary. One was *hoffelijk*. It referred to ceremonies conducted in the courts. The second was *plechtigheid* (from *plecht*), the forward deck of a ship. Maritime law was the legislation by which sea captains lived. It empowered them to bring seafaring under a complex order of discipline and give that discipline a solemnity in shipboard ceremonies that equaled in stature those of Dutch courts. The *zee-rechten* could be grandly codified, as they were earlier by the Hanseatic cities. Or they could be referred to in the simple word used in an Amsterdam publication printed about twenty years before Verhulst's days in and out of the islands. The writer called them, simply, *water-recht*.[11]

Verhulst was also an amphibian because the trading company appointed him as *commis*. In a world that especially honored the *mercator sapiens*, that appointment meant that he was an experienced merchant responsible for the cargo and wider business concerns of the ship's owners. Their cargo pulled him into its own amphibiousness: first stored in a ship's cargo hold, then deposited on the wharf, and from there either consigned to customers or held in a warehouse along a waterfront. At sea and alongshore, the cargo was his responsibility. Because of the cargo he needed to make a public display of shipboard and onshore professionalism (and cunning). Arrangements about the goods and their exchange might continue for many months onshore. So yesterday's supercargo became today's office-bound commissary. Accompanying returning cargo, an officer like Verhulst became a seaborne supercargo all over again.

The commander was also provisional director of the settlement. Or, as the directors wrote, he was provisional director of the *coloniers*. Single persons and heads of families—perhaps ten or eleven—had signed contracts with the company and accepted transportation to New Netherland. Maybe they were seventy men and women in all. Their number may also have included those who were *vrije kooplieden*, that is, free traders such as those who had been moving around New Netherland before May's arrival. The *coloniers* were not directly employed by the company. Between them and the company's personnel, the directors made a clear distinction—and would continue to make it. The differentiation was a crucial one and, over time, often as pejorative as the distinction made in Batavia between company employees and *vrije burghers*.

The *coloniers* were held to be little more than adjuncts to the company and its enterprises. They would have known this from the laws set in place for them as well as the geography planned for the station and the social hierarchy into which they were fitted. Legally, they were the only men and women who might possibly take up permanent residence on the island. Personnel of the company—captains and officers, ministers and ships' carpenters, the seamen and (some) soldiers—had residences at home, where they were subject to local and provincial laws. It wasn't expected that they—any more than East India Company personnel in Batavia, Formosa, or Deshima—would establish permanent residence on the island. Maritime law and *handelsrecht* covered them.

The *coloniers* were different. For them, *een bestuur voor de wal* had to be put into place. Literally, that means "governance alongside"—in this case, alongside maritime law. It was designed for the individuals who were considered simply alongside too: those adjacent to company employees energized by the maritime and commercial law that underpinned the enterprise. The directors distrusted the *coloniers*. They called them free colonists. But nothing good was to be expected of anyone free of the company. When the directors decided to send a second group of emigrants, they avoided *vrije coloniers* altogether. Instead, they chose to transport farmers who would all be in the service of the company.[12]

Verhulst received instructions for laying out a built-up area where these *coloniers* would try to make their living. A contemporary Leiden scholar understood clearly what it would be: "a fort and habitations." Fort Amsterdam was the key building and the key concern. It would be on a trading beach adjacent to the sea. In its orientation and design, it would look outward. Even a directive that there be a hospital within its walls was a maritime consideration. The hospital was not intended to serve the needs of the resident personnel. By the requirements of maritime law, hospitals needed to be made available to sea captains obliged to seek such refuges if they had sick crewmen aboard.

The fort—probably built a year after these instructions were written—was marine architecture. It was not erected inland or on a hilltop position facing the countryside and native people. The makeshift fort erected by English colonists at Plymouth at about the same time was one of these. Rather, like the forts built along coastlines and rivers at home, elsewhere abroad, and even here where Fort Orange stood upriver, Fort Amsterdam was a shore fort built to repel enemies from the sea: Spanish, French, and English. Hadn't Nicolaes Wassenaer, warned that the Spaniard would never allow others to gain possession of the Americas and had made many incursions "in Florida, Virginia, and thereabouts"?[13] Twenty-five years from now, in the mid-1650s, a resident New Netherlander would have one of the fictional characters in his account of the country issue a warning that the Portuguese and other pirates could easily invade.

Far across the Atlantic, the directors could only imagine the terrain on which the fort would be sited. Yet this didn't diminish their concern for detail and their determination that it be seen to. Engineers' plans and builders' models for military fortifications were plentiful in the Low Countries. The wars begun in 1572 and still raging had seen to that. Dutch engineers had learned that simple forts could be built in less than four months. So the directors' orders about the fort were echoes of a science born of war and applied by a people accustomed to building such structures along shorelines. They directed that the engineer mark off a circular moat and major skirts according to a form set out in an attached draft, that is, they added, where the elevation is and the fort "lies open to the waterside." The outer and inner moats would be laid out along three sides and a fourth side open to the sea. About the vagaries of tides that might affect a fort located on the water level, the directors were willing to take advice. But an installation set only a hundred feet from the water at high tide seems not to have worried them any more than fortifications at the water's edge worried the Portuguese in the Indies. Let it be "100 feet from the water at high tide, as the situation more or less requires."[14]

The fort was the material presence of the company. It announced a powerful trading company taking control of its own trading beach. It was taking commercially advantageous space and giving it a proper shape; it had a valuable harbor and merchandise to protect. The embracing skirts and bastions of the fort were the boundaries of the habitations. Their configuration and measurement also merited detailed attention. The salaried employees and the *coloniers* were expected to live at specified locations within the walls. Some were to be housed on the streets of the fort and live within a social hierarchy fine-tuned within a narrow range. As in the Indies, the highest position a man could attain was that of senior merchant. Below him were the company's sea captains and junior merchants, master builders and overseers of farms, skilled artisans and carpenters, the seamen, and (sharing the bottom rung with unmarried men) soldiers. There were, in short, those who were expected to make a major contribution and those who were the losers. These were the *ondienstighe*, the useless ones who, if found to be of no service, were to be sent home immediately.[15]

There were farms—farms designed and measured out; topography imagined by the directors; places where the *commis*'s farm should be. There were concerns for where a ditch should be dug to separate one farm from another and how productive the farmlands might be. But this was not an agricultural settlement.[16] Rather, the farms of the company were an extension of the fort. They were part of its topographically unified design. They lay, six of them, not more than a hundred feet directly north of the fort. In their calculated compactness—their topographical fusion with the fort—they stood for a commercial, not a territorial, presence. The farms' overseers and laborers were seen as maritime personnel. They might work the land, but they were contributing to the welfare of the Netherlanders as a seafaring people.

Coloniers were sent to New Netherland because they were seen to be needed. At times, the directors were prepared to acknowledge this and use a term that encompassed both them and their employees—such terms as *onze troupen*, our people. But the adjunctive nature of their contribution and their status as farmers placed them in a subordinate position.

Netherlanders were generally ambiguous about landsmen. This ambiguity had distinctive cultural forms at home. In New Netherland, it was to have tragic repercussions on the strangers and natives alike. Yet over the years, it went unanswered. The company took colonists to be actively or potentially disloyal. They were the ones most likely to incite conflict with the natives. Given a chance, they would maximize their own short-term needs, stir up unnecessary trouble, and compromise the distance required between the company's employees and the local people. The directors were already warning the commanding officers about what to look for: their provocative words—words mocking the natives, ridiculing, shaming, and humiliating them; their desire for close contact with the natives and then recourse to injury and violence; their trickery—exulting in dishonest bargaining and facile deceit. Such violence did the company no good.[17]

Perhaps the *coloniers* were lucky to be there at all. At least twice before, the company had rejected the notion of sending agriculturalists. Colonization was not a straightforward proposition with the great trading companies. Since 1613, the issue had troubled the directors of the East India Company, about whose business the West India Company men would have had intimate knowledge. For the next ten years, Coen vigorously urged them toward colonization. Coen was only thirty-one when appointed fourth governor-general in the Indies. Direct and arrogant, his insistent remonstrations to the directors about their attitude toward colonization and administration generally could have amounted to impertinence dangerous to career and personal fortune. "Who, "asked one biographer, "has ever written letters like his?"[18]

But the directors didn't take orders. Moreover, they saw no need for colonization. To them, "*agrarische kolonisatie bestond niet de minste belangstelling*," agricultural colonization was not of the least importance. First, the company followed a policy of using indigenous agriculturalists, contracting with (or forcing) local rulers to deliver rice, cattle, and other necessities. The situation in Batavia beginning in the 1630s was seen as ideal. Around the town's environs, Chinese farmers were transforming wastelands into rice fields, kitchen gardens, and sugar plantations. As a second consideration, those men who had served the company and been discharged or who were, for other reasons, not in its employ had invariably proved untrustworthy. Whatever they undertook as *vrije burghers,* they knowingly competed with the company. From earliest reports, they had been a point of contention.[19]

Answering these points, Coen was brutally frank about the colonists he wanted. He was not asking for farmers. Agreed, they were not needed. Nor was he willing to accept unmarried women. They would be troublesome. And women married to Dutch traders? He shared the notion expressed later by the company: they could be expected to induce their spouses to break the company's monopoly. Further, some of the non-merchant personnel already sent by the company were disgusting in their ways. Their ilk should never be sent again. The lay readers sent by the company typified all the others. They were "clownish, uncircumcised idiots."[20]

But middle-class men, those who understood Batavia's ambitions and were merchants like themselves—and here the sticking point for the company—could profit by running the *inland* trade between the Dutch and the Javanese—or Taiwanese, Ceylonese, or Malaccans—while the company continued to monopolize the long-distance trade and in that way still determine the price of exports. Such Hollanders and their families, he was saying in 1614, were essential to maximizing the company's enterprises and profits. They could be the foundation of a *burgermaatschappij*, a truly civic society. They would be like the disciplined Hollanders observable at home. Only a year before May set out for the coasts of New Netherland, Coen was urging the planting of colonies in the West Indies as well as the East Indies. His vision, however, was of a *borgerlijcke politie*, a middle-class society and the kind of civil law it would bring (Fig. 5). Isaack de Rasieres, a company officer in New Netherland, was neither as vehement nor as colorful in his advice to the West India Company regarding colonists. But after taking some measure of those on the island in 1626, his point was the same. "A better class of colonists should be sent out by the Company" if better results were to be anticipated.[21]

Farmers were needed on Manhattan Island. The company would have known by now that the natives would not provide an adequate labor force. But not many colonists were required and not such as would think they could follow their own devices, appearing to put their energies into farming but actually acting as independent agents in the fur trade. So the company gave itself two castes of agriculturalists. Those designated as *bouwmeesters* and *bouwlieden* were included in the company's *volck*. They were counted among those needed to attain its purposes, those such as the sailors in a ship's complement toward whom—if it had any—the company showed some degree of loyalty. The other caste, the *coloniers*, were simply the passengers.[22]

Later generations of those called British Americans or American citizens would seize upon these colonists as worthy of singular consideration. They were generative of New Netherland and then New York. Look to them for the origins, not to men-in-motion. The Americans and New Yorkers were wrong.

*   *   *

For some colonists and free burghers, the restrictive company practices were a provocation to more flagrant disregard of its rules. They might have thought themselves demeaned by the company. It had, after all, decided to subject them to *landsheerlijk recht*, the law that had once reduced farmers at home to the status of serfs—and still did in parts of some provinces. But they could not have been surprised at the identities they were made to wear. The enterprise was, after all, in the hands of maritime entrepreneurs and would remain so until the end. The merchant-adventurers called upon distinctive domains of imagination, emotion, and knowledge. A maritime way of life at home had given them authentication. The same ways of imagining had given shape to the practices of science and warfare, theater and the arts, navigation and colonization, government and agriculture, social hierarchies, relationships between countryside and city, and alongshore and inland. The marine topography of the rendezvous was a consequence of these fields of imagination and knowledge. So was its

Figure 5. A mid-seventeenth-century artist uses the clasped hands of a prosperous couple to say that—as Jan Coen had ambitioned earlier—Dutch Batavia was successfully replicating the *burgerlijk* virtues and lifestyles of home. Aelbert Cuyp, *An Officer of the VOC, Possibly Jacob Mathieusen and his Wife; in the Background the Bay of Batavia* (detail). Collection Rijksmuseum, Amsterdam.

disdain for those who were the least maritime of the company's complement, the farmers.

And imagining the Amerindians? How would it go with them? One Hollander, this man serving in the East Indies, had his own way of summing that up. It all sounded so promising. We are here, he wrote, precisely not as Spanish conquistadores but as *cooplieden*, merchants.

We mean only to trade.[23]

Chapter 4
Natives and Strangers

Cultural ways of imagining, feeling, and knowing shaped the Dutch strangers' encounters with the natives. Or closer to what happened, those ways were about to be tested. They would be clarified and altered in encounters that also activated the imagination, emotions, and ways of knowing of the native people. May and Hendricksz, like Henry Hudson and Robert Juet before them, had already experienced what a stranger's encounter with the natives was like. Each participant maneuvered the other. Each got a skewed understanding of the other. Each drew the other onto his hazy horizon of expectations.

One man who crossed the beach into the Americans' lives wrote down the natives' words for the strangers. And the natives had it right. The Dutch strangers were *winderswaren*, traders who came on the sea winds.[1] And they *were* transients; they were conscious of places to which they would return. Even here on their trading beach, they would stay within their own culture. They would normalize their alongshore enclave. It was the way of long-distance merchant travelers: Persian merchants in Amsterdam, Dutch merchants in Nantes.

It was as outsiders that the Dutch imagined and put into practice the terms of their relationship with the natives. They came as traders with headquarters and interests back home or elsewhere overseas. In time, they would turn their attention to more elaborate alongshore facilities for their extractive and seaborne operations. They would provide for collecting, warehousing, and shipping furs—the same process for timber and perhaps minerals. The future would involve care for the hydrographic mapping of harbors and rivers. It would see the construction of shore facilities for repairing transatlantic cargo vessels and shallow-draft coastal yachts. Personnel would be aggregated to complete these requirements: sailmakers, ships' carpenters, skilled pilots. An island settlement such as Goa or Deshima would emerge: one satisfied to be adjacent to the sea before it and to the continent at its back. Exploiting both. An enterprise abandoned when the riches ran out.

You may think that the desire to achieve adjacency is a curious one. It seems to suggest satisfaction with being on the sidelines to the real field of play, a willingness to be nearby but not central, to be diminished in the presence of something more important, more attention-grabbing or significant. You may think of the parking lot adjacent to the stadium, the baptistery to the cathedral, the tourist traps to Saint Peter's Basilica. Adjacency implies acceptance of a shared border, confinement in a functional but dependent space.

But here on the island, embracing adjacency as a way of making sense of their role in North America was not the Dutch entrepreneurs' way of embracing powerlessness. Awareness of margins was a way of exerting power and, if necessary, the violence of power. If adjacency involved a moral carelessness in personal or social relations with others, so be it.

So a contemporary publicist writing in Holland thought nothing amiss in calling his countrymen "strangers" in the lands of the natives. Starting in the mid-fifteenth century, Dutch merchants had regularly been "strangers" in places such as Bergen in Norway, where they had handled the timber trade for a home port like Hoorn or Enkhuizen. Some chose to become citizens of Bergen but could as readily have remained resident strangers. When the directors were determining the legalities of settling on the island of the Manhates, they chose to describe the indigenes as "native-born people" and themselves as the "strangers" or "foreigners."[2]

Here on the island in 1625 and 1626, the Europeans needed peaceful coexistence on separate parts of the beach. The directors told May and Verhulst to observe care in conducting native affairs. Only they were empowered to enter alliances and secure trading contracts with the natives or, more specifically, with the *vreemde mogendheden,* those in power among them. They still half-expected to encounter powerful American leaders or, as they worded it, "foreign princes and potentates." They had expressed this possibility more than once. Americans might be rulers of "an immense civilized land." So, they instructed, you must arrange meetings with them and extend the proper honorifics. Be careful to present yourselves as subjects of a powerful sovereign—in this case, Prince Mauritz of Nassau.[3]

The directors were already beginning to take on a distinctive way of writing about the natives. They gestured to them as ghosts. Even when they came into view as customers, they were formless shapes: objects, seldom subjects, and never personalized. A name might come ashore on a contract of sale or later in an account of conflict. But it was quickly washed away. The directors were working out trajectories of their own projects and the shareholders' profits. Names—of the *coloniers,* of soldiers and ordinary seamen, of native customers—didn't need to be known.

Now the directors were carefully foreclosing any possible misstep in the process of settling in. They knew well enough that (as they wrote) "force or threats" were always a tempting recourse in concluding a business transaction. But only a contract or treaty that was signed by all parties would prevent future disputes. One day, they warned Verhulst, the validity of such contracts might be "very useful to the Company." Such disputes were, in fact, going to arise on the part of a European rival in about seven years' time. But for now, they were giving instructions for the proper purchase of Prince's Island. Natives living on the island or making any claim on it, or upon other places useful to us, they advised, "must not be driven away by force or threats, but by good words persuaded to leave, or, be given something therefor for their satisfaction." Or else allow them to live among us under contractual arrangements. The natives, they assumed, had their own written language system and protocols. So they added that they should sign such contracts in their own manner.[4]

Those were Verhulst's instructions dated January 1625. Directions written three months later were the same but more comprehensive. Now the directors were saying: we've got to get the geography right. It's crucial to establishing a proper legal footing with the natives. But they were still reluctant to prescribe the exact location of a central rendezvous. They wanted to hold out for a place such as their East India Company counterparts had spent their energies locating a decade earlier: if uninhabited, they'd said then, "so much the better."[5]

So it was with reservations that they put forward their first choice. Consider the west side of the island of the Manhates. But here's a bit of latitude. If no suitable place can be found left abandoned by the natives (on the southern tip of the island), don't undertake the fortifications and outlying defenses in the directives to the engineer but put in place something "more provisional." Meanwhile, survey the other principal places we've favored in case one of them has been abandoned. Should only inhabited lands be found, negotiate an agreement with the proprietors for the best location on the island of the Manhates.[6]

The directors went on to distinguish between their present belligerent relations with Europeans and those they hoped might exist with the non-Europeans. The distinction rested in part on discussions then being aired in Holland and within the offices of the East India Company. What is a just war, and how is it to be conducted? For a war to be just, they agreed, it had to be declared. This was a requirement founded on Roman and medieval law. If it met other conditions, total war against such declared enemies was legitimate. Because injuries had been intended and inflicted, a state might ward off further injuries by declaring war and waging it to its finality. States or peoples who were "*not* the first to lay violent hands upon their neighbors" were not to be proceeded against.[7]

The directors didn't labor the distinction. But they did use it to remind their subordinates of purposes that were clearly never far from their minds. These were the destruction of Spanish imperial power whenever and wherever they encountered it and—again, whenever and wherever—the pursuit of orderly trading beachheads. The Heren XVII of the East India Company had put the same distinction to a fleet commander in instructions issued in 1603. "We are," they began, "an organization for the protection of our people and the places established . . . [by us] on the islands *and others being our friends [andere onse vrienden wesende]* and also for the advantage and assured security of the East Indies trade, enacting everything offensively possible against the Spanish, Portuguese, and their allies."[8]

So here on the island of the Manhates, the West India Company directors were ordering their men to negotiate treaties and accords without force. Twenty-two years earlier, an Indies fleet commander had received orders to respect the religion and culture of the Bandanese and not to cause difficulties. Now another set of directors was ordering: don't resort to trickery or fraud, and certainly not war. We are making a beginning, they reminded them. It must not be a foundation laid on injustice. Right now, we needn't offer reasons for making war against the Hapsburgs and their allies. They are "our declared enemies." Even the English and French could be expected to be predators on our trading stations and need watching. Hadn't they just been warned by the States to take a lesson from the difficulties the East India Company had with them? When you are at your weakest, they'd warned, they'll frequent the places you've established and from which "they cannot be excluded" without armed conflict. With the natives, the company implied, we are not in such a relationship.[9]

The directors' goals went beyond negotiating for an island rendezvous. Legal justification for entering the territories of those they called the several foreign nations depended on wider negotiations. To trade successfully beyond the island and into New Netherland—that is, to wherever the farthest territorial boundaries of the nations living there might be—the company needed to establish monopoly status with each one. Only bilateral treaties or accords agreed to by the parties concerned extinguished the principle that ensured *to other European powers* what Grotius called the natural freedom of trade.[10]

Therefore, the company's officers were ordered to make contracts with natives from (wherever they were) other areas. Promising reasonable prices for furs would encourage them to grant exclusive rights and share knowledge of how they managed the trade. Perhaps because of European practices, the directors anticipated that the coastal and inland people would keep in secrecy information about traffic among themselves. They would have to tease it out. In this and other ways, they would have to depend for success on amicable relations with these foreign nations that, taken together, were masters not of some limited area immediately surrounding the island but of a boundless landscape and on whose sufferance they were being allowed to stay.[11]

*   *   *

For the most part, the directors refused to be deterred by a number of well-documented negative reports about the natives. These were descriptions of them as unpredictable, given to suspicion and vindictiveness, and prone to intervillage warfare. The directors also seemed, as the saying went, to look between their fingers at killings committed by natives a decade earlier. If their intrusion into the lives of Algonquian-speaking people seemed unwelcome and was creating disorder and violence, they were quietly disavowing it. Perhaps they wanted to avoid frightening off shareholders or potential colonists. Perhaps, like the artist's vision in the Prototype View, it had to seem natural that they be there: a piece of Algonquian land is simply beginning to take on the coloration and lines of the Low Countries. Perhaps they wanted to demonstrate that they could match the achievements of the East India Company on Formosa in the same year, 1626. There, the governor-general was able to write, his people were maintaining good trade and friendship with the inhabitants. But his words were ominous if one cared to examine them closely. We do this, he continued, because of the profits that may be expected but also "to keep them from becoming too antagonistic toward us."[12]

There were also powerful legal reasons for insisting that the company was locating itself on peaceful trading beaches. It had to seem internationally non-problematic that they be there. Early in the 1600s, Hugo Grotius had articulated an important principle: foreign traders had the right to enter the harbors of other nations, providing they came without coercion. So now, in 1625, the officers on the island were being told what others elsewhere had been told: don't interfere in the foreigners' affairs, but as far as possible, "maintain peace with one and all." If hostilities break out among them, find the best means of acting as mediators. Remain neutral. This was sound business practice upgraded to treaty law.[13]

These instructions and the determination to maintain separateness were not a humanist's ideal or theologian's moral imperative. Nothing in the documents pretends they were. But neither were they just the expedients of a trading company. The directors' determination to shape non-entanglement into overseas policy and practices could be imagined because coexistence was a commonsense logic that went back centuries. It encompassed humanism, pragmatism, and more. It was a logic that was taking on new forms at home even as the island was being settled.

Well before the time of our story, the Dutch had become aware that cross-cultural encounters involved risks and therefore required vigilance. They called for attention to boundaries, to concern for inclusion and exclusion. Regarding strangers,—Europeans and people overseas—it was best to lay offshore: offshore to their internal political affairs or warring impulses, offshore to their religious beliefs and customs, offshore to their lands and territories. European powers were finding contemporary protestations of this neutrality offensive, especially when combined (as they had been lately) with large measures of self-congratulatory republicanism. It was a hypocritical rhetoric intended to hide the machinations of a people steadily acquiring the riches of the known world by whatever degree of cunning and interference they thought necessary.

The Europeans were correct in recognizing that the ambitions of the United Provinces were far more threatening to their interests than those of a clutch of merchant communities simply plying the waters in their small ships, pragmatically going about their business. And in time, the Dutch vision of noninterference was going to be tragically compromised. It had already begun to be in the Indies. But the Europeans were wrong in assuming that Dutch claims to calculated forms of containment were not grounded in time-honored mythologies and practices. Well before the early seventeenth century, Netherlanders had fused mythic notions of themselves and the landscape with common sense and, taken to be the same thing, good business sense. The result was a powerful, and powerfully spatialized, self-image.

The Dutch counted themselves to be people of islands and coastlines, drowned land, and shifting margins. Geographically, they were not inland to Europe. They were not, as one Englishman derided, bog people living on the "off-scouring of the British sand."[14] But they were alongshore folk. They made their homes on the marshy stretches where Europe petered out and drowned itself along the edges of the North Sea. Well-being meant maximizing the prosperity of these sea-replenishing and marginal places—we have seen it in Hoorn and Medemblik, Amsterdam and the Zeeland isles. It didn't mean expanding inland or getting drawn into inlanders' affairs.

Overseas, the Dutch could be the same alongshore people. In Batavia and at the Cape, along the Coromandel Coast and New Netherland, they could lie alongshore and hope for riches while entertaining a minimum of cultural exchange. They had come to such places to trade, not conquer. They were present to wheel and deal, not to take command of people and territories. Beyond the business of commodity exchange and the need to acquire knowledge of local trading practices, neither natives nor Dutch men and women were under any obligation to appropriate one another's ways, not even to have a close knowledge of one another.[15] In the late twentieth century, multinational entrepreneurs were similarly disinclined to know the natives into whose lands they'd come to set up their offshore factories or mining operations. Only because of public opinion, or world opinion, were some of them forced to extend their knowledge of the indigenous people. They had to undertake environmental impact studies, employ an anthropologist, consult together.

Now on the island, the directors seemed to be reaping rewards from their carefully legalized presence on the island of the Manhates. Or so they presented it. The island has been purchased, they reported to the States in 1626, and "our people are in good heart and live in peace there." Peace was showing itself to be productive. Grain sowed in May had been reaped in August. More than eight thousand furs had just reached Amsterdam, along with timber, oak, and hickory. A Dutch publicist of things European and around-the-world was writing that the Manhates were becoming "accustomed to the strangers." One early Dutch trader there could understand the native languages and was regularly able to trade in a friendly manner. The natives were incorporating the strangers' trading goods into their lives, even if in oddly quasi-religious ways. A native woman, for example, wished to be buried in a skipper's shirt (the same commentator wrote earlier), and the skipper had willingly given it to her.[16]

In 1628, a minister on the island was writing home with similar assurances. The fort was symbolic of the peacefulness of their situation and the natives' satisfaction at being part of the Dutch trading environment. We've built a new fort, he wrote. But it is not so much for protection against the natives with whom we live without fear as against European enemies beyond the island.[17]

In the same year, a publicist was telling readers that those on the island could confidently live outside the walls of the fort because the natives lived peacefully with them. Four years earlier, the minister had written that it was a matter of the natives getting accustomed to the Dutch. And that was happening. Take the experience of going north along the great river to the lands of the Mahicans. You must navigate "up, through divers nations, who sometimes manifest themselves with arrows, like enemies, sometimes like friends." But then "when they have seen the ships once or twice, or traded with our people, they become altogether friendly." Indeed so widely had an unambiguous description of the docility of the natives reached certain churchmen and "many others in the Fatherland" that the same minister, who thought he saw the other, darker side of their behavior, was set to wondering who it was who "had imposed" the accounts on them.[18]

The minister's unease was with accounts that were contradicting the evidence of his own eyes. Yet neither he nor the company men, nor perhaps the natives, were in a position to fully imagine the pattern discerned by a historian some 330 years after his letter. Ironically, the tragedy that was to unfold around the natives also had to do with their either being alongshore or inland. Researching early New York, Allen Trelease had discovered evidence of natives deemed valuable and those who were expendable. The strong position of the inland tribes had convinced the Dutch that for profit's sake, they should be favored and their existing powers increased. The weaker coastal bands, on the other hand, he wrote, would bear the brunt of European invasion, "receiving only transitory benefits in return."[19]

In twentieth-century Dutch Indonesia, there was an old saying: *Hoort gij de donder niet?* Didn't you hear the thunder? Weren't you at all aware—you the strangers and you the people of the land—of the terrible things coming?

PART III

Staying Alongshore

Between 1625 and 1640, personnel of the West India Company appear to have established an amicable presence among the natives of New Netherland. Consistent with the logic of a maritime trading company, they expanded commercial networks but engrossed little indigenous land. At the same time, however, private investors in Holland were demanding the incorporation of privately owned patroonships. These, as some immediately recognized, would undercut the monopoly on furs and introduce the political and territorial consequences of the colonization that they vigorously opposed.

In 1629, a government resolution favoring the patroons moved the venture in a direction that challenged its fundamental character. It forced the company to recognize an altered distribution of power in New Netherland. Rights of sovereignty would not rest solely with the company but within multiple jurisdictions. The district (as they called it) would be a confederated one. Sovereignty would be exercised in the patroons' separate enclaves and in those lands directly administered by the company. It would also be rightfully exercised in the territories of the tribal rulers. This design replicated the political structure then being worked out for the emerging Dutch republic. There the problem of preserving traditional provincial sovereignties within a united Netherlands had begun to be resolved in the Union of Utrecht (1579), which allowed each province to retain sovereignty while granting minimal authority to the States General. The political identity of the indigenous Americans was being constructed for them just as the Dutch were inventing this structure as a large part of their own national identity.

At about the same time, the Netherlanders were defending the Americans as rightful landowners legally independent of intruding European powers. In 1632, they advanced this position before the English court in order to reject claims that New Netherland was part of Virginia. The Americans with whom they'd dealt in order to purchase New Netherland were, they insisted, free to open their markets to traders of their choice and free to either retain their territories and places of residence or sell portions of them (as they had done to the Dutch.) They were free men, subjects of neither the British crown nor the United Provinces.

During these years in New Netherland, the Dutch meant to engage with these free men and women in transactions of things—metal objects, shells, and woolens in exchange for fur and timber. As an anthropologist recently noted, "some transactions appear simply to concern things." One does not, he elaborated, "go into a shop to establish or consolidate a social relationship."[1] Nor does one, I would add, go into the shop to buy it and take over the running of it. But even in these early years, the Dutch were learning that there is a spillover in the exchange of things. Because the boundaries of exchange are porous, unanticipated cultural entanglement occurs. That was to happen in New Netherland in greater and greater measure.

Chapter 5

Sovereign People

In Holland, the business of the company is getting under way. For the benefit of its shareholders and political patrons, it is trafficking commodities from New Netherland. Trafficking has a universal meaning among these burghers. Pieter de la Court put it succinctly in 1662. Trafficking means "buying in foreign countries cheap, to sell dearer abroad."[1] Simple as that. Now it is December 1626, only a year since the company had charged Verhulst to bend every effort to establish a central trading beach on the island of the Manhates.

A public auction is held. The directors of the company's headquarters in Zeeland are managing it in Amsterdam. They have seen to all the details. The commodities landed about fifty days earlier. That's a long period of time to have elapsed between off-loading and sale. Overseas goods carried on Indiamen for the East India Company were often auctioned within days of a ship's arrival: five or six days—and the wares were gone.

In any case, the gentlemen-directors have now engaged an auctioneer, maybe more than one, and seen to the display of the wares to prospective buyers. The principal items for sale are furs: beaver and otter, mink and lynx. Undoubtedly, they are part of a cargo carried by *The Arms of Amsterdam*. Some of these were auctioned earlier this month. Originally, there were more than 7,200 beaver pelts, each one possibly weighing as much as fifteen pounds. There were also 675 otter skins, and far fewer mink and lynx.

A journalist shares the news of the late-December auction. He is accustomed to alerting his Dutch readers to happenings all across Europe. Merchants especially have to be up with the times "in Germany, France, England, Spain, Hungary, Poland, Seven-bergern," he boasts, and also "Wallachia, Moldavia, Turkey, and places in the Netherlands." He calls his comprehensive publication a *Historical Account* (*Historisch Verhael*) and puts it out annually.

About the furs sent from New Netherland and now presented for sale, the journalist has little to say. He describes them as various kinds. Nothing more. There is also timber for auction; oak and the wood of nut trees. To describe these, he leans on the spruiker of the auction. Here are "large quantities of logs, of oak and nut trees, which grow there in great abundance and which with the permission of the natives there are cut down and shipped, being—the spruiker warming to his task—"very useful here for many necessary purposes."[2]

At first glance, the description of the logs may seem insignificant. It's merely a string of superfluous words put together by an auctioneer to attract customers. In fact, the words are attractive but not superfluous. Regarding the wood, the company needs to make it clear that it is "with the permission of the natives" that trees have been cut down. This is, after all, one of its earliest efforts at selling New Netherland timber. The company needs to establish legitimate ownership. Buyers need to trust the bona fides of the original purchases: permission was given; the new buyer has clear title. He can sell them abroad (Fig. 6).

At the same time, the company needs to establish that it has begun to exploit a market in overseas logs. Buyers—and others who will learn of the company's role as a new player in the timber trade—can recognize that because the natives are amenable to selling to the company, it can supply logs over time. As a supplier, it can offer continuity and reliability in an ongoing market relationship. The logs are not illegally gotten goods. They are cut from stands of trees growing on lands owned by natives whose possession of them is unchallenged

Figure 6. Cornelis Jansz Kerfbijl probably owned the planks seen here stacked against a hoarding near houses at the far left of the painting. Timber merchants also operated at the Houtkopersbrugwal (Timber Merchants Bridge) near warehouses along the Oude Schans. On the city's west side, seventy to eighty sawmills were continually functioning as part of the giant shipbuilding industry. Jan Wijnants, *The Herengracht in Amsterdam*, c. 1660–62 (detail). The Cleveland Museum of Art, Gift of Harry D. Kendrick.

and with whom some (undisclosed) mutually acceptable arrangement has been reached. Nor is the timber confiscated goods—items seized overseas on some drummed-up pretext with all the uncertainty about status and ongoing availability that involves.

The auction is only a clue to the way the company men mean to function as foreign traders in New Netherland. But among other things, it brings on stage the shareholders and potential buyers in the home marketplace, players the company dares not treat lightly. In fact, it privileges their interests. In 1621, a government subsidy plus a float of the company's shares had yielded about 6.5 million guilders. Shareholders knew that they were buying into a high-risk enterprise. The company is always playing for high stakes. International competitors make them do so; their own instincts tell them to do so. One expert would write later, however, that the East India Company's policy was never to engage in excessive risks. It avoided risky capital ventures such as voyages of discovery to uncivilized regions and mining activities. Neither did it burden itself with "the founding of agricultural communities" or the supervision of large labor forces. The West India Company was the same.[3]

The home marketplace would give shape to the marketplace in North America. The natives who had given the Dutch permission to log trees on their land are being imagined into their role. The company means to have their timber—indeed, exclusive rights. But it does not covet ownership of the land or rule over their villages. In two, three, and five years' time, trading relationships between it and the native peoples will thicken. More extensive territories than the island will demand strategic decisions about a presence kept within the proper goals and structures of a trading company. Then a wider range of possibilities will require prolonged debate and heated discussion. But the company will remain consistent in recognizing the advantages of extraterritoriality in relation to the natives and their lands. Say it attaches itself to the native peoples like nothing more than a parasite: but that is the reality.

This is the recognition now folded into the words, with the permission of the natives. The Portuguese in the Indies had a word for it: *Precario.*[4] We are there, they accepted, on the sufferance of the native inhabitants. Verhulst had been reminded to take this into consideration in his instructions. During the 1630s, this premise will be a guiding consideration but, even as it was with the Portuguese, ominously fragile.

*   *   *

The company's New Netherland was becoming two entities in the late 1620s and 1630s. On the ground, it was still the island and increasingly the island's immediate surrounds. In 1630, probably only 270 Europeans made up the waterlands' settlements and the trading posts established upriver on the Hudson and along the Delaware. On paper, it was something larger. It was "Nieuw Nederland": two words confidently sprawling over a cartographer's elaborate map. A contrived representation but, for some, a powerful one. It was a place largely unknown but claimed as a sphere of commercial interest. This pictorial wish list was seacoasts and islands possessed from the forty-fifth degree of latitude in the north to the thirty-ninth in the south, from somewhere along the Delaware northeast to the open Atlantic. To defend their claims to both realities, the directors at home and overseas personnel were beginning to bring the jurisdiction into sharper focus. They began to collate better sea charts and maps. They constructed mini-histories of their arrival in North America and produced legal briefs supporting their legitimate presence and purposes. The maps and stories meant greater clarification, especially for the directors themselves. But not the erasure of damaging ambiguities.

Territorially, the company was scarcely altering its limited coastal presence. A twentieth-century scholar using archaeological and documentary evidence stated that in the first ten years, the Dutch purchased only two tracks of native land along the coast. In 1635, the States tried to describe the company's territorial acquisitions. It had a claim to seven parcels of land, each purchased from the natives. The lands included Fort Orange, set at a distance far up the Hudson River, and others within the confined area adjacent to Manhattan Island.[5] Staten Island and the Colonie of Swanendael were two among them. Each was a place about which the company men had some focused definition. They knew them well enough to have given them Dutch names.

The other three parcels of land, at least as they are listed, lack sharp definition. They are locations along coasts we now call the Jersey shore (Map 3). A stranger reading their description could suspect that the company's traders had little knowledge about the land and felt no need to fill it in, at least not for the present. They are presented as the land of Achassemes and Arasick. Another, Hobokina, had been purchased five years earlier by one of the directors, Michiel Pauw, but soon vacated. They seem to resemble the "paper annexation" annexed by Coen near the fort at Batavia. Here, too, the lands were Dutch but only on paper.[6]

Still, they were the company's lands. But in the early 1630s, the company's monopoly was under threat from the same source that had infuriated Coen and later resident directors in Batavia: *vrije burghers*, private traders. To Coen and the directors, such men were miserable hangers-on, a vicious lot who would cheat the natives and cause hatred of the Dutch. They were also a continual source of internal disagreement. At times, policy seemed to suggest the

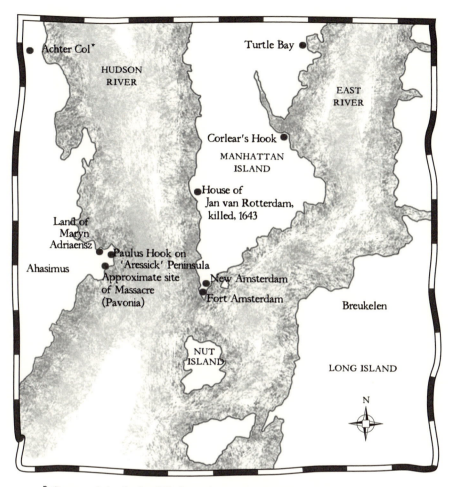

Achter Col*

HUDSON
RIVER

Turtle Bay

EAST
RIVER

Corlear's Hook

MANHATTAN
ISLAND

House of
Jan van Rotterdam,
killed, 1643

Land of
Maryn
Adriaensz

Ahasimus

Paulus Hook on
'Aressick' Peninsula

Approximate site
of Massacre
(Pavonia)

New Amsterdam

Fort Amsterdam

Breukelen

NUT
ISLAND

LONG ISLAND

N

* Coasts and riverlands of Hackensack now Newark Bay, Newark, Middleton
Elizabethtown, Woodbridge, Shrewsbury and Piscattaway

Map 3. Manhattan Island (detail), c. 1640.

need for them. Coen argued at one point that they be given a limited role in the trade. In the years after 1614, the Javanese, who were cultivating spices for them, needed to be provided with food and cloth. Coen proposed a relaxation of some of the restrictions on the free burghers. Others argued that such a move would jeopardize the livelihood of the native traders whom they had now made dependents. An unnamed company official wrote in a marginal note in the 1620s: "Are [the native traders] to be struck dead, or to be allowed to starve of hunger? That would not help us either, for there is no profit at all in an empty sea, empty countries, and dead people." In 1633, another official in Batavia proposed making an exception to the company's monopoly. Allow the free burghers a small space within the city where they can set up their trades. The directors at home wanted no part of it. On the contrary, encourage them to return home. Get rid of them.[7]

In New Netherland, the *vrije burghers* were of the same sort. From the start, the company treated them as a rogue element forbidden to trade or hold land. They were interlopers or, worse, villains such as Jacob Eelkins, who had accepted employment with them but was soon doing his own trading. He'd been trading around the islands and rivers before the company had set up its operations. Now he would not go away, at least not amicably. Once, the company had expelled him for taking a native leader hostage near the Connecticut River. Soon he would be dragging the company into an embarrassing dispute with England: charges would be let loose, depositions taken, courts convened in London, and the king involved. Other interlopers were the early *coloniers*, men ostensibly brought over to farm but surreptitiously—sometimes defiantly—trading in furs with the natives. There were also the "private and poor people" identified in the early 1630s and forbidden to purchase any native lands, let alone freely trade in furs.[8] Even the patroons took it as an insult when the company hinted at a comparison between them and such men.

Desperate to maintain its monopoly, the East India Company had held the line against such traders. Even when Coen came to recognize that the company would profit by allowing them to handle the inland trade of a place such as Java while the company operated at the ports collecting import and export fees as well as charges for the long-distance transport services, the directors would not relent. As for private merchants owning estates inland from Batavia, such ventures were about sixty years away from being legalized.[9]

Now, however, in New Netherland such large-estate owners were an imminent possibility. They would compete for the trade and expect military protection as well. Less than half a decade into the company's operations, patroons were being given approval from the highest levels of government to establish colonies independent of the company's control.

Three years after the auction, in 1629, four wealthy Amsterdam entrepreneurs made their move. They would be alongshore, too. At home, municipal regents and town corporations closely observed such entrepreneurs. Their interests were bound to jostle against those of the commonalty. Still, Samuel Blommaert, Samuel Godijn, Michiel Pauw, and Kiliaen van Rensselaer were successful in their individual bids. The company officials on the island had no option but to negotiate with one of the native bands for lands on their behalf.

In mid-summer 1630, the resident director of the company, Pieter Minuit, began negotiations on behalf of Godijn and Blommaert for land along the Delaware Bay. The subsequent patent makes clear that neither party knew exactly where the lands were. The contract of sale was, however, impeccable. Two natives had come to the strangers on the island. They made declarations about the sale and—noted carefully in writing at the fort—spoke freely and voluntarily. The men were from the same village. Somehow Minuit could write down that they were acting by special authority of the village leaders.

Moreover, they had additional authorization for their mission. Minuit wrote that they were acting with the same authority as would representatives of the early Batavian villages or a contemporary Netherlands town at home. They spoke, the natives supposedly said, with "the consent of the Commonality." They had received back in June of the previous year—and to their full satisfaction—certain parcels of cargo. In return, they had conveyed the land—careful wording again—as "true and free property."[10] The coastal and riverine lands were situated on the south side of the bay of the South River" (Lewes). Somewhere here lay the natives' village (Map 2). Perhaps it was a settlement of two hundred Algonquian-speaking people. More probably, the families were no more than forty people—possibly wampum makers. Like the Dutch, they had a maritime and tidewater culture. In any case, the waters of the bay from which they fished for food and shells in summertime now lapped along Dutch-owned land, whatever that might have meant.

The company's commissary on the island had made some inquiries on behalf of one of the investors two years earlier. He'd asked the local people for some idea of the distance traveling overland from the island of the Manhates to the South River. The questions came to nothing. The natives said they were fearful of enemies there. They would not venture to go there. Perhaps the speakers were Delawares, referring to their enemies to the west, the Susquehannocks. Whatever the case, the men implied that they were at home moving across the bay. But if there were "paths across," they were little used.[11]

As it happened, neither Godijn nor Blommaert ever came to the great delta of the South River, though a small group of colonists were sent out to a place they called Swanendael. But the wording of the patent points to an assumption that would remain in place to the end of Dutch rule: the natives have (but have now renounced) "property . . . command and jurisdiction" over their lands.[12]

This recognition of native sovereign jurisdiction would soon set the Dutch apart from the English. Over the coming years, it would be enunciated on more than one occasion. Especially, it would be called on to give proper order to this district called New Netherland. At home, Netherlanders were beginning to institutionalize the power that was now theirs, since they had declared independence from Hapsburg Spain. Decisions about the sovereignty of the United Provinces were giving rise to questions about the residual sovereignty of the individual provinces within the republic. Netherlanders were bringing into existence a particular kind of geopolitical community. What was imagined for the political structure of the united Netherlands during this time was imagined for New Netherland as well.

Meanwhile, Minuit and his associates were identifying themselves in the patent just as Portuguese traders would have done in the East Indies or Venetians in the eastern Mediterranean. They were acknowledging their status in New Netherland as intruders, as a set of foreign entrepreneurs given the task of evolving an offshore depot and marketplace. As they worded it, they were "the Director and Council in New Netherland, residing on the Island Manahatas and in Fort Amsterdam." They were here with the authority of the States General and the West India Company, chamber of Amsterdam.[13]

Here we see them designating their presence at three places. They put them in this order: New Netherland, the island, and the fort. But I think we get a better insight into how they understood their presence in North America if we reverse the order: "in Fort Amsterdam," "on the Island Manahatas," and "in New Netherland." Construct the view from the fort outward, that is, into the interior. This affords the same understanding of possession entertained by Coen in the Indies. In 1621, he had just negotiated the permanent rendezvous at Djakarta. Writing home, he described it as being within someone else's dominion. It was a city and fort lying in the kingdom of Djakarta. A later commentator put it more powerfully: just because the Dutch made a commercial contract accepting preferential arrangements with the "leading authority of a town or group of places somewhere in a coastal area, this in no sense meant that the hinterland [*achterland*] or a whole island or an island-group was taken possession of."[14]

*   *   *

The new owners of the land washed by the bay opening into the South River were front-runners in a field of entrepreneurs prepared to contest the company's monopoly. Now the directors were feeling the breath of those who were catching up. So for seven years, from 1628 onward, they found themselves engaged in nothing less than a boardroom revolt led by prominent investors they might have thought would be most loyal. Unable to count on a sure majority of the principal shareholders or the States, they were forced to make concessions. These were humiliating but increasingly seen as the company's only hope of survival. In the summer of 1634, the directors were charged with bungling the company's operations so badly that success was "beyond expectation." For all the criticism leveled against it, this had never been said of the East India Company.[15]

On one principle, however, the directors had no need to make concessions. The patroons were in full agreement that the natives of New Netherland had sovereign jurisdiction over their own lands. They had a decidedly pragmatic reason for acknowledging this. But at the same time, their position was supported by the complex and, in many ways, remarkable political developments at home.[16]

The patroons acknowledged the sovereign rights of the natives because they intended to do with them a very Dutch thing: they would buy them. The company had done the same. Now joined in angry dispute with the directors, Kiliaen van Rensselaer and the other patroons were discovering that they could assert sovereignty over their colonies by mounting an argument that the company could not dispute. Van Rensselaer, Samuel Blommaert, Michiel Pauw, and Henrick Hamel put the assertion in grievances addressed to the States in 1634. The patroons, they demanded, had "bought and paid for not only the grounds belonging to the chiefs and natives of the lands in New Netherland, but also their [the natives'] rights of sovereignty [*jura Majestatis*] and such others as they exercised." Now they were successors to the natives in their lands and sovereign jurisdictions. Conveyed to them were, as they continued, "the lands and jurisdictions purchased from the Saccimaes, the Lords of the Country." These were the men having substantive rights that now passed to them.

They carried the argument further. The "prerogatives and advantages" ceded to them by the native rulers "belong absolutely to them." The company "hath no more power over the Patroons, as purchasers of such lands, than it had over the lords Sachems, the sellers." Why? The intention of the States in conveying the company's charter "notoriously was not to abridge *any person in what is his.*" The company therefore could not, for example, justifiably burden the native vendors or the new proprietors with forms of justice and order that may be deemed appropriate to them but that were "repugnant to the right [of sovereign jurisdiction]."[17]

However imprecise, the design of a significant political topography is present here. New Netherland is envisaged as a place of multiple territorial possessions and multiple sovereignties. It is not the unified and two-dimensional space—the already all-Dutch space—that contemporaries' areal and hemispheric maps would seem to be claiming. First, there were the plantations of the patroons. Four separate colonies were envisaged. Had they all eventuated instead of just van Rensselaer's upriver near Fort Orange and the confluence of the Mohawk and Hudson Rivers, they would have been at locations quite separate from one another, lying along two rivers and several bays. Each patroonship would have been an enclave within the lands of New Netherland and, in that respect, similar to the enclaves of foreign princes that familiarly riddled the kingdoms of medieval and early modern European rulers.[18] Each was a domain with the marks of sovereignty.

Alongside these was the confined territory over which the company exercised its jurisdiction: Manhattan Island and its adjacent islands and lands as well as the places where it had erected commercially strategic forts. The dominion of the company over this jurisdiction was agreed to by the States, the rebellious individual investors, and the company. The company was already fiercely protective of them. A visiting skipper stated that anyone registering a claim on them was "taking the property of the Company."[19]

Finally, there were the places in New Netherland where native law and custom existed under the authority of (as they wrote) the many "Sachems and Chief Lords of the Indians." Over these, the Dutch claimed neither jurisdictional nor territorial sovereignty. Internationally, they were not alone in defending the natives' exercise of sovereignty. At one time, Grotius's occasional adversary, Franciscus de Vitoria, had (fruitlessly) reminded the Spanish crown that a hypothetical discovery of Spain by Indians would not have justified a claim to sovereignty over the Iberian Peninsula. The Dutch also knew that in New Netherland, they had no right to imagine themselves as overlords. Nor had they the inclination. Exactly where one of the tribal lands began and another ended was a matter about which the Dutch were ignorant and could be, for the present, relatively indifferent. These were the lands of leaders with some of whom Kiliaen van Rensselaer's agent was already engaged in signing bilateral contracts[20] (Fig. 7).

*   *   *

This structure of multiple sovereignties was not only an arrangement adopted as a result of exigencies cast up by circumstances overseas. It was also analogous to the emerging design of the United Provinces at home. There the uprising against Spain had necessitated a new structure of government. The rebels

Figure 7. This vignette appeared in 1630, the same year in which Kiliaen van Rensselaer ordered his agent to purchase patroon lands. It illustrates the uncritical self-referentiality and hauteur of the Netherlanders in appraising their encounter with the Americans. Here three natives approach a female personification of the Republic. They pose deferentially, bearing bounteous gifts. Their banner celebrates: you have finally come.

In 1630, were the Dutch of such singular significance in the natives' lives? They had entered a complex world of interconnected commercial and political alliances, personal stories, and tribal histories. Except in their own eyes, were the strangers seen as minor players? Joannes de Laet, *Beschrijvinghe van West-Indien,* 2nd ed. Universitietsbibliotheek Amsterdam.

were bringing into existence a federated polity and geography. The story of this political creation is remarkable. It is made all the more intriguing because it is a narrative frame for the co-synchronic story of New Netherland.

In the beginning of the rebellion against Philip II of Spain, the seven northern Netherlands provinces were autonomous political units jurisdictionally separate from one another, each accepting the authority of its own provincial estates. They shared only their status as provinces within the empire ruled by Spain. In 1579 and after seven years of conflict, the necessities of armed rebellion led the provinces to form a defensive alliance. They committed themselves to the Union of Utrecht, a temporary agreement among provinces desperate to defend their local liberties against Spanish oppression. It was not the outcome of a positive and preexisting national impulse. For that reason, the pact was followed by nothing like a declaration of independence or a constitutional convention called to plan the institutions of a unified state. Instead, the Union of Utrecht, as scholars have suggested, operated by default as the republic's constitution.

The United Provinces that emerged was the embodiment of contractual arrangements that carried forward the prerogatives of provincial autonomy ensured by the Union of Utrecht. When Kiliaen van Rensselaer and the other patroons described, although obliquely, a structure of multiple sovereignties within the territory included in the West India Company's charter in New

Netherland, they could as well have been describing the form of multiple territorial and jurisdictional sovereignties legitimated in the constitutional form of the United Provinces and caught in Joost van den Vondel's phrase *'t Bondig Land*, this confederated land. In the case of the States—the assembled representatives of the (more or less) United Provinces—power was theirs only to wage war and make peace. Its authority did not extend to "direct power over the subjects of the provinces, either in taxation or in criminal or civil justice, or in religion." The patroons' parallel wording about the company's authority was this: the company may not justifiably "burden" the natives of New Netherland (who held "rights of sovereignty") or the individual Dutch proprietors "with the *Venia testandi* . . . [or with forms of] justice and police which are repugnant to the right already . . . [held but now alienated by the natives and] acquired by the Patroons." Local law and custom existed in Friesland and, different from it, Gelderland, and different from both, Zeeland. Similarly, native law and custom prevailed in the several parts of New Netherland. Each was legitimated by sovereignties rightfully exercised within the several jurisdictions and territories of the United Provinces and New Netherland.[21]

Still, the nature of the confederation at home posed unresolved constitutional questions about sovereignty. They were a largely unanticipated result of the many decisions by which the people were, without prior intention, slowly institutionalizing a republic.

Sovereignty posed two questions. First, what sort of sovereignty did the government of the United Provinces claim if, as was the case, each of the seven component parts retained its own sovereignty?[22] Was its claim to authority among the European nations merely a sham? The second consideration was perhaps even more many-sided, since here sovereignty was entangled in the contentious matter of self-determination. On what grounds could a popular uprising against a sovereign king be legitimated? Could sovereignty rightfully be located in the people—the Netherlanders called it *volkssoevereigntiet*—whether they were people choosing to delegate sovereignty to a body such as the States convening in The Hague or retaining it in each of the provincial estates?

The Dutch needed to legitimate sovereignty as divisible. This imperative arose not so much from recalcitrants within the provinces. They were, in fact, a minority out of step with patriotic ideology. Rather, Netherlanders needed to gain acceptance in the eyes of Europe.

Hugo Grotius presented his argument for the divisibility of sovereignty in commentaries set out as eleven theses. He was writing from 1607 through 1609, years at the end of what people called the forty murder years. About four decades earlier, in 1572, the Dutch had taken up arms against Spain and experienced the full force of the Army of Flanders, generally mustered at 65,000 men. Now Grotius, as was customary with theoretical works of the time, was dividing his theses into historical and theoretical parts. In the *Pars Historica,* he presented three theses concerning the legitimacy of the Dutch revolt. He subdivided *Pars Theoretica* into four propositions on sovereignty and four on the subject of a just public war. He based both the legitimacy of the Dutch revolt and the justice of a public war on a defense of sovereignty as divisible.

The jurist's case rested, as his philosophy generally did, on natural law and natural reason. It accords with natural reason, Grotius began, that not all princes are fully sovereign lords with true independence from overlords. "Prince" is simply a title. It does not necessarily entail predetermined constitutional powers. Nor does heredity ensure them. Rather, properly constituted popular estates can hold sovereign power. Those who govern the parts of the body politic should collectively govern the whole. They can exercise sovereignty because it has marks. Two of the marks or qualities are the right to appoint magistrates and to collect taxes. They can properly reside in popular assemblies or estates. They are precisely the rights that Dutch provincial estates had been exercising before the outbreak of the revolt—Spain, wrote one contemporary commentator, had allowed the exercise of these rights in Holland (including West Friesland) and Zeeland for eight hundred years. They could not be revoked. Nor had the provinces forfeited them by waging war, since the Netherlands had waged a just war in their defense, especially in exerting the right to collect taxes.[23]

On at least four occasions, Grotius felt the need to find a logic for the singular Dutch position regarding sovereignty. He struggled with the problem during the first decade of the seventeenth century and returned to it in a treatise written in the mid-1630s.[24] For the people of the provinces, finding such a logic was not as insistent a problem. Singular though they might be to the rest of Europe, they were accustomed to living with multiples. They created them in every way and in every possible shape. Those of the deep past they carried into the present. Those of the present they cherished and multiplied. Among these, the disunited United Provinces was ideologically and symbolically just right.

The United Provinces was simply a variation on the disaggregation that characterized the Netherlandish way of life. Only power sharing ensured security, social order, and prosperity. There were local and district boards of polder- and river-regulators as well as overseers of dikes (*dijkreeves*). There were overseers of orphans; councils of ship captains convened on the high seas; Scots and Venetian merchant enclaves in Amsterdam and Rotterdam; five separate admiralties administering the navy; joint ventures for draining polders and insuring a ship's cargo; dual ownership of a water transportation system (*trekvaart*) operating between two cities. Calvinists, Catholics, and Anabaptists worshiped in fairly equal numbers and within a pattern of ecclesiastical liberties that one authority called "benign incoherence."[25] Federation was simply, at the highest level of government, what town councils, vestrymen, and boards of directors were in daily life.

Just as history could be trawled to discover precedents for the exercise of sovereignty by kings and princes, so could it be searched to justify leagues and federations formed by sovereign member-states often existing on as modest a physical terrain as the northern Netherlands. Vondel found a comparison to the United Provinces by reaching back to the glorious days of Greece. In one poem, the great poet and playwright sang of *d'Amfiktyonische raad der vrije Nederlanden,* the Amphytionic league of the free Netherlands. Others pointed to the Hollanders' early forebears, who, although primitive forest dwellers, were allowed to live in union with Rome and, as one pamphleteer wrote, "alongside her lived in peace." The Romans considered our forefathers "as their united friends," he continued, acknowledging Batavia to be a free state "and calling my household servants the Batavian commonaltie."[26]

So it happened that Netherlanders were beginning to put into place overseas the same structures that they were designing for national institutions at home. When the patroons laid claim to rights and attributes of sovereignty on behalf of native rulers and themselves, they were, in effect, summoning Grotian political thought popular at home. Similarly, the West India Company's charter empowered it to form leagues. It was to enter into "leagues with the princes and natives of the countries therein comprised." The word "leagues" was not chosen by accident. And in 1632, the directors reached for "confederating" when they needed a word to express their meetings with native rulers to buy lands. We have, they wrote, gone about acquiring property by "confederation with the . . . owners of the lands."[27]

In the Low Countries and New Netherland, only confederating together carried the promise of social harmony. Concord was achievable because the outcomes were commercially beneficial to all. In both places, it was contracts and markets that glued part to part. A contemporary put it succinctly: the uprising has transformed the Netherlands into *a grosze burgherlicke Handelsgesellschaft,* one great middle-class business-oriented society. Neither custom or language, religion or law held together the seven northern provinces of the Low Countries. Not even a national economy. Markets did. "Markets, more than politics or culture," wrote economic historians Jan de Vries and Ad van der Woude in 1997, "articulated the common space of the Dutch people." Or, as I would prefer, markets, activating a particularly unique politics and culture, articulated the common space of the Dutch people.[28]

* * *

Markets were also the primary concern of the aggrieved patroons in 1634. To share the market in furs with the company—to control it—colonies could serve as a point of entry. So they raised with the States the issue over which Coen and the East India Company had so strenuously contended. The inland trade: Whose was it to be? It is as much ours, they argued, as the company's. Agreed, the company justifiably controlled the fur trade everywhere on the coast of New Netherland. And trading locations circumjacent to the coast were theirs as well. Quite legitimately, the company had reserved these to itself.

But to trade inland was not to be denied. Here the patroons were imagining a trading geography based on elemental differentiations that the natives, as they thought, had made among themselves. They were either southern coastal and tidewater villagers or those of the central and northern interior. Or, better, they were providers or consumers of wampum. Ironically, the businessmen's map was one of spiritual as much as material powers on the move: the spiritual power of shell beads fashioned by south-coast Algonquians and traded in great quantities to those unable to obtain the beads locally, the Mahicans and Iroquoian tribes farther north.

By 1630, the beads—always exchanged in measured lengths and, in the European period, carefully drilled with iron tools—were the accepted medium of exchange among natives and Europeans. But they were not simply commodities. Worn during ritual ceremonies, they signified and invested a political or religious leader with authority. For the Dutch strangers, wampum was the shining comet whose inland trajectory was already there to follow. The Netherlanders called the comet's path the inland trade. As the patroons now put it, that meant access to natives in the interior ready to sell an abundance of furs. They claimed the right to enter the market on their own terms, buying wampum as cheaply as they wished. Then with fathoms of shell beads and other trading goods to offer, inland tribes would be drawn to non-company trading posts, where they would fix their own prices for furs.[29]

The patroons carried their critique of the company further. They had already contended that it could not legitimately enforce Dutch-Roman law in the lands of the native rulers or their own patroonships. Now they extended this argument by raising the issue of territory. Exactly which lands did the West India Company think it had oversight of? Wasn't it the case that, with the exception of the island of the Manhates and its surrounds, it had direct legal oversight only of "uninhabited lands, or lands on which settlements were found of particular Indians, having no chief"? In this respect—as they might well have said—its direct jurisdiction over territories was constrained in a way that resembled that of the States. At home, the provinces had limited the States to direct rule over whatever uninhabited or juridically vacant European and overseas lands the Netherlands might, with the provinces' approval, chance to acquire. Beyond that, it was assigned direct oversight of the Generality Lands, that is, the southern Netherlands districts conquered from Spain but not incorporated within any of the seven northern provinces in the confederation. Let the company be satisfied to conduct itself in a way similar to the States: oversee matters of war and peace across New Netherland and exercise direct rule over the enclaves where it was actually conducting and (by purchases) expanding its trade. Otherwise, let it facilitate the well-being of those colonies and adjacent native sovereignties coexisting with it.

Only a year before, in 1633, the company's resident director had written that there were undoubtedly many native lands empty of inhabitants.[30] Yet no one among them had yet reported finding such uninhabited lands or villagers without chiefs. But that, the patroons were implying, was the company's affair.

*   *   *

Settled natives, natives with sovereign rights. These were words being expressed by the company and the patroons. The Dutch had used them with considerable determination two years earlier in a story set in 1632. It must be told carefully, because in this larger story of ours, we have only begun to know how the Dutch understood what they were doing in New Netherland, and what they were doing and going to do to its natives.

The story begins with a simple description and the name of a single ship, *Eendracht:* "Now it has happened, that a vessel belonging to the West India Company, and coming from the said island [of Manhattan], with quite a number of people, their wives and children on board, arrived at Plymouth harbor through the stress of weather, where she has been seized."[31]

Chapter 6
Masters of Their Lands

Set on the channel coast of England, Plymouth was as important a port to Dutch seamen as any along their own coastline. Its name promised safety amid the wreckage and loss of life that the channel so often delivered to men navigating between England and the continent. Dutch navigational charts were careful to help seamen find the entrance to Plymouth harbor. It lies, they said, behind Meeuws-steen (Eddystone). Sometimes Dutch seamen looked for the nearby headland named Rame Head (Ram's Head).

The same charts marked Plymouth as the entrance to the open seas of the Atlantic. It lay along the passage to the routes leading to the Mediterranean, the West Indies, or Africa thence to the East Indies. In autumn 1636, twenty-two ships prepared to sail from Texel. They had been awaiting other vessels with which, for safety's sake, they would sail in convoy down the channel. Among them were merchant ships bound for France, the Mediterranean, and Ireland, and a ship sailing for New Netherland. "We arranged to sail together as far as *pleijmuiden* [Plymouth]," wrote the Dutch skipper making for North America, "and so put to sea, in God's name."

Weather made Plymouth a place of unexpected arrivals. Sea captains who had no intention of making it their destination ran to its harbor for shelter. Often they were commanding ships broken in the channel's gale-force winds. Or they were skippers forced to haul sails and drift for days, helplessly out of control, with little chance of estimating latitude and usually with westerlies or south-westers driving them inexorably away from the open Atlantic and toward the coast of France. For such distressed vessels, Plymouth was its submerged offshore land as much as its harbor. Even before land was sighted, the seabed before it was a promise of deliverance. Seamen returning from the South Atlantic would take soundings of it, hoping for "good Channel ground." One Dutch captain knew he had found it at eighty-five fathoms and took heart that he could run for one of the other Devon or Cornwall harbors or, if need be, France.[1]

Dutch ships repeatedly limped into Plymouth harbor. On the outward leg of his first voyage, in 1618, David Pietersz de Vries of Hoorn was fighting strong winds but calculated he was somewhere near Seagull's Rock. He made for the harbor and, probably picking up fittings and provisions, took on a ship's surgeon. Ten months later, he was again in the channel and now making for Hoorn and then Amsterdam. He sailed to Plymouth first, went ashore to buy foodstuffs, saw to the dismissal of the surgeon, and in the evening set sail for Texel. In another ten months and on his second voyage, de Vries sailed for Portsmouth and went overland to Plymouth. During the two days before his ship caught up with him, he again bought provisions and conducted what seems to have been personal business.

De Vries was again in Plymouth in 1630. This time he was returning from the East Indies. He'd sailed there in a fleet under the command of Jan Pietersz Coen, a fellow citizen of Hoorn. Now he was serving as supercargo aboard the *Galias van Hoorn* and delighted to be on "a ship of our own city." He stayed in the port for five days. Perhaps with the Dutch and Portuguese shore forts of the Indies in mind or perhaps because no completed bastioned defenses were in place, he took the time to wonder at the fact that, despite England's declared state of war against Spain, there was nothing he recognized as alongshore fortifications.[2]

In the years between de Vries's second and third voyages, one of Verhulst's ships destined for New Netherland began to founder in the channel and made for Plymouth. There it was officially detained until plague among the crew and passengers convinced the authorities to release it. Ships in a fleet under the Dutch commander Jacques L'Hermite also sheltered in Plymouth harbor. Fierce winds and seas had forced them to anchor near Seagull's Rock in spring of 1623 and then maneuver into the harbor and stand out from the shore. For eight days, they were unable to weigh anchor. Before their departure, the fleet's commander entertained the admiral of the king's fleet and the mayor of Plymouth, along with other naval officers. They shared a midday meal aboard L'Hermite's command ship, *Amsterdam*. His fleet returned to Plymouth in June 1626, this time seeking assistance for ill sailors on board. In his journal, L'Hermite recorded that on one day when an English ship broke up in the harbor, the port's customs officers inspected two vessels that had run with the Dutch ships to the safety of the harbor. One was from England, the other from Hamburg. The search was for *onvrije* goods, those that needed to be declared and customs paid. None were found.[3]

* * *

So perhaps *Eendracht* was just unlucky.

First, there was the weather. The captain had encountered adverse weather making for Holland from New Netherland and was forced to seek the roadstead in Plymouth. Next there were tattletales among the crew. The ship's provost wanted his wages paid there rather than at the time of disembarkation in Holland and upon refusal made a point of telling the harbor authorities that *Eendracht* was carrying peltries illegally traded in Virginia. He implied that New Netherland was a part of that colony. The pilot, another troublemaker, agreed.

Next was the anger of the English king and court on a number of disputatious issues regarding the Dutch. Nine years earlier, in 1623 the East India Company had directed an assault on Amboyna, an island where the English East India Company had established trading rights. Twenty-one men lost their lives. In the Caribbean, the island of Saint Martin had recently been seized by the Dutch although the crown had awarded it to Charles Howard, Lord Carlisle. Then, too, the Dutch had challenged the right of certain English merchants to trade in New Netherland. A particularly unpleasant hearing about the case was only eighteen months away from proceeding in the English admiralty courts. There the trespasser would (the Dutch feared) persuade the king that New Netherland was part of his domain.[4]

There was also the unresolved question of the freedom of the seas. Two years before *Eendracht*'s detention, de Vries had encountered an English vessel on the high seas off the coast of Wales. To his surprise, it ordered him to strike the flag of the Prince of Orange and raise the colors of the king of England. Fourteen years earlier, an English lawyer and publicist had argued that the seas to the north and west of England were, in effect, an exclusion zone. They were, in the terminology of the time, a *mare clausum.*[5]

The *Eendracht* dispute was of far less significance than any of these disagreements. The moment of debate over its fate was only that—a moment. Though carefully staged, it was a one-off performance. But in that short time, both parties gave expression to thoughts, customs, and mythologies about overseas imperium that were seldom, at least with respect to one another, articulated again. And native Americans entered the discourse.

A handful of diplomats had to give the natives consideration. Perhaps for Govert Brasser, Albert Joachimi, and the Earl of Sandwich, it was the first time the Americans were needed—to score points. The natives were summoned forth in the hooded statements of international diplomacy. But in some respects, the fate of the West India Company's vessel was to turn less on its own status than that of the Algonquian-speaking people of the northeastern North American woodlands. The Netherlanders insisted that the natives were "free men." Now the Dutch had to use that free status to support pleadings that might otherwise fail.

The diplomatic correspondence relating to all this was a set of inscribed pages and gestures filled with ideologies and mythologies out of which strategic charges and countercharges could be unpacked and laid out. Most of it was finessed in the double-speak of court bureaucrats in London and Newmarket (where Charles I was accustomed to travel) or The Hague. In the past, the Dutch hadn't been particularly careful about the use of "Virginië" or "New Virginia," but they had tried not to inflame controversy concerning it. In 1626, a ship from Virginia had arrived at Vlissingen carrying tobacco. Apparently, the vessel had not cleared at one of the English ports. One of the company directors of the Zeeland chamber had an interest in it. But others declared that the voyage and cargo violated the West India Company's charter and refused to let him take his seat until he had acknowledged his offense. The spring of 1632 was also a time of edginess for the Dutch. They, too, were letting *Eendracht* get caught in a net of larger issues. Its seizure, they alleged, contravened articles respecting the freedom of trade by sea and free ports agreed to by England and themselves fully nineteen years earlier.[6]

The States now called upon these agreements and the free use of the English harbors. For almost twenty-five years, they had followed Grotius in insisting that the North Sea was a *mare liberum* and not a sea closed to all but the English. It was one to whose harbors no one had more right than his neighbor. Yet here in 1632 were disputes that such a principle and more recent articles were meant to prevent. Here was the English king questioning *Eendracht*'s right to seek shelter in an English port and then continue her journey to Holland after conducting trade in a part of North America chartered by the United Provinces to the West India Company—and not encompassed by the king's Virginia. Here were the English denying that Dutch ships from the West Indies had previously freely enjoyed the king's ports and harbors without any objection.[7]

The remonstrances put to the English court went on intermittently for a period of over thirty months, from spring 1632 to autumn 1634. They expressed different perspectives and carried more than one voice. But in structure, they were like Grotius's treatise on sovereignty: they argued for possession and occupation on historical and legal grounds. Procedurally, the company's case was to be carried by representatives of the States. Its own responsibility was to provide enough information to ensure a positive outcome. Short histories of the founding and evolution of their enterprise would need to be pulled together. On at least three occasions, the directors rehearsed the story of the West India Company's role in New Netherland. At the end of May and in mid-June of 1632 and again twenty-eight months later, they presented a story that maintained the same focus but became increasingly detailed.

At first, they kept *Eendracht* as the object of complaint. They put it that the delay was any competent merchant's nightmare. As many as five thousand furs were stored in her hold. Each day of her delay was costing the company dearly. A market in Russia awaited shipment of the furs but had probably already been put in jeopardy. Unanticipated expenses, such as sailors' wages, were mounting. The crew was busily pilfering the furs and trafficking them stealthily into the interior. Yet these furs had been bartered in New Netherland within the limits of their charter, on the South and North Rivers, where there are no "English Colonies or Trading Posts."[8]

Soon, however, the story of the possession of New Netherland moved to center stage and with it the American natives. The tale went back in time. It recounted the exploits of the early navigators to the island and the discoveries of the earliest traders. Except for "Henry Hudson," it was not encumbered with names: not those of Hendricksz, May, Verhulst, or other men from the ports of the Zuider Zee. The tale had a tight chronology meant to serve one purpose: to demonstrate that the Netherlanders' was actual possession of New Netherland and not merely a declaration of possession. That kind of faulty declaration was, the Dutch had pointed out a month earlier, the untenable grounds for England's claim to the island of Saint Martin in the Caribbean. The island was not colonized by the English but "was made use of by the [West India] Company" and consequently possessed. Regarding New Netherland, continual trading with the indigenes had gone on since 1609 between thirty-nine and forty-one degrees of latitude. Such trade was pursued to the present day. After Hudson, several small forts had been built, supplied with people for the security of the trade, and renewed and enlarged. The company had consistently arranged land purchases from the natives, who were, they went out of their way to say, "the indubitable owners thereof." Among the purchases was the island of the Manhates, where they laid the foundation of a city.[9]

Twice more in this 1634 version of the story, the company emphasized land bought from legitimate indigenous rulers. Over a year earlier, they had also insisted to the English that they'd purchased from the native inhabitants a certain island called Manathans, where they had remained surrounded on all sides by them. Now they were referring to purchases made in the areas around the Delaware River and rivers to the east of the Hudson River. They were composing stories we have already thought about: the initiatives of the absentee patroons, the appearance of the two natives before Minuit and his council, and the transfer of alongshore lands around the Delaware and east of it. In this account, investors such as van Rensselaer were men whom the company had assisted in planting colonies. For this purpose, they had "purchased from the chiefs of the Indians, the lands and soil, *with their respective attributes and jurisdictions.*"

This story pointed to others. Let the deeds of conveyance and cession executed in favor of the patroons tell their stories, too. Let them be examined. They would show that "the Sachems and Chief Lords of the Indians" had executed them and obtained approval from the native commonalty, that is, "those who had anything to say therein." So, they concluded, the company had occupied, settled, and cultivated those countries, and carried on trade there "from the commencement of their charter." They made no point about not having received a land patent to New Netherland—as indeed they had not. The English would soon make an issue of this. But for the Dutch, the claim to proprietary rights before arrival in strangers' lands would have been nonsense.[10]

Behind this argument were further stories, decades of them, though here well below the surface. They were all the accounts, some reasonable, some paranoid, of Spanish incursions into the Americas. Listen to Grotius acting as adviser to the East India Company and inching his way toward a definition of the law of nations, with always more than a side glance at the Spanish. Title of discovery, he wrote, was essentially inchoate until it was "perfected by actual possession of the discovered territory." Even then, actual possession was universally legal provided the land was either *terra nullius* in the eyes of the law of nations or available for occupation through purchase. Countries existing before European arrival could patently not be said to have been discovered by Europeans. It was illogical and invalid to declare title to East Indies lands and those of the subcontinent, as Pope Alexander VI had done in 1492. And *alia enim India alia Americana ratio est*: what holds true for India holds true for the Americas.[11]

Wouter van Twiller was no equal to Grotius. But he, too, could speak the language of international law. Only months after the seizure of *Eendracht* and while acting as director-general in New Netherland, he addressed the governor of the Massachusetts Bay colony in defense of Dutch purchases of native lands in New Netherland. He didn't contrast their policy with that of the English. He had the Spanish in mind. It's not the intent of the States, he wrote, "to take the land from the poor Natives, as the Kinge of Spaine hath done by the Pope's Donation." We intend to acquire it "att some reasonable and convenient price, wch God be praysed wee have done hitherto."[12]

Meanwhile, just two days after *Eendracht* had been seized, the Dutch ambassador and commissioner had contacted the king and learned something of his mind regarding New Netherland and Virginia. They prepared their presentation. It opened with arguments about trading zones. These led to the insistence that claims to overseas possessions needed to be put alongside the rights of resident peoples. Possession and occupation could not proceed irrespective of the legal position of local communities.

Since the boundary between Virginia and New Netherland was clearly in the king's mind, they dealt with that directly. The company's charter of 1615 stood as documentary evidence that the thirty-ninth degree of latitude was their southern border. The boundaries under discussion were, they assumed, those separating a Dutch and English trading zone. So they moved to what they thought was the crux of the dispute.

Let the king consider how charters ensure orderly trading with overseas peoples. Let him exercise his authority as the States had done in granting charters to the East India Company and West India Company. Let him "grant his subjects by charter the right to trade with any people, to the exclusion of all others [of] his subjects." But let him not pretend to encroach on the rights of others to manage their affairs within their own legitimate trading zones. Here they reiterated Grotius's point regarding the independent status of residents in countries existing before European arrival. "It is contrary to all right and reason," they argued, "for one potentate to prevent the subjects of another [from] trading in countries whereof his people have not taken, nor obtained actual possession from *the right[ful] owners*, either by contract or purchase." It was therefore against all reason to suppose that the Netherlanders should be denied a claim to property "acquired . . . partly by confederation with the owners of the lands, and partly by purchase." They had maintained actual possession of New Netherland for twenty-three years because they had consistently acquired land by contract or purchase. They had, they could well have thought, met the conditions of the law of nations.

But the directors foresaw a problem. The king and court might well question their assumption about rightful native owners. You need to take this into consideration, they advised the States' representatives: "the inhabitants of those [North American] countries are free men, and neither his Britannic Majesty's, nor Your High Mightinesses' subjects." They are therefore "free to trade with whomsoever they please." We need to assert this principle in order to maintain our sovereignty and defend two related principles of natural law. The first is the freedom of trade by sea. The second is the freedom to make "alliances with distant nations, who are not, by the laws of nature, the subjects, nor have become the property of any other person by conquest."[13]

As expected, the legitimacy of New Netherland was strongly contested. When the remonstrations about *Eendracht* were put before him some weeks later, Charles I reacted swiftly and unequivocally. His answer was an opposing view but also a misreading of the Dutch meaning of being overseas. To the king, it was clear that, unlike them, the United Provinces had never seriously pretended to claim the country. Either they had carelessly failed to meet the requirements of a European power taking possession of overseas territory, or they had not followed first discovery with occupation. Their shore forts and scaled-back mercantile personnel had not amounted to proof that the lands had been invested with settlers who had taken possession of it.[14]

Furthermore, the United Provinces had not issued a patent to the country covered by New Netherland. Had they done so—as the English had done following various discoveries—a patent would have given them title. Lacking this, they hadn't, in the king's eyes, "any power or title thereto." Moreover, the Dutch themselves had said back in 1621 that they had no "plantation." They had only sent out a succession of traders to lands "between the 40th and 50th degrees," put Dutch names to places, and sent ships to look for furs. This did not constitute the "establishment of a plantation there," and clearly they had no intention of doing so. Lack of intent was further obvious in their failure to offer residence to the families who had journeyed from Leiden, also in 1621. Such a weakened authority was no authority at all.[15]

As anticipated, the English king dismissed the notion of the North American natives as free men and rulers of the lands. He began by reinterpreting the Dutch account of the seizure of *Eendracht*. You demand "the release of a vessel seized at Plymouth, returning from a certain plantation usurped by . . . [yourselves] in the North parts of Virginia, which . . . [you] say was acquired from the natives of the country." But first, he went on, "it is denied that the Indians were *possessores bonae fidei* of those countries, so as to be able to dispose of them either by sale or donation." Why? Their residences are "unsettled and uncertain, and only being in common." And second, "it cannot be proved, *de facto*, that all the Natives of said country had contracted with [the Netherlanders] at the said pretended sale."[16]

In concluding, the king revealed his own imagined geography of this place—his place—called Virginia. It was an expanse of land where there was no deterrent to English occupation. Virginia was juridically unoccupied. Because no set of native rulers existed with demonstrable legitimate authority over it, the land was *terra nullius*. English settlers were legitimate occupants of Virginia "by the concessions and letters they have had from Sovereigns" preceding him, and not on the sufferance of any already established native rulers. All of it was the king's colonial dominion.

By inference, Virginia was a cadastral geography, not a trader's geography. Its analogue was the grid map that objectified plenitude and rule spread over a continuous cartographic and jurisdictional surface. It was, as the king said, "his Majesty's plantation"—even as the island from which *Eendracht* had sailed was (in his words) a "plantation" and not a trading beach. Virginia had territorial limits to defend, not multiple sovereignties to consider, each with its marks or attributes of legal jurisdiction. Constituted in what one writer has called "retro-feudal fantasies," Virginia had native chiefs to turn into vassals, not free men with whom to make contracts.

Virginia's enemies were those whom landowners feared. They were predators who would encroach on their properties. Let the Lords States of the United

Provinces, the king admonished, not continue to usurp and encroach on Virginia. It was "one of his Colonies of . . . [great] importance." He intended to cherish it and "maintain . . . [it] entire."[17]

In 1634, the counter-positions put during the *Eendracht* affair appear to have ended. Let the matters, the directors wrote in typical fashion, take their course.

*   *   *

This moment of exchange catches two sets of colonialists contending with definitions of Americans—which, we have to think, the natives would undoubtedly have found meaningless. Being merely an episode, it lacks the improvisational dimensions that constitute actual colonial policies and colonial encounters over time. Still, it is important because the clarity expressed about overseas imperium and the status of resident indigenous peoples was seldom to come again.

Our story follows the improvisations of the Netherlanders in North America. The exchange of views about native rights in 1632 takes us to a doorway where we may ask one question. The natives as free men and rulers of the land, the natives as "neither subjects of his Britannic Majesty nor Your High Mightinesses," native rulers with attributes of sovereignty—did these beliefs work to the natives' benefit? A Dutch scholar writing of these early years has offered something of a positive answer. He accepts that it was Dutch policy not to concern themselves with the government and jurisdiction of the natives. Rather, they chose to assume that the inhabitants were "governed in freedom and [able to] follow their own laws in *politie* as in civil affairs."[18] This would seem to shelter resident pre-European populations under the protection of the emerging law of nations. Or were they not protected? Were they in no less jeopardy than the Algonquian-speaking peoples of Virginia who were not *possessores bonae fidei* of the land?

Put another way, did the Dutch remain adjacent to the lands and the lives of the native New Netherlanders? Did they stay on their share of the trading beaches, content to look out over the skirts of their forts—or later the palisades of their city on the island—into a continental interior variously ruled and administered by native-born people? Were they, in that respect, similar to the early Greeks in their colony at the harbor of Massalia (Marseilles), satisfied to look north into the independent lands of the Gauls? The Greeks were outsiders; they were mostly traders whom the later Romans identified as "non-Gaels in Celtic territory." They survived in the presence of a numerous native population because they promoted trade and good native relations. They were *windersvaren*, too, professional sea and urban traders prepared, as one scholar wrote, to "enhance their economic influence while tempering their pretensions to political domination." Or, as the Romans might have put it, they were merchants prepared to see the natives as they themselves did, that is, as "*externae gentes* . . . [some among them] not usually worth annexing." Were the Dutch in New Netherland the same?[19]

Starting in the late 1630s, the Dutch began to violate much that might be called adjacency. The violations are a story of imprudence, compromise of principles, and violence. They came to a close in 1645, but only partly. Parallel to this story is one less dramatic but equally important and more encompassing. It recounts the impulse to remain alongshore. This impulse endured even during the years when it was being so brutally breached and well into the mid-1660s when the English seized the province.

The strength of this impulse is more mysterious than the willingness to violate it. For we are no longer strangers to accounts of European violence toward native populations in North America. Dutch violence in seventeenth-century New Netherland may be a new story for some but scarcely a surprising one. The parallel story is different. It is not known. In fact, the more strenuously being alongshore is considered as a way of being present in North America, the more illogical it may appear. We are accustomed to accepting going inland as normal, as the unique promise of landownership, of acres of farmland. Inland is valuable beyond anything alongshore can offer. It is a continent to be won, a Turnerian frontier to be exploited and moved beyond, and proper rural communities to be founded. But this is Anglo-American hindsight. Applied uncritically, the view is an Anglo-American anachronism of the North American past. What Netherlanders imagined in venturing overseas and establishing themselves alongshore in North America is not to be excavated in the strata of such an Anglo-American history. It lies in the complex, mostly unearthed, layers of Netherlands history.

One seventeenth-century Hollander was saying that to clear the ground around a place such as New Netherland, take a trowel in hand and look for the remains of a cat. Let's see.

Chapter 7

Inland Drownings

One of the great novelists of the twentieth century caught the mystery of finding well-being in staying alongshore. One of his characters describes it as a fear of the interior of a continent, of drowning inland.

In Thomas Pynchon's *Mason and Dixon*, a Dutch resident of Cape Town introduces two eighteenth-century surveyors to the ways of the small port perched on the southern coast of Africa. As upon a ship at sea, he begins, "we do things here in our own way—we, the officers, and you, the passengers." He goes on. "What seems a solid continent, stretching away Northward for Thousands of miles, is in fact an Element with as little mercy as the Sea to our Backs, in which *to be immersed* is just as surely and swiftly, to be lost, without hope of Salvation."[1]

Pynchon's metaphor offers a valuable insight. It tells us things about the strangers' encounters in New Netherland. Drowning was, as we know, both the daily reality and ultimate terror of Dutch life. The drowning of thousands in floods and sea surges was common: the Elizabeth Day Flood in 1421; the All Saints' Day Flood in 1570; and the late January inundations in Holland and Zeeland in 1682. During the years of the Dutch revolt, more Spaniards in the Army of Flanders drowned than were shot. In the Netherlands, the notion persisted from Roman times that only drowning was adequate punishment for an individual found guilty of parricide. The murderer should be tied in a large sack containing four live animals: in Roman times, a cock, dog, snake, and small monkey. It was then dumped in a river. Because of its monstrous contents, the site was always to be well away from a town or city. Twice when New Netherlanders wanted to express their desperation at alleged native attacks about twenty-five years after the *Eendracht* affair, they compared their peril to that of people facing drowning. Perhaps they had in mind flood victims. Perhaps they were thinking of the prisoner condemned to die in a room inexorably filling with water: the "drowning room." Help us, they pleaded to officials. The water is already "up to our lips."[2]

The reluctance of the Dutch overseas to immerse themselves in the interior of the lands to whose coasts they sailed is another reason that Pynchon's metaphor is far from fanciful. Even in the case of Batavia, they chose not to engross territories just an hour's travel from the fort. They did resemble the Greeks in Massalia. They seemed to operate on the premise that there were no advantages in taking on the administration of lands in zones of trade surrounding their commercial enclaves. Why, as a Dutch scholar wrote, add to economic obligations the acceptance of "sovereign responsibilities"?[3]

Stories we have about early Java, India, Ceylon, Formosa, and New Netherland are the same. Concerning Java, Arthur Wertheim wrote, "for the Dutch, the inland for the most part remained *terra incognito*."[4] It was viewed from the ship's deck or over the wall of a fortress or the high veranda of the director's residence. Or from a sparsely manned trading station anchored on a distant riverbank away from, but dependent on, the central rendezvous. Other historians agreed. Let's gather them together and, as we have done for the words of mariners and company directors, ambassadors and jurists, listen.

The East India Company had little interest in acquiring territory. Having settled a powerful center at Batavia on Java in 1619, it failed to reach the south coast of the island until the end of the seventeenth century, and in 1750— 120 years after the *Eendracht* affair—was exercising control over only one-sixth of it. Only reluctantly and in a piecemeal fashion did it, as Clive Day has written, extend its Javanese control "first over the ports, and then along a narrow coastline."[5]

There was also the fear of drowning in inland politics. This had occasionally happened to the Netherlanders' predecessor, the Portuguese. They had discovered that meddling in the affairs of the Javanese interior, for example, made needless enemies. The Dutch traders also tried to avoid such interference. Because territorial acquisitions in Java were something that "had never been contemplated," the company directors avoided the privileges of sovereignty until the middle of the eighteenth century. When they did assume dominion, it was to protect their expanding markets. Scholars concur that before that time, "never, outside the limits of its settlements and factories did it accept sovereign responsibilities" or aim for the "extension of dominion" over the natives.[6]

For its first 150 years—that is, until about 1770—the company at Batavia had what it wanted most—and what New Netherland was in its earliest decades. It "stood at the head of not a territory but a series of widely scattered establishments, factories, and forts." The Portuguese had put it this way to the queen of Quilon in India in 1519: our king "did not build fortresses in India to conquer territory but merely to protect his merchandise on the seashore." As for dominion, wrote Jan Huyghen van Linschoten considerably later, the Portuguese have none beyond Goa. They have a kingdom (*rijk*) without territory.[7]

The Dutch would follow the same path. They, too, were aware of being subalterns in a highly developed trading world. As in New Netherland, the point was not to overrun it—least of all, to take on the administration of it—but to master it commercially. The Dutch, as Johan van der Woude summarized, "wanted to discover the world, to be able to learn about it and draw to themselves a large part of the world's trade; they did not want to add any territory to that of the Republic, which for them was large enough." He continued: the Hollanders thought continually about maximizing profits. "About the control of territory they thought nothing." And what was true for Java held true for India, Ceylon, Formosa, and New Netherland as well. The historians' stories become repetitious. In India, the company showed not "the slightest desire to meddle in Indian politics." They were "emporialists" rather than imperialists. Their operations never amounted to "a Dutch empire."

In Formosa, commerce, not the island's colonization, was the principal objective. The company had actually situated itself on nothing more than a sandbank some six miles off the coastline. There, the employees built Fort Zeelandia. In the same year that May was cruising the waters along New Netherland's southern coast, it was being erected atop a sand dune. Its purpose was to protect a trading beach that Chinese and Japanese merchants used to engage in secret trade and to develop trade with the Chinese mainland across the straits. In Ceylon, too, the company erected several fortified coastal strongholds to defend shipping routes to southeast Asia. Raja Sinha II gave them rights to forts and trade. They had further convinced him that they were administering his strongholds for his benefit and not "governing them in their own right." "Provided he kept his side of the bargain, they were prepared to leave him alone in his capital in the mountains of the interior."[8]

And New Netherland. Let's listen to Francis Jennings writing in 1984 and then to Raymond O'Brien, who published a study of the lower Hudson valley in 1981. The nature of the Dutch colony's business, Jennings wrote, noting a contradiction, called for "aggressive penetration of the continent, but the Dutch sat still in their villages; there were no Dutch Champlains, Perrots, Marquettes, or La Salles." O'Brien also stressed the Dutch disinclination to penetrate the continental interior. When the Dutch regime ended, he found, there was "not a single Dutch Reformed Congregation on the Hudson for a hundred miles north of New Amsterdam. There was but one village, Kingston (Esopus)." In the lower Hudson valley, occupation occurred "remarkably late." In 1683, Orange County was a howling wilderness with scarcely a single settler located within its territory." By 1693 the total population amounted to about twenty families. . . . In 1702 only 268 persons were in Orange County; 200 in 1698." This is strange, he mused. "No other colony had anything like a Hudson River to allow such easy penetration into the interior."[9]

In the upper Hudson valley (not O'Brien's research field), the Dutch had, however, penetrated into the interior. But they had done it in a way that supports O'Brien's conclusions. The company directors had halfheartedly maintained Fort Orange on the west bank of the Hudson since 1624. In 1643, they were employing fewer than a dozen personnel and permitting perhaps an additional twenty-five men to trade with the Mahicans and Mohawks. The men at the trading station were using (and would continue to use) Manhattan Island exactly as they should have, that is, as the *middelpunt* to which furs were sent downriver and then shipped to Holland. In 1630, van Rensselaer began sending small numbers of settlers to his patroonship, a colony that bordered the company's fort. Called Rensselaerswijck, it was, in its attention to rural development, the single anomaly within the early settlement structure of the trading company. With its slowly but steadily growing number of colonists and farms coming into greater productivity, it was, not surprisingly, the kind of penetration not found by O'Brien in the lower Hudson valleys.[10]

This did not deter later New Yorkers from entertaining the notion that the Dutch yielded to superstition in imagining the land beyond their forts as a "vast and brooding *terra incognita*." They were, many were sure, topophobic. But, then again, one Portuguese commentator, seeking a reason for the Netherlanders' failure to settle themselves in the countryside of Brazil in the 1630s, wrote that God had withheld this aptitude from them. The historian Charles R. Boxer added that in contrasting this failure with Dutch success in developing a distinctive urban civilization, perhaps the writer "was right."[11]

*   *   *

Learned scholars—academic storytellers—have little time for phobias or heavenly designs as explanatory models. Probably not much time, either, for "drowning inland." In 1946, however, a noted Dutch historian looked back over the past 375 years of the United Provinces' history and discovered substantial evidence for what he called the pervasive *mentalitiet* of *kleine nederlandse*. Pieter Geyl was examining the years after 1567, when the Dutch uprising against Spain began. He had never made it his aim to study Dutch overseas expansion. Had he done so, he might have noted that the Dutch carried overseas the same wrongheaded notion about themselves that they accepted at home. They had succumbed to the irrational myth of *kleine nederlandse*.

According to this mythology, the Dutch thought they were destined to be a territorially small nation. They had accepted this as fact. Since the late sixteenth century and as a consequence of the peculiar circumstances of the revolt against Spain, they had, Geyl wrote, seen it to be in their best interests to limit their territorial boundaries to the minuscule lands of the seven northern United Provinces. When the opportunity was offered, they had even refused unification with the southern provinces of the Low Countries. As one writer put it in agreement, the States had at a crucial moment of diplomacy beginning in the 1630s paradoxically refused to contemplate its territorial extension "into the old heartland of the Netherlands."[12]

Many seventeenth-century northern Netherlanders, however, supported such a policy. Joost van den Vondel staged *Leeuwendaelers* in 1647 and called for a marriage of the northern provinces with those of the south. The play pleased no one. To Geyl, this mentality was shortsighted in the extreme. It was further evidence that the preference for a territorially constricted nation was "ten times more intense than . . . [the appeal of] a *groot-Nederlandse*." Calvinists, he argued, played into this. During the siege of 's-Hertogenbosch in 1629, for example, the synod of South Holland had urged the States not to incorporate the city into its territories. They should work to propagate God's church not to "conquer land and towns." But it was Grotius's propositions that contributed most to a sense of inevitability about this. In 1623, he had written that territorial expansion negated the possibility of efficient government, whether at home or overseas. A ship may, he wrote, attain such a size that it cannot be steered. So, too, "the number of inhabitants and the distance between places may be so great as not to tolerate a single government."[13]

In the years before the *Eendracht* episode, the powerful political party of Johan Oldenbarnevelt was openly promoting a *kleine nederlandse* policy. Three decades after *Eendracht* and the confrontation about native rights, Jan de Witt was Councillor Pensionary of Holland. He stepped into Oldenbarnevelt's role and convictions. He, too, was vigorous in fostering a *kleine nederlandse* policy. And his associate Pieter de la Court, a Leiden textile magnate, was taking it as far as logic could carry it.

One day, opinion would have it that de la Court was the best political thinker of his generation, with the exception of Baruch Spinoza. But in 1662, he was writing *The True Interest of Holland, or Grounds of Holland's Welfare*. Brazenly Holland-centered, extreme but uncompromising in its propositions, the lengthy tract urged Hollanders to look to their own interests if they meant to maximize the province's already extraordinary influence in the Low Countries. It far outweighed the others in population and wealth, assuring it a dominance that was overwhelming. But this was not resulting in a desire to extend the province's "formal control over more territory."[14]

On the contrary: Holland's merchant oligarchy intended to avoid the expansionary foreign policy of other European states and instead pursue contractionary strategies. Holland's self-interest was a driving force behind the *kleine nederlandse* policy that Geyl later excoriated. It accounted for the rejection of seventeenth-century opportunities to add territories in the Rhineland and the Spanish Netherlands. It had already showed itself in the adoption of the waterline, a series of defensive works devised to protect Holland from invasion "but none of the other provinces."[15]

De la Court's tract called for an even more secure defensive waterline. His argument elides this and territorial contraction with republicanism. Republics, he began, have a unique advantage in generating urban wealth because "where there is Liberty, there will be Riches and People."[16] Holland will flourish if it engages in manufactures and trade. Seek European markets, certainly. But Europe is too small to sustain adequate commercial intercourse; trade with Asia, Africa, and America must be developed. Such traffic, however, was being jeopardized rather than enlarged by the overseas "monopolizing Companies." The Indies companies had betrayed their original purposes. They had deviated from their original insight that commercial success was always in inverse proportion to "vast and unmanageable . . . [territorial] Designs." They had lost their identity as trading companies and become institutions mired in the requirements of political dominion.[17]

He put the case for *kleine nederlandse* overseas simply. The more lands the companies conquer, the more capital they must spend for their preservation and defense. "And the more Dominion they have . . . [over others] the less they are able to attend to and augment their Traffick."[18]

These were contractionary territorial strategies for successful overseas traders. Those suggested for Holland were even more contractionary—and extravagant. For the sake of her prosperity, let Holland make herself an island. United with Utrecht, Holland could defeat her mightiest enemies. Let the two provinces build around them "a Canal, Trench or Channel . . . [extending] from the Zuyder-Zee and into the . . . [River] Lek." Operate it by sluices capable of flooding the countryside "when and as we wish." Figure the channel's length to be twelve thousand Rhineland rods. Expect the cost to be 1.6 million guilders. Let the other provinces fend for themselves[19] (Map 1).

De la Court's proposal that two provinces make an island of themselves tapped into a mythic Dutch identification with islands and shorelines. It drew upon nothing less than a faith in the political and economic promise of islands—Manhattan Island and the archipelago of the great harbor, Onrust and Deshima, Formosa, Curaçao, Java, Ceylon, and the Moluccas. In 1628, a senior employee of the West India Company in New Netherland proposed creating an island within an island. The point where Fort Amsterdam stood on the island of the Manhates, he wrote, might easily be made a small island. We could cut a canal through a low valley nearby and create a winter and summer harbor for sloops and ships. The resulting island should make "a superb fort . . . approached on land only on one side."[20]

At home, geography and a justification for the uprising also sanctioned de la Court's proposition. Geographically, the Netherlanders of the sea provinces were people of islands. Islands were everywhere to be seen (Figs. 8, 9). Nature created them. Learned engineers and common peat diggers brought them into existence as well. Water entirely surrounded Haarlem. As many as forty islands lay within the rivers and canals of late-sixteenth-century Leiden. The northernmost land of North Holland was once the island of Huisduinen. In the fifteenth century, seas along the coast of Holland threatened to wash away the delta land to the south. Netherlanders had to think of the present day's western Holland as an offshore island.

Being isled was central to the self-identity expressed in *kleine nederlandse*. During the revolt against Spain, the Dutch had discovered a heroic past that authenticated the political and territorial character the rebellion was assuming from 1567 to 1648, when, among other things, each city became, more than ever, an island expected to be self-reliant for its own defense. They came to celebrate their Batavian origins. This early Germanic tribe had occupied an island described by Tacitus in the second century. He had left unclear the island's exact location: it was somewhere between two arms of the Rhine River; or it had "the Ocean Sea in Front, and the River of Rhyne behinde and on either side."[21]

Figure 8. Polders: the elision of water and land. Visscher's farmhouse, thought to be just outside Amsterdam, catches the interchangeability of land and water as part of daily life. Claes Janse Visscher, *A Farm in the Polders*, 1610 (detail). Collection Frits Lugt. Institut Neerlandais, Paris.

Exactness didn't really matter to the legend's vitality. But the Batavii being islanded did. Only by defending the waters around their homeland had they achieved victory over invading Roman forces and enduring independence. In the 1660s, the legend (and a strong measure of nationalistic scholarship) was allowing de la Court to fuse island-ness with liberty and security. As with the Batavii, measures based on naval preparedness were paramount. In this, the real audacity of de la Court's proposition about Holland transforming itself into a sort of Venice with the remaining provinces expendable terra firma was in adding to an already deeply divisive distinction being drawn between the maritime provinces and those inland.[22]

The True Interest of Holland identified the inland provinces as different—and subversive. Physically, it could have been thought, they were clearly different: didn't every one of the navigable waterways stop where the inland provinces began?[23] The war too had created or strengthened any number of territorial (and covertly political) discriminations. People of sea towns and (as one Dutch military leader called them) land towns were learning that they had different

Figure 9. The making of islands. This map of the Schie area shows a meandering canal connecting Overschie in the left foreground to Rotterdam (left background). Another waterway leads directly from Overschie to Delftshaven. Ships move over waters across the horizon. The residents have given themselves an island. Anon., *Map of the Schie Area*, 1512. Algemeen Rijksarchief.

identities. The war had, for example, strengthened the seaward-looking character of the Zuider Zee ports. Hoorn and Enkhuizen residents had had to cope with the loss of many of their men drowned, tortured, or hanged by the Spaniards after an unsuccessful venture organized to obtain salt in the West Indies. They faced attacks on the fishing fleets from Flemish warships and privateers. In 1625, while Verhulst was exploring New Netherland, Zuider Zee folk learned of enemy fleets destroying almost 150 fishing vessels and taking 945 fishermen as prisoners while, in contrast, the rural population of the eastern Dutch provinces was experiencing the destructive presence of land armies.[24] Geyl considered the inland provinces so different that logic suggested to him an east-west divide in the Netherlands rather than the north-south division that eventuated. Let the northwestern provinces separate from those to the east rather than from the southern (now Belgian) provinces.

But de la Court was identifying them as distinctive and as enemy territory. In his view, the Batavian legend had fused liberty with republicanism and tied both to a defensive posture against potential enemies—that is, to a concern for defenses proper to any island: a well equipped navy and shoreline fortifications. Inland—or as the Hollanders sometimes called these lands, "the outer provinces"—had come to have diametrically opposite political meanings. To the Hollanders, the maritime provinces were the core of the Dutch economy. They owed this to their merchant fleets and well-subsidized navy. Navies and trade were never at cross-purposes. Armies and trade were.

Yet the outer provinces were the preserve of the army and—one small step away from that—the monarchical aspirants of the House of Orange. To the people of the *zeeprovincien*, the Dutch army was like any other: odious, a scourge on civilians, a haven for mercenaries eager (like their leaders) for war and spoils, a plague of men made wild and savage in offensive wars conducted in open fields. De Witt and de la Court were not alone in distrusting the army: it took the field under a nobility openly transgressive of republicanism; it was an internal threat more than a defense against foreign enemies. Soldiers did the bidding of the land-owning courtiers of a monarchical party oriented toward territorial acquisition. Vondel had expressed the dichotomy earlier: in Germany and France, localism and absolutism were in deadly combat; in the Netherlands, the struggle was between republicanism and monarchy. And everyone knew the physical terrain that corresponded to that opposition.[25]

De la Court was a practiced political propagandist. He was a master of the literary devices that appealed to Holland's audiences. He chose an allegory to reiterate Vondel's point and to summarize his own maxims for achieving the peace, prosperity, and territorial security that the mercantile republic required. He presented a cast of characters familiar to seventeenth-century audiences, a menagerie of beasts: "Lions, Tygers, Wolves, Foxes, Bears, and, diminutive along-side these animals but of equal cunning and self-interest, the Cat." He saved his venom for the contrast between the lion, the monarch—and the monar-chical party of Orange—and the cat, the republic. Lions live by "conquering and plundering their Neighbours." Republics follow the commendable example of the cat. They live in peace because they "subsist by Trade." Minding their own business, they are careful not to meddle in the affairs of other animals. Republics are shy, fearful, and inclined, if pursued, to seek natural defenses and remain quiet until the trouble is over. They are not aggressive, because in this way they have what they want: they are left alone, and they "live longer and are more acceptable" to others.

His allegory filled out this way: the cat "never converses with strange Beasts, but either keeps at home, or accompanys those of her own Species, meddling with none, but in order to defend her own, very vigilant." She doesn't snarl at those who provoke her. But if she can't by using all available means avoid com-bat, then she is will defend herself "with Tooth and Nail."[26]

De la Court was defending the cautious foreign policy adopted by the republic since the Peace of Münster in 1648. He could justifiably think that being feline was popular and had proved successful. Although the country was under threat from France and, in his estimation, similarly threatened by Nether-landers conniving to raise armies against the republic, 1662 was a year of rela-tive peace, a time of the *Pax Belgica*. But the Netherlands had watched itself engage in war and use force. How, then, did the image of the cat have signifi-cant meaning?

Feline practices were part of the West India Company's policies in the New World. But they can only be read as one side of the ledger of its accounts during these years. That is, on the recto side of the register under "New Nether-land," let us say, the company inscribed its intentions and early practices toward the native Americans. It was all there: the calculated nonaggression, the guile-ful disengagement from the "noise" of contending native tribes, the desire to be left alone in order to be more "acceptable" and thereby trade. The self-interested live and let live.

The verso side of the ledger was otherwise. Encountering Spain and the Portuguese in the New World, the company became the conquering and plun-dering lion. In many respects, and paradoxically, the power of the Catholic Hapsburg Empire to reach across Europe and ruthlessly destroy or subordinate enemy states and principalities has been underestimated because of the shrill hyperbole of the anti-Spanish "black legend" that came to dominate later inter-pretations. Similarly, justification for the detestation—felt even by pragmatic

Calvinists such as the men of the West India Company—has been underappreciated. To get some sense of the terror aroused by the conquering imperial armies, one may read between the lines of W. J. van Balen's study of van Linschoten and the Indies. He published his book in Amsterdam in 1942, that is, during the Nazi occupation of the Netherlands. He condemned the Hapsburg Empire in what must have read as a double entendre. Spain was detested as nothing less than a *militaire wereldmacht,* a militarized world power.[27]

Both sides of the company's ledger were there to be read when its directors pressed their instructions on Verhulst in 1625. Toward the Americans, play the cat. Establish peaceful trade on a foundation of justice. The Portuguese in Brazil and the Spanish in the Caribbean and on the high seas were declared enemies. Toward them be the lion, the beast of prey.

De la Court had written an allegory that expressed both idealism and national self-interest—and, as it proved, a deluded notion about national survival. He concluded with a declaration that a cat cannot be transformed into a lion. "And in the same way, we who are by nature Merchants cannot be turned into militarists."[28]

*   *   *

But if persuasion fails, merchants might well become soldiers. This possibility dismayed some members of the East India Company sixty years before de la Court wrote *The True Interest of Holland.* In 1602, a captain in the company's employ had seized a Portuguese galleon as a prize in the Straits of Malacca. When this became known to the directors at home, some investors argued that trading with the East Indies was one thing, but capturing Portuguese vessels quite another. Some men refused their share of the prize; others sold their shares in the company. Still others considered establishing a new company in France under the protection of King Henry IV, "which should trade in peace and abstain from all warlike action."[29]

Grotius, too, it seems, had blinded himself to the possibility of merchants becoming soldiers. The right to free trade with all peoples was, he had written some thirty-five years before de la Court, a natural right. It could not be denied. Force, by implication, played no role. But this proposition was faulty, rebutted a Portuguese Jesuit. Seraphim de Freitas pointed to the position of a non-European ruler, especially one who might be weaker than the outsiders. Such a ruler "has the right to refuse the admission of foreigners to his territory or commerce and to forbid his subjects trade and intercourse with them."[30] Then what?

In 1634, the *Eendracht* affair had, as we have seen, ended. The States had showed themselves decidedly feline. They chose to quit snarling at the provocations of the English on this and other matters. This state, they announced, cannot interfere in the dispute between the English and the West India Company. Let the matter "take its course."[31]

But in 1640, New Netherland merchants became soldiers. They did not attack the nearby English. They turned on the natives. By mid-1643, indigenous and Dutch settlements were burning.

PART IV

Omens of a Tragedy
Coming On

The Netherlanders with whom the natives began to trade in 1624 were men accustomed to war. They were among the millions swept up by the Eighty Years' War in the Low Countries, the Thirty Years' War in Germany and central Europe, the religious wars in France, and the English civil war. European historians have expressed amazement that the barbarism of the conflicts has been so little studied. For the military entrepreneur and the war profiteer, however, they were the best of days. In resisting Spain, the West India Company put itself among their number as privateers. Its personnel in the New World came armed.

Still, the 1630s in New Netherland were years of relative peace between the Americans and the strangers who in 1630 numbered perhaps 270 men and women, and in the mid-1640s, three to five hundred. They were not the romanticized times some historians have envisioned. But a number of both indigenous and Dutch contemporaries remembered them that way. Their evidence and that of violence recorded as unplanned suggest that the decade was—and not merely in hindsight—a time of omens.

Paradoxically, the company's concentration on the Portuguese and Spanish enemy during this time was beneficial for the natives of southern New Netherland. The company's directors chose to expand the role of New Netherland in its Latin American and Caribbean-based operations against Spanish shipping and ports. In this, they made emphatic who the enemy was and was not (the natives) and enlarged the already seaward orientation of the small *waterstad* on Manhattan Island. This orientation was emblematic of the transience that marked the lives of the men of the trading station. Transience also affected their relations with the nearby Americans. Cross-cultural contacts were those of the marketplace. For the Dutch, they were not entry points onto a terrain where colonization or civilizing and Christianizing missions might be advanced. To such projects, they remained indifferent. Portentously, however, the violence and death that were to afflict New Netherland beginning in 1640 were already signaling their presence.

Beginning in the 1620s, the Dutch were sporadically trading in the Connecticut valley. In 1634, a violent incident there cost native lives. The traders' presence in the area was not as destabilizing as that of the American tribes vying among themselves for supremacy and trading advantages—Pequots, Narragansetts, Sequins, Mohegans, Pokanokets, Massachusetts, Niantics, some refugees, some contending overlords, some meddling neighbors. Nor was it as destructive as the instability and conflict caused by perhaps 2,750 English who were also in the valley in the late 1630s. But it was ominous.

The turbulent environment was defying the unproblematic integrative exchanges the Netherlanders had hoped for. Each group that had made itself a party to the exchange process was experiencing the inevitable excesses of things exchanged: the reranking of values, the construction of new generalizations (about trade and forms of sociality and hierarchy), the acceptance of unanticipated valorizations of locations and commodities, the amendment of ways of exercising diplomacy and peacemaking. During these years, in the valley and elsewhere, the Dutch were not the most important agents or stimuli of change. Possibly, the villagers of the Iroquois League were. We cannot be sure.

In 1637 and in return for protection, the English demanded tribute from the natives of a northern Connecticut native village, Agawam. Two years later, the Dutch put the Raritans and then other Algonquian-speaking people in New Netherland under a similar obligation. They ignited a fire that burned for five years.

Chapter 8
Bells of War

A Pequot man greets a group of English soldiers moving along the coast of his people's lands. It is his watchfulness and fear we must notice. His sense of the ominous.

Somehow he has intuited that the English intend war against them. "What Englishman, what cheere," he cries out. "Will you cran us [burn us alive]?" "Will you kill us, and doe you come to fight?"

Later that night—it is sometime in 1637—his people and others also look into the face of the ominous. They made, said one observer, "most dolefull and wofull cryes all the night . . . fearing the English were come to warre against them."[1]

In 1626, Pieter Minuit wanted to create a space for religious worship near the fort on Manhattan Island. A mill was already under construction nearby. A commodious room for worshipers could be erected over it and, above that, a tower.

There were even bells for it. Everyone among the Dutch on the island would have known their origin. They were booty taken a year earlier in an attack on the Spanish-held port of San Juan de Porto Rico.[2] People would have known that bells, like cannon and other pieces of heavy metal, were prizes seized after a successful siege or raid. Unlike other loot, they became the property of the master gunners or commanding officers.

In this case, the prizes had gone to Boudewijn Hendricksz. Serving in the employ of the West India Company, he had sacked the port and then distributed captured goods throughout a fleet of thirty-four ships bound for Holland. There the men under his command received their pay and were dismissed from service. Hendricksz was from the Zuider Zee town where women feeding their cattle from a small boat had taken the legendary mermaid. The town was Edam. He had been a burgomaster.[3]

In 1627, Holland's greatest playwright, Joost van den Vondel, wrote an epic poem. He titled it *Verovering van Grol door Frederick Henrick, Prince van Oranje* (*The Conquest of Groenlo by Frederick Henrick, Prince of Orange*). The prince had captured a strategic city held by the Spanish and, as it seemed, ended six years of victories won by the enemy's Army of Flanders. Nothing would do but that Vondel honor him by calling on the *Aeneid*. "I sing," he called out, "of arms and a hero."[4]

The invocation preceded almost eight hundred lines of poetry. Vondel laid bare the sufferings of his war-torn land. But now he could set the presence of marauding soldiers and enslaved burghers against the promise of peace and the restoration of liberty and prosperity. "The Spaniard," he cried, "is now a wolf without a bite." He is overthrown, and each class of Netherlanders will now know the joy of that. To the farmer, Vondel gave comfort in nineteen lines flooded with powerful images and harsh memories: the "terror in the woodlands," "roving troopers," a countryside fearful to enter, farmhouses destroyed, properties deserted, cattle "brutally skinned." These were now in the past.

The ultimate blessing of peace would be the end of a practice that farmers feared most from military predators. "You shall no longer," he promised, contribute the *brandschatting* to the enemy's soldiers—or, he might have added, to the raiders of our own armies. The *brandschatting* was extortion money. Euphemistically, it was called a tax but it worked like this: pay up, and we may give you protection (from us and your enemies); fail to pay, and see your animals seized and your farmstead and village burned to the ground. Now, Vondel promised, that was over.[5]

But not for everyone, everywhere. In the Low Countries, the capture of Groenlo was not the end of prolonged sieges and bitter warfare. Peace was still twenty years in the future. More than that, these were years when—some say after 1607—Europe's wars were carried like a virus to the Far East and the Americas.[6] Having at one time or another infected Europe from Madrid to the Baltic, and from the coast of France to Bohemia, the techniques of the continental wars would be cargo transported to Mexico, Florida, and Canada by the Spanish and French, and by the Dutch to Java, Formosa, Banda Niera, the Guinea Coast, Brazil, the Caribbean, and North America: "terror in the woodlands," "roving troopers," countrysides made fearful to enter, farmhouses destroyed, properties deserted, cattle "brutally skinned."

And the *brandschatting* would travel as well. The ways of the extortionist would be hauled out of cargo holds, unloaded, and familiarly put to use. About thirty-three hundred miles away, on and around the island of the Manhates and within twelve years of a victory at a place called Groenlo in the eastern lands of Gelderland, Algonquian-speaking natives picked up the word. They called it "contributions."

* * *

The native people of New Netherland—some recorded as Warenecker and Souwenos and Quinnipiac, others written down as living in coastal or island villages such as Mareckewich and Kestateuw—were receiving traders who came on the sea winds. But the same strangers were acquainted with war and armed violence. They worked for a company whose directors had decided where its future lay. Boardroom papers told the story. It was a different kind of along-shore story to the earlier tales of the Zuider Zee towns. The company had a role to fill as a floating war machine. It would serve the state and its shareholders by disabling the Spanish empire wherever it could be sought out and, piece by piece, dismembered.

The directors were already spelling out the unique contribution they were in a position to make to the States' war effort. Their war fleets and soldiers could, they assured its representatives, constitute a diversion. They could attack the enemy's distant convoys and shore installations in theaters of war such as Brazil and the Caribbean. They would turn alongshore places into war zones. About fifteen years earlier, an allegorist had put these theaters of war in picturesque language. The Netherlands' fleets were like waterfowl. They were able "to swimme over the Spanish seas [of the West Indies and] into the Spanish havens . . . [to] revenge themselves."[7]

The directors' words were more pedestrian. Their operations would deprive the king of Spain of the single commodity without which he could not continue to pursue the war: silver and the raw materials that, when traded, became silver and gold, too: salt, sugar, wood, and tobacco. Their contribution would bring the king to his knees by draining his treasury dry.[8]

The directors knew exactly what they were talking about. The uprising's forty murderous years before 1609 and then the twelve years of uneasy truce had now brought them to a year such as 1625, when all seemed lost: Breda had fallen to contingents of the Hapsburg's 300,000-strong army while two able commanders were suffering considerable losses in the Rhenish campaigns. Spanish enforcement of a river blockade was strangling trade between the northern and southern Netherlands. The sheer duration of all this had taught them and other Dutch citizens what the king of Spain knew as well. Money, and money alone, meant holding out for final victory or accepting ultimate defeat.

So the company's brightest prospects were similar to those of giant companies in the twentieth century that they could not have known about, those of Krupp, Rolls-Royce, and McDonnell-Douglas. For the immediate future profits lay in war. The company would pull back from the goals of trade and navigation that had won it the monopoly on New Netherland when Volkertsz and others were looking out to sea and earlier directors were concerned about ships' logs, places of rendezvous, and trading beaches. Those were domestically oriented ambitions. In many ways, they were aimed at ensuring the country's prosperity by giving employment to large numbers of seafaring people who would otherwise flounder or fail.

In the mid-1630s, the company directors knew that, but the main chance must be seized. So now they were writing to representatives of South Holland and western Friesland, Amsterdam and the waterlands of the Zuider Zee. Profits would be returned to their shareholders by searching for places where the Spanish and Portuguese were most vulnerable: shipping lanes, undermanned harbors and shore forts, and poorly defended sugar plantations. There would be raids in the Americas: hit-and-run escapades, the collection of ransom for a "Vice Roy and his Son, and the Jesuit prisoners" taken from a distant place called the Bay of All Saints. And there would be other booty as well as the human loot called captives—bells and other prizes garnered from privateering or, as a Dutch scholar put it unambiguously, getting into the *piratenhandel,* piracy. They would cripple the king's trade and replace it with their own. Commerce alone would be ineffectual. Spain's power in the Americas was like the well-built dike familiar to them all. "Not a straw of . . . [it] can be weakened" just by trade. But trade together with war, that was another matter.[9]

In 1626, just after the directors were instructing Verhulst to explore New Netherland and invite a people such as the Manhates to sell land on their island, the same men were overseeing the stockpiling of war material at home and increasing the company's armed fleets to seventy-three ships. Optimistic and able to see its bottom line in credit, the directors were pleased to send the States a list of the company's growing assets. They could itemize the value of their fully fitted-out ships and yachts, ample stocks of cargo, and vessels in the port of Amsterdam "provided with metal and iron guns, and all sorts of supplies of ammunition of war, powder, muskets, arms, sabres." They had discovered that—everyone knew that these things mattered—putting this equipment to sea could be managed at less than a fourth of previous costs. Already they had captured the port of San Juan in Porto Rico and large quantities of sugar. The settlement of New Netherland was costing only about 1 percent of their current capital. A cozy relationship had developed with the decision makers in the States' assemblies and committees. They called them their partners. They benefited by way of subsidies, loans, and even the use of large numbers of paid soldiers when needed. The States benefited because, as the directors were careful to point out, the company's fleets and its operations as coastal raiders injured the king of Spain and, not to be overlooked, afforded the partners solid profits. Ten years after Minuit had erected the makeshift church on Manhattan Island in 1626, one of the directors took the time to tally the number of Spanish vessels seized over the past years and do some simple arithmetic. He could account for 547 prizes with an estimated value of thirty million guilders.[10]

The directors were, they confided to the States, learning by experience. They could pinpoint places in the West Indies and the Brazils that were "useful or useless to the Company." They were also gaining knowledge of what could and could not be defended by the enemy and themselves.[11] Nobody talked of following the Spanish example by invading native lands; nobody talked of territorial acquisitions as assets. The gaze was that of the mariner: on alongshore installations and the high seas.

But the directors could foresee a serious danger to the corporation's bright prospects. Another truce or peace was always a threatening possibility. Neither side, for all these years of war, had been able to deliver a knockout blow. So peace parties were strengthening across the provinces. The so-called inland peace provinces and peace cities elsewhere were openly expressing weariness with war, weariness with taxes, and falling prices for products such as cheese and butter. For their prosperity and well-being, they were satisfied to rely on the European carrying trade and inland river commerce. So the company directors, now deeply implicated in the continuation of war and aware that they had gambled shareholders' funds on it, needed to mount their own propaganda warfare.

They used images of native Americans to sell their public relations message. They constructed a portrait of threatening forces in the Americas. But the enemy to attack in the New World was Spain, not the resident natives. In making this distinction, the directors' strategy was simple. They would capitalize on the powerfully nationalistic polarity drawn between Hapsburg Spain and the republic. Alongside this powerful narrative of self-identity, accounts of native Americans' hostilities, even the most vividly constructed atrocity narratives, were either marginal or supplementary.

Americans were primitives over there. The Spanish were a deadly threat over there and over here. We know that in three hundred years' time, the blood of Europeans would run cold at the power behind the Nazi threat to put the entire continent on Berlin time. In the days of Verhulst, Minuit, and Vondel, an English propagandist could incite the same terror and revulsion by pointing to the imperium of Madrid, the capital of Spain's military empire. A Spanish pamphleteer was, he warned, already describing Madrid as "the head Citie of the World." The Englishman had to agree: the sun never sets on Spain's empire. They have more dominion than the Romans.[12]

On at least three occasions from the late 1620s to the mid-1630s, the directors argued for continued war by presenting images of the Americas to the representatives of the province of Holland and West Friesland, and the States. First: their own place in the picture. Should a truce be entered into, the company would be ruined. A multimillion-dollar enterprise would have to be dissolved. It could not rely solely on trade in the Americas and certainly not on undertaking agricultural projects there. The nature of the peoples of the Americas and the presence of Spain saw to that. Earlier experts—"those who thought themselves conversant with the trade"—prophesied that trade would flourish, colonists could be transported, and plantations of various products could readily prosper. But these were visionaries hopeful of duplicating the good fortune of Spain: our trade, they clamored, our colonies, our plantations would be equal to the king of Spain's—and just consider how such enterprises had enriched his treasury.[13]

But now experience had taught the directors otherwise. Trade with the nations and peoples of the Americas? We only get to deal with those in places outside the control of Spain, and with them, the trade is trifling. Agriculture and colonization? The countries "yet uninvaded" by Spain and Portugal are inconsequential remnants of their foraging and unproductive. In the few available tropical lands, the rigors of cultivation and heat discourage our people, who, unlike the Spanish and Portuguese, don't know how to employ slaves even if we could provide them. And consider New Netherland. Nothing seems favorable. It's a colder place than we expected, with frost and—not worth itemizing—other inconveniences. Trade in furs is only minimally advantageous. The colonists sent over face a meager existence. They are, the directors implied, like the unprofitable and clumsy peasant farmers that people here compare with other low-life figures. They haven't been of any profit to us. In fact, they're a drawback.[14]

In all this, the directors knew how to talk the language of corporate earnings and corporate collapse. Without war, they warned, we'll have to sell our principal assets at a loss, lay off employees, write off other investments, anticipate a fall in the value of shares as stockholders sell out, and try to defend our decision to invest the stockholders' capital so lavishly in the public service. They might also have appealed to the lack of interest by many East India Company shareholders in overseas colonization. It was more than boardroom knowledge that "there wasn't the least interest in agricultural colonization."[15]

Ask us to profit on trade and colonization, they argued, and you ask the impossible. Sue for a truce or peace with Spain while we have risked shareholders' funds to go "farther and farther into war," and you mandate the exclusion of the Netherlanders from the Americas.[16] Even as de la Court charged about thirty years later but to make a decidedly different argument, "[we] have made war . . . [against Spain] instead of traffick . . . [we] have conquests instead of colonies."

*   *   *

The company's directors could easily have imagined the propriety of getting into the entrepreneurial business of war. War had made the first eighty years of the seventeenth century the halcyon days of military entrepreneurship. Most military moneymakers were private individuals garnering their profits by owning and often commanding regiments contracted to one of the warring parties: the States, the Catholic League, the Swedish crown, a petty warlord. The highest bidder. Such war profiteers managed their regiments like other well-organized business enterprises that offered certain services. An entire regiment was the entrepreneur's to send into the field, sell off, put into multiple ownership, or contract to a previous enemy if it offered greater profit. Most had neither the reach nor the finances of the giant trading company. But they, too, meant to capitalize on the wars, to profit from the desperation (or stupidity—it didn't matter) of powerful states or weak princelings. Possibly fifteen hundred such men found it lucrative to do so during the Thirty Years' War alone.[17]

The trading company's men had no reason to think that they were out of step in hiring and sending overseas personnel whom they could boast were trained in the ways of war. To handle a vessel bound for New Netherland, they had reemployed a skipper previously hired at Kampen, a fortified seaport on the east coast of the Zuider Zee. They also hired a man for New Netherland who was a *vrijbuiter* from Veere: someone like those—often deserters—who ravaged the countryside or coastal villages for their own benefit. A third man in New Netherland had commanded forces in the Indies for the king of Denmark.[18]

In 1629, the company had made a significant contribution to the war effort at home. It was the year just before the native leaders and commonality of the Delaware delta village peacefully sold lands to Minuit and his council for the use of private investors. In September, the States' armies had captured 's-Hertogenbosch, the gateway to Brabant (Map 1). Twenty-five thousand men had been thrown into a siege that lasted six months. The siege works needed to assault the city stretched around it for forty kilometers. Elsewhere the States were financing a standing army of 43,000 men. The company had allowed twelve hundred of its fifteen thousand troops destined for Brazil to serve in the campaigns as well. Another man, an Englishman, had hired himself to serve the Dutch forces, too. In late 1628, John Underhill had been a cadet (*adelborst*) in the guard of Frederick Hendrik and probably present at the siege and capture of Groenlo. In nine years' time, in 1637, he would hire himself out to the Connecticut colony and take responsibility for massacring some of the natives there. Six years later, he offered his services to the director of New Netherland to repeat the dubious achievement. He delighted, commented one writer, on spreading terror, and was ruthless and without scruples.[19]

In 1629, the revolt was in its sixtieth year. Nineteen years of war would be endured until the Peace of Münster. Were this the duration of the American Civil War begun in 1861, it would be the year 1921 and the presidency of Warren G. Harding—and peace to come in 1940. As it did with the Netherlanders, war would have crept into the lives of four generations, into their habits of thinking, the space of their imagination, the ordering of social action.

So the company's role in the business of war is not surprising. But for the native Americans, it was ominous.

*   *   *

The ominous works as a dark prelude to an oncoming event. It is haunting because it goes beyond the hard edges of logic. It is real but indeterminate and mysterious, filling the crevices unreached by the rational. The ominous is Edgar Allan Poe's brooding midnight reader and an inexplicable and vaguely fearsome someone or something tapping at his chamber door: "only this and nothing more." It is William Turner's dark foreboding clouds. In ancient Rome, the ominous was read in a set of signs more surely trusted than the considered plans of senators or military commanders. With one work to do, to portend good or evil, it was outside the questions that common sense might raise.

The trading company's capacity to embrace the business of war was a portent of the war that would be carried to the natives in New Netherland in the early 1640s. The directors were not being devious when, back in 1624 and 1625, they were instructing May and Verhulst to maintain amicable relations with the natives around Manhattan Island and the Delaware. Nor were they being disingenuous in demanding that trickery and fraud be conscientiously avoided "so that the divine anger of God may not be brought down on an unrighteous beginning, the Company being in no sense intent to burden itself with war or aggressive attack as with the Spaniards." And in 1633, Wouter van Twiller was not deceiving himself or the New Englanders in insisting that the States were acutely aware of Spanish overseas policies and had no intention of taking land "from the poor natives."[20]

But in the coming years, there were omens to be read. There was a dark space in the strangers' imagination for war and aggression. Until 1640, "only this and nothing more."

Chapter 9

"Only This and Nothing More"

In the 1630s, a waterfront way of life was emerging on the island. The war against Spain was making its maritime character even more real. The chase for prizes, the sight of captured vessels brought into port, stories from the Caribbean—all these were focusing a seaward orientation that was already a fact of life among the dominant groups of men on the island. It gave further scope to those whose livelihoods took them to sea more than they planted them on land. In this, it contributed to the transience that characterized the small *water-stad*. And this meant relatively peaceful coexistence alongside the native peoples.

New Netherland officials were now directly involved in the hunt for Spanish prizes. They could bring the ships into the harbor before the fort and settle cases there rather than conduct them home for judgment. Wouter van Twiller brought a prize to the island in 1633, and two years later the company bought two more seized vessels. Private ships were now joining those of the company in ranging along the coast from Florida to Newfoundland. They could seize the vessels and retain the full value of their cargoes. They called it "catch[ing] a fish."[1]

Perhaps by the mid-1630s, Nicolaes Wassenaer's earlier generalization that the Spaniard would never accept rival claims to American possessions was being discounted for what it was, an exaggeration. But it's difficult to think that the islanders were untroubled when David Pietersz de Vries sailed into port bringing stories about the Spanish destruction of an English settlement in the Tortugas and their sudden attack on his struggling tobacco plantation in Guiana. At home, New Netherland was often identified as a part of the West Indies—company clerks filed reports of its affairs in a *locketkas* marked *Westindische*—and they were known to be a favorite Dutch hunting ground for Spanish prey. When young Petrus Stuyvesant signed on for the company's operations in the Caribbean, he made a will assigning his possessions as "salary, monthly pay and prize money." Several years later, advisers to the States would be promoting New Netherland as the rendezvous for vessels of war operating against the Spanish. Think of the abundance of provisions and timber. Think, too, of its location as a safe and easy jumping-off point to all parts of the West Indies. Here, "designs against the enemy can be kept . . . concealed."[2]

Perhaps the New Netherlanders had reason to fear an attack by the Spanish or Portuguese. A story set in the 1640s raised the possibility of such a raid. Adriaen vander Donck presents a New Netherlander and "Patriot" conversing about the settlement's seemingly weak defenses in the face of a Portuguese attack. He gives a possible raid far more than anecdotal treatment.

New Netherland's seaboard, Patriot open, is easily accessible to the Portuguese and other pirates. The New Netherlander firmly denies this, countering that its surrounding waters are not a seaman's ocean. They're the waters of a *loodman,* a pilot acquainted with shifting bars and sand flats and places such as Sandy Hook and Hell-Gate that can easily be made impassable. Ah, responds Patriot, but if I were a Portuguese raiding party, I wouldn't seek your bays and harbors but one of your sand beaches. There I'd cast my ground hooks and attack you from the rear. Impossible, responds the New Netherlander. The whole coast presents double forelands separated by broad shallow waters or islands "two or three deep." And, in any case, where will you find boats to carry your men over the bays? Attack New Amsterdam directly? You'll fail because you don't know the navigable waters. "This is work for madmen." And besides, we reward the natives for alerting us whenever ships appear on the coast.[3]

If the coastal bands of natives were prepared to warn the Dutch of enemies appearing on the foreshores, there is no evidence that they sighted Spanish or Portuguese raiders with landing craft and ground hooks. But they were now familiar with the Dutch islanders crossing over the bays and piloting around the shallows and double foreshores, catching the feel of islands before they were reached, always searching for trading beaches and native traders. Whether they saw them as a potentially dangerous riptide moving along their shores and coastal villages we cannot know. Perhaps if we look at the strangers' ships or listen to their words about sailing and movement, we can catch a glimpse of the native people who also looked and listened.

The Dutch strangers tell us that during these years, yachts for exploring the coasts and rivers were imperative. For a trader employed by the company or trying his luck as a private trader, a boat and a primitive house were necessities. It was expected that he had the skills to build both. Here on the edge of a bay, wrote one observer, two men have built a house and scow "in order to go and look after the trade in wampum."[4]

Residents of all occupations needed sailing craft. In 1639, when there were possibly four hundred Netherlanders on and around Manhattan Island, a ship's carpenter listed the work he and other carpenters had been carrying out on the island's various ships over the past six years. He identified long hours of work on company yachts, undoubtedly those such as the sloops now sent to trade with the Raritans in New Jersey each spring. But he also did carpentry on farm boats and skiffs, a boat for the woodcutter and nine boats the director had ordered be made or repaired: one needing new knees, one "entirely rebuilt and plancked up higher," a large open boat, two yachts fitted out with an "orlop and caboose," a yacht with a mizzen, and "many boats and yawls made for the sloops." This was in addition to constantly repairing and caulking old craft. Any resident director knew that his reputation was as good as destroyed if he was reported for neglecting the company's ships.[5]

Ships' carpenters also repaired the vessels of private owners or skippers visiting the port—careening the timbers, replacing a worm-eaten keel. The directors anticipated that the patroons' future colonists would also be building coastal and river craft to prosecute their own lawful trade. Now a city—that's what they called it—had grown up outside the fort. New Amsterdam, not the English Virginias, advised skipper de Vries, was the place to get a ship properly caulked and made tight.[6]

These were ships for men more accustomed to the unsteady motion of the sea than the rhythms of planting seed, cultivating the soil, and harvesting. Experienced merchants were the highest-ranking employees of the company. Their transience lay in the very definition of a merchant. As a New Netherlander later put it, it's a truism that they come and they go: they bring something to a distant or local marketplace but carry much more away. Without permission, the company's senior merchants were specifically forbidden to own farms or boweries. They were to be content with their wages and refrain from conducting trade for themselves or private traders. They were the only men—not the farmers or missionaries, not the soldiers or patroons—sanctioned to exploit newfound trading beaches, scouting on the company's behalf for native customers farther and farther abroad. And they were the ones quickly relieved of office if they failed to do so. So while Verhulst was still tentatively locating the *middelpunt* of the company's trading station back in 1625, Pieter Minuit was already being instructed to think of the island of the Manhates as an *aanloophaven*, a jumping-off point. Sail with cargo along the Hudson, he was ordered. "See if the Indians . . . [will] trade." Later and as director-general, he facilitated the expansion of the trade by commissioning the hydrographic mapping of the pilot's waters around the island. This he completed seven or eight years before the company's men authorized a survey of the land.[7]

A few years later, in 1636, one of Minuit's successors, Wouter van Twiller, suggested to the directors that he move out to investigate the opportunities for coastal trading even though the island under his supervision was beset by a number of pressing problems. The fort, he admitted, was in ruins, and English settlers were increasingly making incursions into New Netherland. But those were present realities, whereas, as in all merchant ventures, the promise of power and gain lay in the future, in the completion of actions that could only exist there. So he portrayed himself as the restless action-oriented servant he ought to be: let's explore the coast from Newfoundland to Florida to see what trade might be carried out.[8]

The company's hired soldiers were also men who put to sea. Or, rather, they were men who expected to be put to sea by the company. Here were the figures conjured up by the imaginary New Netherlander's reference to boats to carry your men over the bays. A comment made by the directors to the States' representatives at this time hinted at the maritime nature of their role. Our ships and men, they reminded the delegates, have been of great use to you in recent campaigns in the eastern Netherlands. But this, they complained, has depleted our fleets in the Americas. So we have "three thousand men abroad doing nothing."[9]

Soldiers knew that they were contracted to serve the company in two ways. First, they were to defend the perimeters of the overseas trading stations. They were not there to look outward to the local populations: they were not to abuse them, not to act in an aggressive manner toward them, and not to go native. Rather, they were like armed security guards, paid to look to the protection of the products being exploited by the company—sugar, fur, spices—and the stability of the trade. Second, they were shipboard people. They sailed in consort with the company's seamen as marines carrying out raids or other maritime operations where company traders or cargo needed to be safeguarded. One pamphleteer compared them to grasshoppers. Sent across the seas, they have skill to "leape upon the water-sides, and the hard land." In the mid-1630s, the directors brought charges against van Twiller. Perhaps they suspected that he had used for his own private gain some of the one hundred and fifty soldiers they had hired to accompany him to New Netherland—were they sailing with him as he searched for the beaches, foreshores, and riverbanks where he might exploit the trade for himself?[10]

Soldiers were in motion in a more fundamental way. They were transients, bound to the company by the same short-term contracts that bound soldiers to the States at home. Like the fighting men on campaign there, they were often taken on for a single operation, the nature of which was not disclosed to them and about which they probably had little concern, in any case. Everyone knew that they were men of no fixed address, just like the vagabonds and gypsies at home. For their part, they had no intention of tying themselves permanently to an area to which service took them, neither to the confining walls of a captured city at home nor to the operations of a trading station. This could make them indifferent to the locals, or dangerous.[11]

Certainly, they didn't intend to stay on as farmers. A resident director-general later spoke of the company's employees and their transience during this time. No one calculated to remain there in New Netherland longer than the expiration of his bounden time, he related, "and therefore they did not apply themselves to agriculture." Even when campaigning, soldiers considered the use of the spade a task below their dignity. An observer said of the typical Dutch man in the Indies: when he arrives, he thinks, "when my six years of service are up, then I will go home to Europe again."[12]

The company's seamen were, of course, men who lived with the movement of the seas and rivers, tides, and currents. Among them were the pilots employed by the company. The New Netherlander caught in conversation with the Patriot was correct: without their navigating skills and experience, visiting ships could founder making their way to the fort on the island. But all seamen were trained to read the turning pages of the seas, to be restless like Cornelis Hendricksz: altering course suddenly, moving ahead by seeking familiar coastal markings or new sightings. Sailing for home. Like the soldiers, the senior- and junior-merchant employees of the company and even the clergymen sent out, they were transients with no intention or prospect of permanence.

New Netherland's private traders were men afloat as well. Later they and the company's men became known simply as "floating Dutch traders." Working around Manhattan Island in the mid-1630s, an ordinary sailor earned only ten guilders a month, a little over the value of one beaver pelt. Some of the traders cruising the coasts and setting up camps on the bays or along rivers could do much better or be lured into thinking they could. One early private trader, it was said, was using his sloop to meet with natives on the Connecticut River, along eastern Long Island, in the highlands of the North River and farther north in the Mohawks' and Mahicans' lands. Reportedly, he regularly sent valuable cargoes of furs back to Holland.[13]

A rogue trader within the company offered the exaggerated testimony in 1633 that traders moving on the North River could usually exchange goods with the natives in return for fifteen to sixteen thousand beaver skins—by his calculations, pelts worth 150,000 to 160,000 guilders. He himself, he swore later, had once traded upriver for five thousand pelts to the value of 40,000 to 50,000 guilders. The trader was a relatively insignificant interloper, a not uncommon sort of river-rat hustler. Like the others, he was a transient, another entrepreneur with no concern for the native people other than to cut a bargain and run. Still, he was linked by a common occupation to an honored merchant such as de Vries. Both embraced a livelihood linking them to sealanes and seashores. At the end of his life and when he came to identify himself among his fellows, de Vries proudly called himself *Koopman en Zeeman* (Merchant and Seaman).[14]

*   *   *

The waterfront's mode of living, then, fostered the presence of transience. It allowed the Dutch to act out a separateness from the native people. No system for native rule was set in place, no language of command. No one sought to manage his or the trading company's encounter with the natives by devising rituals or insignia of superiority. No employee was assigned to maintain surveillance on native villages. The Dutch wanted incorporation into the local trading network and the knowledge that would effect that. But they didn't seek entry into or control over the natives' political, social, or epistemological worlds. So while a creole or pidgin developed for the purposes of trade, no one sought to appropriate the Algonquian language in order to serve in the construction of a system of rule. From what appears in their writings, the strangers knew of the existence of many autonomous and warring tribes and had made efforts to name some of them and establish the general location of their lands. They traded with the Mohawks and Mahicans, the nearby tribes along the present-day New Jersey shore, Staten Island, and Long Island, possibly the Susquehannocks on the Delaware River, and a range of natives along the Connecticut River. But only a few men inscribed lengthy observations of individual groups. For some reason—perhaps because the fur trade with the southern Algonquian-speaking natives was already falling off and with it their value to the Dutch—descriptions of the southern coastal bands were scanted in favor of the highlanders farther north.[15]

Only a few of the harborside men gave conspicuous care to categorizing the natives as savages. Scant correspondence indicates them learning that some coastal bands were constantly at enmity with others, even frightened of going into one another's lands and forced to enlist the cooperation of friendly villagers to do so.[16] Their reports tell us that political coalitions of villages appeared and disappeared, exercised power and then lost it: some paid tribute to others; some recognized overpowering enemies and moved away. Company officials seemed satisfied to carry on alongside these changing configurations of native rule. We have to think that they knew their trading goods were agents in consolidating some villages and setting others at enmity, impoverishing some and enriching others. One day, they would come to count on this. But for now, they wrote nothing about it. At least on paper, they were content not to sort out the tangled affairs of the natives—as long as the trade was secure.

Nor were there rhetorical or gestural expressions of an ideology of rulership or command. No individual officer sought to manufacture a vocabulary of benevolence in order to legitimate his or the company's presence. No officer expressed concern for a good impression he might or might not be making on the native people. There is no record of narcissistic demands made for heartfelt admiration. No officer looked closely for signs of disrespect or mockery. The neighboring Plymouth colonists had already warned the nearby Massachusetts and Narragansetts that terror, not friendship, would underlay their mutual relations. This either/or was not conceivable among the Dutch. Universally, the strangers condemned the thieving practices of the natives. Yet it seems that most were prepared to follow the advice given to commander Abel Tasman by the East India Company directors in the early 1640s: "Connive at small affronts, thefts, and the like" for the sake of the trade and valuable local information.[17]

Because the trading company was indifferent to colonization and set against territorial dominion—many said negligently shortsighted—there was no need to invent the pluriform language of savagism that elsewhere accompanied a desire to despoliate native lands. Far from coveting additional lands and supporting colonists on them, the company couldn't even succeed with the farms and boweries it had under its control on Manhattan Island. In 1638–39, five of its farms were vacant and the overall number of cattle and horses had fallen to less than half their numbers in 1630. The resident director contracted with some farmers for grain, but generally New Netherland was not producing enough to answer its own needs.[18] This dismal failure, however, enlarged the list of commodities sought from the natives. Paradoxically, it made this a period when the advantages of peaceful trade were as real as they were ever to be.

The company was equally passive regarding the task of Christianization. At home, the call for evangelizing New World natives was increasingly demanding, and certainly the company's many Calvinist backers were concerned that missionizing be a prominent consideration. The reality overseas was otherwise. On Manhattan Island, one minister, Jonas Michaëlius, undertook the task of converting the natives—and let himself come to despise them. Unlike him, no company officials expressed the malevolence toward native religious practices that Christianity seemed to necessitate. At this time in New France, even some Hurons noted the Dutch lack of interest in missionizing. The Blackrobes had introduced disease and other calamities among them, they declared. In contrast, the Dutch had "preserved the Iroquois by allowing them to live in their own fashion." On Manhattan Island, no Dutch resident thought of himself as one among a chosen people. No one considered the trading posts a New Netherlandish Canaan.[19]

Controlled inclusion was policy enough. Town regents at home had long ago recognized that inviting strangers to live among them advanced the locality's commercial well-being. One citizen wrote in the late 1640s that they could use people from places such as Germany and Westphalia "and make them Netherlanders." In 1625, the company directors recognized that they were in the same dependent position in settling New Netherland. They told Verhulst's engineer that should the natives want to work on the fort and other installations, employ them and see that they are paid. Follow practices at home. Pay the sailors the eight to ten stivers that were the daily wage for building fortifications at home. Employ the natives for two stivers a day—perhaps in accord with the Friesland custom of paying slaves one-fourth the wages of a free man. Seven days' work would, they reasoned, amount to fourteen stivers and allow a native to buy a company ax—unless the resident officers, using their discretion, could wangle a price of "less cost to the company."[20]

The arrangements suggest a degree of measured inclusiveness and trust. Stories of friendly natives continued to be taken as creditable. The Dutch encouraged natives to come to the fort, where they could exchange furs for merchandise. Villagers regularly arrived from a place across the Hudson called Pavonia and established a trading pattern that the company jealously protected (Map 3). A Long Island native unhesitatingly came to the fort with news that he and others had rescued a Dutch sailor who had struggled to shore after his skiff had foundered. A skipper told it abroad that, thanks to them, the sailor had been "wonderfully saved."[21] Elsewhere, natives were showing themselves to be as open to innovation as the strangers, accepting employment on farms and as messengers, guides, domestic servants, and traders' brokers.

But these cross-cultural contacts were the usual transactional ones expected of a marketplace. They were not points of entry onto terrain where a Dutch civilizing mission might take root and be cultivated. Such projects could be shams and were not without contemporary Dutch criticism. To impose civilization upon uncivilized people was, as Grotius warned, "a pretext which may serve to conceal greed for what is another's." A marketplace such as the company's emerging waterfront had no need of pretexts. Greed—call it profit-taking or getting the competitive edge—was its driving engine. It was a mechanism for all to see and to admire. It was this market-price *mentalité* that echoed in the Amsterdam directors' indifferent evaluation of the American natives. They were simply "barbarians" offering "trifling trade."[22]

Grotius's distrust of missions aimed at civilizing uncivilized people isn't reiterated in the company's New Netherland papers. Yet its employees on the island consistently lived out its intent. Only once, in 1659, did a resident director-general speak of civilizing the native people. Petrus Stuyvesant, desperate to stabilize relationships with Algonquian-speaking natives by introducing colonists, argued to his council that such settlers would promote civilization. For the most part, however, what has been said of the East India Company officials in Java and places such as the Moluccas was also true for their West Indies counterparts. The well-being of natives, wrote one scholar, "was of no concern." Or perhaps more reverberative than that, they "had no thought for the ordinary [native] people."[23]

* * *

Portentously, however, the violence and death that were to afflict New Netherland were already signaling their distant presence. From the beginning, the Netherlanders' trust of the natives had been stained by a persistent distrust. In the early 1640s, the two would become a repertoire of images clashing disastrously against each other. With diminishing intensity, this ambivalence would remain unresolved until the loss of the province to the English.

Rhetorically, trust and distrust often twisted around each other in the same sentence. Or both might appear in statements separated by only a few paragraphs. So, on first contact: "the people offered signs of their friendship . . . but we dared not trust them." Or, found in Wassenaer's description of April 1625: "the natives of New Netherland are found to be well disposed so long as no injury is done them." But, in the next paragraph: "they are a wicked bad people." Affinities drawn between the strangers and natives quickly dissolved into negation. The native are "like us Dutchmen in body and stature" and commit fewer crimes than even Christians at home. But "they live without laws." In their art, they can fix "fine, lovely and bright colours"—such "beautiful red . . . [as] was never dyed in the Netherlands." Still, their paintings are unimportant, neither "spirited" nor "ingenious."[24]

Distrust led the strangers to test native accounts of the most trivial occurrences and facts. To double-check information, they would travel by horseback to the sites of supposed happenings. One colonist tested the truth of native statements about the planting of corn by repeating the same questions to one native after another. Yet he also acknowledged that they despised lying. The strangers got themselves into contradictions. The natives, said one man, are "quick enough to distinguish between good and evil." But in the same description, he asserted that "the knowledge of good and evil is not given to them."[25]

The strangers didn't know where to locate the seat of their own distrust. Were the natives untrustworthy because they were naturally or by God's foreordination left in spiritual and moral darkness? Were they not this, but willful? They rejected the Christian God, but which was true: they cannot, or will not, understand? Were they devious because they were simply very stupid or, by some quirk of nature, were they uniquely changeable? Sometimes they seemed primitive and sometimes advanced: they were the "most barbarous people," but among them were "few or none cross-eyed, blind, crippled, lame, hunch-backed or limping men: all are well-fashioned people, strong and sound in body, well fed, without blemish." This constant inconsistency: was it a fault of theirs or was it a puzzle disturbingly beyond the observer's wit to understand?[26]

Were the natives getting the measure of them? Of their ignorance? Did they think that the Dutch could be controlled or, worse, laughed at? Two ministers who cared to know the natives thought they did: observe their use of language and you observe their trickery. They know we don't really understand them, and they deliberately keep it that way. They refuse to understand what I want, said one man. "When we pray," he went on, "they laugh at us." We are, another minister agreed, "compelled" *by them* to compose an absurd description of our God using their ill-fitting terms. We are, wrote a third man, not a minister, encountering young natives who refuse to offer any clear information about their belief in God. The elders will engage in discourse, but it's always tangled—this is "curious."[27]

The natives, one minister persisted, use one set of words for trade but another for important matters. These they keep secret from us. The gullible common traders think that their language is easy. But they're "entirely in the dark" when they hear the natives talking among themselves. No use ignoring their cunning by saying that they "probably change their language every two or three years."[28]

None of the company's officers, from what we know, had to accept the taunt that a Javanese was to direct at an East India Company official in 1656: "Your orders are to live with us in friendship and to put up with everything." But in the late 1640s, natives were acknowledging to the Dutch that they knew they "could not understand them" and elsewhere that, as one company official wrote, "We are not allowed to punish them for their ill doings."[29]

Perhaps they were neither barbarians nor heathens. Were they only called wild men because, as one man observed, they often seemed to say the first thing that came into their heads so that we have put the name upon them? Weren't there actually two groups to be distrusted: the natives, and worse still, ourselves, those among us whose cunning and thievery they are increasingly imitating? About this time, the resident director-general in Batavia believed that he knew a different reason for the distrust of the natives whom he expected his explorers to encounter in the southern Pacific and Great South Land. They will act treacherously, he warned, because they think the foreigners have come only to seize their land "which (oweing to heedlessness and over-confidence in the discovery of America) occasioned many instances of treacherous slaughter." They will be on guard because they think the Europeans believe that they are "related to the natives of Spanish America."[30]

The lengthiest of the observations of New Netherland's indigenes were written by men conscious of an audience still being fashioned by the travel literature that originated with van Linschoten in 1596. They, too, would contribute to the genre of eyewitness observations of overseas exotica. But their descriptions were unlike those of van Linschoten, May, and Hendricksz. The explorers' tales were itinerary maps. They related natives to distances—departure points and destinations and sites of past, present, and future actions. The writings of men such as Adriaen vander Donck and Johannes Megapolensis were anatomical explorations of New Netherland, with natives set in an ethnographic present unencumbered by a past or future. So despite offering detailed explorations of native customs that could reveal the indigenes to be powerful and dangerous neighbors, they conveyed little agitated concern for the threatening possibilities that the cross-cultural encounters might hold for the future.

The disconnect of the company's men from a close interest in the natives was different. Theirs was a sustained silence, except in one respect: they concerned themselves closely with the contracts and treaties arranged between themselves and the native people in the interest of trading rights and obligations. In New Netherland, *jus mercatorium* was the only law the company had in place. Mercantile law regulated the marketplace and all vendors and customers choosing to operate within it. The company's directors were willing to admit that they could not oblige the natives to trade with them. But the villagers had come into the marketplace, so they had obligated themselves to its fundamental requirement: agreements made in good faith and duly executed were irrevocable unless dissolved by mutual agreement.

It might all work out satisfactorily. Unlike the French merchants of Nantes whom the Dutch allegedly ridiculed as Greeks, saying, that "the Greeks don't understand business," the natives, for all their shifting alliances, reassuringly did understand business. They often controlled their side of the market by accepting some trading goods and rejecting others, measuring the cut and color of textiles, and appraising metal objects suitable for redesign as jewelry, household utensils, or arrowheads. Some bands of villagers, such as those west of Manhattan Island, had mastered intertribal economies, buying furs cheaply from the Susquehannocks and selling them dearer at the fort. At least north in the Hudson valley, as long as the Mohawks and Dutch both enjoyed prosperity, "what they thought of each other personally was," wrote a twentieth-century historian, "beside the point."[31]

As early as 1624, at least one of the company's agents was alerting the directors to the fact that their own understanding of contractual justice wasn't operating among the local populations and that efforts to enforce it could encounter resistance. The natives would arrive at a bargain with one another, he'd written. But frequently, they would retract it, even using force to do so. A decade later, another employee, a ship's surgeon, also recognized that contracts and treaties had some other meaning or none at all. He was investigating an admission by the Mohawks that some of them were selling furs to natives allied with the French in Canada because they were getting better prices. The surgeon showed no surprise at this breach of an agreement supposedly giving a monopoly to the Dutch. The strangers were, after all, quite prepared to break up a native ruler's monopoly if it suited their purposes. Instead he seemed to anticipate the violation, stating only that it had occurred "so soon."[32]

But a treaty was a notional tool that the strangers could also use for treacherous purposes. One colonist, a minister serving the company on a three-year contract, discovered in treaties a pretext for land seizure. He had obviously thought the deceit through carefully. He assumed it was a half-formed plan of the company's men as well.

North of the island, he advised them, was exceptionally good land waiting for us to exploit. Or, as he worded it to a clergyman at home in 1628, along the river near Fort Orange "lies open for us large tract of remarkably fertile and pleasant land." The Mahicans have abandoned it and we could buy it from them "for a small sum of money" (Map 2). But there is a better way of getting it. We can fabricate a cause for its confiscation. The many offenses of the Mahicans have "never been forgiven . . . [by the company], nor adjusted by any treaty." Instead, they have been reserved for use at the propitious time.

What is ominous here is the minister's ability to call up the age-old, allegedly legal, way of seizing territory. Calculate the fear and weakness of a victim; then, as the supposedly aggrieved party, trump up causes for the expropriation and, if necessary, invasion of his territories. But the minister's proposition was only an omen. We have no evidence that the company's men had deliberately left unresolved past hostile incidents with the Mahicans in order to use them as an excuse for confiscating their lands. Nor is there a basis for accepting the minister's implication that they were redirecting their attention from trade to land ownership. On the contrary, he had to admit that the resident director had given no order to occupy the land.[33] Another threatening portent, however, had showed itself in an account of Dutch violence committed just two years earlier, this time on behalf of the Mahicans.

The company's commanding officer at Fort Orange had agreed to help the Mahicans disperse a Mohawk war party causing trouble in their hunting grounds. His decision went against the company's policy of strict neutrality in native disputes unless involvement was unavoidable or—ominous, too—certain of success. The omen of a tragedy to come was not primarily in the subsequent native killing of the commander and three of his men. Nor was it in the fact that the incident provided the opportunity to air at home stories of cannibalistic practices among the natives.[34] Rather, it lay in the company's error in permitting it to be drawn into local politics.

The commander had used the company's soldiers in an offensive military operation rather than reserving them for strictly defensive purposes. He offered the Mahicans the firepower that they and others would later covet as an assurance of success in cross-village encounters. Rather than helping to maintain the company as a commercial agency of the States, he moved it toward making itself a political player in New Netherland. Metaphorically, it began to move inland. It began sliding into native politics, slipping away from the impersonality of market exchange and into visibility: to being more known. It moved onto levels of entanglement where social, psychological, and epistemological boundaries were more permeable. It gave up being feline: "the cat . . . meddling with none."

Things might have been otherwise. New Netherland might have continued to be like Massalia under the ancient Greeks. It might have been one of those places that functions best by acting as a port of trade enlarging its economic influence while curbing its ambitions for political domination. Or, as a scholar hoped for the East India Company, it could have remained only *une colonie d'exploitation*. The company might have been a strictly maritime operation. It might have been a shipping line profiting from inland trade funneled by native and licensed traders to its portside fleets and installations and conducted on the principles of free trade that were fully accepted at home. It might have adhered more readily to the stated ideals of its earliest years: we must not lay a foundation on injustice.[35]

The actions of the commander at Fort Orange were not a turning point in the Netherlanders' relationship with the natives. But his superior on Manhattan Island was quick to realize that decisions like his would take the enterprise in a direction that was not of its own design. Whether he saw clearly the consequences of using Dutch power to confer political dominion on certain bands of natives in return for commercial concessions is uncertain. Still, he was careful to send one of the company's traders to visit the Mohawks after the incident and arrange a peaceful settlement.[36]

But by the early 1640s, other natives were conniving to get similarly on side with the Dutch authorities. They were learning how to draw them more and more deeply into their own politics. Fragments of stories—the sparse reports of the company men, the serendipitous log of a visiting skipper out of Hoorn, the later testimony of traders who thought they could look back and see something of the error of it all—told of these things. Pacham, a chief of the Tankitekes, was "great with the governor of the fort," wrote a skipper who'd anchored along the island in 1641. In early November, the sachem came to the fort triumphantly bringing a hand, dangling from a stick. He said it was that of a chief who had killed Dutch men on Staten Island. Pacham, the skipper continued, "had taken revenge for our sake, because he loved the Swannekens . . . who were his best friends."[37]

This opportunistic play-acting on both sides was portentous for each. The Dutch, for their part, were giving themselves the impossible task of combining merchant capitalist techniques with those of military rule. They were walking into the contradiction that had already become the frame to Dutch undertakings in the East Indies, with disastrous consequences. They would be a trading company with the responsibilities of political dominion. For their part, the natives, without precisely embracing the process, were giving the strangers more and more power. It would soon ricochet back on them with terrible consequences.

*   *   *

In the 1630s, violence carried to the natives was still something the company's men wanted to avoid. But they could read the evil portents in the dispersed incidents of their own aggression. In 1634, they were forced to use the past tense to describe the harmony between themselves and the natives of the upper Hudson valley. Those among themselves were changing the relationship. We had previously lived together "in good union," they reported. Now "injurious seeds of division" have been sown.[38]

In 1641, the dangling hand was part of the brutal violence that had finally come to the natives. Said one of the burghers two years later, "It was a horror that had to come." Of course, he was wrong.[39]

Chapter 10

The Connecticut Valley:
The Strangers' Ways of Violence

The eruptions of the Dutch strangers' violence against the natives were unpredictable. Each was like a piece of wreckage loosened from a sea bottom and suddenly seen breaking the otherwise calm surface of water: nothing the result of policy, nothing vigorously planned by the company's men; unspecified blunders that English neighbors felt imperiled Dutch-native relations but didn't impede the trade; some encounter with the Raritans, but we don't know what. Seemingly brief but hostile exchanges took place at Pavonia, but again, we have no details. Along the Delaware, a tragic encounter occurred, but the facts are lost and only the bizarre remains: a chief (allegedly) thought a tin plate with a Dutch emblem of possession would make a fine pipe; an officer lost his temper, demanding the thieving man's head and then, too late, regretted it. Thirty-two settlers were killed. De Vries arrived later, had to decide between taking revenge and making peace and doing some trading. He opted for the latter and brought valuable pelts and corn to Fort Amsterdam.[1]

Traders up around Fort Orange tell of young natives mocking the commanding officer's authority by attacking cattle and a few scattered properties. In the same area, Dutch soldiers discovered some English interlopers secretly trading with natives. They had erected a makeshift tent along the river somewhere south of Fort Orange. Conflict ensued. Perhaps the natives noticed an ominous discrimination made by the angry Netherlanders between themselves and the English—but not noteworthy in the company's report. The soldiers drove the English away using threats, brandishing arms, and confiscating cargo. But they chose to beat up on the natives.[2]

More portentous was a site of violence northeast of New Netherland. Although the Dutch traded in and out of these lands, it was a place already greatly different from the trading settlements around Manhattan Island. Or rather, it was many places newly occupied by the English and joined by the name "Conetticot Plantation." In 1636, the plantation was a marchland beyond the control of Massachusetts Bay or Plymouth Colony. English colonists were living under their first year of Connecticut government. Government maybe, but at least one Massachusetts magistrate thought them all to be ungovernable and reckless adventurers.[3]

So Connecticut was, by happenstance, a site of two types of colonialization. During the 1630s, Dutch traders and the beginnings of an English settler society had a presence there. Each left stories of their relationships with the resident native Americans. Each articulated the way a group of European intruders went about living differently with difference, that is, with the cultural manifestations of the indigenous population. Each made of the Connecticut plantation a place of violence. But the modes of violence were subsets of distinctive ways of living with cultural difference.[4] They were enactments of desires and anticipated gratifications, one set congruent with a mercantile project and the other borne of landowning aspirations. The need for self-identity and—perhaps the same thing in the case of overseas intrusion—control was activating two encounter imaginations. These accounted for the number and nature of the personnel on the ground and the forms of their encounters with native people.

Our story of shame and sorrow asks us to be theoretical for a moment. In the valley, the Dutch and English wrestled with the task of accommodating to otherness. There could be an acceptance of cultural differences or refusal. To refuse otherness and decry savagism was to claim that natives needed to obey the rules of the civilized. They were responsible for their own savagery and could be punished for it.

The dominant impulse of the Dutch traders toward the native Americans was for proximity. That is, they allowed the other to remain different. Otherness was neither essentially threatening to their identity nor to the kind of control that they had come seeking. They had constructed a meaning for the native that they could come to terms with. They had a common object: trade. The actions of the English colonists suggest that the dominant impulse was for identity, that is, the erasure of difference. This impulse was exacerbated by the necessarily greater degree of entanglement that came with the settlers' claim to the same survival resource required by the natives: their lands. It was a physical and epistemological entanglement played out within a highly sensitized range of emotions, not the least of them religious. An American anthropologist has put into story what I am trying to say theoretically. He contrasts the kind of knowledge sought by a European merchant in Arab lands with that of a settler or missionary. To the merchant, "it was a matter of little immediate importance *whom* the Arab married. To the colonist and missionary, however, it could be crucial."[5]

The English and Dutch both told their stories about the plantation. The English narratives were voluminous and of a variety nonexistent in the New

Netherlanders' archives. The Dutch traders' accounts were few, and each folded into larger sets of business papers. They sat alongside minutes of the resident director and his council, or papers for the conveyancing of properties mostly on Manhattan Island and Long Island. There was also correspondence to and from the company at home: the legal papers of a commercial society. Those of the company were stylized in the customary way. They were factually reductive, inventive in the ways of withholding full disclosure, and unmarred (the best of them) by rhetorical flourish, narrative device, or the touch of personality. Letters were written with the hooded emotions needed for a certain degree of ruthlessness. Most were secret, inscribed for a closed (and not especially trusted) audience of associates: an official's or clique's intellectual property.[6]

The stories of the English settled in the Connecticut River valleys fitted into genres of a different character. They were sermons and tracts, personal correspondence, the reflections of local leaders, and the notes of a chaplain in a Connecticut fort. Alongside these were the reminiscences of military commanders, governors' journals, and the stories of providential events written by self-styled historians: the words of God's remembrancers. Some were the "true relations" of missionaries to the natives and stories energized by writers who compared themselves to Old Testament figures, while others were the peddled narratives of rumormongers or letters of a trader on the far frontier of the plantation.[7] One was a reprise of the English court's argument in 1632–33 that the natives were legally incapable of being landowners. The Connecticut valley, said the leader of the Dorchester Company (Plymouth) in 1635, was the Lord's waste. And we mean to use it to the "right end for which land was created."[8] One tract invited readers into a theater: the "Late Battell Fought in New England [1637] is the Stage. Let us in a word see the Actors." Officials received one resident's letter accompanied by an arrow drawn from the body of a dead English soldier and offered as proof of native perfidy; still others were applications to the Massachusetts court to buy captured native "squaws."[9] And some were notes made for the day when there would be a need to chronicle God's beneficent design in the plantation's discovery and first settlement.

One among them could only have been written by an Englishman, in the late 1630s, about the Connecticut Plantation. It is as curious a narrative as one could encounter. *News from America* fused two popular but disjunctive narrative genres. It made a pitch to Englishmen and -women thinking of emigrating to the New World. Come to Connecticut and, it beckoned, you can make your living alongside countrymen already enjoying land abounding with rich and profitable meadows along all the rivers, various species of good wood and "varieties of fish . . . [and] fowle in abundance."

News from America was also an atrocity narrative. It chronicled war, torture, and the taking of human lives. Here was a promised land that was, at the same time, literally grounds for a story of alleged Amerindian savagery: settlers viciously slain and their shirts then hoisted in mockery as sails on their native assailants' canoes; a trader "martyred . . . most Barbarously"; soldiers pierced by arrows, "some through the shoulders, some in the face"; a native ally taken by the natives, tied to a stake, his skin ripped off, "hot ambers . . . [placed] between the flesh and the skinne," his fingers and toes cut off and "hatbands" made of them.[10]

More than an account of native barbarism, *News from America* was a narrative of the Englishmen's savagery. But on the author's pages, this was savagery sanctioned by God to achieve what he had accomplished in biblical times: the planting of a chosen people in lands that would be wrenched from the heathen and come to proclaim his righteousness. The old Serpent has stirred up savages in this Bible land, wrote the author, and now they run up and down "as roaring Lyons . . . seeking whom they may devour." They and their villages would need to be destroyed. Think, he wrote, of King David's just war against the Ammonites: "When a people is growne to such a height of blood and sinne against God and man . . . [then] he hath no respect to persons, but harrows them, and sawes them, and puts them to the sword, and the most terriblest death that may bee." The cost of God's wrath was high. After a massacre in which four to seven hundred Pequot men, women, and children were burned alive, one English military leader praised a joyous God. He has laughed the natives to scorn. He has made of them "as a fiery oven."[11]

When John Underhill published *News from America* in 1638, he put on the market a texted continuation of the violence. The tract now made theater of it all: the steady movement of settlers inland onto Pequot lands and the "warre" as the natives and their allies put up resistance; the employment of military tactics learned in the Low Countries: actions, sieges, and laying in garrison, all in the two years of the war; the seizure of booty from native villages; the payment of wages to Underhill and twenty other mercenaries for three months' service—perhaps even storm money paid for attacking the Pequot Mystic River fort. What Underhill failed to see was that he was recounting English fury at insolence more than bloodletting: the natives were "laughing at us"; they shouted "proud challenges"; they were "jeering"; mocking us, they "put on Englishmen's clothes." They knew, some of them, that we didn't know our way around deep in the countryside.[12] And so the script went on, finally dramatizing the seizure of captives meant to be sold later to English families. But first, as one military leader hoped, led behind him in triumphal procession through Boston.[13]

Above all, *News from America* foregrounded the devastatingly successful use of fire. It gave an English audience full disclosure of the burning and total destruction of the village along the "Pequaets' River" (Mystic River) in May 1637 (Map 2). The desolation of the village and the deaths of the men, women, and children enclosed within its palisades were of biblical proportions. Because it was the Lord's foreordained work, Underhill described it in great detail. Native defenders were "scorched and burned with the very flame"; they were deprived of their weapons because the fire "burnt their very bowstrings." Another account became phantasmagoric as it dwelled on the fire: "It was a fearful sight to see them thus frying in the fire and the streames of blood quenching the same, and horrible was the stink and scent thereof."[14]

The natives had anticipated that such fiery holocausts might happen. Underhill describes the Pequot man whom we have encountered, the native offering his double-edged greeting to the English soldiers moving along the Connecticut coast. The native knows how the strangers make war: the recourse to fire. He comes to that first. "Will you cran us [burn us alive] . . . will you kill us, and doe you come to fight." Later that night, the English heard Nahanticots (Niantics) and Pequots making mournful cries fearing the war to come. Other accounts told of them dreading the murder of their women and children. A group of Pequots asked a Connecticut officer whether, when the English finished fighting, they were accustomed to killing women and children. A missionary wrote that "it would be pleasing to all natives, that women and children be spared."[15]

* * *

Underhill was a professional soldier. He considered himself to be an outstanding military leader of local militias and other mercenaries like himself. But in *News from America*, he was a compelling writer. He could script scenes that brought his characters intensely alive: the soldiers as, on one occasion, they "marched up to the [native] plantation, burnt their houses, cut down their corne, destroyed some of their dogges"; other newly recruited soldiers deeply troubled by a native who said he would be equal with God when he killed just one more Englishman; the same men later so moved by the cries of the Pequot villagers that if God had not fitted their hearts for the task, the lamentations "would have bred in them a commiseration for them." He could re-create the terrified survivors as they ran from the conflagration only to encounter English soldiers who received them "with the point of the sword. Down fell men, women and children." He was able to reconstruct a scene of natives forced by the English to engage one another in battle. He used it to mock American forms of conflict and describe warfare properly conducted in the Low Countries, where he had been for about five years: fire at an enemy point-blank, engage in hand-to-hand combat, and fight with the intent "to conquer and subdue enemies." Achieve more killings than the natives are interested in.[16]

Underhill, then, could compose sustained scenes of the groups contending for power in the Connecticut Plantation. The New Netherlanders were contestants for power there as well. The United Provinces had laid claim to the Vresche Rivier (Connecticut River) more than twenty years earlier in 1614. Early Dutch skippers had made contact with natives, and ten years later Cornelisse Jacobsz May landed West India Company personnel. They had later established a trading house called Fort Good Hope (at Hartford) and were making improvements on it just four years before the massacre (Map 2).

There the Netherlanders, too, had taken native lives. Ignoring the power held by the Pequots over the fur trade, they had decided to corner the market themselves. Their trading post would be a place of free trade. Let all come and "not molest each other." But a Pequot chief and some of his followers killed an unknown number of natives making for the Dutch *handelshuis*. The Netherlanders retaliated by killing the assailants in a skirmish that followed.[17]

So the Netherlanders were there in the Connecticut valley and also prepared to exercise violence. But Underhill couldn't make them a presence in his story. They weren't there colonizing. In 1639, they would have only thirty acres around their so-called House of Good Hope. They weren't even there as possessors of the distant Hudson River. Rather, the river was a "garden of New England" ready to receive industrious Englishmen.[18] The New Netherlanders were not present Christianizing the natives. They were not struggling with the consequences of bringing to heel a people confirmed in darkness and sin. They could not be shown as interested in removing natives from useful lands nor as thinking about the imposition of rule over a continuum of lands for prospective settlers.

Instead, they could be found literally floating around in the water doing deals with the natives. Taking their soundings of the trade. The way they are—it's not their smaller numbers—they cannot be fitted in as allies in the Englishmen's war. They have erected no equivalent of Saybrook Fort as a center of military command. As Underhill could do with his English characters, they could not be put into battle, say, alongside himself and his forces at the siege of the Mystic River village. There wasn't a professional soldier among them. Even some of the natives would soon be saying that the Dutch were "something on water, but of no account on land." They had "neither a great sachem nor Chiefs."[19]

Underhill could only stage their actions once. Inadvertently, he constructed a scene that was metaphoric of the Dutch and English sets of aspirations in seventeenth-century North America that we have already begun to reflect on. Taken as a metaphor, the simple account helps us read two forms of colonialization: an alongshore scene unfolds sometime in 1637 before the massacre, perhaps on May 24. A Dutch ship arrives at Saybrook Fort from what Underhill calls the Dutch Plantation. A skipper and a merchant, both of whom would have known of hostilities between the English and the Pequots, are sailing from Manhattan Island to the Pequots' river to trade. Underhill and the officers at the fort need to turn them back because of their own larger plans to fall upon the Pequots any day now. The traders respond, saying that they want to be cooperative—and this would be the wish of the resident director on their island as well. Though it may jeopardize the "peace" they are presently enjoying with the natives, they will, if they are allowed to continue their journey and engage in trade, try to rescue two English captives.[20]

We see two sets of actors playing out their separate identities. Among other things, they are using space differently: as linear in the case of the Netherlanders; as planal in that of the English. The Dutch are voyagers, travelers enacting their transience. They have navigated the coasts from Manhattan Island to Saybrook Fort at the mouth of the Connecticut River. They have disembarked and made it clear that their interest is trade and are soon voyaging again, sailing farther northeast to the Pequots' river. There they conduct their trade, begin the return voyage, and call in again at Saybrook. They navigate home.

The English at the fort are physically alongshore, too. But Saybrook is not a port of call or shore fort built solely to protect traders and trading goods. It is a foothold to inland places, to broad and (allegedly) unsettled valleys suitable for the beginning of rural communities. Just days before the encounter, perhaps as many as two hundred soldiers had been mustered upriver at Hartford. There they listened to sermons calling on God to grant success to the coming campaign. They would leave for the Pequot lands from Saybrook, setting sail with Underhill and the fort's commanding officers. They would disembark, join native allies, and march overland. Two days later—now so deeply inland that they woud soon need native guidance to march out and regain the fort—they would open hostilities against the Pequot villages.[21]

*   *   *

The Dutch traders and the native peoples around Manhattan Island knew of the violence in the Connecticut valley. The Mohawks received some of the defeated Pequots into their villages. Natives only thirty-six miles east of Fort Amsterdam would have witnessed the English pursuit of other fleeing natives. But how closely the natives were reading omens in these incidents or in another that occurred in the valley in the same year, 1637, we cannot know.[22]

In that year, the Connecticut government sent three men to the Pocumtucks at a northern village called Agawam. The inhabitants learned that they were now under the protection of the English. The price of this protection was tribute to be paid toward the costs of the Englishmen's wars. For each male, the village was to pay a contribution of one and a fourth fathoms of wampum. This was the Dutch *brandschatting,* the German *Brandschätzungen,* the French *sauvegarde,* the Spanish *salva guardia.* Thirty years later, when the English were still collecting tribute, one chief knew exactly what to call it: fire money.[23]

In New Netherland in two years' time, it was "the contribution." Actualities were about to erase "only this and nothing more."

PART V

Deadly Encounter

Between 1640 and 1645, the Dutch were at war with at least twelve Algonquian-speaking peoples living near Manhattan Island. Much about the war remains a mystery.

The episode aroused a wide range of commentary, some of it contradictory, all of it fragmentary. We are able to say, however, that once under way, the strangers' military tactics were similar to those employed in the ongoing wars in the Low Countries. There commanders adopted the strategies of *kleine krieg,* that is, low-intensity conflict in which formal battles were the exception. Soldiers operated in small-scale encounters intended to control the countryside. Acting under fractured command structures and frequently with ill-defined goals, they conducted hit-and-run raids, sudden nighttime attacks, and a scorched-earth policy carried out against civilians in villages or whole farming districts. So in New Netherland, Americans became Europe's civilians as villages burned, family members died or became hostages, and women and children were suddenly refugees. Indistinguishable from combatants, they faced soldiers turning their coastal and riverine lands into sites of plunder and murder.

The strange afterlife of the Indian war (as they called it) does little to erase its mystery. Its life in memory and narrative does not follow the so-called law of increasing detail as stories are passed down over time. The Algonquian-speaking people rapidly "disappeared." After the English conquest of 1664, neither the victors nor the subdued Dutch felt the need to revisit the 1640s. Only in the mid-nineteenth century did archivists locate relevant documents and translate them into English. To most Dutch scholars, they were of little concern.

The war did find a place in what might be called the history of an emotion. Seventeenth-century Netherlanders record being haunted by their cruel treatment of overseas peoples. Again and again, they express a self-reproach too little heeded for the causes to be erased but too often enunciated to be wholly insincere. When the government of the United Provinces sought causes for the Indian war, it found certain New Netherlanders guilty. But it also assumed responsibility. Leading New Netherlanders so unanimously blamed the West India Company and themselves that later historians characterized them as an antiwar party.

Nineteenth- and twentieth-century Dutch Indonesians repeatedly expressed shock at their history in places such as Banda and Java. In 1900, they instituted the Ethical Policy, an idealistic set of government initiatives that would tie colonial practice to moral imperatives. Naive as this policy may seem, its confessional thrust was real and preceded a position taken by the Dutch historian H. L. Wesseling in *Expansion and Resistance* (1978). In a characteristic Dutch way, Wesseling emphasized that colonialism was an ongoing moral problem inevitably associated with "grief and guilt."[1]

The impulse to shame and sorrow has a place in the mystery of the Indian war. It does not entirely unravel it. Rather, it deepens it and requires an individual judgment—on the episode and colonialism as well.

Chapter 11

The Indian War Seen

It is 1645. The New Netherlanders have involved themselves in five years of war with the native people with whom they are sharing the island and its surrounding waterlands.

Maybe saying the "New Netherlanders" isn't fair. Some said at the time that the war was the business of the director and dozens of his soldiers and cronies. Others said that it was surely they but also traders and farmers moving out onto distant native lands. Most said nothing, while a few said more than they knew.

The violence found its way into story fragments that had a hallucinatory quality. Or better, they were chronicles. Like those inscribed by Dutch, German, and Spanish observers during the wars in the Low Countries, they were close to the events: they were *bloedwarm.*[1] No one could explain the war, that is, explain it away. Many were horrified at what they had done in killing more than a thousand native people. Some said that they didn't do those kinds of things. Yet they cannot have been surprised or shocked at the war techniques they saw themselves putting so readily to work.

By 1645, war had crawled along the lives of at least three generations of Netherlanders and countless other peoples across western and central Europe. We saw it reach the rooms of the West India Company directors, their wharves and purchasing offices, and their accountants' desks. We saw it reach the alongshore towns of the Zuider Zee. Before it was over, ten to twelve million Europeans had learned to become soldiers. Millions more had learned the role of civilians: expect to be the prey of armed enemies and of your own soldiers as well; know yourselves to be the vulnerable ones, especially if you live in the open countryside, villages, and small towns. Everything you have they'll want.

The Dutch had a melancholy and fatalistic saying for it all: *teeren op den boer,* living off the farmer. One writer tried to make sense of the wars in Germany. But his thousands of words only said that war had made Europe obscene. His curious picaresque hero becomes wise to the ways of war and absurdity; he learns that one is the same as the other. He hears soldiers boast: "In God's name, we're going out on a raid to plunder, loot, shoot dead, cut down, attack, make prisoners and burn." Elsewhere he learns that the purpose of soldiers' foraging is only to torture and ruin the peasants, and "rape their maids, wives and daughters." If a peasant resists, he is struck down or his house is "set on fire." In both Dutch and German, the words describe soldiers and civilians living on the level of the abnormal or, as the German writer wanted us to consider, the subnormal.[2]

Now natives around Manhattan Island had learned what it was to be Europe's civilians. Perhaps the New Netherlanders needed food supplies. Or maybe they wanted the coastal wampum makers to hand over fathoms of shells to exchange for pelts or food. But wampum-making was labor intensive. A hundred fathoms required 750 to a thousand days of labor and supportive assistance. The Dutch knew this. Whatever was happening, after 1639 native villagers were required to pay tribute: maize or perhaps wampum or peltries. The company officers said that they were exacting it because they might have to provide natives with protection against nearby enemies. In Europe, these stand-over tactics were a standard device, a warning of impending brutalization certain to cause terror and get results. Army commanders had their ways of operating this form of protection racket—and so did marauding bands of undisciplined soldiers, roving mutineers, deserters, criminals, and bully-boys waging their own private wars. We've seen it set in motion in Agawam: pay the fire money— or face what need hardly be spelled out.[3]

Brandschattingen was a word used in the Low Countries. Alluding to destruction by fire, it caught in an almost tactile way the menace of what was happening. Anthonis Duyck was a commander in the Dutch forces of Prince Mauritz and active in the 1590s campaigns around Groningen, Zutphen, Arnhem, and Steenwyck (Map 1). He was in the center of the usual predators, "various governors and commanders . . . who collected [taxes] *contributien* on their own authority, and frequently imposed, out of their own self-interest, grievous [levies] *brandschattingen* with the threat of putting everything to the torch and destroying everything by sword." In the campaigns, Duyck himself was ordered to take twenty-five men and collect the *brandschattingen* in the countryside around 's-Hertogenbosch. He would have carried instructions ordering that those who paid properly adhere to obedience, and all those who were not paying be brought to such obedience immediately "by cavalry and soldiers." In the wars in Germany, such soldiers were called "tribulation troops." They tortured the peasants, wrote one man, "with a knife they called contribution."[4]

That was the United Provinces in the 1590s. This was coastal New Netherland in the summer of 1640, the first year of the war. Director Willem Kieft had ordered the "contribution" from local villagers and now looked for compliance. A village of Raritans refused to be held to ransom and allegedly compounded their refusal by killing a farmer's pigs. Duyck might have felt at home:

Kieft sent an expedition to attack them and take prisoners unless they submitted. This force [was] composed of about eighty soldiers and sailors. . . . When it reached the enemy's village the . . . [captain of the men] demanded *payment according to his instructions*; but the men wanted to punish the . . . [villagers] without further ado while they were within reach. [The captain] gave in after a token resistance and left the field to his unruly subordinates. Before he had gone a mile, they put several . . . [villagers] to death and captured and tortured the . . . [village leader's] brother[5] (Map 2).

Looking back on events, an adviser to the director argued that exacting the contribution had been a grave mistake. They had built a bridge over which war would soon "stalk through the country."[6] And so it had.

∗   ∗   ∗

In Holland, the Rhetoricians knew how to stage the movement of war as it stalked across a country. By 1640, these amateur actors had perfected the art of elaborate *tableaux vivant*. Some of their performances were mounted outdoors, where they could stage glittering extravaganzas. Reenactments might include elaborate processions to richly decorated city gates where plays commemorating a notable civic or provincial event often dramatized moral lessons or, more likely, made theater of the daring acts of heroes or villains.

The Rhetoricians (*rederijkers*) also presented tableaux within the walls of their playhouses, or chambers. In either setting, their plays were polytopic in form. A stage opened to multiple compartments allowing an audience to see many scenes simultaneously. If those spectacular effects were not intended, stage art received even more attention, creating the same effects in designs, usually of the highest quality. A theater curtain—possibly sixty feet wide—might present as many as ten scenes. They might celebrate the Truce of 1609 between the northern Netherlands and Spain or "Siege and Relief of the City of Leiden. Tragedy with a Happy Ending."[7]

The stage art for the war in New Netherland from 1639 to 1645 might require, for example, the painting of nine scenes. If people in an audience in Holland were viewing the dramas, they would not recognize the faces of the men and women sketched in. Nor would they be familiar with locations of the actions taking place. But because it was warfare conducted by their countrymen and close to their own lives, they would easily have recognized the familiar techniques of waging war and laying waste an enemy. Among their countrymen, they would see drunks on raiding parties, collectors of the *brandschattingen*, ordinary men committing atrocities, and unpaid mercenaries roving menacingly around streets and wooded paths. They would see purveyors of contraband, corrupt political leaders, gatherers of unjust taxes, men laying in garrison (sometimes fifty, sometimes only four or five), and cynical negotiators promising peace but retaining some hostages—just in case.

The Rhetoricians would have known that none of New Netherland's events took place for their colorful restaging. None of the slowly emerging reports was inscribed for their recitation. But, know it or not, not a word was recorded in New Netherland that was not meant for the eyes of Hollanders—certain ones of them. Or in the case of three accounts, all of them.

Scene One

September 15, 1639. Director Willem Kieft and his council are inscribing the words of a curious resolution. The company, it reads, is carrying heavy expenses. Fortifications require repairs, and soldiers and sailors need to be maintained. They must therefore "levy some contributions . . . [from the natives] either in peltries, maize [corn] or wampum." Their soldiers had, after all, previously protected them against their enemies. If any tribe will not willingly contribute, they will be induced to do so "by the most suitable means."[8]

A decade later, the director, now widely blamed for having caused the bloodshed and destruction of a long war, will be accusing the company of ordering him to exact the contribution. Don't blame me, he charges. The seed of the war was "first sown in Fatherland." The company denies the accusation. And no one believes him, anyway.[9]

Later, a committee on West Indies affairs will speak for the States about the war. They'll lay the blame on the director's shoulders. We, they say, find the news of the fire taxes "strange and unexpected."[10] And they say a lot more.

Meanwhile, the director's local detractors continue to expose his contributions as an act of blatant cynicism. He had, they said, laid his extortionate plans well. He had allowed private traders to sell guns to the Mohawks and Mahicans, known enemies of the nearby natives. Then he had denied the neighboring natives the same weapons and promised protection from the nations that he had armed—for a price.[11]

One man wants all of Holland to know of Kieft's designs. He sees to the publication of a pamphlet. It is a true account, he alleges, of all that has happened. In it, Kieft is an evildoer who intended to begin a war because the natives had on reasonable grounds "refused to give him a certain contribution, alleging they were not obliged to give it." They would not pay for protection offered by the soldiers, they said, since they had done them "no service, in case of war with other tribes." The Raritans' representatives—but soon spokesmen of all the tribes—then hurled back at the Netherlanders the strangers' own initial vision of their place among the Americans. They had allowed the strangers "to remain peaceably in *their* country" and had "never demanded a recompense." For that reason, the strangers "were under obligation to them, and not they to the Dutch."

We, they said, have ceded to you the country you are living in. But we "remain masters of what we have retained for ourselves." They reminded the Dutch of the contractual relationship that the strangers had all along encouraged and that the Raritans appear to have honored with them: why should we supply you with maize for nothing, since in the past we have paid the prices asked?

They would "give . . . no contributions."[12]

Scene Two

A small workplace in the house of an elderly wheelwright, sometime in August 1641. Only two figures concern the artist. The old man's body lies on the dirt floor covered in blood. He has been partially beheaded. Near the body is an open chest. A native is seen running out the door carrying some of the old man's goods. He had worked for his son. Perhaps he holds the piece of cloth he seems to have wanted.[13]

Barely visible beyond the door is a path they call the Wekquaesgeek Road. It runs along the East River and to this place, Turtle Bay (Map 3). Natives with trading goods use it daily to reach Fort Amsterdam, only a short distance away.

The enforcement of the contributions has aroused the natives to acts of resentment and hostility. First the Raritans had refused to pay. They lived in river villages about five Dutch miles southwest beyond Staten Island. It was to their villages that the director had sent a yacht about a year earlier with his eighty men to force them into submission. No one said how many villagers died or were taken hostage. In this summer of the old man's murder, a reward is being offered for the heads of Raritan villagers. Christians on Long Island are voluntarily killing some of them there.[14]

In the summer and fall of 1640, the company's yachts had been again seeking their contributions, coasting the Hudson River and its small tributaries. This time, they were lying offshore a native settlement about five Dutch miles north of the island at Tappan. The director knew it was harvest time. He wanted corn. The Tappans know that the corn planted in the river flats is now ready: among other signs, large black birds would have made their annual appearance. Like the Raritans—and like the Zuider Zee fishing villagers and the strangers at the fort—the Tappans are shore folk who exploit the fertile flatlands as part of a surrounding network of waterways and waterlands. They know how to use the river to trap animals such as deer: form a wide semicir-cle, use bones and sticks to make a terrifying noise, close in until the prey must make for one of the rivers, and then take to lightweight canoes and lasso the desperate animals. They know that the saltwater shores will draw thousands of geese each September. Crabs will appear on the flat shores in summertime[15] (Map 2).

Just as the villagers of Hoorn or Enkhuizen know the ways of the herring, so the Tappans know the ways of the large black-streaked fish that the strangers call "the twelve." They come into the river in late March and continue to arrive until the end of May. They are ready to be dried and preserved when the Pleiades tells the women that it is time to plant out the corn. The men continue fishing.

Movement on the rivers also means trade. But in those late October days of 1640, it meant being intimidated by the company ships lying offshore wait-ing for their fire-money and preventing trade with outsiders. Before the col-lection of *brandschattingen*, things were different. A trader said that he and his ship's crew could stay overnight and watch the Tappans fishing. Now the natives were saying that only if the company ships leave would they trade with him.

The demand for a contribution has lessened their respect for the director. They are amazed, they say, that he is impoverished. He is a chief, a Sackima. Yet he cannot pay for things. Besides, they have only enough corn for their own needs. A chief nowadays, they say, has only two women planting out and car-ing for the corn. They don't say that they are already paying a contribution to the Mohawks, but it is probably so.[16]

Now the number of nations fired with anger is mounting toward eleven. They live on the rivers and bays surrounding the island. Soon Dutch violence will drive them into broad alliances, the very thing the strangers fear. But the native who had killed the old wheelwright was not seeking some kind of com-munal or political revenge, only that perhaps the widespread anger had pro-vided a release for the enmity that he had harbored for over two decades. When apprehended, he said he was avenging the strangers' murder of his uncle twenty-one years ago. He had witnessed the killing as a small boy.[17] No one seems to have witnessed what would now happen to him.

The young native would not be the only man storing up dark memories. Before the war, wrote one New Netherlander, the natives were at peace with us. But now "the loss of their fathers, mothers, wives, children and friends has greatly troubled them." After a particularly heinous Dutch crime, a number of village leaders said the event might never again have been spoken of had the strangers given gifts demonstrating true remorse. That hadn't happened. Now, they said, "the infant upon the small board would remember it."[18]

Scene Three

The audience sees a crowded canvas. Brueghelesque. Many small-scale figures. About eighty soldiers are carrying out a massacre. If the artist has somehow written Pavonia for the place of it, perhaps Hollanders would recognize that it is named for Adriaen Pauw, an influential Grand Pensionary of Holland. It is February 25–26, 1643. Deep snow covers the ground and shoreline. Some soldiers are slaying native men, women, and children at a landing alongside a river. They are using guns. Others are throwing children into the waters and refusing the shore to mothers and fathers drowning while trying to save them. The artist has chosen to base his painting on an account composed by a New Netherlander in 1649. He accepts it as being dramatically powerful (even if not valid in every detail):

Between the 25th and 26th of February, 1643, at night, over eighty Indians were massacred at Pavonia by eighty soldiers, where young children were snatched from their mothers' breasts, and cut to pieces in sight of their parents, and their pieces thrown into the fire and into the water; other sucklings were bound to wooden boards, and cut, pierced, or bored through, and miserably massacred. . . . Children, five or six years old, and also some old decrepit people carrying walking sticks, as many of them as had escaped this fury and secreted themselves in the bushes and reeds, when they came forth in the morning to beg a piece of bread and to warm themselves against the cold, were murdered in cold blood. . . . Some came running past our people living on the farms, with their hands cut off; others had their legs cut off. Some carried their bowels in their arms; others had such cuts, hacks and wounds, that the like can never have happened elsewhere. . . . After this exploit, the soldiers were recompensed for their services, and thanked by Director Kieft, by shaking of hands and congratulations.[19]

The artist has had to be selective in his material. He might have shown the same villagers earlier (many of them Tappans) desperately escaping the armed Mahicans and fleeing toward the Dutch for protection. He might have focused on David Pietersz de Vries as he chose to remain in the director's house in the fort to experience the night from its safe distance—de Vries always somehow describing himself as merely alongshore to hostile events. He sits by the kitchen fire and hears "the shrieks" of the natives and does nothing to investigate. Nor does he look into events occurring less than two Dutch miles farther up the island at Corlear's Hook. There, along another small river, burghers are massacring forty natives, attacking them in their sleep. In the morning, de Vries says he witnesses the return of soldiers proud of their valorous deed[20] (Map 3).

The artist had one other choice. Just for its aura of mystery, he might have composed a nighttime revelry. It is February 24. The director keeps Shrovetide evening, feasting and drinking with three of his known associates in one of their houses. The revelry suggests the excess and dicing with Fate that is typical of the behavior of low-life figures such as soldiers. A mysterious toast is later said to have been proposed by one of the drunken men. A few days after this, "the accursed deed was executed."[21]

Someone's recollection of the debauched prelude to the execution of Thomas a'Becket? Herod's slaughter of the innocents?

Scene Four

The morning after the massacre along the riverbank at Pavonia. A Dutch man and his wife lay slain. They had come to plunder the dead. Or, as soldiers later testified, they had come "to steal corn or something else." Natives had shot them some time after the man was known to have boasted when told to leave, "Even if there were one hundred natives, they would do me no harm." The same trust had been expressed even after the Dutch murders committed along the Raritan River. The natives are sly enough. But "do them no evil mischief, and they will do none to you."

Well away from the riverside where the dead lie awaiting burial, three figures converse about the massacre near a bastion of the fort. One is the director, who is saying that he is not to blame. "You must blame the freemen."[22]

Scene Five

March 21, 1643. A room inside the director's house in Fort Amsterdam. Two figures command attention. Lesser figures occupy the background. One of the two men carries a sword and pistol. Nowadays he is a resident of the island. Previously, he had operated among the lawless freebooters and sailors of Verre on the coast of Zeeland. These were men, often deserters, who roamed the countryside at will, looting and burning farmhouses and whole villages. They resembled gypsy outcasts, bonding together and adopting fearsome names such as the Marauding Brothers. People called them *moescoppen*, men who would beat their victims to a pulp.[23]

The man has come, it is later said, to kill the director who now stands, seemingly unarmed, before the crazed intruder. Fellow burghers have called him a murderer. Kieft has spread it abroad that the man, Maryn Adriaensz van de Veere, and two others petitioned Kieft to allow them to lead the soldiers and burghers on the night of the massacre. Now neighbors whose farms have been destroyed and whose friends and families have been killed in retaliation are blaming Adriaensz. Meanwhile Kieft is openly saying, "I have . . . [proof] wherewith to defend my conscience," and points to Adriaensz and the two others "over there, your neighbor."[24]

Adriaensz is arrested and sent to Holland for trial. Questions will soon be asked about the massacre. An archive of documentation is already being assembled. But no one is ever able to say conclusively who was responsible for it. The States will order Kieft home for interrogation. Eventually, he will bear the blame—some of it.

An observer setting sail from the Manhattans writes of the destruction incited by whoever the murderers were. "Before we weighed anchor mine eyes saw the flames at their towns, and the flight and hurry of men, women and children and the present removal of all that could for Holland."[25]

Scene Six

Eight men are shown putting their signatures to a petition. They represent the residents of the island, possibly only 250 men and women. Nine months have gone by since the massacre. The supplicants are bypassing the company and appealing for assistance directly to the States. They are now, they write, pursued by "fire and sword." Trapped in the fort, they can't sow the autumn seed. The cattle are destroyed. The garrison of fifty or sixty soldiers has no ammunition. The fort is "utterly defenseless." The natives around the island have made alliances with seven other nations. All have guns, powder, and lead. Private traders whom the company has never been able to control sell it. They make a threat. Perhaps they will have to deal with their neighbors in New England. The English "would like nothing better than to possess this place."

The petitioners list New Netherland's future prospects if help is given. They are thinking as maritime entrepreneurs. Think of the value of this place: seacoasts, bays, and large rivers—and the island as a port for the Brazil and West Indies fleets. There is fertile land, produce to victual great numbers of our ships. The farms could "provision and supply yearly 20, 25–30 ships from Brazil or the West Indies with all necessaries."[26] This is November 1643, and only two months ago a prize taken by the company still lay in the harbor.

At home, the assembled company directors have seen the letter and agree with the burghers' last proposition. They, too, envision agricultural endeavors that will fulfill a maritime function. The productivity of the boweries can mean the maintenance of ships carrying full complements of seamen, soldiers, and other company personnel. Presently, there are probably seventeen warships at sea in the area. In two or three years, provisions might be furnished for ten thousand men. In a year's time, the company will turn again to the island of Manhattan as a place of rendezvous for warships. It's better adapted than the island of Curaçao and gives the best access to all parts of the West Indies. Also, plans against the Spanish enemy "can be kept better concealed."[27]

But for the eight burghers, two years of war still lay ahead.

Scene Seven

The artist paints in Captain John Underhill. He, fourteen Englishmen, and eighty Dutch men prepare to attack a small native village on Long Island, just across from Manhattan Island. The attack is part of a joint Dutch-English operation. Together the soldiers will later call themselves successful, attacking two villages and killing about 120 men.[28] No mention is made of killing women and children.

Underhill has offered his services to the Dutch. Perhaps they don't know what to make of him, what role he'll play, or what opportunities he'll seize for himself or for the English on Long Island or the Connecticut Plantation. In one account, he is "Sergeant Major," then "Captain," and then "Gen'l." In another, he is a "foreigner," a soldier negotiating a peace with two tribes without bothering to invite one of the company's officers to be present. But then again, the director is no soldier at all. Some say that he takes care to secure his life in a well-built fort and has not once slept outside it in all the years he has been here. The English think the Dutch are ignorant of—or careless about—things military. Later, they will offer to form a military alliance. The offer will be repulsed. A later Dutch historian will say that Underhill's actions transformed the war from a defensive one into a war of aggression.[29]

Just after the massacre and on the advice of the eight men—or was the director acting arbitrarily?—Kieft had hired Underhill and about 150 English mercenaries. For their pay, a bill of exchange for 25,000 guilders is meant to be drawn and New Netherland mortgaged to the English as security. About a year later, the mercenaries, unpaid, idle, and drunk, are roaming the streets around the fort. The director now demands that the eight men impose taxes and excise on the commonalty as payments for their upkeep or he will discharge them. They refuse, saying it is not within their power to impose taxes. The director shouts in response that it is within his: "I have more power here than the Company; therefore I may do whatever I please." But did they refuse? The signatures of two of the eight men later appear on an ordinance written by him and enforcing the taxes.[30]

Meanwhile, Underhill offers to raid another native village. He shares the leadership with a Dutch ensign. A report about the march portends something terrible to come. It implicates nature in the horror of the impending village attack. Moving in "great Sorrow and Storm" and under a "moon . . . [that] was then at the full and threw a strong light against the mountain," the men locate native huts and set them on fire. Five to seven hundred men, women, and children die. Natives later said that many tribes had gathered for a festival. Such dancing and feasting ceremonies often cemented new alliances of friendship—and perhaps common plans for war. They said nothing about this. A deliberate extermination of the people occurs. In Dutch, the word is *vernietigingsmethode*.[31]

"What was most wonderful is," the report relates, "that among the vast collection of Men, Women, and Children, not one was heard to cry or to scream."[32]

Scene Eight

October 6, 1647. Petrus Stuyvesant is the only figure drawn on the canvas. He is the new director of New Netherland and is writing to the States in autumn, four years after the massacre.

Resentments aroused by the war will not go away. He must deal with them. He composes a letter to the directors and encloses documents dating from 1644 to three months before his own letter, 1647. He marks each document with a letter of the alphabet: A through R. Careful merchants are accustomed to doing this.

The matter of the initial cause of the war will not go away either. Among other things, two men, Cornelis Melijn and Jochem Pietersz Kuyter, have already sent letters to the directors in Holland about the contributions. So document M is intended as a step toward determining culpability. It proposes interrogatories for seven men—five of whom were officers of the company at the time. Two were burghers, supposedly directly involved.

To Treasurer Hendrick van Dyck:
"Is he not well aware that . . . Director General Kieft did, on the night between the 24th and 25th February, in the year 1643, send a party of soldiers over to Pavonia . . . and behind Curler's plantation on the Island of Manhatans and cause them to kill a party of Indians, with women and children, who lay there?"
"Did not the general war between our Christians and these Americans follow the next day?"
"Is it not also true, that all those Indians had fled to the above described place . . . in the hope of being protected by our people from their enemies?"

To Mr. Cornelis van der Huygens, Councillor:

"Did he approve the levying of the contributions which . . . Director General Kieft imposed on those Americans in the year 1639?"

"Did not he (the witness) well remark that this tax had excited great animosity among those natives, so that the Raritans shortly after killed four of our people on Staten Island?"

"Did not the Dutch nation in this country live in peace with those Indians before the cruel deed [the massacre] had been committed against them?"

To Dr. Johannes la Montagne, Councillor:

"Did he vote for, and approve of, the maize tax in the year 1639?"

"Was it ever before proposed in their Council, and now when Mr. Kieft had imposed contributions on those natives, . . . that by those proceedings . . . war would soon stalk through the country?"

"Did he know from what cause originated the first troubles between our people and the Raritan Indians?"

"By whose order were the Indians, with their wives and children, killed over at Pavonia, and behind Corlear's Hook on the Island of Manhatans between the 24th and 25th February, 1643?"

"Did we not, up to this time . . . live in peace with all these Americans?"

To Secretary Cornelis van Tienhoven:

"In what year was he sent to those Natives to collect the contribution of maize from them; if he was not employed, who was then?"

"To how many tribes was this done, and how are they named?"

"Did those Indians willingly consent to this contribution, or did they protest against it—and what were their debates about it?"

"In what year was he, deponent, sent by Mr. Kieft to the Raritans; did he not go there with a party of armed soldiers and sailors . . . ?"

"For what reason, and by whose authority did he, the Secretary, insert the words—'the whole of the Commonalty or free people and by their order'—in the petition, [of Maryn Adriaensz and two others] when he, indeed well knew that no person either without, or on, the Manhatans had any knowledge of it except Director Kieft, he the Secretary, and those three petitioners?"

Interrogatories for Jan Claesz Damen and Abram Planck: "By whose order and by what authority did they . . . [present a petition along with Adriaensz], and who prompted them thereunto, that they inserted in the petition the words—Of the whole of the freemen?"

No native is to be interrogated.[33]

Scene Nine

The artist poses about twenty men gathered at Fort Amsterdam. He makes an effort to suggest the whole Dutch community's presence. They look on from a distance. Seven of the assembled men are native chiefs. Perhaps the artist has mistakenly posed the Americans in the high-feathered headdresses and costumes of Brazilian or Caribbean natives. David Vinckboons had done so in 1608 when depicting the Rhetoricians' preparations for an open-air performance at a village fair that year. By now, the native peoples have had to bury about a thousand bodies—later, it will be said to be sixteen hundred. Many women will come daily to the graves. The Dutch have seen this.[34]

The chiefs represent their own tribes and, some of them, neighboring chiefs. Aurange Sesekemus and Willem (as someone thinks they call themselves) are there for the Tappans. John Underhill is present. Maybe he understands the Dutch words. He has a Dutch wife. A Mohawk has been invited to act as mediator. Perhaps a translator is there for him. Perhaps it doesn't matter.

Kieft is presiding. Solemnly, he reads out a declaration of a "firm, inviolable peace." A piece of paper, or vellum, waits signing. It is August 30, 1645.

Promises are made. Ways of maintaining "friendly intercourse" are agreed upon. Kieft reads on: the trade we've taught you to keep with us on and around Manhattan Island will be continued but regulated. Nothing is said of contributions.[35] But at least some of the native leaders now know how the Dutch work the system and have bought into it. Just three months ago, four native chiefs from Long Island had appeared before the man now reading the proclamation. Earlier, one of them had offered to take on the role of military entrepreneur, offering his own services and that of forty-seven of his men to—as Kieft's secretary curiously wrote it—the government. Within a week, they said they had "taken under their protection" five villages. The director handed over a present. He received as proof of successfully enforced compliance a head and hands of the enemy.[36]

Now in August, the Dutch have plans for tomorrow. They'll send soldiers to do some alongshore work. The natives have thrown some of their ammunition in the river. It's at one of the massacre sites. They'll "fish for it" and bring it to the fort.[37]

This is not the occasion for reciting aloud the costs of the war to the New Netherlanders. But later, the company directors will give the most insightful estimate of its price: the war has been a learning experience for the natives. They have gained in knowledge. They now have a better measure of their own military strength—and ours.[38] They know us better. It's dangerous.

Four years later, in 1649, a native's misdemeanor prompts another meeting of the Dutch with several of the same nations. The Raritans need to be spoken for. They have, a leader offers, no chief. The Tappans' chief, Aurange Sesekemus, is still around and doing what others are doing—selling his river land to the new director. Nine years ago, de Vries had judged it especially valuable maize land. Aurange Sesekemus calls it something like Wiequaeskeck.[39]

Eighteen months later, Govert Lookermans is reported as owning extensive lands of the Raritans. He was among those who had attacked the Raritan village in 1640 seeking the contribution. There he had used a piece of splintered wood to mutilate the genitals of the village leader's brother. He was also present at Corlear's Hook.[40] He was from the town of Turnhout in Brabant, a north-south Netherlands border province of continuous and extreme violence. Among other things, it was a mustering center for the Army of Flanders, a zone made dangerous by its unpaid outlaw soldiers. Perhaps the violence in Lookermans was some kind of legacy.

Or perhaps the Raritan village and its chief's brother were just unlucky that he chose to join the attack on them. He was, wrote a later commentator, sexually over active and knew it.[41]

Chapter 12

The Indian War Given Words

In 2001, a poem entitled "To the Words" appeared. The first line read: "When it happens you are not there."[1]

Words were not there when the massacre happened—or when soldiers fired into American villages or Amerindian children drowned. Not the words we have. They all came later. After the events, thousands of words were packed into ships headed for Holland. Some were meant for the States at The Hague, and others were packaged for the burgomasters and directors in Amsterdam. A few lay in the hold for the Zuider Zee towns. Many important ones were lost at sea. In later accounts, some words spread themselves over many pages of print. For a public that cared to read them, there were *Breeden-Raedt aende Vereenichde Nederlandsche Provintien . . . Antwerpen, 1649* (Full Information to the Netherlands Provinces) and *Korte Historiael ende Journaels . . . gedaen door D. David Pietersz. de Vries . . . Anno 1655* (Brief Narrative and Journals written by David Pietersz. de Vries). For the government in The Hague, there was an eighty-three-page tract, Remonstrance of New Netherland . . . by the People of New Netherland, 1649. It appeared in print as *Vertoogh van Nieu-Nederland . . . 's-Gravenhage, 1650*.

The words had something in common. Whether they were destined for the high-ceilinged rooms of West India House in Amsterdam, the moated buildings of the Binnenhof, or the chamber of the watermen from Hoorn and Medemblik, they were used as proof of the murderous effects of the Netherlanders' intrusion into North America. But they were used for other purposes as well.

Three men wanted the story told. Each had put together thousands of words. Cornelis Melijn was circulating his words throughout the 1640s. They went to the States—which sent a copy of them to the company directors who sent a copy to their board of accounts. Then they went directly to the company at Amsterdam. Later they reached the incoming director of New Netherland. More than once, some of them slid into someone else's text.

Four years after Kieft's supposed peace with the native leaders, Melijn published a pamphlet in Antwerp—or did someone else publish it?[2] Six years later, in 1655, David Pietersz de Vries published his stories. They found their way into the travel literature initiated by young Jan Huyghen van Linschoten in 1596. And to Adriaen vander Donck is ascribed the Remonstrance. This past war, he wrote, was unjust.

Why these men wanted their words listened to and why they knew they would be may lead us to what they did not say: we need to leave New Netherland. It's not working out. We are merchants competent in the ways of commercial exploitation—but we have become soldiers. We are the restless ones, but here we are becalmed, dying in the doldrums of our own violence. We're acting the lion, not the cat. For our own sake, and that of the indigenous people, we need to try our luck elsewhere.

In a curious way, Cornelis Melijn is a metaphor for "Kieft's war." The war cannot be understood without him. But that's not because he gives it clarity. Rather, his lifestyle and writings reflect the shadowland of deceit in which the war was conducted and reported. He moves in the same shadows where those responsible hide and where victims also are briefly seen and then cast into darkness. Like the war, Melijn is an object of concealment—and was from the time he first turned up in 1641 to tan hides, raise goats, and distill brandy on Staten Island, to the last time a librarian or archivist bracketed his name as the likely author of *Breeden-Raedt*.

Melijn seems to have been someone who gambled with his life. He was a trickster and an opportunist. He gambled on bringing down the board of directors of the West India Company—and Kieft and then Stuyvesant—by writing scurrilous reports to The Hague. He gambled on his chances of not being convicted in New Netherland for sedition. (He was convicted.) Later he gambled against being caught smuggling guns and ammunition onto his island along a hidden beach.

Often he held a winning hand. When pirates seized the ship bringing him to New Netherland, he was among those who had goods or coin enough to buy their freedom. When he sailed to Holland in 1647 to appeal his conviction for sedition, the ship hit a reef and broke up off the coast of Swansea. Eighty-one people died, including Kieft. Melijn survived. The directors, lamenting the loss of their ship, wondered at the perversity of Fate. They were grieved, they wrote, that those saved were Melijn and his friend Jochem Pietersz Kuyter. They were among the most loathsome types in the still-war-torn Netherlands—"bandits, rebels, and mutineers."[3] But in The Hague, the court upheld his appeal.

Melijn filled each of the roles: bandit, rebel, and mutineer. On the island of Manhattan, he was a petty trader probably selling illegal arms—and certainly brandy—to the natives. He was not of the stature of other merchants who were just coming to prominence. Nor could he compete with the overseas traders whom the company was supposed to control but some of whom had won Kieft's favor and were selling the natives arms openly and in great quantities. But being small and being tyrannized and humiliated by Kieft and his cronies were what drove him. He was unexpectedly and therefore dangerously political.

Melijn wanted Kieft's war known. When he stumbled ashore at Swansea and into the company of its Welsh scavengers, he worried for his papers floating in casks on the seas. Later he worried about the outcome of the litigation that finally went his way and allowed him to return to New Netherland and then back to Holland in 1649. There *Breeden-Raedt* appeared. It was the politics of New Netherland spread out for all to see. At the center of it was "the Indian war"—because the war was the grotesque dramatization of the company's tyranny and failure.

*   *   *

Françoys van Duynen published *Breeden-Raedt* in 1649 from his bookshop near the bourse on Erasmus Street in Antwerp. The pamphlet announced itself as being true and trustworthy recollections and was considerably longer than most—forty-five pages, compared with the sixteen or fewer that was typical. It was printed in heavy close-set gothic lettering and unadorned with the illustrations that might have marked it as a well-financed publication. Only two of its ten characters had significant speaking lines. Given these disadvantages, the pamphlet was probably not the best seller that two historians thought it to have been.[4]

But the author did strive for a readership. His pamphlet, he recognized, needed to be the "speaking pictures" that made vivid and powerful the best plays of his time. He also took care to follow some of the rubrics of attractive prose: let there be dramatic dialogue; let the pace of prose be interrupted by poetry since poetry is best for conveying strong emotion; include even the smallest detail; in some scenes, make it an atrocity narrative. Construct a morally instructive epilogue—*Breeden-Raedt* dutifully closed citing six verses from the Second Letter of Timothy, urging readers to true godliness. Give it all a patchwork quality: passages from a letter, a prayer, Latinisms. All of these are good.[5]

So *Breeden-Raedt* had every chance of being successful. It turned the Dutch experience of the North American war into a readable text. In every detail, it was believable. This was not because it was or pretended to be true. Instead, it combined truth and illusion. It made use of tall tales, gossip, scurrilous reports, wise sayings, and innuendo. It set the war within startling pictorial effects that would wound, startle, and shock the reader. But the pages also asked readers to think about a just war, just rulers, and peace. More important, in denouncing the betrayal of the Americans, it recalled them to the violence that seemed to lie at the heart of the Netherlands people. In short, it complemented the many other Dutch narratives that had been addressing these anxieties and issues since the outbreak of the revolt against Spain.

In 1648–49, the pamphlet also complemented the months of intense public debate on war and peace as the Peace of Münster came closer to reality. In the beginning, the happenings of the uprising were simply a multiplicity of disconnected and formless appearances. There was no history. There were only things happening. The accounts were *bloedwarm maar onbegrepen*, bloodwarm but incomprehensible. As in *Breeden-Raedt*, readers heard and saw things through the voices of unskilled commentators—the cries of civilians and threats of soldiers, the reports of strange supernatural lights in the heavens just before a conflict. As a later historian wrote, "You've got to read . . . [them] for yourself."[6]

The same events aroused a frenzied interest among contemporaries. The war began to find expression in the many forms of popular literature already available. Colloquial ballads and songs, treatises, sermons and chapbooks, remonstrant literature, schoolbooks, plays, and pamphlets all served as readymade outlets for a clamorous voice that began to question the seemingly endless costs of war and at the same time announce a new kind of patriotism. Alongside this literary output were writers pouring new wine into both old and new wineskins. A Dutch public could encounter classical tragedies and lofty poetry that now sounded with themes generated by the war and its nightmare consequences. After 1625, the newspapers of the day carried military reports from the field such as those of Broer Jansz, the "courantier in the Army of His Excellency Prince Maurits." A pamphlet describing a siege might appear well before the event was over. In Antwerp, Pieter Snaeyers was specializing in realistic war paintings. Pamphlets debating the war increased an already remarkable volume of publications.[7]

During the eighty years of the rebellion, a distinctive genre had emerged. It drew the public's attention to the violence suffered in the Netherlands countryside. Today it is called "peasant sorrow." The horrors of war experienced by ordinary civilians—peasants, farmers, rural villagers—became the subject of song and verse. Visual artists took it up as well. The public got images of war as meaningless and surreal. Pieter Brueghel had portrayed the ultimate mercilessness of war in the later-named *Massacre of the Innocents* (1563–64?). Sebastien Vrancx and David Vinckboons as well as J. M. Molenaer, Philips Wouwerman, and Jan Steen took up the theme, depicting the ugliness of civilian-soldier encounters well into the 1650s. Earlier, in 1633 in Paris, Jacques Callot published *Miseries of War*. No series on the butchery, oppression, and savagery of peasant-soldier enmity had ever been seen in art before[8] (Fig. 10).

By 1648–49, the excesses of war in the northern provinces had lessened. But northern Netherlanders still had close experience of it. They paid war taxes;

they encountered roving soldiers, many of them disbanded but now made penniless tramps and crippled beggars. Some now found themselves able to interpret events such as the siege of Leiden as past history.[9] Others went as tourists to reflect on a recaptured city. Netherlanders began to take the jumbled incidents and look for causation and national meaning.

Breeden-Raedt appealed because it had a place within this ardently read war literature. War for some, however, was more than memory, more than family and civic history, more than curiosity. It was still a reality. In the year of *Breeden-Raedt*'s publication, the Spanish were still recruiting infantry in the southern Netherlands and at places such as Limburg and North Brabant. The Army of Flanders mustered at 88,000 in 1640 and still stood at 42,000 in the early 1660s. Eleven thousand men were around in 1664. Only a decade earlier, 33,399 States soldiers were garrisoned at 208 places along a defensive line from Dunkirk to Ghent. Netherlanders driven from Solms in Utrecht hoped to take

Figure 10. Bolswert symbolizes the violence of war in an act familiar to us today. A soldier viciously kicks open the door of a peasant's house. Armed men accompany him, one of whom holds a document seemingly justifying the attack. The woman on the left is a sutler. Generally a prostitute and pawnbroker, such a woman accompanied an army on the move. Bolswert after David Vinckboons, *Boereverdriet*, midseventeenth century (detail). Collection Rijksmuseum, Amsterdam.

up a new life in New Netherland. In Holland a year after *Breeden-Raedt*, Amsterdammers waited in fear as the Prince of Orange marched his forces toward the city, determined to replace its regents with a government willing to do his bidding. Vondel invoked the fire-god Vulcan ready to bring universal devastation. And just returned from drawing up plans for a new fort in the area of Sas van Gent and Hulst was the engineer who had planned Fort Amsterdam in 1625.[10]

Breeden-Raedt was in the form of a *praatje*, a casual dialogue or conversation. That alone increased its chances of popularity. Such *praatjes* invited readers to overhear the exchange of several characters on topical political issues. Frequently, the speakers were passing the time on a canal boat or yacht. They could be three passengers or as many as twenty. The *praatje* was open-ended: always propagandistic but with the appearance of presenting several competing points of view.

Breeden-Raedt's characters make their appearance on a ship and as strangers to one another—a French merchant, a Swedish student, an English nobleman, and others. Predictably, they determine to pass away the time by sharing the latest news. The Dutch skipper and one of the travelers, a Portuguese soldier, move the discussion forward. They immediately enter a heated debate about the military blunders and corruption of the West India Company in Brazil. The subject is a topic of popular discussion. It is one about which seventeen of the fifty-one publications on the New World will be printed in the Low Countries in the same year, 1649.[11]

The Englishman abruptly redirects the conversation to New Netherland. He knows of an incident two years earlier when "two brave citizens, shipwrecked in the Channel" came from there. What stories they had to tell! Could they, he asks the skipper, be true?

The query allows Melijn to explore the mismanagement and brutality that characterized the administration of New Netherland and—as he will go on to make clear—led the Americans to rebel against the Dutch even as Netherlanders had, for the same reasons, rebelled against the Spanish. He poses questions already raising alarms about the existence of the West India Company in its present form—notably, in Brazil. Should it be allowed to operate without state supervision and pursue the misplaced belief that war and trade are codependent? Are merchants the wisest men to entrust with government overseas? They know, says the skipper, how to govern at sea, but are they suited to governing on land? Won't the wealthy merchants use the powers of administration "so that all the fat may drip into the kettle of some few of them?"[12]

Wealthy merchants were untrustworthy. They waited their chance—says the skipper—to crush less powerful traders. But more dangerous were those with the characteristics of New Netherland's director, Willem Kieft. He was occupying a position of high authority but was a bankrupt, an impecunious upstart who somehow managed to assume power by lifting himself above his station. Netherlanders enjoyed identifying such men in plays and crude doggerel. Typically, initial admiration is expressed for the populist folk-hero-as-ruler. But soon, foundering and becoming tyrannical, he is deposed. About twenty years after *Breeden-Raedt*, Thomas Asselijn staged a story carrying just such a plot. *Op-en ondergang van Mas Anjello, of Napelsse berooerte* (The Rise and Fall of Mas Anjello, or a Naples Uprising) invited an audience to see that an ordinary fisherman is incapable of ruling. Asselijn's plot was similar to Melijn's: the impecunious man becomes a tyrant, turns to evil councillors, imposes unjust taxes, and provokes righteous resistance. To Melijn, bankruptcy made Kieft a "pickpocket." To the Tappans, his tax marked him as a leader without his own resources. It made him strange, and a thief.[13]

The illicit acts of Kieft—together with the corrupt ways of his council, soldiers, and mercenaries—become the driving force for lawful resistance among colonists and natives alike in the faraway Dutch settlement. They make *Breeden-Raedt* an antiwar tract. It asks for a moral opinion and an emotional response.

Kieft had for a long time, begins the skipper, designed to make war upon the natives. Dutch readers would not have needed Melijn to explain what the making of war meant. The strategies of combat and the tactics for the victimization of noncombatants were the same among themselves and in New Netherland. In both places, war was excessively cruel because civilians occupied the physical terrain where most of the combat occurred. Inevitably, but especially when military discipline was absent or abuses officially sanctioned, noncombatants became prey to indiscriminate victimization. So readers of *Breeden-Raedt* could find wholly believable the cries of natives in New Netherland: you war "against our innocent women and children."[14]

Breeden-Raedt's readers would have recognized in Kieft's war the military structures of *kleine krieg* within which their own lives had been lived over the past decades. To militarists, it was low-intensity conflict with pitched battles as the exception. Soldiers operated in small-scale encounters. They carried out guerrilla warfare aimed at controlling the countryside, towns, and villages. Hit-and-run raids, skirmishes, sudden attacks at night, ambush—these were the tactics that played out over the landscape of the Low Countries and, had our artist painted in many more scenes, New Netherland. They were actions conducted under fractured command structures and often with poorly defined goals. This made them especially dangerous for civilians. And once in the countryside, soldiers couldn't find the line of demarcation between combatants and noncombatants. Or they chose not to. The operation dissolved into rural plunder and murder.

A committee in Holland found each of the elements of *kleine krieg* in reports of the overseas war: small-scale action, fractured command, and poorly defined goals. The Raritan raid was reported as the enemy attempting to steal a yacht and afterward killing some pigs. So we, it reads, "dispatched eighty soldiers thither to avenge the act, who burnt the corn and killed three or four of their people. Both sides then desisted from further proceedings." Or again, in a journal of later events: our forces looked for and found three encampments of the enemy. They burned two and saved the third for our retreat. They went eight or nine leagues farther, found some huts but they were abandoned. They came back "having killed only one or two Indians, taken some women and children prisoner and burnt much corn." Another ends: our men "got 5 or 6 hundred skepels of corn and burnt the remainder without accomplishing anything else."[15]

The overall aim of *kleine krieg* was to create terror among both the enemy's armed personnel and civilians. The Duke of Alva—of all the Spanish military men in the Netherlands the most hated—employed terror in the way Kieft did. With exceptional mercilessness, he successively brought Mechelen, Zutphen, Naarden, and Haarlem to submission. Just as he calculated, once two or three towns were made to suffer, other intimidated rebel communities would sue for peace. Although Kieft lacked Alva's calculated designs, he did the same. First he terrorized the Raritans, then the Hackensacks, and soon the tribes on Long Island and the Wekquaesgeeks (Map 2). He employed Underhill to spread terror among the natives of Connecticut. By 1644, he was, wrote one Dutch man, sending soldiers to destroy villages in places "which were unknown to us."[16]

So it is not by chance that Melijn allows one of the travelers to discern more than the customary operations of war in New Netherland. He encounters the presence of evil. He uses the skipper's description of the Pavonia and Corlear's Hook massacres to challenge one of the Netherlanders' national sacred myths. "Has the Duke of Alva," he challenges, "done more evil in the Netherlands?" Perhaps by implication: if we are the same evildoers as the Spanish, upon what may we pride ourselves as a new nation?[17]

Two figures personified the terror that characterized war in the Low Countries and New Netherland. They were princes and petty rulers such as Alva—and his Dutch, Spanish, German, French, or Swedish equivalents. And soldiers. In the year following *Breeden-Raedt*'s appearance, Vondel branded the warring rulers "monsters of our age": "One needn't travel to Africa/ Europe breeds them in her palaces/ Wholly merciless." Frederik Hendrik became the *boerenplager* (punisher of country folk) for his deliberate warring against noncombatants when he raged into the Flemish Netherlands in revenge for unpaid protection money. Commoners in the Germanies and Bohemia thought that Albrecht von Wallenstein, a general feared and hated by them and his officers, let himself be carried on his "golden isle through a sea of filth" that his wars had created. He was a man "contemptuous of the human race."[18]

We can't know whether the American natives were terrified of Kieft as an individual. Perhaps he was as distant and shadowy a figure to them as he is to us. If they had actually encountered him, they were nevertheless reported as having been unable to find him a leader. They said that the Dutch had "neither a great Sachem nor Chiefs." Even the colonists accused him of failing to get around the island: he preferred to remain safely in his fort.[19]

In the deep silence that characterized the encounter of the natives and the strangers, we have to think that their response to Kieft was one of terror but also of calculation and manipulation. After the massacre, native leaders kept their distance from the fort. A few came suing for peace but (so he writes) under the protection of de Vries. Others fled, one sachem moving off to Rockaway with two or three hundred men. The Raritans seem to have continued to refuse the payment of the contribution, but others paid up. Natives called "allies" learned to collaborate, bringing heads and other body parts directly to him. Whoever Kieft was to them, the alliance of villagers that formed against the Dutch wanted him—and not necessarily the strangers—removed.[20]

For the victims of the wars, the primary figure of terror was the soldier. His approach meant indiscriminate plundering. Generally, the loot was of little value. Not that it seemed to matter. In Holland, soldiers tore planks off houses and stole dogs. In New Netherland, all the goods taken from the natives wouldn't, wrote Melijn, "be worth the cost of a gallows for the thief."[21]

The attacking soldier also could mean the coming of fire. It meant farmhouses, a church or convent, the local mill, each reduced to ashes. In Overijssel, soldiers created a wasteland as far as the eye could see. For twenty years after their rampaging, it was land unsown and infested with wild animals. To the south, 29,000 Bohemian villages disappeared from the map. In New Netherland, sixteen hundred natives were thought to have been killed. If we accept the figure of 18,500 Algonquian-speaking Delawares, Mahicans, Long Island natives and Wappings living in New Netherland at the time of European arrival, then about 9 percent of the population was lost and must be added to the very much higher numbers lost to diseases, perhaps 90 percent. As in Germany, the Netherlands, and France, noticeable areas of the countryside must have been left virtually without civilians.[22]

As the Dutch revolt got under way, the Spanish king could somehow imagine his soldiers setting on fire the whole of the waterlands north of Amsterdam. He expected them to burn rebel villages and towns, including those along the Zuider Zee, twenty-four towns in all. In 1649, the year *Breeden-Raedt* appeared, the prince of Liege felt he needed to reassert his authority. He did the usual thing. To persuade other villages to allegiance, he sent men to burn two towns to the ground. Five years earlier, English officers fused the soldier's already frightening image with that of fire. Soldiers massacred a surrendered garrison of parliamentarians in a cellar. The house over them was then set on fire. Officers gave the word: let the common soldiers handle this.[23]

When writers or simple versifiers wanted to depict wild savagery, they turned to words for soldiers as incendiaries. One writer captured the ferocity of Frederik Hendrik's drive into Flanders by portraying the Spanish forces fleeing "in smoke and flames." The ferocity of the same campaign, however, also incited an anti-States ballad. *Expedition of Arsonists* depicted the troopers as nothing more than a "gang of firebugs."[24]

Firebugs were, as they still are, agents of devastation. But fire, once lit, has agency of its own. It spreads unpredictably, devouring without purpose or discrimination. So, to invoke fire was to call upon the capricious, to summon war as ruled by chance. Rains arrive, and suddenly farmers must shelter hostile cavalrymen and their mounts. An officer plans a siege, and unexpectedly a local farmer's house near city walls is incinerated. Natives set two houses on fire that just happen to stand near a place where Dutch men are caught stealing maize. Or nine natives, under no obvious command, kill three or four soldiers and burn houses and: "thus began a new war."[25]

In New Netherland, fire was the weapon of choice of all belligerents. Getting it to lick up the walls of a house or to blow across a field of corn, however, was dangerous work. It required a close-in attack—taking a position no farther than the distance of a flaming arrow, silently reaching the perimeter of an unsuspecting village.

The Dutch made no pretense of knowing why a native raiding party laid their plans as they did. If there were leaders, they couldn't—or didn't bother to—pick them out. If there were causes, they didn't bother to spell those out, either. Invariably, they wrote that the natives' successful torching of a barn or yacht meant revenge sought and satisfied. Repeatedly, revenge stood in for motives beyond knowing—or caring.[26] But no one recorded the motives or feelings of the European soldiers, either. With the exception of three or four men, all are nameless. They're staffage: the tiny figures drawn in after the features of a landscape painting are in place.

Often fire came to a town or farmhouse as payback for failing to hand over the *brandschattingen*. Sometimes, as in New Netherland, the racketeering finally drove rural victims to group resistance—usually viciously put down. The insurgents generally had far less effective weapons than their tormentors. But they used cudgels, knives, poles, and guns with the same mercilessness as their overlords. Accounts from Overijssel after the 1590s would have read like those in *Breeden-Raedt*. Locals sought vengeance by seizing hostages, killing unwary soldiers, and using the woods, thickets, and well-known paths for cover and attack. Their efforts, however, resulted in disproportionate losses. Several thousand rebels were savagely put down by the States' troops. Six or seven hundred country people, went another account, were massacred. In New Netherland, the count of the dead after an encounter near Stamford was five to seven hundred natives slain as against fifteen Europeans wounded. At Hempstead, it was 120 as against one European killed and three wounded.[27]

Often the population of a village or town fled. Better to lose everything than endure the horror of extortion, loss of property, and starvation. Such an exodus was not localized. All the order of Europe, a contemporary Dutch historian observed, "is filled with refugees." Just as many European country people fled to walled cities, so Raritans and others had fled from the Mahicans to the safety of the Dutch at Fort Amsterdam. Later they were fleeing the Dutch—moving "7 leagues away" or into the interior. One observer said that the many native plantations once at Marten Gerritsen's Bay (Martinhoeck) were now lying "waste and vacant." But no one admitted that, as much as disease, this was also the consequence of the war. No one recorded the many who left the waterlands around the island of Manhattan and never returned.[28]

* * *

Melijn identified the natives on and around the island as nations. Kieft and the island's burghers also thought of them as nations and, for the most part, treated them as foreign people. But now they were also called rebels. On one occasion, they were "malcontents." In the Netherlands, the Malcontents were a particularly despised group of rebels. Early in the revolt, they had betrayed the cause of the States, fighting as a third force and soon joining the king's Army of Flanders. Whether the natives knew it or not, identification as rebels put them in added jeopardy. Being a rebel—or a rebel village—licensed forms of brutalization beyond those adopted in the course of ordinary warfare. Across Europe and in the British Isles, wars defined as civil wars sanctioned lawlessness and modes of torture otherwise supposedly outlawed by the rules of war.[29] Seventeenth-century writers and artists constructed representations of torture and atrocity over and over again. In a world at war—which Europe had made itself—vile enemies were everywhere. Their outrages deserved stories. The punished body became the object of intense interest, if not prurience. Melijn was there to make his contribution.

The ways of assaulting the human body were seemingly endless. The practice of severing heads in order to induce fear, to provide trophies, or to dishonor the enemy was, as we have seen, commonplace in the Connecticut Plantation and New Netherland. After the Pequot war, Englishmen paraded heads of warriors in Boston. Seven months after the massacre, Kieft paid natives to bring him the heads of his enemies and later accepted the head of a Connecticut chief. When the heads of a number of slain natives were brought to the fort on Manhattan Island, an elderly woman used the occasion to kick them around with her foot. The States angrily demanded further information about the incident.[30]

Meanwhile, Kieft determined to teach a lesson to rebels among his own people. He reportedly beheaded a supporter of Adriaensz and erected his head on a pike. In Europe, such displays were commonplace. Twelve years before Kieft had accepted the heads of Long Island natives, those of a dozen rebels were taken down from a bridge tower in Prague. They had been left there for ten years as a lesson to others. In Ireland, an English commander ordered that the heads of all Irish enemies killed in a given encounter be severed and brought to his encampment. Then all the rebels who sought him would have to "passe through a lane of heddes of their dedde fathers, brothers, children, kinfolk and friendes."[31]

It is no exaggeration to say that practices of torture among the Amerindians, including the Mohawks, were not in excess of those in the Low Countries, or France, Ireland, and Germany. About a decade before *Breeden-Raed*, the caption of a woodcut depicting cruelties in Germany read, "Men's guts pulled out of their mouthes." Johann Grimmelshausen's hero tells us that soldiers commonly split a peasant's head down to the teeth. They put fuses up peasants' anuses until "the red juice began to flow out of them." He hears of peasants retaliating to cruelty by severing a soldier's ears and nose before burying him alive in a barrel. A lone soldier was fair game for peasant revenge. If he were a deserter captured by the authorities, he faced hanging or burning at the stake. He might be tortured on the wheel or dropped from the strappado. If he survived, he was a cripple for the rest of his life.[32]

Cannibalism became a believable horror. Especially during protracted sieges, it became a reality. At Tournais in southern Flanders, locals believed that soldiers of the surrounding Catholic forces intended to eat the flesh of Calvinists. In 1623, Wallenstein lay under siege at Goding in southeastern Bohemia for twenty-two days. "So our resolution must be," he wrote, "to perish in this place, one eating the other."[33] For Michel Montaigne, writing in 1603, cannibalism was a metaphor for the ultimate in human degradation, a state of depravity played out more by the combatants in Europe's religious wars than the New World's primitive anthropophagi. Constantijn Huygens was more specific. He wrote of the desperate Netherlands farmer. He'd been made a brute who "wishes in his mouth/ Not cream nor cheese but human flesh and blood."[34]

Thoughts of cannibalistic practices also gave heightened euphoric dimension to moments of victory. About a quarter-century after *Breeden-Raedt*, a New Englander wrote of the success he shared with fellow militiamen in the Narragansett Great Swamp: our men "had now a Carnage rather than a Fight, for every one had their fill of Blood." Another Englishman at the same bloodletting wrote, "had we been cannibals, here might we feast."[35]

Englishmen and others outside the continental war zones used stories of cannibalism, starvation, and torture to remind themselves of the costs of such civil war. Books such as *The Woeful Miseries of Civil War* made popular reading. De Vries promised that his journal would make readers voyeurs by learning "what people eat people." He had faraway people in mind. But the ship of his words might have been kept anchored firmly at home in the grotesqueries of popular experience, storytelling and story reading.[36]

Melijn's New Netherland natives are not cannibals. If anyone is acting irrationally, indeed unnaturally, it is the Dutch. On one occasion, the natives point this out. De Vries records a meeting soon after the massacre between himself, a comrade, and sixteen chiefs. Fleetingly, we hear the natives' interpretation of the war. They remind the Dutch of the strangers' intermarriage with them. They accuse them of being unnatural parents. Once, there had been peaceful relations, one of the leaders recalls. So now "there rove many an Indian who was begotten by a Swanneken." In indiscriminately killing natives now, they were "so villainous as to kill their own blood."

A number of the leaders had also kept in memory a cold-blooded and unnatural proposition Kieft had put to several chiefs about the "young madcaps" among them. You kill the youths, he had offered, and I will see you compensated.[37]

The soldier, then, embodied the savagery of war. His image made readily believable those pages where Melijn's pamphlet became an atrocity narrative. His scenes of soldiers out of control in New Netherland could as easily have been set in Brabant, Overijssel, or Gelderland. He knew how to present their familiarly depraved ways: they test an innocent native's manliness by measuring the amount of wine that he can consume, and then they laugh sadistically at his efforts to stay in control. They mock the burghers on Sundays.[38] They see themselves as a breed apart. So Melijn expects an absorbed audience when telling the story of their murder of four Long Island (Canarsee) natives. It is not a North American story. It is not even exotic or unique.

His account begins with a defeat of natives at the hands of Dutch and English soldiers. As a coda to this event, readers are taken to a place called Hempstead (Map 2). It is the spring of 1644. The Dutch soldiers, together with Underhill and his English mercenaries, have seized four men for killing some hogs. Possibly they are native fighters, perhaps civilians. The soldiers are taking them by yacht to Fort Amsterdam. The captives are useful booty. But, like their European counterparts, the soldiers are prepared to forfeit their value in favor of making sport of them. They decide to tie two of the men's necks with ropes and throw them overboard. Towing them behind the boat, they watch them slowly strangle and drown.[39]

The yacht continues to the fort. Here the men quarrel over the ownership of the remaining loot, the two natives now under guard. Legally, Kieft could have kept them for himself. Earlier, he had given captured natives to soldiers as gifts and sent others off to the Bermudas as a present to the English governor. Now he does the same. He turns them over to the highly agitated soldiers, some of whom—iconic of the usual transitoriness—are preparing to return to Holland. Without reason, they attack the first man, repeatedly plunging a knife into his body until he dies. They then torture the other, cutting strips from his body, from the buttocks up his back and shoulders, and down to his knees. They allow the dying man to struggle out of the fort but then throw him to the ground, cut off his genitals, and force them into his mouth while still alive. Placing him on a millstone, they "beat off his head."[40]

Melijn is invoking here the topos of innocence versus evil. Throughout the pamphlet, he has missed no opportunity to do so: some of his natives had never seen any Dutch, "much less done them any harm"; Dutch children taken hostage and returned to their parents clung to the necks of the natives if they had been with them any length of time; native women cried out: may the Dutch feel shame for their fowl and unspeakable villainy. It was "never heard of, or seen, or happened among us."[41]

In this invocation, Melijn's pamphlet resembles Brueghel's canvas and other instances of peasant sorrow literature and art. He makes certain to write that the four men were illicitly arrested: an Englishman had committed the crime. He presents readers with the two prisoners as "poor, naked Indian prisoners," and again, one of them is a "poor, naked, simple creature." He makes sure that his readers see the knives in the soldiers' hands, long knives deliberately designed by Kieft to be "more handily plunged into . . . [natives'] bowels" in surprise raids on their villages. He reminds readers that one of the Dutch soldiers on the yacht had once been banished from Utrecht as a notorious murderer. He gives a presence to Kieft as befits the cause of it all: the director stands with one of his councillors "laughing out loud." Readers observe Dutch men taking pagan delight in their deliberate display of cruelty while each of the natives strives against unimaginable agony to perform a dance "as a religious rite." They catch the dignity of the first dying man as he begs his persecutors to let him fulfill this spiritual ritual.[42]

The natives were made analogues for any Dutch citizen who could, by way of anti-Spanish national myth or experientially, identify himself or herself as an innocent victim of unjust oppression. In the scene of dignified acceptance of unprovoked cruelty, the Netherlander might see his or her better self. But what the scene represses are all the untold silent killings: the two or three here and four there; the many half-Dutch natives anonymously killed; the sixteen hundred dead with no story.

The immorality of the incident and its possible revelations about Dutchness were not lost on the members of the States. Six years later, in 1650, they were expressing their repugnance at its barbarism and recoiling from the fact that this atrocious cruelty had, as they judged, happened "before the whole world." They had summoned Secretary Cornelis van Tienhoven to The Hague and prepared questions: "Did not the soldiers, in cold blood, and before all the world, cut and stab with knives, one of the two Indian prisoners at the guardhouse who had been brought from Heemstede, and were not living slices cut from the other's body, and whilst he was still alive, were not his privy parts cut off in the Beaver's path where they afterward cut off his head?" Have the Indians done the same to "our people whom they took prisoners?"[43]

*   *   *

Netherlanders had no reason to question Melijn's benign portrayal of the Algonquian-speaking nations around Manhattan Island. This was not because they had a good deal of specific knowledge but because they had so little. Some might have seen images of Carolina Algonquians drawn by John White and later engraved and widely distributed by the Flemish printer Theodore de Bry.[44] Fewer might have seen a Munsee Delaware brought to Amsterdam from New Amsterdam and then identified in print as coming from "Virginia." Those who read Nicolaes Wassenaer's *Historisch Verhael* would have found themselves more fully, though unreliably, informed. Others could mistakenly think they knew something about southern New Netherland people by consulting Johannes Megapolensis's 1644 pamphlet, *A Short Account of the Mohawk Indians*. In any case, the representation of Indians in the Dutch imagination may well have been a conflation of South and Central American people with those of North America. They were a source of great wonder: Are they really cannibals? Do they wear tight white silk stockings on their legs? Did they all populate from Lake Titicaca in Peru?[45]

They were also a source of compassion. Long before Melijn composed his picture of European savagery and American innocence, Bartolomé de Las Casas had done so. Melijn's work did nothing to match the Dominican friar's passion and scope as he scourged Spain for its Indian policies in the New World. But let's make ourselves flies on the wall at a meeting of Holland's leading historians held in 1966. Dr. Professor J. W. Schulte Nordholt is delivering a learned paper. Soon there will be the usual questions of colleagues, then matters of business. Schulte Nordholt begins and is soon finding similarities between Melijn and Las Casas. He is saying that the significance of Melijn's bitter portrayal of the war lies above all in this, that it is "the first public accusation put abroad about the mistreatment of the natives since the famous tract of Las Casas, from the time of 1552."

Schulte Nordholt continues: "It is also worth noting that in both cases the ferocity of the whites was recorded very deliberately and in great detail in order to awaken a universal outcry." For this reason, emphasis was laid on the senseless rage against women and children. We then hear: "It is not at all clear that the author, Cornelis Melyn or whoever it may have been, had knowledge of Las Casas whose pamphlet was, wasn't it, published again and again in our country as part of the psychological warfare against Spain, but it appears that our writer intended to proceed in the same direction."[46]

Melijn's pamphlet fed into a Protestant and Catholic literature that gave primacy to Las Casas's presentation of Indians as martyrs. Huguenots feeling the scourge of religious persecution were able to overwrite the martyred natives and point to themselves: the pitiable savage is suffering in us.[47] Native Americans as innocents were also believable because in 1649 Melijn could use the term *de wilden*, expecting a non-pejorative reading. As May had done thirty-seven years earlier, he used it interchangeably with *inwooners* (native residents), *ingezetenen* (inhabitants), and in phrases such as *alle natien der wilden* (all the peoples among the natives). He never wrote *Indianen*. More important, his natives didn't act savagely. Other New Netherland contemporaries were saying that they did, though the ambivalence we saw in the 1630s was still in evidence. But especially when the colonists were asking for financial assistance, they were given to exaggerating their perilous state and turned to the natives' savagery and (more often) insufferable arrogance.[48]

Melijn wants his account to move in an opposite direction. He is wily. In the passage where he must describe the sustained violence of the natives immediately after the massacre, he turns to its results rather than the process of its happening, which—given tomahawks, hatchets, guns, arrows, and firebrands—must have been horrific. He writes that the actions were in retaliation for unjust treatment. But although they amounted to a declaration of war, the violence had its moral limits. As soon as the natives were aware of the Netherlanders' wicked actions, he wrote, "they killed all the men on the farm lands whom they could surprise." But they did the women and children no harm. He concludes that they began "a declared and destructive war."[49]

*   *   *

Melijn could have been telling his readers that the Americans were carrying out a just war. Two themes would have drawn them to the logic of his argument.

They would have recognized in Kieft's policies two kinds of injustice that patriots had denounced since the start of their own rebellion: tyranny and taxation. From 1568 forward, Netherlanders had linked the king's abuse of power with the exaction of taxes. The fundamental declaration of that year, the *Waerschouwinghe* (Admonition) was the early rebels' vehement—and soon to be mythical—remonstrance against taxes. They were not renouncing their allegiance to the king any more than Christians and *wilden* under Kieft's authority were drawn to do. They were rebelling against the corruption of the highest authority's distant *local* representatives.[50]

In the 1560s, Alva was collecting a direct sales tax of 10 percent, the hated tenth penny. But to the rebels, direct taxation was the prerogative of the provinces and cities. It had been a privilege of the Batavians and then a right exercised by the late-medieval towns and cities of Holland and Zeeland for 800 or more years. Assemblies collected taxes and then might or might not elect to make a "contribution" to the empire's treasury. The free decision making was a mark of their sovereignty. The Americans in Melijn's pamphlet were defending their rightful sovereignty in refusing the contribution. More, they were outside the jurisdiction of any imperium. They were (as he gave them words to say) people who had ceded some of their country to the strangers whose residences they had thereafter never threatened. The strangers could have been content to remain in peace, while they, the natives, remained masters of the lands they had retained for themselves.[51]

Melijn lets his readers observe Kieft's every move as he illegitimately tries to raise revenue. He is shown imposing contributions on non-Dutch people without lawful precedent, prior consultation, or a declaration of war. When the *wilden* assert their rights, first by various remonstrations and then by a declared war, Kieft responds like the Hapsburgs—with violent repression. He also demands that the committee of burghers raise taxes from the commonalty. They refuse because he has no authorization and, besides, he will use the income to fund his war, particularly the hiring of English troops. He claims the right to tax because he is as sovereign "as the prince in Netherland." He is—as Melijn thinks he has now shown—no longer amenable to reason. Another cause for the just resistance of "Christians and *wilden*."[52]

Melijn's argument is like a portolan chart. In some respects, it is poorly constructed. Some coastal markers are indistinct. Others are missing. Some are drawn in twice over. But subtly, he guides his readers to the landmarks of a just war: it may be prosecuted only to repair a wrong done or to prevent one—yet before Kieft's contributions and administration, the Americans had done the Dutch no wrong, and no native leader could be named whose actions had caused the war. A just war might be entertained but only if there were a possibility of success—yet Kieft had neither the means for the war nor the support. A just war might be undertaken by a leader acting according to his conscience—yet Kieft accepted that everyone believed his conscience was troubled. And there is the peculiarly Dutch reading of war: we ought always to wait until others make war upon us. Kieft had not waited.[53]

Melijn continues laying down his chart, directing his travelers from port to port. A lawful war may not be the plaything of personal ambition—yet except for Kieft's corrupt ambitions, there were "no reasons" for the war. So there is a place on the chart that Melijn letters "murder." The king's war against the Low Countries from 1568 to 1609 was called the forty murder years because it was unjust. Kieft's attacks against natives were murder as well. Carried out in "a needless and unjust . . . war," they could be nothing less.[54]

Melijn's words about an unjust war were bellicose, emotional, and selective.[55] Perhaps in carrying on his campaign against the company, he was doing too many things. He was defending the natives' war, legitimizing the burghers' resistance to Kieft's authority, and putting a case for his own innocence. Yet the mystery of Melijn remains his concern for the natives. It is an irony—it is one of colonialism's ironies—that the Americans' cause should be taken up by so complex, distasteful, and contentious a man.

Less than two years before *Breeden-Raedt*, in 1647, Melijn and Kuyter had composed a letter to Stuyvesant urging that the loss of native lives in New Netherland should be measured against the law of nations. Let us see "what the law of nations thinks of it." For "in the exacting of punishment, this law must first of all be observed."[56] Another resident, the young lawyer Adriaen vander Donck, sent the same message to the States in 1649 but with greater force. First, this war was "unjust and begun *contra jus gentium*." Why? The Americans gave us no pretext for it. Second, it was unnecessary. Third, those against whom we waged war were more than ten times stronger than we "who commenced hostilities."[57]

*   *   *

What happened overseas in the 1640s was not an overseas affair. At home, the Netherlanders were inventing a tradition. However brittle and self-regarding, it was becoming one increasingly difficult to step outside of. Dutch men and women were embracing pluralism, antimilitarism, and tolerance as a matter of national pride. Distant settlements were meant to be outlying theaters of this

Dutch rectitude and humanism. So Melijn was on sure grounds in giving *Breeden-Raedt*'s skipper words that indicate that Kieft's treachery against the natives was "a disgrace to our nation." Then he gave the Portuguese soldier words baiting the skipper about the Hollanders' practices in Brazil. The soldier set them against the requirements of a clear conscience—as though he knew that's what the Dutch would do. "Can you Hollanders," he questions, "digest all this in your conscience?"[58]

Chapter 13

The War's Haunting

It had been on his conscience for eleven years. Back when it happened, a hundred Dutch soldiers and some native Formosan allies had landed on the offshore island of Lamay. He, Robert Junius, missionary, had taken a part in encouraging the expedition.

The island's villagers, maybe a thousand of them in all, had been resistant to Dutch efforts to control all aspects of the trade. They were known to have killed the crew of a trading vessel and raided both the Dutch and their allies. In 1636, the captain of a punitive expedition was following his orders: tell them to leave the island. If they resist, starve them into submission and, if necessary, gas them out of the caves they'll use as hiding places. Use "sulphur, tar and other nauseating malodours."

The soldiers did as they were instructed. They ignited fires and set the poisonous gases in place. Then they sealed off the entrances to the caves. After three days, forty-two people crept out of the caves. When the soldiers entered to take inspection, they found the corpses of two to three hundred asphyxiated men, women, and children—at least, they thought that number was about right. We couldn't count accurately, they reported, "as a result of the great stench."[1]

In 1647, Junius offered himself for several interviews with the East India Company directors. Three years earlier, he had let himself be the recipient of a triumphant homecoming in Delft. After all, he'd worked in Formosa for a remarkably long time, ten years. He had converted thousands of natives—someone later told a reading public that the converts were "five thousand nine hundred."[2] But now he felt the company should know the truth about the terrible crimes. The Gentlemen Seventeen were appalled at his words. They recorded that a brutal act of revenge had been undertaken against a people—"simpletons," they said—who "cannot understand what it is that one desires from them."

They made their own inquiries. But four years after initial interviews with Junius, they were still greatly disturbed. They blamed the massacre on a natural characteristic of their own people. "It is a natural shortcoming of the people of our nation," they wrote reflectively to officers in Batavia, "to be either too gentle or too severe in their actions when governing the areas that are under their rule; this is amply proven by those living in the East and West Indies."[3] At the end of the four years of obtaining copies of various earlier instructions, scanning reports, and holding committee meetings, they buried the story in their locked archives.

In 1655, David Pietersz de Vries was feeling that Netherlanders at home should know of a mass murder committed by their countrymen overseas. Maybe he wanted to see justice done. Maybe he knew the story would enhance sales of the journals he published that year.

The date was twelve years earlier, February 25 and 26, 1643. The place: Fort Amsterdam on another island, Manhattan Island. As de Vries told it: standing around the director were "all his Soldiers clearly ready to march over the River to Pavonia, in order to commit the Murder." About midnight, "I heard a terrible shrieking and mounted the Walls of the Fort and looked toward Pavonia, saw nothing but [heard] shooting and heard shrieking that the Natives were dying in their Boats. . . . [Then] there came a Native and his Woman whom I knew well . . . [who] told me . . . that the Natives from around Fort Orange had fallen upon them, and they were seeking protection here at the Fort." I warned them not to seek help there because "it was not natives who were slaughtering their People but *Swannekens*, as they called the Dutch."

"When daybreak came," he continued, "the Soldiers returned to the Fort and had massacred or murdered eighty Natives. . . . [They boasted] that many Natives had been dispatched in their Sleep." [And now he plagiarized the detail and moral message of *Breeden-Raedt*.] "Even young Children, some still sucking at their Mothers' breasts . . . [were] decapitated or limbs chopped off directly in the sight of their Elders and the pieces thrown into the Fire or into the Water." They were, he repeats, killed "in cold blood." Still plagiarizing, he repeats Melijn's reference to the barbarism of the Duke of Alva. "Has the Duke of Alva actually committed more evil things in the Netherlands? Yes, it is a scandal for our Nation."[4]

Matters of conscience, overseas people ignorant of why they were punished by us, "scandal[s] for our Nation": this sense of being haunted by one's own or one's countryman's crimes is something we are overhearing in two singularly individual stories. It is part of a peculiarly Dutch language of culpability that can also be heard as it spills into a national discourse of self-identity. The reality of the Dutch involvement in the Indian war in New Netherland was going to be produced within that language, a language of betrayal.

Junius and de Vries were setting conscience alongside evidence of a Dutch capacity to punish innocent overseas people at a time when Netherlanders were closely measuring their individual and communal behavior against the emerging ethical goals of the new republic. Civic virtue, tolerance, and a regard for common humanity as well as the many advantages that came from staying alongshore; these qualities were us and they were not to be compromised here at home or—what little they knew of it—overseas. In such places, they had a right to imagine the institution of a humanistic, antimilitarist and moral order equivalent to that emerging at home. Not surprisingly, alarm, shame, and outrage as well as condemnation of "our people" and calls for peace washed across the hundreds of pages written on the Indian war. Just as a Dutch historian could write to his countrymen in the twentieth century that from our overseas settlements we garner a knowledge of ourselves as a people, so the same conviction was abroad three centuries earlier.[5]

The war seemed to answer a national impulse to locate the cause of a particular instance of behavior in a shared ethico-national trait and to assign blame accordingly. The "cruel massacre perpetrated against the Indians," the States demanded, must be investigated so that "punishment for blood unlawfully shed may be warded off this State." Four years later, they were writing that the war was illegal and "contrary to all public Law." It had involved "murder, massacre and other abominations that . . . must startle the Christian heart that hears of them." "What is worst," they continued, "the Dutch name is through those cruel acts, despised to a most sovereign degree, by the Heathens of those parts." Association of the Dutch name with war and oppression contradicted a way of life meant to be—and meant to be seen to be—a beacon of irenicism and tolerance. A popular tract of 1659 carried the message: "Townsman: But our Nation, it is said, is too merciful [for such tyrannies]. Skipper: Nonsense!" Adriaen vander Donck, writing in Amsterdam in the spring of 1650, informed an associate that Kieft's war was public knowledge in Europe. The actions of Kieft and van Tienhoven, he wrote, "are damned by the whole world."[6]

By mid-century, many European commentators were articulating a reevaluation of war itself. A number of later writers said that Europeans were experiencing war weariness. Europe had wasted itself on a century of military adventurism. No party involved in it was free of culpability. Representations particularizing the horrors of a siege or military campaign invariably mutated into a universal condemnation of war. In 1625, Vondel invited listeners to applaud "my Hollanders" going bravely to the field. But soon he was putting before them a universal denunciation of war and its participants on all sides. "We are," he cried, "weary of fighting." "In the figure of the soldier God has cursed us all."[7]

In 1650, in *The Monsters of Our Age*, Vondel surveyed Europe's Christian nations and found that Virtue had become universally deathly pale. Christian monarchs had shamed even the Church itself. In *De Getemde Mars* (*The Shackling of War*), Vondel had also taken up the theme. After acknowledging the

Amsterdam burgomasters as *Vredevaders,* Fathers of Peace, he painted a continent drunk on opulence and avarice. Jupiter had sent Mars to punish it until
the earth shook and wept while sinister omens appeared in hideous plagues.
The chastised people of Europe could no longer find themselves guided by the
stars, the sun, and the moon. Rather, the fires of war leaped across the lands,
beginning in Spain and reaching Lisbon, Catalonia, Ireland, Britain, Italy, even
the gods' home on Crete. "That was Europe's sorrow. Oh, it is time, it is high
time," Vondel lamented, "to awaken ourselves."[8]

Vondel's contemporary Pieter Cornelisz Hooft was also writing that war
and guilt were coextensive on the continent of Europe. Our times, he wrote in
Nederlandsche Historiën, "are the night of virtue." In the wars, Christendom
divided against itself. In the Netherlands, states on all sides had committed barbarous crimes. Townsmen drove local leaders from their magistracies; anger
raged in the courts; laws, local custom, and privileges fell beneath murderous
feet; men raped churches and destroyed one another in deadly party politics.
They committed murders outside the rules of war. The Dutch nation's history,
Hooft believed, was about good and evil. Thankfully, the evil of the past was over.[9]

Few could miss Hooft's purpose in writing the history that was to be his
life's work. He would help create a people forever careful of initiating war and
too easily abandoning avenues of peace. Vondel put the same ideals in his allegory of the gods. The Netherlanders, among all the Europeans, would bind
Mars not with bands of iron but with gentle ribbons of peace or, synonymous
with peace, Orange. In a land where it was national mythology that no person
should be "constrained or aggrieved in his conscience," pamphleteers also
found audiences prepared to discuss the demands of conscience within rules
for the avoidance of war. The triumph of the Peace of Münster was producing
an outpouring of peace *praatjes*, debates and tracts. In New Netherland, parties
on all sides were not immune to this impulse. They, too, appealed to the need
for a clear conscience if the pursuit of a war were to be moral. In 1643, even
Kieft presented himself to the company directors as a man of careful conscience. "We cannot at present resolve to attack the Indians at Mareckkawich
[perhaps Brooklyn]," he wrote, because they have offered us no provocation
and to do so would "draw down an unrighteous war on our heads." Several days
earlier, he had defended his war against other natives as a "just cause."[10] Meanwhile, his enemies continued to condemn the war, his war, on the grounds of
conscience and morality.

The moral grounds were well marked out for Netherlanders by Hugo
Grotius just fifteen years before Kieft began collecting his contributions. Not
everything about the laws of peace and war in *De Jure Belli ac Pacis* were going
to find favor or be put into practice. But Netherlanders embraced Grotius's

humanizing of the laws and, even as Grotius intended, accepted their breach as a cause of shame. In the prolegomena to the treatise, Grotius took the stance that Hendricksz and May took as world-voyaging navigators. He was an eye-witness—and therefore reliable. He had observed in the Christian world, he wrote, "a lack of restraint in relation to war, such as even barbarous races should be ashamed of." He observed that "men rush to arms for slight causes, or no cause at all, and then when arms have once been taken up there is no longer any respect for law, divine or human; it is as if . . . frenzy had openly been let loose for the committing of all crimes."[11]

* * *

Set within the sounds of this polyphonic score played over and over again, the States accepted as complementary the notes struck by the antiwar party in New Netherland. By the 1650s, they were taking as fact a war against the natives that was bloody, unnecessary, and never properly deliberated. It was everything the burghers said it was, including unnatural. It was a fact, too, that the Americans had been "friends there of the subjects of these United Netherlands." In 1649, the States accepted without demur the Remonstrance specifically addressed to them by the people of New Netherland and agreed to its publication in The Hague the next year. In it, they were made to read and accept their share of blame for the unjust war as well as the betrayal and alienation of the peoples living near the Dutch. They were also reminded of their obligation to redress the wrongs committed.[12]

In its early pages, the Remonstrance took a path across the geography, climate, and productivity of New Netherland. Then it traveled through a description of the aborigines, finally arriving at the history and present shameful state of the Netherlanders. Here the authors adopted an inclusive "we," confidently sweeping all Netherlanders into responsibility for the moral failure of the North American venture. All were included in a confession of sinfulness that fused legal, religious, and pragmatic considerations. It unexpectedly erupts in a section on the "Convenience and Excellence" of the waterlands. The oddly inserted prayer is uncharacteristically missionizing. It suggests that sharing with the natives the Eternal Good can right the wrongs of the war and Dutch ingratitude for the blessings of land and trade received from them. But at least one sentence seems to show the hand of vander Donck, one of its authors and a man whom one Dutch historian called a precursor of the eighteenth-century enlightenment.[13] That is, the prayer finds a place for the natives before the throne of God on the day of final judgment.

We have not deserved this land, the prayer begins. We are unworthy because of our manifold sins in mistreating the natives during these years when we have been beholden to them "in the highest degree." They "surrendered this rich and fertile country, and for a trifle made it over to us." They enriched us with their valuable and mutual trade. For this reason, no one in New Netherland "*or trading . . . [from these provinces of the Netherlands] . . . to that country*" is free of an obligation to them.

But because of our war, "great is our shame." Our good fortune in New Netherland now requires that we acknowledge our debt to them. "In return for what the Indians had shared with us of their substance" we must endeavor "to divide with them the Good Eternal." Yet we need to fear that for the injury done to them "they will stand up against us at the last day."

The authors conclude with a final plea: "Lord of Hosts! Forgive us that we have not hitherto comported ourselves better in this matter." Grant us the means and the desire in the future that our own souls and theirs may be saved. And may thy Holy Name be glorified "for Christ his sake, Amen."

The Remonstrance's message was the same as Melijn's. Europe would see Dutch wickedness overseas as wickedness at home. "If the Netherland United Provinces, their High Mightinesses, and his Highness, do not see to it in time," Melijn wrote, "the names of Netherland, their High Mightinesses, and Orange, will stink, not only with the Indians, but with all Christendom."[14]

* * *

If some in the Netherlands were beginning to see the first traitorous deeds of empire, the West India Company directors were also prepared to agree that the American natives were innocent victims of an unjust war. The guilt, however, did not rest with them. Let the States assign them responsibility for "blood unlawfully shed . . . [and called down on] this State." Let the New Netherlanders say that the company hadn't even authorized an investigation into the causes of the war. Let them say that "the seed of the war was . . . first sown in Fatherland." Let them infer that the company's incompetent leadership provided the grounds for violence, even sadism. They knew better.[15]

The guilt lay with Kieft, and the contributions laid on the natives. Kieft rashly pursued an unnecessary war without our knowledge and against the will of the commonalty on the island. The colonists—those non-company farmers and traders whose ilk had excited the company's distrust in the 1620s—were also to blame. They were furtively moving over the land, settling "far in the interior of the Country." Here they were conducting unsupervised trade with the natives, luring them to their houses by excessive familiarity and promises of liquor. For those natives not similarly courted, this was the cause of the enmity. Such colonists had taken the rules of trading out of the company's control and, exerting themselves as the duplicitous *vrije burgers* they had always wanted to be, were living by no rules at all.[16]

But to the directors, the guilt of the colonists was not so much for the murder of hundreds of natives. Even Kieft's guilt was not for the injustice of the contributions and the subsequent killings. In the Indies, forced contributions—call them *leveringen* (tribute in kind), call them *contingenten* (quotas), call them delivery contracts—were already a common practice. The colonists' guilt was in jeopardizing the future of the company's operations in New Netherland. The value of the company's shares was already bouncing all over the market: 43 and 44 in August 1644, then up to 58 with the rumor that the States were demanding reforms; down to 44 and 45 eleven weeks later, due to speculation that the States would soon withdraw its subsidies. Where to turn? The East India Company would not accept a merger. Abandoning New Netherland was worth considering, but the company had contracted with the patroons to remain and provide defense for their people and properties. Just five years before Kieft began collecting his contributions, the private investors had let the directors know that they half-expected the company to induce them to abandon their colonies. They were ready with bills for damages then, and would be now.[17]

So the company would stay. But now, the directors were saying, the wars have convinced us that the natives must be treated with greater kindness. Hostilities may not be opened against them without our knowledge and that of the States. The natives have now learned that "we are forbidden to oppose them." But we must bear with this insolence because the States have expressly commanded us not to begin a conflict with them. We will have to think of some restructuring and small profits.[18]

The natives' lives were going to be thought out within an Erastian language of tolerance and justice. But like two offshore currents crossing each other as they move toward the shore, this discourse was going to be cut across by a corporate language of market prices, profits, and expediency. Occasionally, the crisscrossing of the two currents can be observed. Back in 1644, the natives were merely one datum examined by accountants summoned to salvage the ruined company. They divided their report into three tidy sections: abuses arising from opening the venture to free trade—four points; suggested remedies— seven points; and recommendations—eight points followed by total estimates of probable expenses, 20,040 guilders. Under point two of the first section, the men had to make a judgment on whether a particular action, if undertaken, would be both Christian and financially advantageous to the company. Specifically, should they support Kieft's advice to exterminate all enemies by force? They thought not. "It is impossible and unchristianlike." Moreover, it would provide minimal profits and incur great expense for an uncertain result.[19]

Here was a language murky in its messages but carried in Dutch ships to the Indies, the Caribbean, and Brazil—to Junius's Formosa and de Vries's and Melijn's North America. In 1588, Michel Montaigne was already condemning the practices it authorized as mercantile cannibalism, the rule of plunder. From it, every shred of magnanimity had been expunged. Therefore it was God's work when the seas swallowed up the "great pillages and ill-gotten goods" being transported across them.[20]

Many Dutch men were saying the same thing. To the playwright Gerbrand Adriaenszoon Bredero, the Indies companies were the metaphor for exploitation and the Netherlanders' way of excusing it. They veiled it in a laughable self-righteousness. One of his characters, in self-mockery, claims that they were virtuous and sober: "We chat so nicely with our fellow shareholders about our affairs, about the trade of the Indies and of the Guiana Company." Other Dutch men working overseas for the shareholders were counting even more closely the cost of exploiting foreign markets and distant people. The price was violence and war. And the dead. An experienced officer serving in Java concluded that all wars and similar actions meant total ruin for the company's operations and people. His conclusions echoed a hard-edged voice we heard back in the 1620s: "There is no profit in an empty sea, empty countries, and dead people." So they rebuked themselves. They examined their consciences and looked for solutions to their Christian brutality. But they didn't turn back the ships.[21]

The East India Company was becoming synonymous with mercantile cannibalism in southeast Asia. The seas and countries were not emptied of the company's plunder and profits until the States terminated its rule in 1795 and took the administration into its own hands. But there were dead people—and there was the haunting. From the start, those telling stories about the East Indies were in greater numbers and had more exciting stories to tell than those recording the affairs of the West India Company. They also recorded the haunting of conscience in greater detail than we can hope to find in our relatively fewer stories. Extortionate contributions, killings, and conscience came together as early as 1617 and under Coen's administration. The tale has been told again and again.

In 1617, four years before Cornelis Volkertsz and his associates petitioned to send a trading ship to North America, Coen set in motion the savage punishment of the Bandanese islanders for refusing to submit to the delivery contracts demanded of them. Nearly the entire population of Banda—about fifteen thousand inhabitants—were, to cite a Dutch historian, exterminated. Coen was bitterly condemned when news reached the Low Countries. We have been far too ruthless, his critics charged. We should remember that the victims fought for their country's independence as we "sacrifice[d] our lives and goods for so many years." The company chose to take an amoral and rationalist position. We had wished, they said, that it could have been accomplished by more moderate means.[22]

Perhaps the directors were undisturbed by the specter of the dead. But later Dutch historians were greatly disquieted. In 1886, the archivist of Batavia wrote that there was blood on Coen's name. If Coen's statue had not already been erected in Hoorn, he doubted very much "if it would now be done." In the same year, another historian publishing in The Hague pointed to Coen's cruelties and the "cold-blooded manner in which he eradicated a prosperous people." Still another spoke of the "all but ineradicable blood spot that sullied the name of the Netherlands."[23]

Taking up this late-nineteenth-century voice, subsequent Dutch historians, wrote George Masselman in 1963, vied with one another in relieving their guilt and expressing their horror. The conquest of Banda became one historian's "tale of murder and manslaughter, destruction and extermination which, in its shocking simplicity, exceeds all others." For another, it was "inhuman and bestial judicial murder." The balance of major historians agreed. "It will be difficult to find, in the historiography of nations," wrote Masselman, "a similar example of censure of a national figure by his own countrymen."[24]

Far fewer Dutch historians turned their attention to Kieft's war. J. W. Schulte Nordholt, however, did. Let's return to the room in Holland where he is delivering his learned paper. The meeting will close at four o'clock in the afternoon. And the chair will thank the speaker for an especially learned exposition covering a great deal of terrain unknown to most of them. The paper was learned. But it was also a passionate expression of conscience and corporate guilt.

Schulte Nordholt returns us to 1643 in an exceptionally moving passage. "In 1643 a war broke out with sudden fury, a small war in our eyes, a conflict of hundreds against hundreds, nothing more, but in the circumstances a great war which enveloped everyone's life and changed everything thereafter." He goes on to give details of the war. They are the details we now know. He speaks of the months after the massacre when Kieft set a bounty on the head of every Raritan. "That then," he read out, "was the first occurrence in American history." It was not, of course. Long before Kieft, the English had paid bounties for the heads of native Americans. Schulte Nordholt's judgment about his countrymen was not, however, the result of careless scholarship. It was the result of guilt and shame. "What happened [in New Netherland] was more than a mistake; it was a moral failing."[25]

*   *   *

Willem Kieft, Dominee Evarardus Bogardus, and Cornelis van der Huygens drowned when the *Princess* broke up in a storm off the coast of Wales in 1647.

Cornelis van Tienhoven retained his office as company secretary until 1653 and for an additional three years continued to serve Petrus Stuyvesant as the company's highest law-enforcement officer. In that year, he suddenly disappeared. He is thought to have committed suicide. His hat and cane were found in the river. His body was never recovered.

Johannes la Montagne continued to hold public offices. He was appointed commissary at Fort Orange in 1658 and surrendered the fort and Beverwijck (Albany) to the English in 1664.

Govert Lookermans played a leading role in the affairs of New Amsterdam until his death in 1671. In 1644, he carried the complaint of the Eight Men to the company's directors in Amsterdam. As a private trader, he grew wealthy operating around Fort Orange and at the Delaware River. In 1648, he was accused of selling arms to natives while on a trip from New Amsterdam to New Haven but in 1653 was serving on Stuyvesant's council. Three years before his death, he was appointed lieutenant of a military band.

Cornelis Melijn was living in New Haven after 1655. He settled there as a free colonist. Jochem Pietersz Kuyter was killed, allegedly by natives, in 1654.

John Underhill died in 1672. In 1653, he turned against the Dutch, gathering soldiers and seamen to seize Dutch vessels and drive the Netherlanders from Long Island. In later years, he was appointed high constable and under-sheriff of the North Riding of Yorkshire on Long Island as well as surveyor of customs for Long Island. In 1908, an obelisk was raised to his memory at Locust Valley, Long Island. He had long before had a coat of arms designed for himself. A biographer called him "The Savior of New Netherland." J. W. Schulte Nordholt said he was a "*condottiere* without scruples."[26] He died in 1672 at his Killingworth estate at Oyster Bay on Long Island.

David Pietersz de Vries returned to Hoorn after his fifty-eight months in New Netherland. He embarked on no further world voyages. He lived to be one of Hoorn's honored citizens, though he did not accept public office.

J. W. Schulte Nordholt remained a devoted scholar of the early American republic. He served with distinction in the Dutch resistance during World War II and was a greatly loved professor at the University of Leiden. He died in Leiden in 1995.

No one was ever brought to justice for the 1643 massacre and subsequent killings of native Americans. No native, as far as we know, was ever interrogated. No one, including this writer, has told their story fully.

PART VI

Cross-Colonization

The 1650s were New Netherland's time of transformation. The natives had a presence in Dutch lives that they had not commanded before. They were there in memory (of the war and the dead) and on a landscape of destroyed or empty villages. Some were present as survivors selling lands or buying guns, challenging Dutch legitimacy in sly words and silences, in gestures made and gestures withheld. Their positionality, to dip into today's postcolonial discourse, was not merely one of effects but agency. Both sets of actors were fitfully guarding themselves from the will of the other.

Manhattan Island, and especially New Amsterdam, remained firmly within the merchants' definition of what New Netherland would be. But increased numbers of colonists began to challenge their priorities, not least their nonaggressive and non-expansionist policy toward the natives. By 1664, the population had increased eighteen-fold. On Long Island, a number of farmers sought to reorder the ownership and control of native-owned property. In the neighboring English towns, they had the example of aggressive, often rapacious, appropriations of indigenous lands. Petrus Stuyvesant refused to sanction such policies but not always successfully. Meanwhile, the peopling of native lands on Long Island and on the Jersey shores west of Manhattan Island went steadily ahead.

In September 1655, River Indians and New Amsterdammers confronted each other on the city's streets and waterfronts. Historians have named the events the Peach War. Neither side had planned the violence or its repercussions. Both were maneuvering within something that could be called the structure of the fur trade. But all knew that they were hostage to contingency: a drunken Dutch man or native with a grudge and a gun; a gesture misread; a skiff or canoe sailed up the wrong river; a tribe with its own reasons for seeking revenge. Each party to the conflict felt the pressure of unpredictable intersocietal rivalries: Susquehannocks against the Delaware villagers (and the Dutch); English against Long Island tribes; Dutch against the Hackensacks and Wekquaesgeeks; Mohawks intimidating each of these groups and the Esopus as well. In these years, the Dutch and the natives were not two sides. Each was many— unable to master the others, capable only of diminishing their certainties.

Stuyvesant was also learning that New Netherland was hostage to the West India Company's indifference to its fate. Along with others, he had become aware of the promise of New Netherland. It had a history to chronicle. Now within its grasp, it had futurity. The directors in Holland had little realization of this. They refused to provide military assistance. They were prepared to abandon the defensive military posture traditionally adopted in dealing with enemies. Instead, they encouraged the English model of militarized colonialization. Organize the country people into militias; let them be ready to move out offensively against the natives.

In 1657, Stuyvesant and his councillors wrote a page in the history of the emotion I cited earlier. They conducted deliberations to determine whether a just war could be waged against the River Indians. The consultations turned into moments of self-reproach. They acknowledged themselves as cause of the violence. Again, as in the Indian war, they were the aggressors. The natives had simply seized the legal right to retaliate. A war against them could not be justified.

In closing off the option of a just war—and postponing any kind of final settlement—the administrators were facing the reality of being militarily weak. But they were also seeking a dual legitimation. They wanted to endow their own authority with righteousness and believe that the original determination to respect the rights of the surrounding inhabitants still had some force. Both hopes—and they knew this, too—were vain.

Chapter 14

Watchful Waiting

It is the afternoon of the last day of May 1658. Petrus Stuyvesant is meeting with natives in the scatter of houses called Esopus. He is upriver, far to the north of New Amsterdam on Manhattan Island. There have been disturbances between the natives and farmers. Stuyvesant is suing for peace.

He knows he must listen to a long speech delivered by the native spokesman. He sits with the others under a tree near a hedge surrounding a Dutch man's house. The natives have chosen the spot, and he has gone over to be with them. The messages he hears might have been anticipated. But they cannot have been welcome. The native orator reminds him of Kieft's war. He calls on Stuyvesant to remember how the war had been waged "between them and our nation in Mr. Kieft's time, how many of their people had then been killed." Stuyvesant replies that it had happened before his time and therefore did not concern him.[1]

But it did concern him. In pursuing the war, a shift had occurred. The Dutch had given the natives a presence that they had not previously commanded. Now was the time of cross-colonization. Hybridity, entanglement—call it what you will—had become their lot. First there were the native dead. They had not lived at a distance and perhaps by that offered themselves as forgettable. They had lived in close proximity to the strangers' administrative headquarters in the fort, their wharves and warehouses, their waterfronts on the island. Close to most of their people. Where they had been massacred, residents were settling the town of Bergen. The Dutch kept reviving the subject of the war and the dead: how the old inhabitants talked about it all, how it was better not to go into detail about it. The natives, those of different tribes, kept inspiriting the present with the dead; they could not leave it empty of the "people [of theirs] killed."[2]

Even if punishment for the injustice of the war had not been meted out, the conflict and its consequences were still bleeding into public discourse. The growth of trade and agriculture had been deferred for years. Everyone's profits in furs, timber, and grain had been lost. Lost, too, was the promise of all that Manhattan Island might have become as a successful West Indies rendezvous. In the late 1640s, only three hundred to five hundred Europeans were living on the island. Some residents were now spending years rebuilding their Manhattan Island properties. Jochem Pietersz Kuyter had taken eight years to build his—a house now found to have been destroyed not by natives but Dutch men. In 1653, Newtown was just about where it had been ten years before, when the natives attacked.[3]

These were only some of the undeniable results of the company's failed policies. But a few men found a positive purpose in them. Non-company burghers now used the need for new leadership as an argument for winning a charter defining the city of New Amsterdam as free of the company's control. So the dead became part of a usable past: an advantage to the free burghers, a haunting shadow for Stuyvesant. Rather than being a frame to the picture of the enclave, the natives had become an element within its composition. Too much of their culture (whatever it was) was washing up on the beach of the strangers' culture. In their own way, the native leaders who had reminded de Vries that the strangers were surely killing some of their own offspring were recognizing signs of this hybridity. They were intimating that, like it or not, the ways of the Europeans and Americans were not entirely incommensurable. Now the identities of all would be even more strongly natives and strangers bound together[4] (Figs. 11–14).

Those natives who survived Kieft's war were galling because—not always, but often enough—they were behaving as insiders. They could make telling discriminations: this house, they would say, belongs to us except for the nails. They were even pretending to stand inside the Dutch mind. One of them (later, in 1663) said he knew how they came to decisions about ransoming prisoners: first, demand them on the grounds of conscience, then make threats, and finally "wring the prisoners from . . . [the enemy] by war." They said, we know that you cannot understand us. One of the Mohawks said: you trade with us and then you do not want to know us. They said they knew the local director and merchants had orders to "conciliate and to satisfy" them.[5]

They sidled into the legal system. They appeared as witnesses in court cases involving serious crimes as well as misdemeanors—and (so it could seem) their testimony was being accepted over that of Dutch residents. Stuyvesant and the council said it in the mid-1650s: violators of the ordinance forbidding the sale of liquor to them will be punished "on the declaration of the Indians." Some were making themselves knowledgeable about the current market price of land and demanding resale of lands that they had sold earlier. They sat in judgment. We "are now waiting to see what you will do," they chided the resident director. Or they would say that they lacked confidence in one of his appointees or policies.[6]

They were filling up more places in Dutch memories of New Netherland:

telling stories of their welcoming reception of the *Half-Moon*; reciting their tales of grieving for a boy killed soon thereafter. Some were saying they remembered Minuit's farm and "Wouter." Others spoke of the beginning of the troubles under Kieft. (But of course, all was now forgotten.) They were giving themselves and the strangers a mutual past. They were entering the company directors' anxieties. The war, the men feared, had brought them to a greater knowledge of their strength relative to us. They might have entertained deeper anxieties had they known how extensive the coastal natives' knowledge was.[7]

The natives' unwillingness to be submissive was getting to the Dutch. They seemed to know exactly what style of authority the strangers wished to display and how most painfully to refuse it. The Dutch wanted to appear—the directors said it in 1660—awe-inspiring. But the natives were continually letting them know that they were not. In 1652, seven years after the purported peace, the directors seemed to be at their wits' end regarding their pacification. Natives murdered, seized children, and stole animals. But they could only make sense of it by identifying it as insolence and, by that, charge the natives with the effrontery of making their own interpretations of things and drawing their own (inappropriate) conclusions. "All the letters" from Manhattan Island carried complaints about the "insolence of the savages." Three years later, in 1655, a resident councillor said simply, they have made fools of us.[8]

Most infuriating, the directors were discovering that the natives had an inside track to those who wanted to diminish the company's power and knew how to turn the information into ridicule. They know "we are forbidden to oppose them." Or later: there are "evil-minded persons who make the savages believe that we are not allowed to punish them for their ill doings." Still later: someone among our people is telling them that the director general and council had sent for five hundred men but they could not get any soldiers. The States—they were throwing this at us, too—have expressly commanded us not to begin a strife with them "under any consideration."[9]

The natives were especially enjoying the experience of belittling the Dutch for their impotence as a military force. Kieft knew that the natives' observations had led them to conclude that the Netherlanders were cowards—"you might indeed be something on water, but of no account on land." Now they were mocking them for the insignificant number of their soldiers and colonists. Their insufferable arrogance arises, wrote New Amsterdam's representatives in the late 1640s, because our numbers are smaller than theirs. They will continue to exhibit such arrogance and hostility until—written elsewhere—we promote greater emigration. But they laugh at us for warning of a day when we will outnumber them. They don't seem to understand or accept their position of weakness. They seem to evade it. They say, "the Dutch do nothing but lie."[10]

12

Figures 11–14. Perhaps we can never know what
Algonquians and Europeans saw when they looked
at one another. The iconography of the seventeenth-
century middle colonies is generally misleading
because natives appear as classical or otherwise
stylized figures, according to the intent of the artist.

13

11

Few natives would have seen the body language and elaborate attire of the European strangers in Figure 11. Equally, no European Pennsylvanian would have encountered natives feathered and clad (or unclad) in the encounter shown here. Nor would a Dutch man or woman of the mid-1650s have seen anything like the native woman and children shown resting under a southeast Asian tree in a state of untroubled innocence (Figure 12 and see also Figure 4).

By 1658, New Amsterdammers were seeing natives wearing coats of several different colors. Perhaps the wearing of such clothing created a space for individuation. Perhaps it closed a cultural divide insisted upon in Figure 13 but unintentionally undercut by the native orator's woolen leggings. Wasn't it also probable that by 1656 natives, rather than seeing elaborately attired colonial leaders, were more readily seeing ordinary Dutch men and women such as the tailor and his two assistants depicted in Figure 14?

Figures 11, 12. Thomas Campanius Holm, *Kort beskrifning om provincien Nya Swerige uit America. Nova Svecia Seu Pensylvania in America Descriptio (Swedes and Indians in New Sweden)*, 1702 (details). The Library Company of Philadelphia. Figure 13. William Smith, *An Historical Account of the Expedition against the Ohio Indians in the year 1764. The Indians giving a Talk to Colonel Bouquet in a Conference . . . Octr., 1764* (detail). The Library Company of Philadelphia. Figure 14. Quiringh Gerritz van Brekelenkam (active 1648, died 1667 or 1668), *The Interior of a Tailor Shop* (detail). Worcester Art Museum.

But the laughter said something more. Too often, the Netherlanders singled out instances of natives ridiculing them not to suggest that they were worrying: Are we laughable? In the Dutch official who said that they had been made fools of, are we seeing, even if momentarily, a man pausing to wonder: Is there something about us, something about our ways here, that is foolish? Why can they make fools of us?[11]

The natives were also colonizing the resident director's records. Itemized lists of commodities sent home were still drawn up: the columns of exports that constituted the proper marketplace accounts. But now the natives' activities demanded description: what mischief they were up to; their relations with the English; their vulnerability as a target of newly arrived farmers' aggression and unrest; how the colonists used them against him when he refused to sell them guns and liquor; the Christians, one man wrote, "are treated almost like Indians."[12]

Large numbers of natives were being bought out as proprietors of the coastal lands. By chance, location around the waters of a district gave form to both the culture of the strangers and the coastal New Netherland natives. Both knew how to read the demands of the land beside the sea. But now the domination of alongshore was an uneven competition. Entire tribes were being displaced. Many seaward-looking villages once busy with water traffic and wampum-making were now deserted (Fig. 15). The tides of Jamaica Bay that once flooded the natives' low-lying meadows now drowned the lands of farmers in Flatbush. To fish in the river at Haarlem, natives needed to acquire a permit. One chief, Corruspin, was lucky: he acquired four permits.[13]

But other natives were around, making themselves known by demanding guns, questioning land sales, stealing, moving about with their half-lit purposes, and generally exhibiting the effrontery of people who seemed to think that the deep meanings of their social and personal lives lay well beyond anything to do with the Dutch. Seeking to understand and control their behavior only amplified inexplicable differences. This was the shadow world of the inland, one onto which a moment's light had been thrown when a sachem told de Vries in 1643 that his people would execute a fellow Amerindian guilty of murder "but not at the will of foreigners." In the mid-1650s and when they were taking captives, their threat was always that they would take them into the interior. In many ways—and probably to no less a degree than they hid their identities from the feared Mohawks—they moved in the dark interior all the time.[14]

In the 1650s, Adriaen vander Donck was already writing a memorial of the original native inhabitants of the land. May it be preserved, he wrote, "after the Christians have multiplied and the natives have disappeared and melted away." It is difficult not to think that the natives also knew of their melting away.

Vander Donck reported that natives believed that "nine-tenths of them" had died of smallpox. About thirty years after Kieft's war, the coastal families and Mohawks knew that diseases brought by the Europeans were destroying them. They were also living in the violence of competition for beaver in circumstances of devastating ecological changes. Some of the survivors had to know that they were losing their independence to the Dutch and English by incurring debts. In 1657, the English fined a Long Island tribe three hundred pounds in wampum. This required work on something like 1.008 million beads and presented them with a debt that they were unlikely to discharge. In the same year, Wyandanch, a local Long Island leader, learned that he must pay the English "fire money." Terrified, he ceded land as part payment. The burghers of New Amsterdam once expressed the hope that the natives would soon disappear. Adriaen van-der Donck, however, saw the disappearance of people who occupied a uniquely unified moral universe and, more than the Dutch, had accommodated to what we would call cultural change. But the burghers said, if we become many they'll be "of little consequence."[15]

Figure 15. The photograph suggests loss. Only the beautiful design of the canoe remains to be admired. However natural, the setting is somehow a museum. Anon., *Algonquin Canoe* (detail). The Mariner's Museum, Newport News, Virginia.

The natives still outnumbered the Dutch. During the two decades follow-ing Kieft's war, the strangers would learn that they weren't yet the walking dead. Inexact accounts tell of natives killing ten Dutch men and women in seemingly incidental encounters and at different times and in different places: Manhattan Island, Long Island, Manhattan Island again and then Staten Island. Meanwhile, insolence would continue to show itself not least because, while they acted as though they knew the Dutch inside out, they kept themselves concealed. They carried out what we (trying to put it all into some kind of order) call the Beaver Wars. But the ways of these they left unexplained. They hid who they really were, refused to be predictable, were not readable.

There were moments when they seemed to be teaching the strangers things about themselves. You'll know if we've done any mischief, they said, because we always boast about it. But generally, they slid out of easy understanding. None among the Dutch was now going to make the mistake of the minister who, twenty years earlier, had looked for kings and thought he saw each chief com-manding several hundred warriors.[16] Certainly, the resident director and other company personnel were still satisfied with the merchant's minimal knowledge of their strange worlds. But it mattered to know exactly how the nearby sachems organized themselves, shifted in and out of their alliances, and controlled the selling of furs—who knew that?

Back in 1634, when the company's surgeon was visiting villages along the Mohawk River, a chief showed him his idol, a cat's head dressed in duffel cloth. Something cross-cultural, yes, but unreadable, too. How to keep peace with such unknowable people? Or how to accept an identity inclusive of them?[17]

*   *   *

The natives were confronting the Dutch with concerns that they were already entertaining about the viability of New Netherland, at least until the mid-1650s. There were, however, two sites of discourse the natives didn't enter.

They made no comment about a religious zealotry shown by the strangers. There were no words reminding them of their professed role as Christians in order to then confront them with being hypocrites. They accused them of being lazy and treacherous. One man among the Mohawks stated that they were cruel. Others scoffed at them for being pusillanimous. The Raritans accused one man on Staten Island of killing them through sorcery. But they had apparently been given no reason to taunt the Dutch for parading Christian pieties while living lives of dishonesty and violence. A vocabulary employed so piteously and effec-tively by other Algonquian-speaking people against the New Englanders dur-ing this time and in the 1670s went unused. In 1676, during a merciless war between natives and Puritan settlers, a Nipmunk killed a settler after crying derisively, "Come Lord Jesus, save this poor Englishman if thou canst, whom I am about to kill." Elsewhere natives laughed at the Puritans' self-styled solemnities, calling out to a group of them, "Come and pray, and sing Psalms." A native then killed a man, ripped him open, and thrust his Bible in his belly.[18]

In these instances, the natives were savaging the same sensitivities that were providing Puritans with categories of loathing for those who had stubbornly resisted Christianization and now needed to be, if not exterminated, dispossessed of their lands. By 1676, the Massachusetts settlers were conducting a holy war against an overwhelming number of Satan's minions. The conflation of natives and Lucifer was reaching a peak of versatility. But the fusion was in evidence before that time and in a wide diversity of accounts. The Pilgrims had a dread of the New World natives even before leaving Leiden. They seemed to imagine them as the primitive devils portrayed so luridly by Theodore de Bry. Later, a chronicler of the Pequot wars described the English fighting not only men but devils. Two years before Pavonia, in 1641, William Bradford was asking himself why evil was so readily breaking forth in southern New England. Satan, he concluded, "has more power in these heathen lands."[19]

This was not the case with the Dutch. The language of Kieft's journal is typically resistant to the entry of the divine or the diabolical. Written in the late 1640s and at a time when a poet such as Jacob Revius could identify the war against Spain as a holy war, it scarcely casts God in an interventionist role in the American war. Nowhere are the natives cited as devils. At one point, the writer takes time to list their character traits but the portrait is a more ambiguated than categorical portrayal of them as nonhuman. They are hypocritical, treacherous, and vindictive but also "brave and pertinacious in self-defense." The journal carries no references to citizen-soldiers assembled to hear sermons or listen to themselves being urged on as God's saints. Rather, the commonalty pointed to the soldiers as the company's hirelings and generally despised them as vagrants and miscreants. In one passage, the Father of Hate is invoked. But the identification is not a reference to Satan. The father of hate is contempt, the response of a group who, having been dismissed as worthless, will then, fired with hate on this account, take revenge on their persecutors. So it had been with the many natives incited by the Father of Hate to take revenge upon Dutch men and women denying them the liquor and weapons given to others. The author quotes a burgher calling Kieft devilish and denouncing his devilish lies. In neither case does the term carry theological weight.[20]

The other area of discourse in which the New Netherland natives seemed to be disinterested was the matter of Dutch movement onto their lands. By the 1670s, the New England aborigines under King Philip had drawn an identity between the English and their insatiable thirst for lands not their own. Some passed judgment on their avarice in 1675 in a grotesque burial and single-sentence epitaph. They buried several English captives alive. "You English since you came into this Country have grown exceedingly above the Ground," they taunted. "Let us now see how you will grow when Planted into the Ground."[21]

A curse such as this never fell upon the Dutch. Even in the clash of words during and after Kieft's war, neither natives nor anti-company burghers ascribed the war to the occupation of native lands. Nor had Kieft and his supporters used it as a justification for the war. Territorial ambitions had not been the cause. No one had said that the natives failed in law to possess the lands they tilled or from which they fished and collected shells. It would have been inconceivable that a contemporary commentator would have valued or wanted as one of its outcomes the fruits of English killings in Virginia that so heartily pleased one Englishman. He was writing of its unexpected benefit to English agricultural settlers now numbered, he estimated, at thirty thousand. The victors, he wrote, "shall have those bruites their servants, their slaves."[22]

Throughout the 1650s, the natives knew that the Dutch were capable of harboring visions of dispossessing them. One can only suspect that they would have been unsurprised to learn that in 1644 the States had to dismiss their extermination as one party's way of recovering peace in New Netherland. But they knew, too, that the Dutch had neither the will nor the power to do so. That was the danger in revealing to them that someone in high office was telling the resident authorities to "conciliate and to satisfy" them.

The Dutch still wanted control over clients and not mastery over territories. They needed chiefs able to command followers prepared to deliver trading goods peacefully and with regularity. Contracts and perhaps payments of tribute could be negotiated. The tribes would be controlled without the need to annex, administer, or enter their lands. Again and again, complainants— even "all of . . . [us who] without exception had or could have good employers in Fatherland"—were refused permission to begin outlying settlements. The administration, they complained, mock us if we try to possess the land.[23]

The natives of the southern waterlands were not offering themselves as partners to these arrangements. They were not guaranteeing the expected loyalty and predictability. So while the Dutch retained control over the market in peltries and could enforce a good deal of native cooperation, they continued to look in vain for leaders who could command widespread allegiances and by that ensure the orderly delivery of pelts, wampum, and maize. Perhaps Kieft's war had taught them that the native groups' hunger for autonomy was a madness that they could not cure.

Perhaps they knew (as we think we do now) that the people they called the Raritans were—they alone—divided into two sachemdoms and about twenty chieftaincies. Perhaps they knew that subdivisions of people immediately north and south of Pavonia were themselves subdivided—and no one knows to this day whether one group was equal to another in size and importance. On Long Island in 1653, colonists were saying that they couldn't deal with the natives who were committing murders under the pretext that they had not been paid for their lands. We don't know "to what nation these murderers belong." Two years later, Stuyvesant echoed their frustration. The sheer variety of tribes and subgroups meant that he kept as prisoners natives of one tribe in order to exchange them for hostages kept by another tribe. It was, he said, dishonest.[24]

This was defeating them. In 1650, the company conceded that market controls on furs were not holding. The sellers could not be managed. We would exert our rights, they wrote, if only we could think of the proper means. The situation had been the same in 1644 when the community was debating how to force the natives to cooperate. But the solution was not a redirection into success measured by occupancy of the native lands. That would suggest that a people could release themselves from self-identifying mythologies and satisfying ways of living. An analogue offers itself in the decision making of Jan de Witt and the Amsterdam burgomasters regarding the Netherlands army in the third quarter of the seventeenth century. The army desperately needed to be strengthened. But, as we have already seen, army and navy were emblems of a continental military policy versus a maritime one; they lay on the surface of complex polarities that constituted Dutch self-identity. So the grand pensionary and regents embraced indecision. They could not, as one writer put it, shake off the determination "never to sacrifice the strength of the navy for a reinforcement of the army."[25]

Writing his *Description of the New Netherlands* in the early 1650s, Adriaen vander Donck created a character who tells us why shaking off alongshore ways was essentially impossible. The Patriot makes only a brief appearance. We have met him before. Here vander Donck gives him the lines of a wise man: "Places which will suit us must possess convenient situations for trade; otherwise they will not please us, although the territory be ever so great." The Patriot's commonsense wisdom rings through the stories of the Dutch and the lands of New Netherland. The strangers were still maritime people. In 1638 Kieft, for example, referred to colonists killed by natives at Swanendael on the South River. By their deaths and our strategic forts, he wrote, a river is ours. Sixteen years later, Stuyvesant and his council faced a dilemma in strengthening Manhattan Island against the threat of an English attack. They could either recall soldiers at Fort Casimir on the Delaware River or leave them in place. We need to retain the distant garrison, the council decided, lest we lose the beautiful river to others.

A year later, they had ejected the Swedes from some of the lands we call Delaware. But Stuyvesant's words were: we have reduced "that river . . . to the jurisdiction of this Province."[26]

Back in the early 1650s, the island's burghers were saying that control of a river established legal possession to land. They considered Connecticut. The English, they argued, have invaded it "because, as they say, the land lay unoccupied and waste, which was none of their business, and, besides, was not true." Why untrue? Because "on the river a fort had already existed, which continued to be occupied by a garrison."[27]

Officially, the company continued its mantra about coasts, shorelands, bays, rivers, and islands. When the directors complained to Stuyvesant that the English had seized Dutch lands west of Cape Cod, they gave priority to four islands: Rhode Island, Martha's Vineyard, Block Island, and the island directly in front of Sloop's Bay. Meanwhile, they knew how to accommodate their kind of colonists. No one, it decreed grandly, shall be excluded from using "the public waters, creeks, bays and rivers, and from appropriating any islands, sandspits and dry marshes" (all belonging first to the Company). In 1650, the directors were anxious because the English were proposing a war with the Wappings north of Manhattan Island. If they won (which they would), they would be masters of—a river. They would control "the whole North river and with it . . . the fur trade." Much better the Wappings as nearby landowners.[28]

One of the characters in Melijn's pamphlet was a traveler from the seaport of Naples. Melijn lets him speak as wisely as vander Donck's Patriot. "You know well," he says to the Dutch skipper, "that you must live by the merchants."[29] In New Netherland, the question of living in any other way never arose. The war against the natives had borne the deadly marks of maritime entrepreneurs. The places of violence—the exceptions are inland sites to which Underhill led Dutch and English forces—could best be closed upon by the steersman of a yacht (Map 3). The clash between Kieft and his accusers was one of traders versus traders. The new resident director was one of the company's most skillful and experienced merchants.

*   *   *

Petrus Stuyvesant was born at Peperga in the waterlands of western Friesland. His father was a supercargo for the company and had hopes for his son's advancement in its overseas ventures. When a commission came to the young man as director-general of New Netherland, it obliged him to take an amphibious role. It allowed him a title redolent of Coen's East Indies and, in its wording, the wonderworld of Jan Huyghen van Linschoten: "Petrus Stuyvesant, director-general of New Netherland, Curaçao and the islands thereof, commander in chief of the Company's ships and yachts cruising the West Indies." Soldiers under his command would be the company's grasshoppers: when necessary, his orders read, "inflict a much injury as possible on the enemy in his forts and strongholds as well by land as by sea."

On Manhattan Island, few cared to praise Stuyvesant. When he was mocked, it was as a merchant, a petty dishonorable one. Melijn wrote that he sought to share in the profits of every merchant's trade. "He is a brewer; he is a ship-owner; he carries on alone all kinds of business which we all do."[30] Stuyvesant was not, however, a petty or dishonorable man. He often called upon a metaphor to express his image of the honorable man. Not surprisingly, his model was the ship's captain. Not surprising, either, given his professional career in New Netherland from 1647 to 1664, he considered such an officer to be most honorable when taking decisive command, fulfilling his oath of loyalty to his superiors and conscientiously acting to avoid loss of his ship. As he wrote, the admirable man refuses to suffer the shipwreck of his honor and oath. Elsewhere: he keeps "good watch and an eye on the sail."[31]

In the third year of Stuyvesant's administration, in 1649, Hollanders at home were eagerly buying seventh-edition copies of the journal and log of Willem Bontekoe. The skipper from Hoorn was possibly the Netherlanders' most beloved hero. He was bold in his adventuring and loved by his men, some of whose lives he saved when his ship caught fire in 1619 and sank off the coast of Madagascar. Bontekoe's journal also sparkled with his exploits as merchant voyager in the islands of the Indies. Like Stuyvesant, he was the most ordinary man thrust into and required to surmount extraordinary circumstances.[32]

Six years later, David Pietersz de Vries was marketing himself as another heroic voyaging figure, publishing his journal as *Korte Historiael ende Journaels*. To Dutch men and women, his was the best of all possible worlds. He was a businessman who owned his own trading vessel, a practiced supercargo and a superb seaman. Sailing out of Hoorn—he was about six years younger than Bontekoe and, like him, would one day meet up with Coen in the Indies—he had completed six long-distance ocean voyages, three of them to the West Indies and New Netherland. De Vries was a master of self-promotion. He presented himself filling many admirable roles. He was master of a trading vessel and not a ship of war (he was, he pointed out, from too prestigious a family for that); he was the skilled coastal navigator whose journals would, he promised, tell of "dangerous strands and treacherous shallows to watch out for." He was also the religious man, the patriot ("advancing and improving" the country's prosperity by his navigations and explorations), the ideal Hollander loyal to his own values, his province, and city; and the picaresque figure, "a Person who has worn himself out on the wild fierce wastes of the sea."[33] As much as he made himself eyewitness to the things of the far-flung world, he made himself the object of his eyewitnessing. "Here I Go on my Third Voyage to New Netherland and America," he told readers, announcing his 1638 voyage. Or, of the journey begun in 1634: "This is My Second Voyage to the Coast of America and the Wild Coast of the West Indies." For those who wished to take his lead, he made himself the subject of his remarkable and exotic stories.[34]

Stuyvesant's captaincy of the ship of New Netherland was on wild, fierce wastes of the sea as well. He encountered the turbulence of recalcitrant burghers, hostile natives, and treacherous English and Swedish neighbors. He was buffeted by disloyal councillors with whom he was under oath to share decision making, and by the distrusting and shortsighted bureaucrats of a near-bankrupt company. Many thought, often with good reason, that his own reluctance to share power would be enough to drive the vessel aground. In all the stories we are going to hear now, that is, during the seventeen years of his administration, no one was going to call him (as Bontekoe's crew did) "beloved skipper." In many respects, the company should have done so. But, as in all things, it was too niggardly to praise its servants. However extraordinary their contribution, it preferred to put a price tag on their services. The East India Company itemized Coen's service in 1623: commander of the *retourvloet* (return fleet), 100 reals; director-general, 500 guilders per month and for "good service rendered," an added sum of 3,000 guilders; founder of the general rendezvous and Batavia, 7,000 guilders. And a small sum to forestall any additional claims he might think up.[35]

Stuyvesant was consistently obedient to the company's directives regarding the natives. These moved between two extremes. First, the directors wanted to implement the irenic vision expressed in an East India Company directive of 1650. "Company trade over the whole of the Indies," directed the Amsterdam chamber, must be based on "the common right of all peoples, consisting in freedom of commerce, the which being granted in neutral places by free nations where we find laws and do not have to bring them, we may not appropriate the aforesaid trade to our own ideas and constrain such nations thereto by force." Consistent with this and adhering to company policy regarding the nearby native traders and landowners, Stuyvesant wrote in his first year to Governor Winthrop in Boston, "I reallie indeavoured to establish a firme peace."[36]

At the other extreme, the company's policy was tainted with treachery. Generally, Stuyvesant was told to bide his time until a stronger military Dutch presence might persuade the Americans to engage in further years of undisturbed commercial intercourse or face a decisive military defeat. Once, in 1657, they made explicit the duplicity enfolded within their forbearance: woo the

Long Island natives since we understand them to be conciliatory; attack the more dangerous tribes whenever the friendly natives can be used and the time is most convenient. Stuyvesant read their intentions clearly. When they directed him in 1648 to control the natives with kindness, he knew that he had little choice but to do so. He invoked the same policy a decade later when considering hostilities against the Esopus. For prudence's sake, he reported to uneasy settlers, we've deferred taking action "to a better time and chance"[37] (Fig. 16).

Stuyvesant's repeated peace efforts were the theater of this realization. But his own uncertain position together with the unpredictable circumstances affecting the Americans' decisions made for a dangerous game of situation politics. In 1655, he was negotiating from a position of weakness. More often (1649, 1659–60, 1663–64), he could deal from a position of strength. But this was only the case if he exercised the diplomatic skills necessary to bring the Mohawks on his side in an alliance that kept the waterlands tribes subservient to their more powerful northern neighbors. He was generally a careful negotiator. Opportunistically he listened, gave gifts, made concessions, and strove for a wearying equilibrium that would ensure orderly trade.[38] On one occasion, he agreed to a bizarre arrangement for the release of about forty-five captives. Forty-four Mohawks would travel to the place of their captivity and each take a prisoner's hand to lead him or her away. For their part, local Dutch leaders wanted no part of peacemaking. Too much, wrote one man slyly, would have to be accounted for. On at least one occasion, Stuyvesant broke his promise to native representatives. Assuring them of their chiefs' release, he nonetheless sent them to Curaçao. It was an unforgivable act of cruelty. As we'll see, it was still causing repercussions when the province was lost to the English in 1664.[39]

* * *

Stuyvesant's negotiations with the Americans threatened to be blunted by two realities. The first is copiously detailed in the archives. The second is subtextual but more powerful because it encompassed the first while embracing much more. Stuyvesant's conciliation of the natives regularly incited antagonism among rebellious groups of colonists variously recorded as villagers, the patroon's colonists, disloyal English farmers on Long Island, and *boers* seeking, as he wrote derisively, their distant and lonely places. In 1649, some wanted guns. He refused because the company wanted peace. In the same year, he refused military aid to a group of Long Islanders on the specious grounds that their alleged native antagonists lived at a great distance and, by implication, engagement with them would require a major expedition. A year later, in 1658, settlers at Esopus wanted him to begin a war against the local natives.

Figure 16. Petrus Stuyvesant is one of our most important informants on native lives on and around Manhattan Island. As New Netherland's administrator, he observed the Americans for seventeen years, from 1647 to 1664. His descriptions of them are inconsistent and contradictory. Perhaps in that they are a faithful response to cross-cultural encounters, necessarily in constant flux. His policies ranged from vengeful raids into native lands to genuine efforts at peacemaking. Perhaps his only unchanging policy was for native relocation and separation—as we would call it, (nonracial) apartheid.

Black-and-white reproductions of this portrait harden Stuyvesant's features. They legitimate an interpretation of him as autocratic, intolerant, and (always) "stubborn." The painter's original colors soften his appearance especially around the eyes and upper face and suggest a different interpretation. Hendrick Couturier (attributed), *Peter Stuyvesant*, c. 1660. New-York Historical Society.

Again he refused. He called upon the past, acknowledging to them what he refused to admit to the Esopus natives the following day. Kieft's war did concern him. Five years earlier, he had admitted to the jealousies, troubles, and quarrels that had arisen during Kieft's time. Now he was more specific. This is not the time, he argued, "to involve the whole country in a general war." We have previously experienced "massacres, incendiary fires, sustained losses, injuries and insults." But we have been patient. We must be that now: bide out time, negotiate, cut a deal for the sake of peace.[40]

But a second reality was threatening to deaden the efficacy of watchful waiting. Some colonists as well as the directors at home were voicing the possibility of altering their fundamental military posture vis-à-vis those natives who continued to act as their enemies. The voice called for taking offensive military action against the natives rather than maintaining a defensive position. Its sound was intermittent, it disappeared (but reemerged), and it was opaque and ambiguous.

It was opposed. But it was there.

Chapter 15
Alongshore Compromised

The story is told of a captain navigating around an island south of Yemen. He is steering by the stars. Every three hours, he tells a passenger, you must change to a new pair of stars, as the old ones fall away. The Polynesians called it way-finding.

In its own way, the West India Company had been steering by the stars since 1619. More than once, it had looked to a new pair of stars for profits—and often for survival. Setting out, the directors had considered (and rejected) a scheme for colonies, then steered in the direction of commercial exploration and the founding of trading stations. Then they adjusted course following the allure of privateering. In the 1650s, the steersmen were taking direction from the promising glimmer of colonization.

Between 1645 and 1664, the threat made to the natives was slowly coming true. The European population of New Netherland was growing steadily. From about five hundred residents it would increase eighteen-fold, to almost nine thousand. In 1652, the directors were reading the skies, catching the direction of things, and calculating their future prospects. New Netherland's growth, they wrote the burgomasters of Amsterdam, is strong and will apparently continue. To Stuyvesant, they wrote that it now appears that we'll soon "have a large population there."[1]

Three hundred and forty-four years later, a scholar gave poetic (if melancholic) expression to the future into which the directors and other Netherlanders were now about to move the strangers and natives of New Netherland. "There is something uneasy about empire," he began. At first, it requires no homes. The authority from which it derives its form, function, and purpose "is easily sustained by forts and barracks and offices." But soon, he continued, settlements and towns grow as empire is "seized by the urge to make a home of its territory."[2]

The company was slowly and reluctantly coming to realize that colonization could be the pot of gold denied them by the peace with Spain. The presence of thousands of residents would create commodity markets from which it could skim off the profits. It would provide income from the sale or leasing of urban and rural lands. Taxes on real estate could be laid. Its expertise in seagoing transport and communications would also come into play and be turned into profits.

Imagine it. Several thousand overseas people in need of goods from the Netherlands. The same people with products to export. You, the company, control both ends of the ocean trade route: yours are the convoy and customs fees and all incidental charges. Imagine the numbers of people wishing to emigrate and then make return voyages to Holland to attend to business and family affairs. Skippers not in your employ will be allowed to carry such passengers. But your skippers and ships are in the majority. In any case, the private charters have to pay your charges and fees when the sea gives way to wharves, roadsteads, and lighters: the alongshore of a trading company.

In Amsterdam in 1656, the procedures of this colonizing decade were moving into place. A good way to watch them get under way is to pick up one of the permits filled in by a skipper intending to voyage to New Netherland. By the mid-1650s, they were no longer handwritten but printed. The skipper need only fill in his name and that of his ship, then add the date and his signature before returning the form to a company employee.

Note the fees that must be paid: warehousing, wharfage, import and export duties, fines for infringement of company regulations—just some of the control mechanisms and income possibilities in a maritime world business. The skipper may make a voyage to "New Netherland within the limits of the Company's charter," the permit reads. Before taking any merchandise aboard ship, he must bring it into the company's warehouse to be inspected and imprinted with the company's mark. He must immediately pay "sixteen percent on the Indian goods such as duffels and blankets, and ten percent on all other goods and merchandise."

After fulfilling these requirements and crossing from Texel (and touching no other place), he must anchor at the roadstead before Fort Amsterdam, where the goods and merchandise on board must be brought into the company's warehouses, after which the skipper or supercargo is free to "remove them in order to sell them within the district of New Netherland, New England and Virginia." On his return to Amsterdam, the skipper must again pay warehouse fees and duties: eight percent on goods and merchandise but special charges on furs and tobacco. All the while, he will have carried on board a company supercargo whose "board and lodging in the cabin" were at his expense. He will also have carried company soldiers and emigrants, as many as the company demands.[3]

The permit documented the bureaucratic project into which the company had now thrust itself. It caught the role of ships in New Netherland's colonization—and the place of wharves and cranes, roadsteads and necessary waterside buildings. It caught colonialization as a maritime affair. It did not capture its danger to peaceful relations with the Amerindians. But the threat was there.

Another moment of imagination was inscribed in a plan for trade and emigration devised in 1656. The city of Amsterdam and the company were working out a joint venture. Given the many sorrows and defeats that the Dutch had already experienced in New Netherland, the plan may seem utopian. But it was part of a world imagined by tough-minded entrepreneurs.

In mid-summer of 1656, the council of Amsterdam drafted a plan to encourage trade and emigration to New Netherland and sent it for approval to the West India Company and the States. Both offered support, and the project went forward. A new North American center of trade would replace the neglected fort and settlement along the Delaware River and be named New Amstel (New Castle, Delaware).[4]

Perhaps the Amsterdam plan was not very imaginative. It simply replicated overseas what the Amsterdam merchants were observing all around them. What they saw in Holland was a compact cluster of prosperous mercantile cities—Amsterdam, Delft, Dordrecht, Haarlem, Leiden, 's-Gravenhage, Rotterdam—each on a harbor or river and all crowded onto about sixty square miles of land. About 60 percent of the residents were city dwellers, that is, about 480,000 of between 825,000 and 900,000 people. So perhaps it was not surprising that the investors planned to create in North America a site that would one day deliver a similar prosperity. They intended to establish a walled trading city on a strong and navigable river. ("Fiat" agreed the company directors. But its purchase must not disturb their amicable relations with the natives. Any lands selected but belonging to the natives must be made known to the resident director so that they may be received "after the Indians are satisfied.") A large warehouse, a building suitable for religious services, and houses for a school and the minister would frame its marketplace. Roads would carry local products from nearby fields. Netherlands towns and cities, as one authority has written, were not chance growth. They were almost always planned. This was an American one.[5]

The river and its traffic along the strand would seal the city's character as a trading center. Accessed by deep-draught ships, it would ensure the widest possible orientation toward Manhattan Island and Amsterdam, the Virginias, and Boston—and in that was its hope for prosperity. It would double the identity of the imagined colonists—as city dwellers and as *oeverbewoners*, tidewater people.

The Amsterdam authorities were not supporting emigration for flag, honor, or overseas territorial dominion. Rather, they foresaw a commercial partnership mutually beneficial to the emigrants and themselves. They explicitly abrogated any role in governance abroad, stating, "the government of Amsterdam hath no intention to extend any authority or power abroad." It "merely designs to promote commerce, which is the life of this City."[6]

*   *   *

This vision of New Amstel can be read for two messages. First, it is an announcement of trust in New Netherland as a site for the promotion of more than one viable commercial center. Second, it is a statement of lack of interest in colonizing a strictly settler society. A mid-nineteenth-century editor prefaced a document regarding the regents' project as a "plan to colonize New Netherland." But the plan was, as it reads, "for the encouragement of trade."[7] The Amsterdam regents intended, as they said—and who in 1656 could have been surprised at this—to avoid any assumption of power and authority abroad. Amsterdam was a municipal corporation setting up a potentially useful overseas trading center. It was not in the business of setting up an agricultural colony requiring the West India Company to annex and then administer the territory of others.

Reluctance to initiate such a pattern of colonization was the outcome of many cultural factors. We have already considered a number of them. It was tied to distrust of those who offered themselves as colonials: petty and transient traders looking only to their own interests; cashiered company soldiers staying overseas as hangers-on; ignorant, mischievous, and usually useless *boers*—not to be trusted either. Let us, demanded an early East Indies official, make ours the wise distrust of Romulus regarding colonization. Meaning? No women, and distribute no more than two acres of land to our personnel and soldiers.[8]

Over the past years, the West India Company directors had openly expressed their distrust of New Netherlanders who were not expressly company personnel. In Verhulst's time, their distrust fell on free burghers and non-company colonists. Later, when they had lost their contest with the patroons and been forced to open the inland trade, the directors continued to differentiate between the patroons' colonists who were *inland* and its servants on the *island* of Manhattan. In 1634, they pointed out that such colonists were an added and onerous obligation: if necessary, they had to be provided with military assistance.[9]

For many years, the patroon's agriculturalists and those working on Manhattan Island were considered a necessary evil. They were a peasantry or, if not that, unpromisingly poor. One officer of van Rensselaer's *colonie* wrote home in 1630 saying that land was plowed daily on the island. He looked abroad, however, and saw it in the hands of a peasantry. Until the mid-1640s, the landsmen were also described as peasants rather than farmers, as men and women bonded into service. They were the poor, those forbidden to buy native lands and whose description fitted alongside people from almshouses. Kiliaen van Rensselaer dismissed them as poor beggars. The best people, he wrote elsewhere, "seldom go so far across the sea."[10]

Kieft's war taught the directors a lesson. Or, better, they were forced to read lessons from a primer thrust at them by the States and representative New Netherlanders. Promote emigration or lose everything. But who? Of what sort? New Netherlanders were warning them in the early 1650s that the country was overrun with people of small means. We need to bring to New Netherland the willing and poor people "who are in each other's way . . . [in the Netherlands] and almost perish of want." But we also need, agreed others, traders with some capital. The company's directors were beginning to entertain the same thoughts. We hope, they wrote, "wealthy people might take a fancy to these lands." It was a repetition of Coen's cry for a genuine *burgermaatschappij*.[11]

That kind of society was steadily emerging. Two distinct groups of New Netherlanders had voices in the records of Kieft's war. They were the company men and the *gemeente*, or municipal commonalty of burghers. A third group was present but without a voice. The country folk were spoken for. When Kieft failed to alert them to imminent danger from native attack after 1643, there was, except for the burghers' criticism of his dereliction of duty, silence. Nor were they among the men allowed to air their grievances before the company or the States in Holland. No one seemed to think they should be.

Boers were politically inconsequential. They seldom appeared in the records and, when they did, seemed to have been numerically insignificant as well. Two years after the peace of 1645, it was expected that "all the farmers" who had cultivated and occupied land for over ten years on Manhattan Island could fit inside the walls of the fort. The war was not, in anyone's estimation, the result of such agriculturalists advancing onto some sort of native frontier. A later historian was going to use the word "pioneers" for such non-traders in early New Netherland. They were nothing of the kind: not numerically, not by intent. Not even later.[12]

The commentaries on the war are specific. One of its causes was the proximity of natives and strangers. The natives' complaints about cattle straying onto their unfenced lands were frequent enough to reach into the records, find their way to Amsterdam and The Hague, and call for remedial measures. But who were the cattle's owners? Who had this complaint made momentarily visible? Were they landsmen engaged in illicit trading? Or were they traders keeping a few cattle? Everyone knew that settling in the country's interior meant getting an unsupervised foothold somewhere as a trader. Kieft probably had it right when he or one of his supporters suggested that, unfortunately, the opportunity to trade (and not to farm) was the cause of increased population in New Netherland.[13]

That was the late 1640s. The farmers from 1652 to 1664 were different. But how significantly would their numbers and aspirations compromise the maritime interests of merchant entrepreneurs? Those interests depended on, among other things, native tribes having reasonably viable economies. Wouldn't a large influx of agriculturalists mean dispossessed natives and, rather than the success of both economies, the complete failure of theirs for the profit of the strangers? By now, it was clear that the intensive agriculture characteristic of the province of Holland was not going to be duplicated here. The environment had determined that farming would more closely resemble that of the eastern provinces, where sustainable yields would come from larger properties. Were they worth it? Representations of *boers* at home invariably leaned on notions of them as inherently violent. Would they be violent here, and destroy the already brittle relations with the natives?

Contemporary Dutch representations of the *boer* ranged across extremes. But the *boer* as primitive recurred insistently. They always, one critic wrote, "seem to drink, vomit, make crude remarks and fight." Learned men dismissed them as slow-witted, similar to brute animals, mentally and temperamentally incapable of being political rebels, the mad dogs despised earlier by Martin Luther. Jan Steen learned to paint "visual noise" when portraying them. He created deliberate disorder by composing canvases with crisscrossing diagonal lines and obtuse angles rather than the parallel lines and right angles of restful genre paintings.[14]

Maerten van Cleve's painting *Peasants Attacking Soldiers* pulsates with the animality of the landsman. The enraged face of the *boer* is feral. The forehead slants downward to excessively heavy eyebrows raised over crazed eyes. Not surprisingly, his wild face matches that of his victim, the soldier. Each seems to recognize in the other a shared primitiveness. Van Cleve takes care to liken the head covering of the attacking peasant to that of a soldier in the background, with the *boer*'s cloth cap replicating the metal helmet glinting on the head of the man on horseback. The anonymous peasant carries a knife, a symbol of the *boers*. But all take pleasure in using weapons (Fig. 17).

In *Peasants Attacking Soldiers,* van Cleve represents the sharp divide between the social universes of country people and those whom Dutch society had constructed into persons of civic rectitude, those considered *burgerlijke.* The Dutch had worked diligently to ensure the distinction. Legislation gave special protection to the *burgerrecht* and courts merchant; laws ensured the economic dominance of cities over their hinterlands; popular propositions circulated, such as "if it goes well with the merchants, then it goes well with one hundred thousand common laborers." The Dutch could worship at the altar of *civitas* and their own bourgeois elitism partly because there were the *boers* to personify everything they didn't want to think of themselves as being.[15]

Netherlanders welcomed comedies that placed the *boer* within a wholly different social structure. Doggerel and plays ridiculed farmers, often holding up for examination their allegedly uncontrolled sexual appetite. Alternatively, they denied the rustic presence. He is not dignified in Hooft's *Historiën* as

Figure 17. Holland's burghers often identified peasants with soldiers. Both were animalistic, deformed by the labor they did, and prone to the violence of savages. Maerten van Cleve, *Raufhandel (Peasants Attacking Soldiers)*, mid-seventeenth century (detail). Kunsthistorisches Museum, Vienna.

patriotic rebel or heroic victim of the wars. As we have seen, much the same could be said of the commentators on Kieft's war. Similarly, surprisingly few Dutch landscapes showed farmers at work. Dutch landscapists seldom elucidated what rural social and economic conditions were actually like. Rather, anonymous men, women, and sometimes children inhabited their works, their unimportance suggested by the term "staffage," referring to figures often added by an apprentice artist after the completion of a landscape. Dutch pictures of such colonies as Java and Brazil—so full of flora, fauna, and exotic peoples— show little of rural colonial working life.[16]

The *boer,* then, teetered on the edge of typologies whose negativities the merchant or artisan-tradesman needn't have feared. Distrust, while among the least malicious of the attitudes toward him, was a residue of the others. There were moments when pamphleteers allowed peasant farmers to slide out of the category of the primitive and into that of the literate body politic with interests in the international and economic life of the republic. And well they should: men from the rural marshes of the waterlands whose storytelling we've glimpsed were only some of the landsmen who, for example, went to sea and returned with profits from overseas trade. But they were not part of the *gemeente ing-hesetten,* the decision-making community of burghers. To those in New Netherland who wrote the remonstrance of 1649, they were "simple and uninformed."[17]

* * *

Generally, from 1652 to 1664 the New Netherland *boers* joined the soldiers as staffage in the pictures painted by company personnel. Like the hired soldiers we met earlier, they appear as incidental figures on a larger mercantile landscape. Occasionally, however, they are drawn in some detail—and made to look neither simple nor uninformed. One such verbal painting depicts those on Long Island between 1653 and 1657. We need to consider them because they adopted positions of violence and disloyalty to the provincial authorities as a result of desiring native lands.

The determination of the Dutch farmers on Long Island to take a free hand in engrossing native lands made itself known in 1653 and 1654. The year before, in 1652, England and the United Provinces had engaged each other in a naval war over navigation regulations. Dutch overseas trading stations were immediately in danger, especially in places such as New Netherland, where they were in close proximity to the English and were already rivals.

In New Netherland, the director-general and council began the usual preparations for what they believed would be "a surprise attack and massacre." They strengthened water and shore defenses and paid city burghers to assist the soldiers as a defensive force. Collecting grain and other provisions for a protracted siege, they canceled the departure of all ships. They put their situation simply: if Fort Amsterdam and New Amsterdam are lost, "the country and all is lost, and if held with sufficient assistance, the country also is held."[18]

But the months of war preparations allowed interest groups to make demands. In exchange for desperately needed assistance, New Amsterdam's officials demanded extended municipal privileges: to farm the excise on beer, to collect the taxes on immovable property. In early December 1653, they won major concessions from Stuyvesant and by the next spring were supportive of his defensive strategies for the province. The crisis months also forced Stuyvesant to recognize the Dutch farmers on Long Island as a distinct interest group. He and the New Amsterdam burghers learned quickly enough that however perilous their situation, no assistance could be expected from them. They had refused to help repair fortifications and denied requests to bring grain into the city. They have their farms to protect, wrote Stuyvesant. But their steady refusal to man construction works has instilled a fear among us. We are certain, he later wrote, that "country people will not come to help us."

By now, the leaders of New Amsterdam had also come to distrust the villagers. Even though they had organized three or four expeditions onto the island for their protection, they had received no assistance in return.[19] Stuyvesant's anger and sense of danger went deeper. The farmers were crossing the border into English ideas about local autonomy and landownership. Traitorous farmers "of our own nationality," he wrote, have sided with the English Long Islanders, using this dangerous time to join the English in questioning the legitimacy of the provincial government.[20]

They wanted greater political autonomy. Stuyvesant knew exactly what that meant. Among other things, they wanted a right that Englishmen enjoyed: to settle on native lands wherever they pleased. He would have known as clearly as the Dutch delegates who had met with their English counterparts back in 1632 just where they and the English disagreed on native rights. He could see the practices that Dutch farmers were now observing in their neighbors' villages. It was commonplace English behavior, and he laid it out with merciless clarity. They take an already "liberal patent" and "make . . . [it] cover more than its contents allow." Just the reverse of official Dutch practice. As long as Dutch policies contradicting arbitrary appropriation were in place, that was not going to happen here—not legally.[21]

The farmers presented their complaints to Stuyvesant in December 1653 before sending them to the States in Holland. He shot back a response within forty-eight hours. The Dutch signatories were simply ignorant. They were a herd filling their heads with ideas essentially English and threatening to disrupt carefully poised Dutch-native relations. They (and some from New Amsterdam) had signed a document that was not even originally written in Dutch. Its foreign "tenor," he wrote, was immediately obvious. The fact that it was inscribed in English and then badly translated for presentation to him was additionally infuriating. Was there, he sneered, "no one of Dutch origin intelligent enough and capable to draft a petition to the director-general and council"? Were the delegates from among the Dutch so stupid that "an Englishman must prescribe what they should remonstrate and demand"?

He had immediately summoned the New Amsterdammers who had signed and those he identified as "most of the signatories"—perhaps not bothering with the farmers. He made them squirm in their ignorance. What do you understand—he had his secretary record—by "an arbitrary government"? "There was no response." They couldn't state, he reported, why the present government here is contrary to the principles of all "well-regulated states." At least with the burghers, he was willing to talk. To the Dutch farmers of Flatbush, Amersfoort, and Breuckelen, he concluded dismissively: your participation in any sort of assembly is illegal. Keep your people at home.[22]

The farmers were not, however, losing every altercation with Stuyvesant. About eighteen months before their ill-advised petition, one of them, a farmer from Flatbush, had cornered him in a dilemma. Again and again, the company directors had instructed him to keep the peace with the natives. He was to make only those purchases of native lands necessary for the company and residents but certainly not with large sums of company money, and certainly not if they'd already purchased the land.

But now, he had promised five hundred guilders to a farmer, Jan Snediger, as payment to some Canarsee natives for a parcel of land in Flatbush within lands previously purchased by the company. Leaving the matter of previous purchase aside, five hundred guilders was an extraordinarily generous payment. Only five years earlier, he had purchased much of Westchester County for 6 fathoms of duffels; 6 strings of wampum; 6 kettles, axes, and adzes; 10 knives and some corals and iron; a gun; 2 staves of lead; 2 pounds of powder; and a duffel coat. The usual thing. But the Flatbush farmers had him cornered. If he wanted them to leave their dispersed farms and move into a compact settlement, they needed (so they said) the whole of the land. So he needed to explain his decision to the council. More seriously, he needed to have his reasons and the council's approval minuted for the directors in Holland, who would one day almost surely see the records concerning the expenditure.

Presenting reasons for his decision, he wavered on the matter of the land's ownership. "I was somewhat in doubt," he let his secretary record, "whether the Indians had a better claim . . . than the other Christian people." He asked himself what constituted proof of ownership. As an answer, he did not adopt the English position that the natives could not be bona fide possessors because they were somehow nomadic. Rather, he worried that the passage of time from earliest purchases together with the indeterminate membership of contemporary natives in one tribe or another pointed to the impossibility of determining descent of title. "What proof and assurance could be produced that the Indians had a better right and title to the parcel of land than other Indians, even more than the greatest sachem or chiefs who a long time ago had sold, given and ceded the whole piece of land . . . to . . . the honorable company"?

In over a year's time, the farmers were taunting him with his insistence that only the company could purchase native lands. Perhaps so, they said, but it wasn't paying up. Now murders had occurred, and a war was looming because the natives had not been paid for their lands. Stuyvesant denied this. He blamed the farmers for inciting the natives and exonerated himself and the company. You, not we, are cheating them. They think they sold land too cheaply earlier because you're telling them the current price of an acre among the Dutch and English. You're the ones provoking war. You're also wrong and in bad faith in asserting that they committed murders under the pretext of not having been paid for their lands. You're lying and haven't bothered to investigate. I have investigated, and it has to do with Staten Island and natives (as they claim) cheated there. "We purchased the soil with our own money," you insist. That's an absolute falsehood. No private party, he reiterated, can "purchase land from the natives without the consent of the director-general and council."[23]

But here were new arguments. Customary for the English. New for the Dutch farmers who were now moving within the same discourse.

Stuyvesant undoubtedly knew he had failed to quiet the disaffected farmers. Their openness to English ways had been real and disturbing. To oppose pirates raiding the Long Island coasts at this same time, Dutch and English villagers (and others from New Amsterdam) planned to act together against them without Stuyvesant's knowledge or authority. They were still saying that this place might require new laws and orders "resembling as near as possible those of the Netherlands."[24]

* * *

The instances of rebelliousness and the failure to consider the consequences of seriously undermining Dutch authority were undeniable signs of newcomers' willingness to contest the company's control of land policy and destabilize relations with the natives. During these same months, another canvas caught Stuyvesant in dispute with the *boers* who had come to live among them.

He had charged ten farmers and farm servants with pulling the goose on Shrove Tuesday, the day before the beginning of Lent—or the feast of Bacchus, as Stuyvesant preferred. It was a superstitious and crude rural custom in which a goose, with its neck greased, hung suspended upside-down on a rope set between two trees. Contestants mounted on horseback strove to pull off the goose's head. Such a practice, he declared, has never been the custom of this country. We do not want it introduced here, even though some might claim that such evil customs are tolerated in some places in our fatherland.[25]

He might have said, in some places "in the outer provinces" of our fatherland. For six of the ten men whose origins can be traced had arrived from farming communities in the eastern provinces. Three of their villages lay within twenty-five kilometers of the present border with Germany.[26]

One man, Jan Jacobsz van Gietere (Gieteren), came from Drenthe, which was already a place of desolate moors, swamps, and scrub. The wars had made it a wasteland sustaining nothing more than a peasant economy. Isolated from the rest of the Netherlands by impenetrable peat bogs and the lack of surface roads, the district was described as "ordained by the punishing hand of God as a plague to the people." Farmers from Jacobsz's district were inordinately poor and considered foreign. Outsiders ridiculed them for lacking imagination and living with superstition. Later, Drents people also felt they were backward; they feared being laughed at and were therefore evasive. And laughed at they were. When seventeenth-century playwrights wanted to incite side-splitting glee, they created the Drents farmer. In Samuel Costers's comedy, he is a farting German—fat, obtuse, feckless, and lacking in virility[27] (Map 1).

But Jan Snediger was a Drents farmer, too. Perhaps he was unimaginative and feared being ridiculed. Perhaps he and the others felt the distancing of Stuyvesant and his municipal merchant associates. But he had the wit to get the best of him and would be one of many to get the best of the coastal native Americans on Long Island. The danger was not that they were introducing such folkloric practices as pulling the goose but that their numbers represented a social anomaly. In 1654, the resident director and his council had done their sums on the occupational distribution of New Netherlanders on and around Manhattan Island and found: the farmers "number the most." In a maritime province such as New Netherland, that shouldn't be.[28] It wasn't so in Holland.

Yet the company itself was aiding other Netherlanders in bringing over farmers. Opportunism and a growing disregard for the rights of the natives were undermining a care for the spatial compactness essential to an overseas trading enterprise. The earlier image of factories as beached *handelsscheepen* ready to be cut loose wherever advantageous was less and less a reality.

West beyond Staten Island and along the continental coast, groups of Algonquian-speakers farmed, fished, and hunted. They seem to have excelled in hoe gardening, planting six kinds of maize on probably two to three acres for each family. We have encountered them many times. The Nevesinks (later Navesinks) lived in the highlands south of Sandy Hook. (On a clear day, their lands could be seen from Manhattan Island.) In the river valleys north of them lived the Raritans. To their north, the Hackensacks lived on lands watered by the Hackensack and Passaic Rivers. Still farther north were the Aquackanonks and Tappans (Map 2).

But now the lands ruled by men and groups with these strange names— and there were many more—were being claimed by men and groups with new and equally strange Netherlandish names: strange because they were those of a councillor from the city of Utrecht and a titled nobleman from an eastern province with colonists to settle.

Baron Hendrick van der Capellen toe Ryssel's seat was at Zutphen, a city little more than twenty miles from the German border and situated on the Ijssel River in Overijssel. His title also identified him with a chapel near Rijssen, a farming center in the eastern district of Twenthe (Map 1). He was wealthy, well connected in government circles and—so said the company directors— suddenly interested in New Netherland. He had written repeatedly, expressing his intention to send colonists. So you, Stuyvesant, the directors insisted, will accommodate him with favorable lands.

Nine months later, Cornelis van Werckhoven wrote to the directors from Utrecht declaring himself patroon of two colonies. He would, he said, expect to have confirmation of a colony north from the Nevesinks's lands to those already assigned around Pavonia. That was one colony. Another would continue north from Pavonia along the Hudson to the Tappans' lands, then through the Highlands, and (as it seemed) to the lands of the Esopus (Kingston). The company approved.

The men were buying rivers, bays, and coasts with the fertile land breaking back from them. Van Werckhoven claimed that he had purchased "the Raritan kil and the land contiguous." In a conflicting claim, van der Capellen toe Ryssel had paid for the same Nevesink lands in order to ensure the safety of another alleged purchase on Staten Island. He also claimed a bay and land on Long Island as well as the coastal land from Sandy Point to the Nevesink Bay, where good farmland was there for the taking.[29] Van Werckhoven soon discovered that the company had somehow forgotten purchasing the Nevesink and Raritan lands for van der Capellen. The directors wrote Stuyvesant, uncharacteristically acknowledging their ineptitude and admitting that they knew that he would disapprove of the extravagant alienation of native lands. But the baron was a member of the government, and besides, they wanted to avoid the familiar charge of "being opposed to the influx of population."[30]

Stuyvesant was indeed angered. He had assumed that they had awarded the Utrecht official lands extending a full twenty miles up the coast. The directors assured him now that no colonist could receive more than four miles on one side of a navigable river. But they had clearly lost control of the land claims: we had better keep more precise records, they decided.[31]

Still, the company had facilitated the very colonies that it still distrusted. In early November of 1657, two of van der Capellen's sponsored emigrants reported to him in Zutphen. Entering the region of Overijssel, they could have pointed out—but, of course, did not—a tragic coincidence. In the 1570s and 1580s, States troops had descended on the province like the proverbial swarm of locusts. Its peasant population had finally risen up, only to be viciously suppressed. As a result, lands were completely deserted. In some areas, fields went unsown for over twenty years.[32] In 1640, only seventeen years before reporting to the baron, Dutch troops attacked the villages of other farming people, the coastal natives among whom these emigrants had come to live. They, too, had resisted. Afterward, some natives stayed on, working their lands and gathering at fishing stations—but not on lands and rivers that were still theirs, and not alongside the hundreds who had been killed.

The increasing number of farmers presented dangers. Except for the English, Stuyvesant knew that he could cope with the rebelliousness of farmers on Long Island—and, in any case, he was cautiously giving them the local authority they wanted. New Amsterdammers were coming to value the farming settlements as their "outer villages," or nearest subordinate colonies or, again, "dependent bordering colonies."[33] The danger was to Stuyvesant's policies regarding the natives and their lands. The days of the company threatening natives with the *brandschattingen* were over. But not the days of natives needing a permit to fish or a native getting a small corner of land once his own but now farmed by a Dutch man who, feeling the pinch of conscience, gives him the useless acres while "keeping the best for himself."

Or Stuyvesant speaking in 1658 to the Esopus chiefs: move away.[34]

*   *   *

In 1660, a councillor of New Netherland, Nicasius de Sille, constructed a remarkable document. He had arrived in New Amsterdam in 1653. By 1660, he was putting together a verbal map of New Netherland for the company directors.

He was able to list the Dutch possession of three forts, two cities, three colonies, and thirteen villages. He counted 342 houses in New Amsterdam as well as the fort, city hall, company gardens, hospital, church, warehouses, fish market, windmill, and cemetery. A number of houses were valued at over a thousand guilders. In five years' time, the city's burgomasters would claim that its citizens had made the city a place of so many fine houses that "it surpasses nearly every other place in these parts of North America."[35]

Politically, New Netherland was prospering because of two integrated kinds of politics. The first was the politics of a profession, that is, administration by professionals engaged in international mercantile occupations, goals, and legal codes. This was the input of the company's Council of New Netherland, a consultative body headed by the resident director, Petrus Stuyvesant. Alongside this—and successfully alongside it—was the politics that activated the old medieval Netherlandish principle of municipal liberty. Burgomasters and courts in New Amsterdam were now governing according to this principle.

Stuyvesant and the council imposed a regime on New Netherland that was frequently authoritarian. But it was a government that also served the rule of law. It imposed the prescripts of *lex mercatorium*, the mercantile law handed down in courts merchant. It called upon Dutch-Roman law, the customary law the full extent of which, as we saw, the West India Company had been reluctant to introduce in earlier years.

These politico-legal structures worked because New Netherland was an integrated maritime economy. The forts, cities, colonies, and villages unified New Netherland not because they were (or were expected to become) contiguous territorial elements of the province, that is, those that would (soon or eventually) leave no place for independent indigenous domains. Rather, they were elements in a geography where, as in Europe, the holdings of other princes or potentates customarily interpenetrated those of another ruler's kingdom. Such penetration left the ruler with dominion over "a concatenation of places rather than two-dimensional space." Often such a ruler knew the geographical extend of his dominion only by a listing of his possessions.[36]

In large part, what unified the elements of de Sille's list was the New Netherlanders' intention to integrate the components of this maritime economy. Overwhelmingly, the burghers in New Amsterdam's fine houses were engaged in seaborne occupations. Water traffic, as the resident-director used the term in 1654, was not an adjunct to a Dutch identity. It was its lifeline. Only integrated water traffic—between towns, between the colony of Rensselaerswijck and New Amsterdam, between remote native forts and fur-trading towns—allowed participation in an economy that was now fulfilling the definition of a successful overseas establishment as Pieter de la Court set it out. How can you tell when a colony is taking hold? he asked. When it can maintain itself out of its own products, "begin to trade and go to Sea."[37]

De Sille could not make cartographic the most outstanding achievement of the New Netherlanders. They had given themselves a structured moral community. That is, they had constructed a society dominated by family, law, religion, and educational institutions. It was the moral community that residents in the 1640s, men such as Melijn and Kieft, Kuyter and de Vries never knew.

Haltingly, the island of the Manhates had made itself something new. In the 1650s, it had gotten its New Netherlanders. The American natives were its New Netherlanders, too: now in history, they could never be otherwise. But among its different forms over time and even in 1655, none appeared that made it resemble the trading emporium that was the envy of Dutch voyagers to the east, Portuguese Goa. New Amsterdam was a growing city and a busy port, but it was not exactly the wonder that Jan Huyghen van Linschoten had seen along the coast of India. One element was missing. There he had seen in amazement the nearby native Indians, the Xaraffas in every corner and street in Goa. They were Christians who acted as moneychangers, he wrote, adding the sums for buyers and sellers with astonishing accuracy and speed.[38]

In September 1655, a year before Amsterdam's burgomasters were entertaining a vision of New Amstel and our hypothetical skipper was filling in his voyaging permit, natives were also in the corners and streets in New Amsterdam. But they were armed, out of control, and, some said, murdering innocent citizens.

Chapter 16

Considerations on a Just War

They knew exactly what to do. The Swedes were to be displaced from the South River. They had established two forts on its western shores and one on the east in order to dominate the fur trade. Elsener (Elfsborg) was southernmost on the river. North of it were Fort Casimir (previously Dutch) and Fort Christina, about fifteen miles south of Fort Nassau. In early September 1655, Stuyvesant was ready to act (Map 2).

Nothing was left to chance. The fleet—on loan from Amsterdam and the States—sailed from Manhattan Island. On the flagship *de Waegh* (the Balance)—they called it the admiral—Frederick de Koningh carried command. As overall commander, Stuyvesant directed a force of 317 soldiers supplemented by a company of sailors. He had command of seven ships: *de Waegh*; two yachts; a French galiot with two cannon; a flyboat mounting four guns; the yacht *Dolphijn* as vice admiral, four guns; the yacht *Abrams Offerhande* (Abraham's Sacrifice) as rear admiral, also carrying four guns. Perhaps a knowing observer would have mused that in seeing the departing fleet, he or she was glimpsing the aesthetics of military power most dear to Dutch hearts.

The soldiers were properly deployed. Stuyvesant took responsibility for the strongest contingent, ninety men under a captain and ensign bearer. He also commanded a company of sixty men, following a captain and ensign bearer. Nicasius de Sille held the marshall's company: a captain, ensign bearer, and fifty men. The major's company was sixty-two men. His second company included fifty seamen and pilots under a captain, ensign bearer, and, as lieutenant, a sailmaker.

The fleet left the Manhattans and arrived before Fort Elsener on September 8. They found the fort already abandoned.

On September 10, they were ready to invest Fort Casimir. They anchored a cannon-shot's distance from it. Stuyvesant landed the troops and dispatched to the commandant a captain along with a drummer and white flag. The flag signified a willingness to negotiate. Had he intended an immediate assault, he would have raised the blood flag and commenced hostilities. He gave orders to occupy an outlying guardhouse, where he placed a company of soldiers for the night. On the following day, the fort's commander sent a flag agreeing to meet. After their conference, he surrendered the fort. The commanders signed papers aboard the flagship.

On September 13, the fleet sailed north, closing on Fort Christina. The next day, they landed the soldiers who were now prepared to lay siege. De Koningh's troopers and sailors took position on the south with a battery of three guns. De Sille commanded northwest of the fort with two twelve-pounders. Stuyvesant threw up a battery north of the fort, opposite the land entrance and only a hundred paces from the walls. He commanded four cannons.

For almost six days, he made preparations. Otherwise, he deliberately did nothing. Then he sent a letter to the Swedish governor commanding the fort. After the governor agreed to meet, Stuyvesant erected an elaborate tent midway between his quarters and the fort. As was customary, the meeting place would have been punctiliously arranged to be exactly midway. The governor surrendered there on September 24. With him and some of his officers aboard, Stuyvesant took the fleet home, anchoring at Manhattan Island on September 28.[1]

In the voyaging and siege, everyone had known, as if on instinct, precisely what to do.

*   *   *

Another river scene. About two weeks after the fleet's disembarkation. Stuyvesant doesn't know what to do, how to carry on. He is not in command of the proceedings.

Again, there are flags of some sort and the shores of a river, and the Dutch and their enemies. But this time, the western shores of the river are not the stage of an action that will be completed there. They are not the geographical and political beginning and end of it all. They're just the proscenium. Beyond the riverbank, as it is now pointed out for their consideration, are the frightening recesses of the unknown "interior." In this case, it is the inland to which captive Dutch women and children will be taken—never to return unless a ransom is paid, and perhaps not even then. It is unvisited lands somewhere west of the river. Or perhaps the captives will disappear into native villages west and north. In any case, they will go into the native Americans' distant country.

Stuyvesant has returned to an island drowning in panic and disorder. The surrounding coastal communities are living in terror as well. Not for the first time, it is of their own making. Gossip about what had happened is still circulating wildly. Some stories have become fifth-hand and sixth-hand accounts.

Rumors are intersecting with lies and touching corners of guilty silence. Only slowly is something like the truth settling in.

During the early hours of September 15—perhaps the night before—"river Indians" had descended the Hudson River in sixty-four canoes. They were possibly five or six hundred men of the Mahican, Hackensack, Esopus, and Tappan lands. The northern natives were said to be armed, undoubtedly most with arrows and clubs, and a few with guns. Their purpose was (they later said) to proceed around the Manhattans, hug the coast of Long Island, and reach its eastern shores. They then intended to attack tribes with whom they had been rivals for at least twelve years. (Two months later, a son of Tachpaussan, a chief from the eastern end of the island, said that they had for many years been enemies of "those bad river Indians.")[2]

The natives had pulled their canoes to the northern shores of Manhattan Island. This was still as much their land as Dutch, familiar and often frequented. A few landed their canoes at the strand outside the walls of New Amsterdam. The riverside had been a known place of trading for twenty-five years. If the native men had somehow marked their river craft as war canoes and decorated their bodies with war paint, that would have been understandably terrifying. The presence of large numbers of canoes, however, need not have been alarming. During a good trading season up at Fort Orange and Beverwijck, as many as 190 native craft might lie along the riverside, and during August 1677, about two hundred Mohawks encamped around the town. But that was spring and summer, when the Mohawks came with furs, and the trading season, *handelstijd*, was getting under way. This was autumn, and people might have expected the natives to prepare for winter and generally turn to their own affairs.

Routinely, the city was open to the natives. Since the 1620s, they had been encouraged to trade in or near the fort. In August 1654, just a year ago, the trading season and the departure of the summer ships for Holland had heightened the tensions of the city's strands, inns, and streets. The director-general and council had expressed alarm that many Indians were seen daily in the city. Everyone knew that they regularly obtained brandy in exchange for furs and wampum and were soon running wild along the streets, breaking into houses, pilfering and shouting insults. Only four years earlier, they had been reported to be running all over the Manhattans, some with guns sold by the residents. From time to time, ordinances forbade selling them liquor and lodging them overnight if they were carrying guns. These ordinances were generally ignored. Five months after this awful day, two natives would be free to run about on the streets and even enter the fort before being arrested. They knew a couple from whom they could get liquor for wampum: the woman would bring a jug of it out to the garden, and then it's a quick run to the strand.[3]

Knowing a couple selling illegal brandy and knowing the contours of the fort and strength of the city's burgher guard were incidentals familiar to the natives because they knew something more elemental: the structure of the water-front way of life. They knew how the strand and beaches served the burghers as marginal places of boundary crossing, of restlessness and adventuring out, of living with the crimes of smugglers and adjusting laws to the needs of trade. During these years, Thomas Baxter absconded from his place on a beach near the fort and became a pirate, the waterfront's most notorious lawbreaker. The natives would have understood this.

Clearly, they knew the streets well. They could find the house of Isaac Aller-ton, an Englishman known to smuggle English goods into the city, merchan-dise traded with their enemies from Westchester, eastern Long Island, and New England.[4] They could observe very well that the city was carelessly guarded.

The city was open during the early hours of September 15. Soon natives were again running through the streets. This time, however, if they were intox-icated they also had a purpose in entering one house after the other. They were searching for northern Indians—possibly Wappings and Wekquaesgeeks—whose allies they intended to encounter on eastern Long Island. Upon the com-plaint of residents, sometime in the afternoon, they were driven to the strand where their canoes lay. They had not killed or injured anyone.

In the evening, native leaders entered the fort. They were responding to a Dutch request to avoid further disruptions to the city's peace. No one accused them of killings. According to one account, the sachems promised to leave the island before sunset. As far as the Dutch were concerned, they needn't go far—only across the narrow strait to Nooten Eylandt. Presumably, from there they could continue on their way to eastern Long Island and their desired warfare. It wasn't the Netherlanders' concern.

But sometime earlier, in the late afternoon—as jumbled accounts had it—Hendrick van Dyck, a man who eleven years earlier had joined John Underhill in leading the massacre of natives near Hempstead and who was known to be a dangerously volatile man especially when drunk, had killed a native woman. Allegedly, she had been stealing peaches from his garden. In the evening, then, rather than paddling away, the natives remained on the strand and from there shot and wounded van Dyck and threatened to kill the captain of the city bur-gher guard. Someone, probably Stuyvesant's secretary, Cornelis van Tienhoven, who was later said to have been drunk, cried, "Murder the savages who kill the Dutch." With that, citizens who were guarding the fort fell into confusion and, as one official declared, rushed through the gates and over the walls to the strand. Two Dutch men died, and three were wounded. On the riverside, officials later found the bodies of three natives. The remaining men crossed over the river to Staten Island where, unpursued by the burgher guard or (few as they were) soldiers, they reportedly began three days of burning houses and boweries, slaughtering cattle, killing settlers, and taking captives.[5]

When Stuyvesant and de Koningh brought the fleet up from Sandy Hook and closed on Staten Island, they saw the burned-out houses. They stopped to recover the body of a Dutch man still lying in a canoe.

*   *   *

The precision with which Stuyvesant had effected the Swedish surrender on the South River was in sharp contrast to the disorder of September 15 and the rituals of negotiation he soon had to conduct with the natives on both sides of the Hudson River.

His amphibious attack on the three forts was everything an overseas trading company was organized to do and its officers trained to carry out. The Swedes and Dutch were rivals over a river highly strategic to the fur trade and claimed by the Dutch on the grounds of prior possession. If dominance in such a trading zone were challenged, then plans must be laid to dislodge the contender. In the naval engagements and amphibious raids required, contingencies always arose. Wise commanders allowed for these. But bloody and ruthless as they were, everyone knew the rules of conduct in such engagements. A commander could be decisive because he knew the structures within which he was fighting.

The disorder of September 15 was a matter of contingencies and structure as well. Stuyvesant, de Sille, and most of the soldiers who had generally guarded the fort were away. Had they been present, things might have been different. Moreover, each of the two officers left in charge had washed their hands in Amerindian blood in the 1640s. The recently dishonored and dismissed fiscal, van Dyck, was a third. Within weeks of the event, Stuyvesant was blaming them for the entire affair, calling them hotheads.[6]

Basically, the events of the day occurred as they did because the Dutch— and perhaps the natives, too—had no consistent rules of conduct governing their encounters with each other. The indeterminacy among the Dutch existed from top to bottom: from the rooms of the directors in Amsterdam to the house of the woman who—one among many—flaunted the ordinances and crept into the garden with the natives' liquor. Among the River Indians, perhaps contingency lay, among other things, in pressure from the Susquehannocks to join them in punishing the Netherlanders for destroying their trade with the Swedes.

Ambiguity was the most dominant feature of the terrible day. The island was in the hands of a government knowingly driving natives to ever more distant places by buying up their lands. But contradictorily, it was regularly inviting them to bring their canoes to the riverbanks, enter residents' houses, and come inside the fort. For the sake of trade, it was allowing them to count its soldiers and take the measure of its defenses. Even three months after the killings, the authorities delayed implementing an ordinance forbidding natives to enter boweries and plantations, lodge overnight, and conduct trade except in specified places. They agreed to forbid villagers to own or repair guns without proof of ownership, but Stuyvesant's plan to assemble them monthly to discover those selling guns to natives failed to be adopted. No one suggested the monthly muster as a way of training an armed rural militia. Back on September 15, the request that the natives leave the island by sunset was another emblem of this pervasive ambiguity: leave, but gathering in numbers from seven hundred to possibly nineteen hundred on Nut Island, an island only a short distance away, was all right. Again and again: settle nothing[7] (Map 3).

Finally, the men charged with keeping order while Stuyvesant was at the South River fell before the demands of governing. They were hired on as merchants and, if need be, as soldiers in amphibious raids. But a trading company was not meant to be a government. Stuyvesant struggled with the same ambivalence and the same contradictory demands. He was far more successful than the company deserved. But the meager correspondence sent from the directors and the more complete minutes of his council reveal the structurelessness of these days that now dragged into a year or more of further indecision.

But on October 16, 1655, Stuyvesant was monitoring activities on both sides of the great river. This was another waiting game—like the days of calculated watching before Fort Christina. This time, he was not the impresario of how the action would unfold. The River Indians were the masters of time's slow, strategic passing.

The theatrical acts are being enacted on both sides of the Hudson where it is narrowest, between the shoreline of New Amsterdam and Paulus Hook on the Jersey shore. The natives on the west bank have been displaying a flag of some kind. With it, Stuyvesant writes, they have been taunting us. They are luring our negotiators to cross and recross the river but cannot be brought to state clearly the terms for the release of the prisoners. The chiefs are, he writes, bogging us down in trivial matters.

By now, he had had eight years of experience learning that it was not the way of the chiefs to come to terms quickly. There would be oratory, then silences, dispersal into small groups, and reassembly—more oratory and probably an indecisive treaty of peace. He must also have known that the natives, too, were in a perilous situation, vulnerable to the rigors of the oncoming winter and already facing the autumn months, when disease struck the hardest. Their resources would be further tested by the need to feed the captives, probably for months. For that reason, and not simply to confuse him or protect themselves from his retaliation, they would disperse them to many distant villages. But Stuyvesant was irritable. Tell the chiefs, he ordered, that we are tired of it all. Tell them to become specific and (an accusation passed often between the natives and himself) to quit lying.[8]

On his side of the river (and, as we'll see, even along the strand) were enemies as real as the natives. Two of his three councillors had proved themselves to be reckless and violent. The ex-treasurer was the murderer of an innocent woman. In open defiance of Stuyvesant's orders, Long Islanders and others were going into the countryside in small parties. He had already refused to ransom four who had chosen to go inland or, as he described it, to distant and lonely places. They were among the many willing to gamble on safely bringing in a harvest or, equally probable, selling liquor to natives just as was being done a year earlier: "on the rivers, streams and kills, out of sloops or by any manner or by any means."[9]

The English, meanwhile, were making a war zone of western Long Island, southern Connecticut, and Vreedland, the lands of the Wappings and Wek-quaesgeeks just north and east of the island (Westchester County) (Map 2). It was not a zone of overt military contest between the Dutch and English, not a no-man's land saturated with armed men. It was a place where natives moved silently in small numbers against the Dutch—or perhaps it was the English moving them against the Dutch, at least at Gravesend and around Stamford. Wouldn't the English try to get all of Long Island and Vreedland by inciting the natives or fabricating horror stories about Dutch intentions? They had done that sort of thing before.

Rumor was as effective at creating panic as was the appearance of hostile natives. English neighbors were warning the Dutch residents at Gravesend to get out of the town and move to the Manhattans. They said that the natives had told them that they would be picking out Dutch families in the town and inadvertently injuring the English, with whom they had no quarrel. Now the English were telling the Dutch: for the safety of us all, leave quickly. Said the Netherlands residents to Stuyvesant: but then there will be no more Dutch on Long Island. They disbelieved the reports but were hearing them daily. They couldn't understand their changed circumstances. Still, they also saw natives all around the limits of the village and English fellow residents letting them enter and leave.[10] They guessed that they should gather their belongings and leave. They seemed not to have known that the Englishman who was now writing them a warning to remove had met with the local natives on the same day as the River Indians had landed on Manhattan Island.[11] Why?

So it was Stuyvesant's task in these autumn days to look west across the river to natives signaling with a ragged flag but also east and north to sort rumor from reality. In about three months' time, in January 1656, an English schoolmaster, a Mr. Weyls (Wheeler) from Westchester County, composed another warning, delivering it directly to Stuyvesant. It was a barely disguised effort to establish enmity between the Dutch authorities and the local Wekquaesgeeks. He suggested that the Dutch, using the defensive tactics they did—or having no effective tactics at all—were going to be lost in a quagmire there. He had interviewed a local Wekquaesgeek whose people had killed and taken Dutch captives immediately after September 15. The informant insisted that they were not the first cause of the hostilities, but once begun they were afraid the Dutch would retaliate. Now their captives were a heavy burden but protection against attack. Weyls asked him whether his people would now make peace with the Dutch. The man's alleged response was the schoolteacher's invention, meant to sow trouble. It had none of the Americans' usual evasive laughter or equivocation. There'll be no peace. We'll "hide in small parties in the underwood, to surprise anyone who came out, hinder those in planting and kill their cattle . . . until they finally would have no more food."

Weyls identified the events of September 15 as a "massacre." Although initial exaggerated reports had drawn Stuyvesant to identify it in a similar way, he was now referring to it in a familiarly Dutch and less inflammatory way as "the troubles." As for the Wekquaesgeeks, Weyls concluded, they would only be subdued by accepting English settlers and their plantations.[12]

But in October, the distant natives and the river separating them from the strangers needed to be brought under Stuyvesant's control. Natives he called "bad men" and "ragamuffins" were crossing at will to the strand: paddling to the shore with stories, none of them speaking for the chiefs. Burghers were crossing the other way, hoping to bargain and drink with the natives and, as he charged, feed them false stories, perhaps like those fabricated ten months later: the director-general has sent for five hundred soldiers; or, the director-general could not get any soldiers; or, no settlers come here. Disloyalty was nothing new. But these men were escalating an already present danger. Stuyvesant didn't want them on the strand.[13]

On October 17 and 18 negotiations came down to the wisdom of two men, Stuyvesant and Pennekeek, a chief of the Hackensacks. If only out of necessity, they seemed to respect each other. They had met six years earlier. Pennekeek, the sachem of Achter Col (vicinity of Newark Bay), had come into the council chamber of Fort Amsterdam in mid-summer of 1649 (Map 3). Although two of Stuyvesant's councillors had been present at the peace treaty of 1645 and met Pennekeek the day before the signing, Stuyvesant had first encountered him in 1649, two years after arriving on Manhattan Island. The sachem had come with three other notable chiefs. He, however, took command of the natives' side of the negotiations. Although he was in the presence of two leading burghers and a minister, he directed his words solely to Stuyvesant.[14]

Pennekeek established his authority ceremoniously, interrupting his own words on five occasions in order to present gifts. He was there to request that the Honorable General excuse the recent mischief unknowingly committed at Paulus Hook by a native of the Mechgachkamics (possibly the original owners of present-day Brooklyn).[15] Pennekeek said that he spoke for the Raritans. Calling on ancient history, he chose to identify them as formerly living north of Manhattan Island at "Wiquaeskeek" rather than identifying them with the lands they occupied south and southeast when Kieft demanded tribute from them. He said that they now had no chief, so he was conveying their pledge of friendship. He also made himself spokesman for other nearby peoples. He represented Meijterma, who held a sub-chieftainship on land east of the Narrows at Nyack. He also had the right to speak for the people of Remahenonc, probably the Rumachenanck of Haverstraw. After each declaration, he established silence and presented gifts of beaver.

If Stuyvesant had not already heard the highly inflected eloquence of Algonquian oratory, he heard it now. Again, he was Pennekeek's only audience as the leader moved toward a statement that was not an empty phrase. "I wish you could see my heart, then you would be sure, that my words are sincere and true." In the name of all, I say that we desire to live in friendship, "forgetting on either side, what is past." We are, he affirms, ready for it. He adds that the Mohawks—to whose subordination he now refers either gratuitously or out of obligation and fear—wish it.

Pennekeek knew that Stuyvesant had wanted to meet with him and the other leaders. He mentions this and hopes that now he sees their good intentions. We know you cannot understand us, he continues. But we trust your goodwill.

Stuyvesant responded with equal courtesy. No other Dutch man spoke. He promised to live in friendship and to treat with justice any native complaint. Stuyvesant and Pennekeek exchanged gifts, and the natives retired from Fort Amsterdam in the manner the Dutch enjoyed recording, amicably.[16]

Now Pennekeek and Stuyvesant were negotiating again, this time through intermediaries. Perhaps neither man remembered a meeting of six years ago—and certainly they could not know that they would deal with each other again in two years' time, when Pennekeek would release lands on Staten Island to the Dutch. There were many chiefs at Paulus Hook, and again Pennekeek assumed a commanding voice. He responded immediately to Stuyvesant's message, asking when they would return the prisoners: within forty-eight hours, he had sent fourteen captives across the river.[17]

Stuyvesant's response was immediate and remarkable. Remarkable because it was a tangible show of respect. He isolated Pennekeek and himself from the malign associates with whom each had to contend and sent him a token of mutuality. For a moment, he made a gesture that occluded the asymmetries of power that the strangers' long-ago intrusion had irreversibly caused. A messenger carried Stuyvesant's expression of gratitude for the "kind heart and affection" shown by Pennekeek and the other sachems in releasing the fourteen captives. In return, he sent two captured natives, admitting that they were not of the chief's nation but asking that they be accepted as a token of goodwill and returned to their own people. He advised Pennekeek that he would not make payment for prisoners but would honor their return with gifts of powder and lead. Where are they, and when will they be returned?

He then acknowledged certain sensibilities that he and Pennekeek shared. That is, he admitted that he had among his people those he could not trust, just as Pennekeek had untrustworthy men to deal with. You, he stated, are sending bad men as messengers, whereas they should be sachems whom I can believe. But I have men who are crossing over to you without my authority and carrying false stories of each of us to the other. My representative therefore brings you this token, a reproduction of the West India Company insignia made by my own hand. Believe only someone bearing this sign.

In this exchange Stuyvesant and Pennekeek communicated in the way that was theirs: for Pennekeek, throat to ear, and for Stuyvesant, hand to eye. Each gave to the other a credible performance of his limited power. Each would have known of the other's subordination to higher superiors: for Pennekeek, it was to the Mohawks who later boasted that they had gone down to Manhattan and worked to bring about a peace. The Dutch man's obedience was to company directors who sat at their desks in Holland and would hold him accountable should the captives somehow not be returned. Stuyvesant admitted his weakened authority in sending the token; Pennekeek tacitly admitted his humiliation in requesting a ransom that would not enlarge the fighting power of his men but merely see his people through the winter. Each knew that it was a short moment of truce. The Hackensacks, and possibly the Raritans and Nevesinks, would aid the Esopus against the Dutch in several years' time. The Dutch would await their chance.

During a further week of negotiations, Pennekeek released fifty-six captives. Twenty children were still held by River Indians in late March of 1656. Neither man crossed the river. The River Indians and Dutch did not have a war—even though the happenings of these weeks have survived as the Peach War. Stuyvesant (from what the documents reveal) saw to defenses but chose to send out not a single raiding party.[18]

*   *   *

During these days of adversaries on all sides, Stuyvesant felt deeply the betrayal of the directors at home and even the States. Two weeks after sending his token to Pennekeek, he was telling authorities in The Hague that he and the New Netherlanders were in an impossible position. They were victims of the natives' depredations and denied assistance or even counsel from sources that they had a right to call on, that is, the company and their lordships of the States. In five years' time and for the same reasons, he would be writing, "We have fallen into this abyss."[19]

For now, he portrayed them staring at "the final total ruin of the country." He recited a brief history of their relations with the natives. He began with Kieft's war, disingenuously describing it as waged by "various barbarous Indian tribes against the Netherlandish nation." The natives, he continued, repeatedly broke the subsequent peace treaty and since that time had murdered ten citizens while he was loyally passing over the breaches of the treaty to avoid hostility or revenge. But now circumstances had changed. Antagonistic parties were buffeting him and his council, one for peace with the natives, the other for war. In late September, he had conceded that the River Indians had no intention other than to fight the natives of eastern Long Island. He now opposed initiating a war—it would be unsuccessful in any event. He awaited the noble lordships' speedy advice and assistance.[20]

The burgomasters and council of New Amsterdam sent the company a remonstration that accompanied and duplicated Stuyvesant's complaint. It presented the directors with an either/or proposition. Either, after reading our petition, you instruct us regarding the assistance you'll offer, or we will (like the director-general) have to expose our abandoned situation to the States and officials of Amsterdam.

Their demands were an opening gambit in an anticipated tug-of-war with the company directors. They were unrealistically excessive. From an organization that generally hired on far fewer than two hundred men—two years after the first settlement, the company had fewer than forty and in 1639 not enough to send against twenty-four men at the Swedes' Fort Christina on the Delaware—they wanted three to four thousand fully armed soldiers. The men would offer immediate assistance and then be required to stay in order to increase the population. They also wanted thirty to forty thousand guilders in clothing, food, and drink for the soldiers. Perhaps they had visions of matching the land forces available in New England. In any case, they charged the directors to answer their needs and also consider the list of required arms. Let our petition be taken seriously, recommended favorably to others, and, together with good advice, quickly acted upon.[21]

Where the burghers would have housed three to four thousand men on and around Manhattan Island is an interesting hypothetical question. And would the soldiers have been different from those whom Stuyvesant typified as ready to harm the natives? [22] The directors appear not to have responded to the New Amsterdammers' remonstrance and delayed their answer to Stuyvesant for six months. When their letter to him finally arrived, it must have rubbed salt into open wounds. The options arising from your recent misfortunes, they offered, are either to make some arrangement with the natives or revenge the bloodshed and inflict damages accordingly. We, however, can't as yet come to a final conclusion about one or the other. We'll discover what help we can get from the States. Meanwhile, you are "on the spot there and better informed of everything." It would seem advisable to make a provisional treaty with the natives. Do insist upon restitution of any stolen goods and extorted ransom.[23]

In the summer or autumn of 1656, they wrote again. They had now received sufficient verbal and written evidence to accuse van Tienhoven and van Dyck of instigating the hostilities. They chided Stuyvesant for failing to bring van Dyck to justice as a murderer. The colonists, they added, were clearly indulging the natives with excessive liberties and freedoms or, in their words, caressing and cajoling them, even arming them to their own destruction. Only in late December 1657—about twenty-seven months after the bloody day on Manhattan Island—did they promise a thousand pounds of powder and—because they thought that ought to be sufficient—fifty soldiers instead of three to four thousand.[24]

In the course of this correspondence, the directors had introduced the possibility of Stuyvesant arranging a military alliance with the English. Such a proposal had been considered twice before, in 1648 and 1652–53. In neither case had the propositions borne positive results. In 1648 and within months of his arrival in New Netherland, Stuyvesant made a series of diplomatic overtures to the governors of Massachusetts, New Haven, Plymouth, and Connecticut. Hoping to secure a formal accord, he proposed a league of amity and cooperation. Among other considerations, he reiterated the benefit of a mutual league, or, as the pro forma words went, an alliance "both offensive and defensive, against a common enemy." The New Englanders chose to defer their decision.

The New Englanders had their own reasons for spurning the alliance proposed by Stuyvesant. As to the Dutch, their response in 1650 to the Englishmen's delayed willingness to consider a league is highly instructive. It suggests how firmly the Dutch distrusted the English and, more significantly, distrusted their ways of waging war against the natives. Stuyvesant had taken the position that within the terms of a possible league, the English should, when necessary, bring into the field at least twice the number of forces as the Dutch. The New England negotiators agreed but conditionally: they would do so but exercise twice the number of votes regarding the declaration of war and any peace settlement. Stuyvesant refused, offering the excuse that he needed to consult with superiors at home.

In 1652, Stuyvesant again proposed an alliance. He feared that the hostilities of the Anglo-Dutch war in Europe might be repeated in North America and weaken both sides to native attack. In response, the New Englanders appear to have considered the offer but posited a war against the natives that was not as the directors and Stuyvesant intended. They rejected it. The directors informed the Amsterdam regents and Stuyvesant that the English were proposing an "aggressive war." Clearly, their identification of it as aggressive was (for whatever other reasons) meant to cancel any participation in it.[25]

The New Englanders were inviting the Dutch to adopt military tactics with which the Netherlanders were generally deeply uneasy. Perhaps in this case, the directors were fearful of aggressive campaigns that would call down retaliatory actions that New Netherland, in its usual weak military posture, would not be able to repulse. But the Netherlanders also had, as John Shy has written, an "attitude toward war." Aggressive offensive military campaigns organized to bring men (as they often used the phrase) "into the field" were adopted with great circumspection and only after being weighed against the wisdom of defensive measures. When Stuyvesant discovered in 1653 that English and Dutch Long Islanders were intent on forming a "defensive and offensive" alliance in pursuit of a band of English pirates, he angrily rejected the plan. He had neither been consulted in the plan nor would be countenance offensive measures against the bandits. His approach to the disturbances had been characteristically defensive: to arrange discussions of the problem while excoriating those living in remote places who might foolishly house the pirates. On at least five occasions, he sent out yachts and soldiers but "only for the protection of the trade, and the rivers and streams between us and our neighbors." He expected the villagers to take nothing more than measures of self-defense.[26]

Three months later, he learned that the English at Gravesend had heard rumors of the Dutch hiring the French and natives to kill the English living among them. In retaliation, they were preparing a preemptive attack acting as, they reported, the aggressors. Not only was Stuyvesant not interested in following this example, but in this instance he urged: let's resolve "to close our eyes at the present time."[27]

In the lives of the Dutch and Amerindian New Netherlanders in our story, the Dutch determination to maintain a defensive military posture is of central significance. If being a successful trading company meant purchasing a foreign enclave along with the right to trade beyond it and defend it, then in dangerous times Kieft's defensive plan for the enclave on Manhattan Island in 1638 was entirely logical: all persons in the service of the West India Company were ordered not to leave the island without expressed permission of the Honorable Commander. Penalty: three months' wages. [28] Only the intention of abandoning the fundamental military character of a maritime trading company in favor of another sort of structural presence gives a logic to land troops, soldiers, and country people trained for offensive action in the open field.

Change in this direction was threatening to come. In 1662, Stuyvesant was in open dispute with the company directors regarding the structure of their military presence in New Netherland. A letter sent in mid-July is the angriest we can read in his correspondence. It is a letter equal to Jan Pietersz Coen's 1614 letter of reproach to the directors of the East India Company. If, as historians have written, Coen put his career on the line writing it, perhaps Stuyvesant did, too.

Stuyvesant's anger with the men in Holland turned around the role of offensive and defensive military tactics. Particularly, it centered on the directors' recent enthusiasm for a policy supporting settlers moving out to attack native enemies in the open field. Rebutting this, Stuyvesant insisted that security was a matter for the company's soldiers. In order to discourage or repel aggression, let them continue to be settled in garrisons and their numbers properly maintained. His position clearly subverted any plans that the directors might have had in mind for the formation of rural militias. His was the traditional Dutch posture toward war. Theirs was the stance that was changing.

He came to the point immediately. If you "persist absolutely upon this principle, namely, total abolition of the military and reliance on the inhabitants alone for the offensive and defensive maintenance of this territory," it must be feared, and indeed expected, that it will come to a bad end. Of course our inhabitants are, as you've pointed out, bound to defend themselves. Nature and necessity compel it. And they are willing, he continued, to guard their own and other settled places.

He became more vehement. The same inhabitants are unwilling "to attack the savages in the open field and . . . [engage in] bringing help to other outside places." Bring help to outside places? Attack the enemy in the open field? Who among the burghers of Amsterdam—or Haarlem, Leiden, or Dordrecht— would accept being compelled to such a thing? As Stuyvesant put it, "We do not remember . . . that citizens and inhabitants in the Fatherland were held or compelled to it." And summoning sarcasm: some parties have obviously put it to you that this place is best maintained without hired soldiers. Listen if you like. But do so and we'll lose the province.

He called for additional soldiers and condemned the directors for their shortsighted parsimony in failing to supply them. They were unwilling to imagine the realities of life in New Netherland. He began a list of those realities by citing something he must have had on his mind for seven years—he held them responsible for the terrible happenings on and after September 15, 1655. If, he charged, you had from your own experience some perception of the "interests, losses, sudden attacks, unexpected murders, manslaughters, [and] different incendiary fires" that our inhabitants have experienced, then you, too, would consider means of increasing the number of soldiers rather than, as you seem determined upon, reducing the already small contingent. It is not even economically reasonable: "twenty-five men more or less will not make the public treasury richer or poorer."

In any case, in 1655, the damage we suffered could have been prevented if we'd only had twenty-five to thirty additional enlisted soldiers remaining here in defense on Manhattan Island. But: "we will not go further in these inferences."[29]

Perhaps back in 1655, Stuyvesant had experienced a moment of trying to find out where they went wrong or, as one twentieth-century writer has put it, "where the rain began to beat us." Perhaps, still wading in the flotsam and jetsam of the incident and then their subsequent abandonment, he was recognizing that his and the settlers' New Netherland was something different from that of the directors. We can only think that he had some sense of a gap when he received a useless letter from the directors in 1657. By all means, they wrote, build blockhouses at strategic points, as you continue to suggest. But we cannot contribute. Send us profits and we'll invest them. With the income, we'll then send some soldiers.[30]

*   *   *

On November 10, 1655, Stuyvesant convened the council and requested opinions on the advisability of a just war against the River Indians. We look and listen, even though in a sense this will be more of the same. That is, the deliberations are in miniature the thousands of words expended on the legality of the Indian war and the hundreds more that will be rolled out just five years from now. They repeat the search for causation and the hope for justification to be found in scholastic distinctions between remote and immediate causes. And they record expressions of self-recrimination.

Stuyvesant is meeting with his councillors in the fort and asking questions to which he wants written replies. Can we justify going to war with the natives? If the war is justifiable, is it timely and if not now, when? If the war is both justifiable and timely, can it be brought to a successful conclusion? Outside are, as Stuyvesant acknowledges, parties angrily divided, one for peace, the other for war. He needs to let them see that extended deliberations are about to address and settle their concerns. He must present them with a decision so carefully weighed as to quiet (in his words) "the unpleasant feelings and dissentions" on every side. The outcome is scarcely in doubt. Stuyvesant's determination is already firmly against a war, and he means to bring the councillors around to his position. The outcome for the natives is determined, too: their fate is not dramatically hanging in the balance. It is already settled, at least this time.

Stuyvesant seeks to establish causes. He offers no preliminary disquisition on the natives' savagism. On the contrary. The Indians, he opens, cannot be considered the cause of recent events because they intended nothing more than to proceed to eastern Long Island. "Various indications, too long and too manifold to follow up here" make that clear. "Careless watching" and "hotheaded individuals diverted the Indians and gave them cause" for all that followed. The Indians have exhibited sauciness, and we need to curb that, but not by declaring and beginning an open war. Even if I cannot absolutely contradict the lawfulness of a war, he continues, the present is not the time for it. We still have captives to rescue. And the proposition put forth by a few that we should capture some Indians in order to exchange them for our hostages is dangerous and impractical. Besides, it is "dishonest . . . to seize and keep as prisoners Indians of one tribe, to exchange them for prisoners in the hands of another tribe."

Is a war likely to be successful? Let us simply say to the commonalty: we have written to the States and the directors for advice and assistance but received no answer. Should we proceed now, we would be reproached for following our own caprices. Meanwhile, we must take preventive measures. We must, among other things, erect blockhouses for garrisoning soldiers. Since the Hackensacks and Wekquaesgeeks have the best fertile land, our people will want to go there. To prevent conflict, we can hope to dislodge the resident natives or use the garrison to keep them under closer control. In case they initiate hostilities, our raiding parties can reach them more easily.

Nicasius de Sille delayed two weeks before delivering his opinion. It was brief and equivocal but basically in agreement with Stuyvesant's. He did, however, support the idea of taking native hostages if their own captives were not returned. Johannes la Montagne was one of the two men left in charge of the fort in mid-September. He wrote at greater length, agreeing with Stuyvesant that they lacked the military capacity to pursue a war. Still, he refused to exonerate the natives as the cause of the hostilities. If they were not the immediate *causa movens*, they were instigators of the remote causes. He offered a benign version of the September day's happenings and then truculently questioned the value of their present investigations, since they had been sent no advice or assistance and a war was clearly out of the question.

Cornelis van Tienhoven was probably one of the most intelligent men in the province but known to be devious. Certainly, his response was just that. A war would be "just according to the law of nations." The natives deserved punishment for repeatedly breaking the treaty of 1645. But now such a war had to be deferred. The coming months of December to March would have been the proper season to inflict punishment. But they had not heard from Holland. Without assistance, he conceded, the just war could not be favorably concluded.[31]

Stuyvesant had his answer for the anxious burghers. But he had neither war nor peace. He had only an unpredictable, draining insurgency. In any case, time was running out for the Honorable West India Company.

PART VII

Final Logged Entries

From 1655 to 1664, the intertwined cultures of the Amerindians and Netherlanders continued to constitute what it meant to live in New Netherland. Natives around Manhattan Island acknowledged the strangers' dominance, alienated traditional lands and traded—with fewer and fewer available pelts. But they resisted the Dutch in ways that were effective because they were unpredictable and (to the Dutch) sly: they harassed farmers; disturbed travel on the great north river by committing sporadic acts of violence; and were able to terrify settlers living on the South River and Long Island as well as those within the defenses of New Amsterdam. The Mohawks continued to operate as power brokers. Desperately defending their diminishing power and numbers, they heartlessly destroyed some tribes while opportunistically succoring others and serving the Dutch. Stuyvesant and his council continued to act within the creaking structures of a native policy that ensured market profits while—if they had thought it out, which they had not—creating apartheid conditions supposedly beneficial to natives as well as strangers. When the English came in 1664, they inherited a feline mix of cooperation, hostility, and indecisiveness.

In the final seven years of Stuyvesant's administration, New Amsterdam and Beverwijck were becoming successful urban centers. Their residents constituted the majority of the eight thousand to nine thousand Europeans in the province. Commercial houses in the Netherlands recognized the stability of their financial and mercantile enterprises. Newcomers were arriving in steady numbers. Stuyvesant and his council, however, were forced to attend to episodes later called the First and Second Esopus Wars (1659–60; 1663–64). "War" is (as it was regarding 1655) a misleading word for the conflicts at Esopus (later Wiltwijck/Kingston), some eighty miles north of Manhattan Island. Rather, the hostilities were the maneuvers of opponents adventitiously raiding vulnerable villages, repeatedly negotiating peace but only to buy time to regroup and rearm: again, watchful waiting. The native insurgency soon brought into conflict the administration on the island and the farmers on the Esopus plain, the opposition of island and inland. Esopus was a cultural borderland. It existed on native lands but was still oriented to the Hudson River as a satellite dependency of merchants who lived along the river in Beverwijck and controlled the settlement in order to monopolize the fur trade and see to the production of grains for their distilleries and breweries. The insurgency also led the administration to another set of deliberations on a just war. Again, the Dutch had provoked the initial violence. The officials declared a war but almost immediately called upon the Mohawks to negotiate peace. The Esopus problem had not been settled, even under English rule.

In August 1664, an English squadron under the command of Richard Nicolls seized Manhattan Island. The English occupation of the province ended forty years of Dutch presence in New Netherland. But it did not bring closure, at least not in the sense of a moment when the Dutch appraised what that presence had meant, how it was best defined, and what its impact had been on the native Americans. There was no postcolonial moment closing off the years from 1624 to 1664 and by that making them a historical category, a colonial period. A new West India Company, formed in 1675 after the collapse of the old trading company, said nothing about the end of empire or colonialism. Instead, it voiced what must have been general opinion: that New Netherland had been part of the old company's experiment in commercial maritime expansion. And they had botched it.

Chapter 17
Cultural Entanglement

In the summer of 1659, the affairs of the Dutch farmers at Esopus must have been a matter of indifference to most people on Manhattan Island. No one on the island seemed to have friends there. No one took an Esopus resident to the court of New Amsterdam on legal matters. Except for administrators, no one is recorded as having visited the place.

The Esopus was a remote plain eighty-three miles north of the island. Boatmen reached it by navigating up the Hudson before going three miles inland. In fair weather, the river journey took a single day, but it meant avoiding hazardous sandbanks and tacking through dangerous shoals and tidal currents. When the winds blew from the north, a sailor had to think of three days of sailing. Winter ice closed the river even into spring. Very few went overland.

About fifty years earlier, Dutch traders had entered the river and seen the plain and the highlands that upheavals and soil deposits in the Middle Devonian Period had lifted sharply above the riverbed. Five years later, in 1614, it was nine letters on a map kept secretly in Amsterdam: *het Esopus.* About this time, some later said, a Dutch fort stood on a creek near the Esopus. Long after this summer of 1659, an old man called the place "Yopus." Perhaps that is how the strangers pronounced it. The natives living there seemed to call it Atkarkarton, the great field[1] (Map 2).

The native-born people of Esopus had been farming the fertile lands for generations. As fishermen, they also found sustenance in the Esopus, Wallkill, and Rondout Creeks and the great river nearby. They had no single name for the Hudson. Cohohatatia was the waters where the salmon were caught. Mahicannittuck named the places where the Mahicans lived. Where the natives farmed, the river was a mile wide. They were small bands of families, perhaps five hundred inhabitants, when the strangers came. They were active traders and brokers between peoples to the south and north. With other Algonquian-speaking bands of families south along the seacoast, they exchanged maize for dried fish, venison, and wampum. These they exchanged with Mohawks and other people to the north.

Now they were trading with the sixty or seventy families of the strangers who had come among them. They were also sharing the arable lands. The strangers were still struggling to establish their herds and bring in their harvests. But the natives seemed to have been careful and successful agriculturalists. In 1663, they were said to have had 215 acres of corn under cultivation, with yields of 1,483.5 bushels. From some of their fields, they could walk onto those being plowed by the strangers. And the strangers' wandering animals were close enough to dig up and ruin their corn mounds.[2]

In the mid-1650s, Stuyvesant and some Beverwijck merchants had recognized what the natives already knew: that the Esopus was an ideal base for trading in furs. Along its creeks, native trails passed between the Hudson and the Delaware Rivers. To ensure the trade, Stuyvesant had accepted that the resident traders would be farmers as well. They could exploit trading opportunities but also make New Netherland self-sufficient in grain. He had authorized a limited number of land grants. In the beginning, the landowners were fewer than a half-dozen freewheeling land speculators. Now there were fifty to sixty. They engaged in farming or running a few cattle or horses. But as everyone would have known, each was also a trader. They seized every chance to exchange goods with the natives. They passed cloth or tobacco across to them—or, just as readily, illegal goods such as gunpowder or brandy. These they exchanged for furs, wampum, and basic necessities. No one among them would have thought to look where one role left off and the other began. The same could be said of the natives.

Most farmers were living within a palisaded settlement built in 1658 (Wiltwijck, later Kingston). But while the upright logs bound some of the families together physically, no other structures did. The place was dysfunctional. The enclosure was not an incorporated village. It had no magistrates or court, no minister or law-enforcement officer. It had no name. The authorities on the island simply called the people there "the farmers." Some of the residents had scoffed at the boundaries of the settlement. These included men who took leading roles in its affairs—when it suited them. They stayed in isolated farmhouses, some on the far side of a small stream. They could not be compelled to move in. Their affairs were their own business.

About fifty of the men around the place were soldiers lying in garrison. Their officers, junior as they were, constituted the authorities of the place. Like others we've met, the soldiers were mercenaries scrounged by the company from across Europe. They had no intention of taking up farming as an occupation. "We have not learned any trade nor farming," they said. "The sword must earn us our subsistence. . . . If not here, then we must look for our fortune elsewhere."[3]

The soldiers were not guarding a strategic point along a distant northern frontier. The administrators on the island had never entertained the notion of a frontier line, not in correspondence or reports, and not in the form of a straight line laid across a map or a zigzag or broken one. Rather, the soldiers were protecting a place that was in between: fifty-eight miles south of Fort Orange and the fur-trading town of Beverwijck, eighty-three miles north of the island. West were the mountains and uncharted lands of natives. Immediately east was the great river. A few settlers had scattered themselves north of the settlement and along the river at the foothills of the highlands and at remote places whose names were a giveaway to scarcely remembered violence, such as Murderer's Creek. Others lived on some of the islands, again, to the north. Otherwise, there were no Europeans for miles and miles.

The administration on the island had sent the men of the garrison to be the boundary between the natives and settlers that an undefined geography and the careless farmers failed to provide. They were guarding the farmers against a native attack. Yet they were also policing them, restraining them from undertaking their own forms of violence. Supposedly, the troopers were a peacekeeping force, but they too often crossed the line into violence of their own making.

* * *

In late September of this year, 1659, the authorities on Manhattan Island were alerted to just how entangled with the natives the men and women of this settlement were. During the evening of September 20, a young native man was savagely murdered and six or seven others badly beaten. Worse was to come, although a period of about three weeks passed before the full facts concerning the incident and the terrifying subsequent events reached Manhattan Island.

The murder seems to have happened this way. Eight natives were entertaining themselves after a day's work picking corn for one of the Dutch farmers. Contrary to the law, they had been paid in brandy and were soon looking for a place to rest and enjoy it. One suggested that they take it to a place they called the "liquor house." Another wanted to stay near a little kill and build a fire. They agreed and settled in. By midnight, they had finished the brandy and began to make what were later described as wild noises. They decided to replenish the liquor. One of the young men returned to the farmer for a further supply but was refused. Before long, he encountered a soldier inside the Dutch settlement who gave him some liquor. The native said, "I'm much obliged to you." Another soldier asked him where he meant to drink it. Nearby, he responded, "near the little kill."

The young man returned to his friends but found them "lying about, crying."

He tried to rouse their spirits, saying, "Why do you cry, I've brought brandy." Soon they began to quarrel. During the brawling, one of them discharged a gun. Another announced that he was "too small to fight" and left, along with a friend. A fourth man cried out, "Come, let's go away, I feel it in my body that we'll be killed." The others answered, "You're crazy. Who should kill us?" "We would not kill the Dutch. We have done them no harm. Why, then, should they kill us?" That's true, replied the other, "but I'm nevertheless so heavy-hearted." He repeated, "Come, let's go, we'll surely be killed . . . my heart is full of fears."

The men fell asleep. Then a number of Dutch men suddenly arrived and without warning fired on them. One young man was killed and another seized. A third man who was moving about drunkenly received shots so continually that his clothing was torn away. Surrounding him closely, the Dutch men listened as he moaned, "Come, kill me, I'm not afraid." One of the assailants then attacked a final victim, who had passed out with drink. He, too, managed to get away.[4]

Within twenty-four hours of this evening's violence, natives had attacked the settlement. Allegedly, they ranged from four to six hundred and kept the settlement's defenders under siege for twenty-three days. By one account, thirteen men were taken hostage, and nine or ten of them were killed. The trapped villagers watched in horror as the natives burned surrounding houses and barns, slaughtered farm animals, and plundered food supplies. What the Esopus casualties were, no one said.[5]

In the following weeks, the people of Manhattan Island were drawn into the conflict. Initially, only the highest authorities needed to concern themselves with the distant violence. At least seven letters and two reports came into Stuyvesant's hands. They had made their way from a settlement now reduced to panic and desolation. They came from farmers, soldiers, and natives. They presented evidence that was contradictory. In the end, only one explanation was going to be left standing. It was a version offered by three natives. The director-general and council accepted it, even though it pointed the finger of guilt directly at the farmers. In fact, the finding was something the officials had anticipated.

Thirty-one men felt it necessary to forward accounts of the events. Some produced their own individual versions. Others cooperated with friends in constructing stories that vindicated themselves and indicted others. Almost always, the storytellers suppressed more than they said. Their clumsiness betrayed an awareness that someone else would certainly be reporting on the happenings as well—someone among the military, a native or farmer, or just a mischievous rumormongering outsider. They needed to cover their backs.

Not for the first time, the farmers and soldiers were playing contestants in a game of disclosures played out for the provincial authorities. They shared two assumptions. First, the authorities on the island would begin their investigations:

they would take depositions, send an elaborately written report to the directors at home, and put the care of the village well below the wider interests of the company. They would dig around asking questions. If it became necessary or even convenient, they would use the answers to exonerate themselves. Particularly, they would look for causes—the immediate causes, the remote causes.

Second, they would begin by reminding everyone that their own dreadful sins were the cause of the present punishment inflicted by the natives. Everyone should examine his or her conscience. Then, if they went ahead as they did after the troubles of September 15, four years ago, they would point the finger at the farmers, those in the open country whom they characterized as being like the natives, quick to appropriate "separate places" either already "burned or deserted."[6] They would entertain a series of more specific questions: Were the Esopus farmers' initial actions revenge? Who initiated the hostilities or, more specifically, was it true that one of the locals had lied to the natives about the director-general himself, saying that he planned to wipe out the Esopus? Was the native attack on the village sufficient reason for the provincial authorities to mount a just war? But certainty about the events and their causes would almost surely elude the authorities' grasp. Or they would fudge the matter of accountability, postpone it, make it ambiguous. They would put together their version of the reality of things, but it wouldn't stick anyway. Everyone was playing the same game of evasion and partial truths.

The testimony of twenty-eight informants reached the resident director within ten days of the assault on the settlement. One was an account written by the ensign who had been in command of the garrison. He wrote as a frightened and cornered man, almost certain to be charged with negligence. Somehow he knew that the director was furious at the self-serving violence that had incited the attack. Now he admitted that well before its outbreak, he had Stuyvesant's direct order "not to act hostilely against the savages unless they begin first." Even if they did, he should "attack defensively."[7]

Further reports of the event soon crowded Stuyvesant's room. Little-known figures from the settlement spoke their lines. Twelve farmers and soldiers offered their declaration. The ensign had written that one of the farmers had asked to lead out four or five *boers*. A sergeant had agreed. The farmer who had taken the lead admitted responsibility for the killing and beatings, but he became abusive when questioned. He retorted with a statement used by Kieft about sixteen years earlier. "We wanted to slap their mouths," he boasted. "[T]he dogs have vexed us long enough."[8]

Others admitted that they had been among those searching for the young natives sleeping outside the gates. Now, however, they were trapped within the settlement and wanted to explain their part in what was surely an unexpected tragedy. They wanted to keep the ensign among them and firmly exonerated him. Someone had given the order to fire, but it wasn't he. They said nothing more. Another letter carried the voices of twelve other farmers confined within the fort. These were men ready to blame one of their neighbors and identify others. They classified the night's incident as mischief: the farmer who had taken the lead in going outside the fort's gate caused it; the sergeant who had accompanied him was also guilty. Now it was done, and they looked for relief. They were still not certain whether the natives would return to engulf the settlement in flames.[9]

Finally, the director had to deal with a letter signed by four farmers, among whom was the man who had, as two accounts read, boasted of assaulting the natives. He had volunteered to confront them, saying, "Please let me go." But the young natives had fired immediately, and the farmers had simply retaliated. Besides, native informants had warned him that the Esopus were planning to attack the settlement. They were anticipating the sight of fire consuming the soldiers' bones and flesh. As he put it, they intended to "roast and burn the soldiers" inside the fort.[10]

Informing his superiors in Holland, Stuyvesant quickly collated these accounts and assigned responsibility. He blamed the farmers, abetted by the soldiers. He might easily have stated the conclusion that one of his councillors reached on much the same evidence four months later, in February 1660. The people of the Esopus, he wrote, "very thoughtlessly and without having any lawful reason . . . attacked some of [the Esopus natives] with an armed force, killed one and took others prisoners." With good reason, the natives had every right to presume that this was "a general design of all the inhabitants at the Esopus to kill all the savages." We, the authorities here on Manhattan Island, had promised to live in peace with the Esopus the previous year, and the natives had accepted that. But our people have betrayed our promises and us and "very rashly broken the compact." In the mirror put up to savagery, the face was that of the farmers.[11]

For his part, Stuyvesant reported to Holland that the disaster was "the result of the inconsiderate action committed the night before against some drunken savages." Still, the undeserving farmers and soldiers left him no choice but to relieve the besieged settlement.[12]

* * *

On September 30, Stuyvesant set plans for a campaign in motion. He followed the same procedures adopted by military commanders in the Low Countries for the relief of besieged forts or cities. First he bargained with the magistrates and populace of New Amsterdam for financial support. He seems to have had only twelve soldiers in Fort Amsterdam, so he needed volunteers.[13] They would have to do what the States hired soldiers had done in the Low Countries: cross into the countryside, move into place, and lift the siege of the settlement. Then they would enter the countryside cornering stragglers, punishing armed natives and civilians alike, and pursuing the enemy to his hiding places in villages or fortified strongholds. No one could predict how long such a campaign could last. The men would live off the countryside. They could hope for a small monthly wage and profits earned from officers prepared to buy prisoners or other kinds of booty. All this was very familiar.

Stuyvesant first called on the city's leaders for their advice and assistance. He could not have been surprised at the resistance that greeted him and continued to mark the subsequent negotiations. Such belligerent sparring was customary between the magistrates of cities in the United Provinces and military commanders charged with extensive, and always expensive, campaigns undertaken in their area, often for their own defense. New Amsterdam had no reason to make itself an exception just because it was a city in a province that bordered the Atlantic rather than Gelderland. If anything went forward, it would be because a contract favorable to both parties had been worked out. Just as he expected, Stuyvesant had to buy his citizen-soldiers.[14]

He won the magistrates' approval to beat the drum for volunteers. Assembling the city's residents, he addressed them in terms that carefully distinguished them from the country people of Esopus, those who had now gotten themselves into an impossible situation. He conferred on them the highest possible status within the social structure of the Netherlands, acknowledging them as citizens of a chartered city.

That done, he followed precedent and spelled out the terms of the coming campaign. Prizes seized along the way were now, as always, negotiated in advance. Captured natives could be turned over to the authorities for a price and then exchanged for a ransom that would see the government reimbursed. Captains of the city's militia bands would have their chance for additional rewards. Each was now given the freedom to incite as many of his men to enlist as possible. In Europe, it was called "enticement money."[15]

Death and danger became real. The New Amsterdammers called it peril to body and life. "Body" was not an abstract term. On a similar occasion later, Stuyvesant tried to induce other burghers to do their duty. He needed to talk about maiming and mutilation. He promised that those mutilated in the campaign would be given the same relief afforded to the company's soldiers. He set a monetary value on the parts of a man's body: for the loss of the right arm, 800 guilders; for the loss of the left arm, 500 guilders; for the loss of a leg, 450 guilders; for the loss of both legs, 800 guilders; for the loss of an eye, 300 guilders; for the loss of both eyes, 900 guilders; for the loss of the right hand, 600 guilders; for the loss of both hands, 1,000 guilders; for the loss of the left hand, 400 guilders.[16]

After two days of cajoling and arguing, only six men volunteered. No one offered himself because of a concern for the Esopus farmers; no one spoke a word of sympathy for the beleaguered villagers. No one said that he had friends there; no one seemed to care about the garrisoned soldiers. Rather, the citizens were, as the director recognized, concerned for their own safety and terrified of the nearby natives. Infuriated, he resorted to an unwelcome, but not unprecedented, expedient. Since none of the three city militia companies would come forward, he chose one by lot—and set a date for its embarkation. Anyone trying to abscond or failing to make his appearance faced a fine of fifty guilders.

The mustering of the volunteers and their river journey to the Esopus took place from October 3 to 10. On the evening of the men's departure, a sense of fright still prevailed. Panic took hold when a dog suddenly barked as the men were about to embark. Citizens took to the water, fearing that natives were about to swarm over the island. By October 10, the men had scrambled ashore near the river landing at Esopus. For about ninety minutes, they trudged from the strand up to the plain and the stockade.[17]

The natives had left two and a half days earlier. The land was drenched with rain.

An ineffectual military expedition turned into more of the same: prolonged negotiations for the exchange of prisoners and terms of a peace almost certain to be short-lived.

*   *   *

On Sunday, October 12, two days after the finish of the campaign, a native runner delivered to the director-general one of the final accounts of the murder of the native. The letter told a story from the young men's point of view. The statements were those of three Katskill natives. Two Esopus had insisted that they dictate the words to a Dutch man acting as scribe. He was the sergeant who had led the farmers and soldiers to the site of the assault. Now he was a prisoner of the natives. He knew that his captors were Katskills and Esopus. He was with them somewhere in the northern forests. He didn't say, or seem to know, exactly where.

Having been overcome by the natives, he had now been made their accomplice in producing a letter that carried their version of the affair. In many ways, the unnameable and unmarked forest that was home to none of them was a metaphor for the pages that were written there. They were neither entirely Dutch nor native. They were both: stories intertwined, hybrid. The natives, even as they had made themselves masters of the sergeant, had also buried their voice in the scribe's Dutch language. Once the pages found their way to Stuyvesant, he was, even if only for the time it took to read them, tangled in with the natives as well. He was made to absorb their thoughts, made to think about their understanding of the events. Like it or not, the pages drew him inland into their lives, and drew them into his.

The narrators told a universal tale of youthful innocence gone awry. Here were young men working all day, then tired and aimlessly rousting about and drinking, getting less and less careful for themselves, finding themselves set upon by men who may also have been drinking, finally engulfed in unanticipated and unprovoked tragedy.

At some moments, the storytellers seemed to be constructing an uncontrived description. It flowed out of their own world; it was one drawn without care for how it was read by the strangers. They described a world of dreaming and spirit presences. Twice, one man gave himself over to crying. Together they acknowledged the presence of death. They started keening in a strange way and accompanied it twice with expressions of dread. "Come, let's go away, I feel it in my body that we'll be killed." And later: "Come, let's go, we'll surely be killed. . . . my heart is full of fears."

At the same time, the narrators telegraphed messages meant for a Dutch reader. They and others had come to affect mendaciousness when dealing with the Dutch, and now it was present. So Stuyvesant was meant to find in the account of a young man who received brandy from the soldier and timidly replied, "I'm very much obliged to you," a youth who had an untroubled relationship with the soldier and who politely and cravenly accepted a place—even if only momentarily—in a community dominated by armed strangers. Stuyvesant was even made to read that the youth gave the trooper a friendly embrace. Yet the director-general knew that the young men were more than wary of the soldiers. About a year ago, he himself had reported that they were "very much frightened and hardly dared to appear because there were so many soldiers." Later, he had minuted that the soldiers were beating them. Only sixteen days before the episode, the chiefs had told his officers that the soldiers' guardhouse had been erected squarely on a path that they had long ago marked out and needed. For trying to use it, the soldiers had beaten up on a chief and others. They were lucky, the elders said. Had the young men been attacked, they would have "lustily fought for it."[18]

Stuyvesant was also expected to read as sincere another young man's assertion that trust existed between the Dutch and the natives. "You're crazy," the young man was supposed to have said. "Who should kill us?" We wouldn't kill the Dutch, and "we've done them no harm; why should they kill us?" The young men also had firearms in their possession, or at least one gun. Yet they seemingly never thought to turn the weapons on their Dutch assailants, despite the fact that they were among those whom the elderly chiefs had repeatedly denounced as undisciplined "barebacks," disillusioned youths easily provoked to lawlessness and violence, and beyond their own control.[19]

The director-general may also have found messages about masculinity encoded within the lines of the account. They may have been pointed directly at him. In many ways, the theme of male prowess or males raped of power stitched together the scenes. When the youth returned with additional brandy, his friends took pleasure in distinctly male behavior, engaging in fisticuffs with one another. At the end of the story, one of them gave clear expression to masculine courage in the face of death. "Come," he invited. "Kill me, I'm not afraid."

Yet fifteen months earlier, Stuyvesant had humiliated the same young men, or friends of theirs. In the course of speaking with the elders, he had challenged the young Esopus men to meet his troopers in combat. "I would match man with man," he challenged, "or twenty against thirty, yes, even forty." The old men had made no response. A day later, he reported them as saying that they were ashamed because he had challenged the young men and "they had not dared to fight and that therefore they requested, not to say anything about it to others." Eight weeks later, he reported that they were talking about it every day.[20] The unnecessary challenge was a dangerous and foolish action on Stuyvesant's part. It was dangerous because the young men were the very ones whom the Dutch intrusion had brought to power or at least loosened from the control of their elders. They saw the elderly chiefs beaten and humiliated by the soldiers. They reacted with overt anger and spite, perhaps at the madness that their cultures had become.

It was a foolish action, too. Stuyvesant's intention had been to keep a distance between the natives and himself and his administration. But fighting with the natives roughhouse, man to man, was to open a space for more than a physical encounter. It was taking a step, however small, into a relationship of physical and temperamental closeness where earlier the trading company had no need or desire to go. So perhaps the taunt "Come, kill me, I'm not afraid" was a reminder of the stranger's insults and the young man's violated pride. Perhaps Stuyvesant's own words were being thrown back at him in the mock self-description of another of the men, "I'm too small to fight."

There is no reason to think that Stuyvesant shared the letter with the citizens of New Amsterdam. He was, however, obliged to continue to report home on the violence of the farmers and soldiers, the immediate financial costs, and the long-term repercussions. What he reported was the last thing the company would want to have heard: again there were hostilities, and they were not of the company's making. Rather, they were the result of hotheaded actions by farmers against natives who were not even organized for some malevolent purpose but drunken.

*   *   *

Other evidence about Esopus also disturbed Stuyvesant and the company directors at home. The farmers had created a scene of murder in a social, moral, and physical space where too many margins were becoming increasingly permeable. Hybridity in the sense of deep mutual engagement was probably not abroad. But the settlers and natives were interacting in too many discernible ways. They were trafficking at will, in and out of the palisades. They were working the same land, the Dutch as bosses and the natives as paid laborers. Native children were running onto Dutch farms. The trading in liquor was making a mockery of provincial laws meant to set boundaries around liquor, its consumers, and the violence that was its predictable consequence.

Liquor, now consumed in abundance by the natives, had absorbed new and unexpected meanings: as something spiritual, a mystical source of solace. It made the natives dependent on the Dutch—another way of being bound together. Natives and Dutch farmers and soldiers got drunk together in what they called "liquor houses" and in other dark places where (some reported) they were learning each other's ways, each enjoying some unspoken but purposeful unguardedness. The soldiers played tricks on the natives; the natives made lying promises to Dutch men with whom they were now familiar. Sometimes the natives were the collective enemy, sometimes not. One farmer boasted that he knew when they posed a danger and when they did not. He would drive his cattle through their lands all the way to Fort Orange: he would run the risk for less than nothing. Like the others, he was both laconic and aggressive.[21]

When they weren't drunk together, they were thieves and tricksters to one another. The natives told Stuyvesant in 1658 that they wanted even more strangers among them ploughing the fields. But at the same time, they said that they wanted the strangers only at a trading post—probably the shanty where a stream ran into the Hudson River and where soldiers, farmers, and natives could get liquor. They listened to rumors that each would massacre the other. Stuyvesant, the Dutch told them, would see that it happened to them. Native men remembered being at the Manhattans in autumn of 1655—maybe they talked about that. The house of Christoffel Davidsz was in a secluded valley where he slept drunken natives and engaged in (as one soldier reported to

Stuyvesant) "his old tricks of selling liquor and tattling" with farmers and natives alike. At the bowerie where the young Esopus were working, furs, liquor, and stories were also regularly exchanged. Stuyvesant saw the danger of such conversation and forbade it. But it was the elusive coexistence that going inland was bound to breed.[22]

The natives' story of a single murderous encounter had inadvertently shown Stuyvesant that with the exchange of things, there was an unintended spillover of non-things. Beliefs and feelings seemed to be undergoing exchange; there were unintentional borrowings.[23] The narrative also exposed a landscape of deceit that was not entirely new to him. In 1658, the farmers had played him for a fool. They reported a murder committed by the Esopus. Firing from the shore, intoxicated natives had killed a Dutch man standing in a boat. The farmers wanted a war of revenge. Yet Stuyvesant's investigations of the incident proved that he had been misled. The victim had been shot accidentally and by a native of other families, not Esopus. Meanwhile, as he expected, the farmers maintained their pleas for a war or the removal of the Esopus from the whole country.[24]

They would have understood that war had only one meaning. It would be as it was in Europe or in New Netherland earlier. Once justified, it was total war. The farmers' knowledge of the European wars was not expressed in the vocabulary of moral justification used by Grotius and other jurists. It found expression in the commonplace barracks-talk of soldiers. We hear it only once, when an enraged soldier accused one of them of being a sutler. "I don't want . . . [this place] turned into a home for you sutlers." The sutler (*soetelaer*) was a figure as emblematic of the continental wars as the soldier himself. She (or he) was a camp follower who fleeced the trooper of his booty and wages (if he had received any) in return for provisions the army felt no obligation to supply, pots and pans, blankets, and, in the case of women, personal favors. Usually a woman, the sutler symbolized on a low-life level the trilogy of war, booty, and venality that, ironically, jurists blessed as well. "Everything is lawful against an enemy," wrote a renowned eighteenth-century Dutch jurist. The only question is "whether the loot rightfully belongs to the captor or the warring state"[25] (see Fig. 9).

As he would be forced to do a year later, Stuyvesant responded in 1658 by sailing upriver to Esopus. He announced his refusal to undertake the much desired war. Instead, he insisted that the farmers distance themselves from the natives, relocating within a defensible settlement. He and his men would join them in erecting palisades. He would initially provide the settlement with a garrison of men. He, too, talked the language of war. The farmers could buy his soldiers' protection just as peasants had done for decades in the Low Countries. In return for twenty-five men garrisoned at their expense and billeted among them, they could pay him a yearly contribution of grain. He reduced their call for a war to a whining complaint. Do not disturb us in future with your "reproaches and complaints."[26]

*   *   *

Affairs have now moved forward nineteen months, to February 1660. The young men with their brandy and premonitions of death have been slain or wounded. The Esopus have retaliated. Nine or ten Dutch men have been slain, and another fourteen taken captive but most of them released. The authorities on Manhattan Island meet to consider how to proceed. We can predict the scene that now opens before us. These are the last considerations on a just war that we will hear.

Chapter 18
No Closure

In early February 1660, Stuyvesant summoned to Fort Amsterdam his councillors and the burgomasters of New Amsterdam. They were to debate whether a just war could be waged against the Esopus. Their considerations were shadowed by threats of hostilities from nearby natives. But Esopus demanded immediate attention. So the three sets of players we have encountered are in their own way present: administrators on the island, farmers, and the native people.

Once again the council chamber is a theater not of facts but of emotions, stratagems, and uncertain justifications. Stuyvesant delivers opening statements. He may have given nine or ten minutes to reading them out. He has taken care to have copies made for each of those present. The burgomasters are going to say they have no interest in responding. He will make them do so.

He begins by citing the disturbances at Esopus but then steps back. Setting aside decisions about this officer, that set of farmers, or those informants, he challenges his advisers to consider a just war by placing the events in a European context. Or, rather, he infuses his words with force because he speaks as a northern Netherlander of 1660, that is, as we might say, a postcolonial. We are, he says, a new nation. We are newly emerged from the imperium of Spain, free of the yoke of political and religious tyranny. We deserve a righteous reputation. The Dutch, not the natives, are the injured party in these affairs. Injuries have been done to reputation as much as to human lives and property. Over the past years, he reminds the officials, we have earned respect as a "nation loving honor and liberty." God has delivered us from "Spanish tyranny and inquisition." But now we face hostilities at Esopus too dreadful and unbearable for us as such a nation. Our enemies there have jeopardized our Batavian reputation, denying us a future we deserve in this place. They have made it impossible for us to farm the most productive land in New Netherland. We have fallen into an abyss. To climb out of it, we must wage "an aggressive war . . . against the Esopus Indians."

He seems to consider the just war a philosophical subject too wearisome to rehearse once again. Because he knows the law well, he must realize that in

Grotian doctrine, the prosecution of wars is like the prosecution of court cases: to be just, they must be pursued with due scrupulousness. But now, he seems finished with justifications—theological, legal, or commercial. He has only a plan that it is marked by war-weariness as much as resolution.[1]

He proposes invading native territory and driving its people out by force. In this, he makes the move of any expropriating colonialist as well as one uniquely Dutch. As he had not done before (and, one must suspect, is not wholly convinced of now), he essentializes the native as a being naturally unamenable to rational negotiation. He can then rethink the positive value of the aggressive war that he had thus far rejected. On the first matter, he breaks with Dutch humanism and denies the natives the capability of making laws and governing themselves, qualities that the company and patroons had accepted in the 1630s and that his countrymen had affirmed during the *Eendracht* affair. To support this, he calls upon a binary world that he knows he does not inhabit. It's a world the natives have never allowed him to experience and one disallowed by his own often indefatigable efforts to negotiate with tribes he knows differ not only from the Dutch but also from one another. We are, he implies, bound by law and the dictates of religion. They, however, are not fettered by "any form of government or laws or divine service."

This re-description of the natives as a species apart allows him to urge the others to rethink their military posture. Haven't we, he argues, been ruining ourselves by maintaining defensive positions while anticipating and waiting for improvement in the capacity of these "barbarous savages" to understand our legitimate intentions? Mustn't we now abandon this posture of hoping and waiting and instead give ourselves the freedom of moving over the open country?

He considers two meanings of the open country. First, he takes the voice of the administrator concerned for the security of the whole province and especially the places he guards most closely, those immediately around Manhattan Island. He is thinking in terms of the deployment of his limited number of troops to the many nearby trouble spots either already in evidence or likely in the future. Mespath Kil is one such place. Only a month after these deliberations, he has to sign another treaty of peace with the chiefs of the Hackensacks and Wekquaesgeeks as well as those from Staten Island, the Highlands, Haverstraw, and Queens County.[2]

The open country are those acres immediately around the many new villages where farmers, Stuyvesant insists, have a right to run animals without fear of native depredations. For their security, he suggests mounted patrols. Let their numbers be filled by a limited number of available soldiers and, as needed, six to ten men of each village "for attack or defense." Such patrols were common in Netherlands villages, even during peacetime. But here he evokes a picture of vulnerability resembling Camus's urban citizens in *The Plague*. A disease is abroad and cannot be checked. No one, neither the doctor nor the priest, can predict where it will appear and do its killing: here in the home of a solitary man; there in the mayor's house; someone living near a restaurant. You can't find it to end its treachery.[3]

Second, as for the Esopus, Stuyvesant advises, the Mohawks now press them into seeking peace. But they must be punished. They show no remorse for killing colonists; they say they're superior: one savage, they jeer, is "as good as two Dutchmen." Their peacemaking is a grand act of deceit.

Stuyvesant's proposal is one freighted with illegalities and dubious historical precedents. Let us determine, he is saying, that we can justify an aggressive war and with that carry it to "their dwelling places and wherever they may retreat to." Legitimation was possible. But equally available were counter examples of illegal trespass. Aggressors carrying war into the lands of others were the hallmark of seventeenth-century European warfare. Ironically, it was realized in the army that operated with such devastating effect against Stuyvesant's own rebel people, the Army of Flanders. Again and again, enemy troopers carried war to the Low Countries along the Spanish Road, a military route stretching seven hundred miles from Lombardy to Brussels.

Unsurprisingly, carrying war into another state's or people's territory was a point of contemporary legal discussion. In *De Jure Belli ac Pacis*, Grotius had quoted Cato on such an invasion in Roman times. Julius Caesar, he wrote following Cato, ought to have been satisfied with driving the Germans out of Gaul, the province that had been assigned to him. Without first consulting the Roman people, he ought not to have carried war against them into their own territory.[4] Whether this example was known or not, these early February deliberations were such a legitimating consultation. If justified, soldiers will invade the territory of a people who had not initiated hostilities and who, by the administrators' own repeated words, were living under independent rulers and were legitimate landowners before the strangers came—only to trade. But now they come to remove.

Councillor Nicasius de Sille echoes Stuyvesant's concern for the safety of Manhattan Island and its villages. He directs his response exclusively to its security, seemingly unconcerned about Esopus, which he mentions not at all.

Cornelis van Ruyven's response is calculated to demolish Stuyvesant's position. He refuses Stuyvesant's regression into stereotype and essentialism and returns to the realities of the present. The natives' outrages are, he agrees, unbearable for a "liberty-loving nation." But no war can be waged against the Esopus until we are certain that they "have given us sufficient and legal cause."

Like some twenty-first-century critic of colonialism, he alludes to its penchant, in the end, to be driven by desire, not reason. Let Stuyvesant consider that his anger and frustration are driving his proposals rather than reason. For we cannot, he continues, justify "a *wish* to punish . . . [them] for the deeds committed by others." He has examined the facts in order to establish causation—including Dutch culpability—and concluded: we have insufficient grounds to support the legality of a war.

Stuyvesant's points, he shows, are flawed. Look at events from the natives' side. Wouldn't the natives surely have grounds for seeing, as we know *we* have facts to see, "a general design of all the inhabitants at the Esopus to kill . . . [them] all." Stuyvesant might also think about his own compact of friendship with them. It was dated June 1658 and agreed upon by the council. Now we have broken it. Since the causes are insufficient, we would be blamed for initiating an illegal war. Try once more to keep open the question of peace. Maintain the present posture, frustrating as it may be: keep "war in the background and in suspense." We have, after all, deferred seeking revenge when even more seriously provoked.

The meeting concluded after prolonged deliberations. Perhaps van Ruyven spoke again as Stuyvesant's moral conscience. Perhaps he summoned the humanism that a Rensselaerswijck merchant had four months later, stating, "on both sides people had been killed." Perhaps Stuyvesant took the position he had in 1656. He, too, would in effect accept a truce and keep war in the background. We don't know. The majority voted that war was unavoidable but would have to be deferred until fall. Its legality was not mentioned. Van Ruyven's conviction that the natives' hostilities were justified because they were defensive was never enunciated. Perhaps someone dared to suggest that in initiating the Esopus settlement, Stuyvesant had gotten them into a contradiction. He had, after all, colluded with Beverwijck traders in promoting the expansion inland that would surely incite conflict and destroy the native communities upon which the trade depended.[5]

The correspondence, proclamations, and communiqués of the following months referred to war and peace. The Mohawks, Mahicans, Katskills, Hackensacks, and Esopus as well as the Dutch leaders all used the words. Actually, diplomacy, especially sophisticated and purposeful on the natives' part, created conditions for a truce. Stuyvesant vacillated about waging a war. Officially, he proclaimed a war six weeks after the deliberations in the fort but almost immediately entered negotiations with native tribes as eager as he to see the Esopus disempowered, if not entirely driven away. Dutch raiding parties sporadically attacked Esopus villages and took captives. Native raiding parties did the same and for the same purpose. The fact that the Esopus held Dutch prisoners from

1659 to the end of his administration in 1664 meant that at no time during those years could Stuyvesant pursue an all-out war.

Stuyvesant continued to evaluate war (and truce and peace) through a merchant's eyes. He weighed its worth against the profits of trade. In winter 1664, he shared his thoughts about war with the magistrates of Beverwijck. He needed to give directions about the ongoing conflict between the Mohawks and Seneca against the Hurons. So it was about their conflict that he was writing. But his opinion and advice expressed a position that he had held about his own responsibilities over the past seventeen years. Their war, he warned, will stifle the trade. Use your powers of intervention to bring the parties to peace.[6]

*   *   *

In 1660, the unstable encounters of the Esopus and the strangers had about four years to run their course, that is, until the English carried war to de Sille's three forts, two cities, three colonies, and thirteen villages. A nineteenth-century editor refashioned the Dutch-Esopus encounters by calling on the romanticized stories of the frontier wars between American soldiers and the Plains Indians. Dramatically, he flagged an attack in 1663 as the work of people on the warpath. Were the Netherlands Rhetoricians (*Rederijkers*) invited to perform some scenes of those final encounters, however, they might have seen through such romanticism and shown some degree of reluctance to stage them. The story up to November 1664, when the English occupation of New Netherland began, offered no climactic moment followed by a denouement and closure. In fact, so much was repetitious. An audience wasn't going to be treated to scenes of an enlightened redirection of Dutch policy toward the Esopus or other indigenous peoples. They would simply see the strangers' and natives' war begun in 1660 followed by another in three years' time. They would be viewing the same sort of staged characters—military leaders and their armed but often disobedient and halfhearted followers. They would again view the plight of the weakest individuals on both sides: the elderly, women, and children who were either killed or, more likely, used as pawns exchanged in these conflicts. The strangers and natives would be seen continuing to wear each other down in the same ways—by terror, predation, dishonesty, or their mere presence. They'll provide little new material for the players to work with.

Looking back from 1664 to the assault on the young Esopus men in 1659, the *Rederijkers* would have caught the tediously repeated actions. Company directors continued to blame the overseas administrators and colonists for the unrest—and spoke their tired lines about lack of funds for soldiers. Stuyvesant and the council remained squeezed between the company's shameless neglect and the disloyalty of distant villagers. They continued to denounce isolated habitations but failed to use the law to protect the natives. The treaty of peace made in March 1660 between the Dutch and the Hackensacks and other chiefs offered all sides a chance to repeat pledges that murderers would be brought to justice. It provided a well-trodden platform for one chief's predictable lines that all would henceforth live as brothers.[7]

The strangers, especially those supposedly guiding the enterprise from Holland, continued to be uneasy about colonization. In the year when the young natives had been attacked, Stuyvesant had become anxious about a possible English settlement competing for the northern fur trade. His solution was similar to the one seized upon at Esopus. He would settle a number of colonists, "some good and clever farmers, about 25 or 30 families." He had in mind Polish, Lithuanian, Prussian, Jutlandish, or Flemish emigrants. Many were refugees from the wars to the north and east of the United Provinces and from Flanders in the south. Such a settlement would—and this was original, at least in its enunciation by a New Netherlander—promote civilization. He wrote that he hoped to select the appropriate lands soon and purchase them from native owners. From what we can tell, he never did and nothing came of it. Five weeks later, the directors told him that they meant to prevent all future colonies established by private investors. They offered no colonization plans of their own.[8]

The Esopus did sue for peace—but it was much like the earlier scenes of the Raritans, Tappans, Hackensacks, Mahicans, Wekquaesgeeks, Canarsee, and Nevesinks doing the same. The director-general played the cat, entering negotiations with them but also leading his punitive expedition into their country. Mercenaries were sought among the English and (again) a military alliance proposed but carefully hedged with reservations about aggressive wars. Nothing came of it.

Meanwhile, the Esopus said that they were afraid of the Dutch and wanted peace. But other raids followed. In April 1660, soldiers moved off from the settlement to about three miles inland. They came upon a house and perhaps as many as sixty natives. A trooper recorded that the natives made no resistance but started to flee. Three or four men were killed trying to escape. The *Rederijkers'* audience would have seen it all before. It could be the expedition against the Raritans in 1639 or the march in snowy weather near Hempstead in 1644.[9]

The Esopus were still wedged between the Mohawks and the Dutch as well as caught in an economy where pelts were in short supply. As for their lands, their loss could be predicted, too. In 1658, Stuyvesant told them it would be better to sell him the whole country of the Esopus and move inland or to some other place. We're too close together, he said. In 1659, he put their removal in terms of the sentence of banishment familiarly handed down to criminals in the Low Countries. Let them depart and join another nation "without ever coming, much less planting, again on the land." He said, again, "sell me the land," and they had promised to do so. Then, just after he'd met with his council and peace had been negotiated, they agreed (he reported) to "abstain from . . . [using it] and leave it." He told his superiors that the seized land—the audience would have heard European warlords say this—were reparations for damages done.[10]

As for the Esopus natives, their words about dispossession carried some originality. They admitted that they wanted to get away from the Dutch; they wanted to be given a small piece of land "at a great distance." The adult men, once estimated at four hundred to six hundred and numerous enough to be represented by ninety-six leaders during these years, soon were described as no more than sixty. Once berated for cherishing their plantations and haggling too strenuously over beaver prices, they were described by the farmers as malingerers, drunks, and vagrants good for nothing but spying on the village and visiting everybody's house in it.[11]

*   *   *

On two levels, the encounter episodes in Esopus failed to be marked by closure. After a year of hostilities, peace meetings in May 1664 failed to deliver a moment of final resolution. The English assumed authority over the area just three months after the peace and the surrender of the last captive taken by the Esopus. But their military occupation was not co-synchronic with an end to hostilities. Rather than constituting some kind of new beginning, a policy-driven break with the past, the new administration simply provided new bureaucratic desks onto which the old problems might fall. The Euro-American encounters now became the responsibility of an English commissioner. A rumor was drifting among the northern and river tribes that the Esopus and Dutch had been sold out by the Mohawks and English well before the Dutch left in 1664. Some Mohawks, said one native, had heard an Englishman say that the Mohawks should now offer gifts to the English to kill the Dutch. So they gave the new strangers some wampum and promised them the lands of the Esopus. But exactly how the Esopus assessed the replacement of one set of strangers by another, we cannot know.[12]

The farmers continued to abuse and distrust one another. Not surprisingly, they resisted English troopers in 1665 and carried out a mutiny against the English garrison in 1667. From what we can tell, it was the most sustained rebellion in the province. The terrible shared happenings of 1659 to 1664 had done nothing to make the families into a harmonious community. Farming went ahead apace. English authorities quickly reconfirmed lands purchased by settlers and the Beverwijck merchant-entrepreneurs. Men accustomed to serving as interpreters and those known to have sold illegal brandy and arms to the natives continued to do so. A confederation of Esopus sachems continued to make decisions for their people. They renewed the peace signed with the Dutch about a year after the English occupation. In the earlier peace conferences with the Dutch, they would have heard their lost lands described vaguely as "all the land" and as "payment" for losses they'd caused. Fourteen months later, they would not have listened to a three-word description but one 127 words in length and carefully composed by men with a keen eye for the acquisition of territory. Now they were hearing (or, unless the interpreter were skillful, perhaps not really hearing at all) about land on "a direct line," or a hill as "the true west" bounds of the land—just an inkling of the surveyor's language that was about to help colonialize New York in a property-centered English way.[13]

The year 1664 marked the end of what later commentators would call the Dutch period in New York's history. Yet in relation to the formulation of a workable Amerindian policy or the resolution to native insurgency, it ended inconclusively. There was no closure, certainly not in the sense of an evaluative or reflexive moment. The after of Dutch New Netherland came too quickly for a critical overview of a forty-year encounter with the natives, too quickly for reflecting on how traditional Amerindian values and ways had melded (or not melded) into those of the Europeans. Some men and women experienced trauma because the province would now be English. Of course, none needed to cope with the distress felt by twentieth-century colonials such as the English when the subcontinent they had constructed into the Raj had to be returned to the colonized first peoples. Nor did they seem to need the sense of shame and regret that saturated many Netherlanders' remembrances of their colonial past in the Indies.

The year 1664 preceded by about three hundred years the voices that found international expression in terms such as "decolonization" and "post-colonialism." These terms made colonialism a historical category. By deconstructing this or that colonial project, scholars and political figures had framed such sites as units for critical inspection.

The assessment of the Dutch period as a closed-off colonial or imperial interlude was not available in the 1660s. In 1665, Stuyvesant submitted hundreds of papers to the company in order to defend his stewardship of New Netherland. He was not required to assess the impact of Dutch policy on native Americans. Nor did he think to do so. The Others—to what "investigative modalities" they had been subjected; whether subduing them had been a cultural project of control; the degree to which colonial knowledge or modernizing capitalism enabled their domination—these contemporary ways of understanding the subtleties of imposed power were not central to an understanding of what had transpired in New Netherland.[14]

Today it is difficult to determine what sort of Dutch colonialism Stuyvesant might have been able to identify in 1665. Even if he'd had the inclination to do so, he did not have the term "colonialism" to think with. In a conversation with contemporary scholars of colonial and imperial formations, he might well have rejected colonialism and empire as applicable to New Netherland. The terms, after all, identified a centralized authority neither contemplated by nor put into place by the Netherlanders. He might, however, have accepted his conversationalists' insistence that European colonies and empires were of various forms and that within that variety, two distinctions stood out. First, early modern structures differed from those of late modernism; and, second, empires aimed at full-settlement colonization differed from the maritime empires of traders.[15] He might well have agreed with a third insistence found in the discourse of colonialist scholars, namely, that the foreign intruders did not establish domains of unimpeded hegemony.

Let's say our imagined discussants first consider the matter of hegemony. (Stuyvesant is listening and, in my judgment, at times nodding in agreement.) The scholars would concur that rather than colonialization and imperialism being coherent and able to produce internal substantial transformations according to changing circumstances, such projects were often incoherent, torn apart by allegiances to conflicting values, and (some) only epiphenomenally effective. Inevitably, they were unable to appropriate crucial sites of imagination, personality, and spirituality. Even the strongest of them was vulnerable to endless possibilities for fragmentation. All this places a question mark over hegemony as an adequate descriptor for the highly complex and, because of that, more destructive and suppressive force of imperialism.

Insofar as colonial empires were fluid and multidimensional webs of relationships, both the exertions of power and resistance were characterized by complexity and contingency. Relationships across alliances—those the Dutch, for example, formed with the Pequots, Mohawks or Hackensacks—were necessarily unstable and created limits of rule rather than the expansiveness of rule at will. Such untrustworthy boundaries were set by indigenous societies as well as the mechanisms of exchange that repulsed the colonizers' efforts to reshape the natives along uncontaminated European lines. Instead, exchange entangled European cultural ways with native traditions. There was no alterity: all were bound together.[16]

Stuyvesant would have experienced in New Netherland what Bernard S. Cohn described in 1996 as the experience of the British in coming to India. They entered a physical territory, he wrote, but an epistemological space as well. They thought they could make known the "unknown and strange unknowable." In many ways, they failed. Stuyvesant would have recognized, too, the sly civility of the native population, the cunning David frustrating the giant's certainties. What he would not have played a part in was the cause and effect of British imperialism in India, that is, the construction of an imperialistic ideology that preceded and caused colonial expansion. The seventeenth-century imperialism of the Dutch was like its nationalism. It was an outcome of prior endeavors, experimental and often undertaken only reluctantly. The Dutch seaborne empire was the result of such loosely coordinated mercantile experiments. In terms of imperialism, it was, wrote one scholar, "the reverse of what was to be expected." In that, it was beyond Stuyvesant's knowing.[17]

Pushed to recognize his conversationalists' reasoning Stuyvesant, I suspect, would have further recognized that a colonial history—the story of his New Netherland—was not simply a chapter in the history of the mother country. It was chapters in the histories—singular and entangled—of the Raritans, Hackensacks, Mohawks and Esopus. Here were oral histories in which far more than relations with the Dutch would have been recited and where the Europeans might not have even been accorded a dominant role.

In 1978, the Dutch historian H. L. Wesseling published his reflections on European colonialism from the sixteenth through the eighteenth century. He argued that the colonizing efforts of this period differed greatly from those that succeeded it. The earlier adventurers, for example, knew of no superior Occident. They recognized the East as a "rich fabric of a strong broad weave with a more fragile Western warp inserted in it at broad intervals." The Portuguese and Dutch acceptance of a subordinate presence in the East testified to this reality. George Winius took up Wesseling's perspective in 1991. He questioned the value of applying the notion of empire to the Portuguese presence in Asia. The word, he wrote, conjured a "misleading mental picture." The correct one must somehow be of a maritime presence, that of a people "wedded to the sea." Portugal's *Estado da India Oriental*—their eastern estate—consisted of a "number of enclaves, the largest only a few dozen square miles in area and the smallest no longer than the foundations upon which its fort rested." From these, he went on, they strove to control, for example, the sea lanes of the Arabian Sea and its commerce. Winius also called for a review of the matter of intentionality—again, one can envision Stuyvesant signaling limited agreement—and argued that historians have often erred in finding more plan and pre-design to the building of colonies and empires than they actually involved. "In the Portuguese case, everything seems to have been ad hoc." They were not seeking an independent role in places such as India but entry to the spice trade and magnificent profits.[18]

The Dutch also expected to be subalterns in a superior Orient. It is less certain, however, that they anticipated a subordinate presence in North America. The line drawn at one time by Grotius through his own words, setting up an identity between the two trading spheres, is perhaps as valuable a trace to this uncertainty as we need. *Alia enim India alia Americana ratio est* ("What is true for the Indies holds for the Americas") he had written and crossed out. But certainly, the Dutch knew that they were in North America by way of being wedded to the sea. They were alongshore to legally ordered societies. They were there on sufferance—living in what Ann Laura Stoler identifies for a later period as white enclaves. And they were moving ahead as the markets led: without pre-design but confident of their prowess as traders whose changing relationships with markets and customers were design enough.[19]

Additionally, the apparatus of a Dutch state had only recently been imagined into existence. With respect to overseas ventures, the States were expected to be coexistent with, if not dependent upon, the great trading companies. The nationalism that fueled nineteenth-century European imperialism was yet to make its appearance. By the mid-seventeenth century, overseas company personnel and settlers felt a belonging to a Netherlandish (Batavian) people. They did not yet, however, give allegiance to a Dutch nation-state grounded in some primordial force dividing one people from another. A twentieth-century historian such as C. A. Weslager might direct readers to find a character fault in Pieter Minuit for leading the Swedes against the Dutch on the Delaware on one occasion. But Minuit's loyalty to the Swedish queen was unexceptional in an era when societies expected loyalty to be bought and sold.[20]

The West India Company closed down its operations in New Netherland because the English forced it to do so. What, we might ask, did they think they were walking away from? Publicly, neither the directors nor Stuyvesant wrote of having walked away from part of an overseas empire. Later scholars, cogitating on this question, have admitted to semantic difficulty forming a satisfactory definition of the presence of the early seventeenth-century Netherlanders overseas. Expansion, diaspora, overseas presence, far-flung trading and naval power, international trade and maritime power, seaborne empire: all have seemed fitting descriptions. George Keyes employed the term "empire" in the title of his catalog of Netherlands marine art published in 1990 as *Mirror of Empire*. With the exception of a single reference to a seaborne empire, however, the word then vanished from the catalog's pages. Elsewhere, he settled for two maritime empires, one in the East and the other in the West Indies. In 1973, Charles Boxer surveyed the possibility of a Dutch empire in the South Atlantic in the first half of the seventeenth century. He rejected it. Such a formation in northeastern Brazil seemed "on the verge of realization in 1644." It did not, however, "come to fruition."[21]

Perhaps the new West India Company, a corporation floated by the provinces after its predecessor's demise in 1674, best understood the mentalité of the West India Company. The new directors evaluated the defunct company not in terms of failed political imperialism but of botched commercial expansionism. The collapse was not an affront to the pride of a humbled aristocracy, military class, or centralized state. It was simply an example of what incompetent businessmen could do, even with millions of guilders. Echoing Pieter de la Court's words, the company, they said, had gotten into reckless privateering and risky "colonization schemes." But their own attempts at colonization—those made in the 1680s—were as halfhearted as the efforts of the organization they were replacing. They were, in one scholar's words, "uncertain and lacking in real *élan*."[22]

In 1664, the States and the West India Company left behind the possibility of political dominion over an extensive territorial domain in New Netherland in favor of navigation rights and speculative ventures in the slave trade and sugar production in Surinam along the northeastern coast of Latin America. It was a choice against territory suitable for settler communities. In 1992, Peter Hulme drew a distinction between the practices of territorial and maritime imperialists. He reminded readers that in considering colonialism, a curious division separated "the discursive practices which relate to occupied territory where the native population has been, or is to be dispossessed of its lands by whatever means from those pertaining to territory where the colonial form is based primarily on control of trade."[23]

Hulme did not go on to specify the discursive or nondiscursive practices of traders. But there is no reason to think that Portuguese and Dutch administrators were ignorant of the distinction he had in mind. Nor were they unaware of the traditions and deep cultural orientations always at play. Among the Portuguese, a landed aristocracy, always eager to play out its hidalgo tradition, pitted itself against the aims and purposes of seafaring traders such as Vasco da Gama and his financial backers. To meet the demands of this feudal tradition, Luis de Camões in *The Luciads* (1572) under-described the peacefulness of da Gama's voyaging in search of Eastern markets and instead created adventures that supported the hidalgo's warrior identity. In 1674 at a council meeting in Batavia, Pieter van Hoorn asked whether the Dutch ought not "turn their commercial and maritime empire into a true colonial one, that is, one based on the settlement of white people in the tropics." The love of the soil was something deeply implanted in mankind the world over, he continued. Even in commercially minded Holland, successful merchants seek to buy a bit of landed property. But then, proving the opposite of his argument: they then "engage in farming or gardening, if only on a small scale and as a hobby."[24]

Stuyvesant and his councillors increasingly considered territory a major concern. They referred to New Netherland as a newly opened province. They also contemplated an offensive military posture toward the natives. But stopped in our tracks in 1664, as it were, we haven't certain evidence that either a vision of lands saturated with Dutch dominion or a policy of aggressive warfare against the Americans would have become a reality.

The demands of reversing into such a vision or policy—of abandoning ground saturated with exchange for ground saturated with dominion or, equally, social stratification based on land rather than money—would have been a break with deeply seeded cultural ways, as I hope these chapters have shown. The validity of Francis Jennings's conclusion about Amerindian-Dutch encounters up to about 1661, namely, that they occurred in an environment where the Dutch "lacked the desire to extend domination over distant tribes," was dramatically reinforced by two well-known decisions of the States taken about New Netherland after 1664.[25] First, in July 1666, the Peace of Breda ended the Anglo-Dutch naval war during which New Netherland had fallen to the English. The States abandoned it in favor of a naval peace in the East Indies and unchallenged rights to Surinam.

Second, the hand of alongshore entrepreneurs also steered the wheel of events over the next eight years. In the course of a third Anglo-Dutch war (1672–74), a small Dutch fleet unexpectedly found itself in command of the fort on Manhattan Island and indeed New Netherland. Had it not involved Netherlanders, the episode would have been little short of bizarre. As it was, it was a story of restlessness, of seeking the opportunities of the next bay or sea lane. Zeeland (and not the States) had seen some value in sponsoring an expeditionary squadron commissioned to raid English ports and attack shipping at Saint Helena, then in the Caribbean and waters off Newfoundland. The fleet would then return to the Azores and home. Of the two squadron commanders, little, if anything, wrote one scholar, separated them from daring sea rovers such as Piet Heyn, Francis Drake, and Jack Hawkins. The raid into New York harbor proved successful, but they, understandably intent on following their instructions, remained on Manhattan Island only long enough to put the fort in good repair. Then they went a-roving, north to the fisheries of Newfoundland and thence to a rendezvous with other vessels at Fayal in the Azores. Meanwhile, a marine captain found himself elevated to governor-general on

Manhattan Island and served honorably until, after fifteen months, the States again returned New Netherland to the English. No one among them or in Zeeland had, in any case, envisioned a conquest of New Netherland.[26]

Native Americans were not a presence in these maneuvers as the English and Dutch traded New Netherland back and forth. A cruel silence seemed to say: they go with the territory. In 1673, when Zeeland's raiders found themselves coming ashore on Manhattan Island, they were making landfall on sites that only two generations earlier were the waterlands of native villagers. But neither they nor their superiors cared to state what had been insisted upon only thirty years earlier: that the Americans were sovereign owners of their lands, free men and women. The silence about them resembled what enveloped the Maroons living along the mysterious and treacherous coasts and rivers now opened for business by the Dutch in Surinam. The natives there were on the periphery of another theater of adventure capitalism. The coastal and riverine lands were first in the custody of Zeeland and then, twelve years later, under the control of the refloated West India Company, Amsterdam, and the Aerssen van Sommelsdijck family. They were expected to produce tropical commodities (largely sugar) for the profits of the owners. The entrepreneurs had the Surinam River and its tributaries to bring its plantations into productivity. They worked slaves under Dutch supervisors. The Guianese natives were on the margins of an enterprise that had no need for colonists—mostly no need for them, either, except to get out. They were inland to a place where members of the board appointed all officials—the governor, auctioneers, even teachers.[27]

*   *   *

Petrus Stuyvesant died at his bowerie on Manhattan Island in February 1672. In 1799, New York's authorities affixed a plaque to one of the walls of Saint Marks-in-the-Bouwerie, where his body rested. Their words seemed to re-create New Netherland as the island that so satisfied the earliest voyagers. "In this vault lies buried Petrus Stuyvesant, late Captain General and Governor in Chief of Amsterdam in New Netherland now called New York and the Dutch West India Island."

Praising Stuyvesant but offering only a teasing sort of closure on New Netherland, Dominee Henricus Selijns wrote an epitaph shortly after his death. "[H]ere lies Stuyvesant, Who once commanded all that was New Netherland."[28]

Weighing Up

Weighing has always been a concern of Netherlands people. Constructing weights and measures, weighing anchor, weighing up income and debits on the recto and verso pages of an account book, weighing a jar of spices, two lengths of timber, one quarter of a beaver pelt, a half-barrel of herring, holding things in balance: these have been the necessary preoccupation of a dominantly mercantile and, in the seventeenth century, seagoing people. New Netherland was a matter of weighing up during each of its forty years.

Weights and measures could serve as a metaphor for the spirit that lay behind the Netherlanders' encounter with the Algonquian-speaking people. Dipesh Chakrabarty reminds us that a society makes weights and measures exact so that the business conducted is strictly economic, not social. Prices do not reflect in any way a concern with trust and familiarity. We have seen, I hope, that the Netherlanders expected such commercial measuring to dispose of the need for familiarity, for full presence. The expectation was a chimera. Their economic exchanges entailed social elements and social consequences for the unanticipated outcomes of which they could not avoid holding themselves answerable.[1]

The story of New Netherland is not a tale of tragedy. The record of the Dutch encounter with the native population is a tragedy. The Dutch did not intend to reorder the natives' construction of daily realities. They felt no metaphysical obligation to bring them to a Netherlandish worldview. They didn't mean to impose models of time and space. Yet time, space, the construction of social reality and a worldview did change. Stuyvesant, van Ruyven, de Sille, Jeremias van Rensselaer, farmers, and Beverwijck's land speculators could all could see it. They experienced it firsthand.

The need to subordinate the natives provoked moments of contrition. The tragedy lay in the awareness of error but stubborn persistence of illegitimate violations nonetheless. The Dutch came to realize that, among other things, staying in New Netherland asked for the practices of a military culture that was not theirs. In 1780, Sir John Dalrymple sought to console himself after England's loss of the thirteen North American colonies. "England might very well put up with the loss of America," he wrote. "For she would then exchange an empire of dominion which is very difficult to be kept for an empire of trade which keeps itself."[2]

Seventeenth-century Netherlanders knew that empires of trade—or spheres of commercial influence—did not keep themselves. They were kept by the traders' schemes, visions, and greed. As much as empires of dominion, the indigenous peoples kept them. Theirs were the lives and resources exploited. They were the ones who faced cannon fixed to the decks of cargo ships and arms carried by company soldiers hired to protect a trading monopoly. Theirs were the cultures carelessly destabilized, disfigured, or destroyed. Empires of trade did not simply crank over smoothly, one deal, one trading season, one fleet departure after the next. They required ruthlessness: all it took to procure (as we would say) the deliverables. In weighing up and then enacting such a culture of dominance, the Dutch acted out a betrayal of ideals and accepted values: betrayal of themselves and others. They reaped the shame and the sorrow.

I do not pretend to be untroubled at this betrayal, nor at my inability to wholly understand it or explain it. If you, as a reader, are also troubled, that, it seems to me, is honest and to the good. But because I have often in this story used the Dutch East Indies as a context for getting a better understanding of the Dutch in North America, let me share with you the mind of a similarly troubled historian writing of those islands in 1995. In trying to recover the reality of the Dutch East Indies society, Frances Gouda wrote: "[H]istorians must read in between the lines of every narrative and apply personal, moral judgments, even if the images they are impelled to construct reveal a murky mixture of black and white." It was a moral murkiness of which the seventeenth-century Netherlanders were aware as well.[3]

As we end, think again about New Amstel. You'll remember the Amsterdam regents' high hopes in 1656 for its establishment and prosperity. Jacob Alrich agreed to be its first overseer and was also optimistic. "This is a new beginning," the merchant wrote in 1657. But within two years, he was despairing at the failure of his city. When he died of fever in December of that year, the Amsterdam officials were already trying to sell the colony to the West India Company.

He'd written little about the natives. One of his few recorded statements is metaphoric of the intentions of Netherlanders we've heard expressed so often over the province's previous years. "Little is thought here of the inhabitants or natives. . . . [W]e'll keep ourselves peaceful toward them."[4]

Notes

Soundings

1. In writing these paragraphs, I have been inspired by John Stilgoe's *Alongshore* (1994). For a reproduction of the Prototype View, see Stokes, 1915–28, 1 (Frontispiece), and analyzed, 119–31. For later interpretation, de Koning, 1999.

2. "Quiet possession" was also a diplomatic term referring to undisputed possession of territory.

3. *The Sorrow and the Pity* screened on television in 1981.

Chapter 1. Alongshore

1. Fernow and O'Callaghan, 1853–87, 1: Resolution of States General, September 24, 1621, 26 (hereafter, *CHSNY*). States General is hereafter States. I will clarify when States refers to a provincial assembly.

2. Stilgoe, 1994, 9.

3. Goedde, 1989, quoting William Temple (1673), 108.

4. Davies, 1961, 6; Lambert, 1971, 172.

5. Unger, 1971, 191–94.

6. Guicciardini, 1593, 11, 63; Le Petit, 1609, 101, 102.

7. *CHSNY*, 1: Memorial of Gerrit Jacobsen Witsen . . . Read August 18, 1616, 13; Resolution of States, August 18, 1616, 12. See also Stokes, 1915–28, 2: First Dutch Surveys of the Vicinity of Manhattan Island, 63–75, and plates 23, 24. I have not reproduced the Figurative Map of Cornelis Hendricksz (1616) because it is an areal map of New Netherland and, in that respect, too easily read as a representation of territorial dominion and occupation. For the same reason, I have not included the Figurative Map of Adriaen Block (1614).

8. *CHSNY*, 1. Memorial of Gerrit Jacobsen Witsen . . . Read August 18, 1616, 13. For *Onrust*, see Stokes, 1915–28, 2: First Dutch Surveys, 69, 72.

9. Goedde, 1989, 62. See also Stokes: the Dutch were too unimaginative to read prophetic meanings into *Onrust*, 4: 39.

10. Seed, 1995a, quoting Grotius, 151. See also 102–3.

11. *CHSNY*, 1: Hendricksen's Report, August 19, 1616, 14. See also Seed, 1995a: making charts and highly detailed descriptions was linked to the unique Dutch meaning of discovery, 160. The Minquaes were possibly Susquehannocks (Kupperman, 1995b, 96).

12. Nijhoff, 1909, 33. See also Muller, 1909, XLIX, L.

13. Naber, 1921, Bijlage D . . . *Contract met Henry Hudson*, 89. The East India Company may have particularly distrusted Henry Hudson, even anticipating that he

might foment mutiny (Nijhoff, 1909, Chamber of Zeeland to Amsterdam Chamber, March 11, 1609, 113).

14. For excitement aroused by seamen's stories and the return of the Indies fleets to Dutch ports, see von Saher, 1986, 10, 11, and Rinkes, 1927, 261, 262. For the vessel detained in Medemblik, see van der Zee and van der Zee, 1978, 82. For references to May, the Monnickendam ship, and the view from the quarterdeck, see Jameson, 1909j, under December 1624, 78, and 1909b, 41.

15. Brugmans, 1973, 3: 207; Prudon, 1968, 63, line 322.

16. Van der Heijden, 1971b. See also I. B. Berckhout, *Sonnet op de Beschrijvinghe van de Gedenck-weerdighe Oost-Indische Reyse van den Vermaerden Schipper Willem Ysbrantsz Bontekoe,* 70, line 1, and see sonnet immediately following, *Klenck-Dicht op de Wonderlijke Reyse van W. Y. B.,* 71. For the popularity of sea stories in cheap pamphlet form, see Goedde, 1989, 23.

17. Van der Heijden, 1968b, *Hij Leut, Die 't Leut; Ick en Leut Naet* being no. XXXIV in *Derde Schock van de Sinnepoppen van Roemer Visscher* (Willem Janse Blaeu, Amsterdam 1614), 135.

18. De Veer, 1978, 153. For Coen as *een legende,* see van der Woude, 1948, 50.

19. Muller, 1909, 9.

20. Ibid., XXXIX; 27, XLIV, and see 36 n. 2.

21. Ibid., 6, 4, 37, 42, 54, 41, 55.

22. For these references, see ibid., 36–59 and XLIX.

23. Ibid., 41. See von Saher, 1986, using the journal of the first Dutch fleet to the Indies, dated September 30, 1595, 35.

24. Kern, 1910, xviii; van Balen, 1942, 7, 14, 54, 27, 56, 73, 78.

25. Van Balen, 1942, 19; van Strien, 1998, quoting William Lord Fitzwilliam, May 1663, 292.

26. *CHSNY,* 13: Dirs. to Stuyvesant, February 16, 1650, 26 (emphasis added); 2: Alrich to Commissioners, April 13, 1657, 6. See Wieder, 1925: the "founding of New York made little impact at the time," 3. For excitement about voyaging tales, see Beekman, 1988, 27, and Klooster, 1997, 41.

Chapter 2. "The Island"

1. *CHSNY,* 1: Resolution of States, October 4, 1618, 21; Resolution of States, February 12, 1620, 22, April 11, 1620, 24, and March 16, 1622, 27. For "Manhates," see Stokes, 1915–28, 2: First Dutch Surveys, 71. For *Prinsen Eylandt,* see Wieder, 1925, 12.

2. Instructions for Willem de Vlamingh and Broad Council from Dirs. of East India Company, April 23, 1696, quoted in Schilder, 1985, 166 (Hereafter, VOC). For Manhattan Island as the *middelpunt,* see Wieder, 1925, 6. For the term's use, see Muller, 1909, 3 n. 1, 10 n. 2, 98, and *Annotatiën,* 1 n. 1, van der Woude, 1948, 349, Kern, 1910, 1: XVIII, Cannenburg, 1964, 107. For Ijszee rendezvous, see Muller, 1909, 3, 96, 98, 120, and map opp. 226.

3. Van Balen, 1942, 58, 93, 92, 113; Beekman, 1988, 7.

4. Masselman, 1963, 159, and 322; van der Woude, 1948, 80, and see 349; Boxer, 1965, 211.

5. Van der Woude, 1948, quoting VOC Instructions to Governor-General Pieter Both (1610), 98; Masselman, 1963, 319.

6. Boxer, 1965, 211. This account is carried in van der Woude, 1948, 99; Masselman, 1963, 322, 361; Colenbrander, 1934, 159; and Colenbrander, 1911, under February 25, 1629, 127.

7. Nijhoff, 1909, 56. For voyaging to coasts and islands, see *CHSNY*, 1: Organization of a Company, July 18, 1614, 6, Grant of Exclusive Trade, October 11, 1614, 11, Resolutions of States, October 9, 1618, 21, October 4, 1618, 21, and August 29, 1620, 25. For Isaac Jogues's comparison of New Netherland with the Low Countries, see Jameson, 1909e, 259. For multiple voyages, see Jameson, 1909j, under December 1624, 78.

8. See *CHSNY*, 1: West India Company Agents at Hoorn to West India Company Assembly, March 29, 1624, 31, and Petition of Traders, September 13, 1621, 25 (hereafter, WIC).

9. *CHSNY*, 1: Resolution of States, September 28, 1621, 27. For Carleton, *CHSNY*, 3: Privy Council to Carleton, December 15, 1621, 6, and Carleton to Lords of the Council, February 5, 1622, 7.

10. *CHSNY*, 3: Carleton to Lords of the Council, February 5, 1622, 7. For Carleton's eventual protest to the States, see Rink, 1986, 80 n. 22.

11. *CHSNY*, 3: Carleton to Lords of the Council, February 5, 1622, 7 (emphasis added).

12. Jameson, 1909b, 34, 36, and see 37–39. For *ontdekking*, see Seed, 1995a, 161. In *Nieuwe Wereldt*, de Laet is emphatic that between 1610 and 1615, Amsterdam merchants navigated the Hudson River, traded, and "*our people wintered there,*" 38 n. 4 (emphasis added). For Isaack de Rasieres's mistaken belief that English notions of possession were something like his own, see Jameson, 1909c, 109–10 (emphasis added).

13. *CHSNY*, 1: Petition of New Netherland Company Dirs., February 12, 1620, 23, quoting Remonstrance of Dutch Ambassadors to Charles I received by States, June 11, 1633, 56. For Adriaen vander Donck's grounding Dutch possession on the "long and peaceful trade" that grew up in New Netherland, see Seed, 1995a, 155.

14. For European nations' different strategies for claiming overseas possessions, see Seed, 1995a, 2.

15. *CHSNY*, 1: Petition, February 12, 1620, 23, and see Resolutions of States, April 11, 1620, 24, and November 6, 1620, 25. For the petition rejected to avoid trouble with the Crown, see Rink, 1986, 74; [Robert Cushman], *Reasons and Considerations Touching the Lawfulness [Rightfulness] of Removing out of England into the Parts of America* [1621], quoted in Arber, 1897, 501.

16. For lack of interest in forming a nation or state at the time, see Klooster, 2000, 9, and Schama, 1987, 62. For glory, see Harline, 1987, quoting *Munster Chat* (1646), 215.

17. *CHSNY*, 1: General Charter, March 27, 1614, 6.

Chapter 3. The Quarterdeck and Trading Station

1. Wieder, 1925, Doc. C, "*Instructie voor Willem Verhulst (Januari, 1625),*" 125 (hereafter, Doc. C), for *Prinsen Eylandt/Verhulsten Eylandt*, 12; for *Nooten Eylandt*, 14.

2. Van Laer, 1924, Doc. C [48], and Wieder, 1925, Doc C, 125. For May's use of *logie* when describing the Russians in the Arctic, see Muller, 1909, 23. See also van der Woude, 1948, 91 and 338, and de Veer, 1978, 128, passim. For *Nooten Eylandt* as strategic and useful, see Jameson, 1909b, 45, and 1909j under November, 1626, 83, and 1909c, 104.

3. Stokes, 1915–28, 2: First Dutch Surveys, 74. For the Buchelius Chart [1640] as accurate as a modern chart, 1: 137.

4. Jameson, 1909j, under December 1624, 76, 77.

5. Guicciardini, 1593, 74, and see 75, 76; Le Petit, 1609, 159, 160.

6. Hoogenberk, 1940, 102.

7. Wieder, 1925, 22. For the legalities of *handelsrecht* in greater detail, see Hoogenberk, 1940, 87, 88.

8. Wieder, 1925, Doc. C, 121.

9. Schiltkamp, 1964, 21. See von Saher, 1986: the Broad Council might also include supercargoes and ordinary seamen, 21. See also Colenbrander, 1911, under February 18, 1630, for de Vries identifying the assembly as *den Breede-Raedt,* 134. For Curaçao, see Schiltkamp, 1964, 21. For the Indies, see de Klerck, I, 1938, quoting Instructions to Pieter Both (1609), 339. For New Netherland, see *CHSNY,* 1: Remonstrance of New Netherland, July 28, 1649, 308.

10. For messmates, see Hoogenberk, 1940, 88, and Wieder, 1925, 24. For Verhulst's residence on the South River, see van Laer, 1924, [64]; Wieder, 1925, quoting Doc. C, 130.

11. For a third word, *vormelijkheid,* the performance of empty formalities, see Seed, 1995a, 49. On *zee-rechten* (1603), see Schiltkamp, 1964, 50.

12. Quoting Schiltkamp, 1964, 86. See also Wieder, 1925, 32, but for directors sending some free emigrants and thereby raising the colonists' numbers to 270 in 1628, see Jameson, 1909j, under March 1630, 89. For ministers under short-term contracts, see Jameson, 1909h, 120, and Stokes, 1915–28, 4: Jonas Michaëlius to Johannes de Foreest, August 8, 1628, 72, and Michaëlius to Adrianus Smoutius, August 11, 1629, 73.

13. Jameson, 1909j, under February, 1624, 73. For Plymouth fort (1622), see Arber, 1897, 111.

14. Wieder, 1925, Doc. E, *Particuliere Instructie voor Crijn Fredericksz, April, 1625,* 149, 150 (hereafter, Doc. E). For fortifications in the Low Countries, see Westra, 1998, 11.

15. Wieder, Doc. E, 157, 158. For useless folk, see van Laer, 1924, Doc. D, *Naerdere Instructie voor Willem Verhulst, April 15, 1625,* [105] (hereafter Doc. D).

16. Wieder uses *der Hollandsche kolonie* but is generally careful to distinguish between terms such as *handelsnederzetting* and *factorij,* 17. For the Provisional Orders as plans for a factory or garrison "instead of colonies," see Condon, 1968, 73.

17. For "our people," see van Laer, 1924, Doc. D [109], and Wieder, 1925, Doc. A, *Provisionele Ordere Maart 30, 1624,* 113. For distrust of colonists, see Wieder, 1925, Doc. C, 122.

18. Colenbrander, 1934, viii.

19. Van der Woude, 1948, 336. For a damning critique of the company's policy of non-colonization and rejection of *vrijeburghers,* see de Klerck, 1938, 1: 266–68, and also Masselman, 1963, 358. For description of the Chinese farmers, see de Klerck, 260.

20. Colenbrander, 1934, Coen to VOC Dirs., March 19, 1613, 43, and see 54, passim. For distrust of women, see Meilinck-Roelofsz, 1962, 238. The WIC also preferred that its personnel and colonists marry local women; see Boxer, 1973, 130. For Johan Mauritz's fruitless pleas for middle-class emigrants for Brazil in the late 1630s and early 1640s and a despair at unsuitable colonials, see Boxer, 1973, 145, 146, 132, 133.

21. For Coen's hopes for a middle-class society, see de Klerck, 1938, 1: 234, and Colenbrander, 1934, 43, 54. For ascetic Hollanders at home, see Wertheim, n.d., 6. For Coen's doubts about successful colonization in Java in 1628, see Boxer, 1965, 244, and for

his plans for the WIC, see van der Woude, 1948, Coen to VOC Dirs., January 1, 1614, 345; Stokes, 1915–28, 1: Report of de Rasieres to WIC, September 23, 1626, 134. For "idiots" as unqualified preachers, see Jacobs, 2005, 269.

22. For this distinction, see van Laer, 1924, Doc. C [60].

23. Coen quoted in van der Woude, 1948, 337 n. 17.

Chapter 4. Natives and Strangers

1. Seed, 1995a, quoting Adriaen vander Donck, 160.

2. Jameson, 1909j, under October 1628, 88; Wieder, 1925, Doc. D, 142, 143, but see also identifying the natives as *Indiaen*, 141, 142.

3. Wieder, 1925, Doc. A, 113, and *CHSNY*, 1: Resolution of States regarding Voyage of Discovery, February 21, 1611, 4.

4. Van Laer, 1924, Doc. C [52]. For the English crown questioning the contracts, see *CHSNY*, 1: Answer to Dutch Ambassadors, April 1632 and found as appendix, May 23, 1632, 58.

5. Masselman, 1963, 319.

6. Wieder, 1925, Doc. D, 136–37, 141. For the accomplishment of some of these arrangements, see *CHSNY*, 1: Pieter Schagen to the States, November 5, 1626, 37.

7. Alexandrowicz, 1967: the Dutch-Ceylon Treaty (1612) announced a declaration of war as essential for opening hostilities against a third party, 239 n. H. For a just war as a result of injuries, see Grotius, *De Jure Belli ac Pacis*, book 2, chap. 1, no. 1 (hereafter *JBP*), Bull, Kingsbury, and Roberts, 1990, 23, and for an example of illegal territorial invasion, 5 (emphasis added).

For the acceptance of Grotian precepts regarding a just war across polite and popular culture, see Schama, 1987, 238–39, and iconographical evidence, 239, 241.

8. Hoogenberk, 1940, 74, quoting J. K. J. de Jonge, *De Opkomst van het Nederlandsch Gezag in Oost-Indië*, III ('s-Gravenhage, 1862–65), 28–29 (emphasis added).

9. Von Saher, 1986, 7; Wieder, Doc. C, 122 and Doc. D, 142; and van Laer, 1924, for translation of the same document [106]. For predation, see *CHSNY*, 1: Secret Resolution of States, March 22, 1624, 29.

10. Wieder, 1925, Doc. C, 127. For monopoly status and bilateral agreements, see van der Woude, 1948, 61; Alexandrowicz, 1967, 58; *CHSNY*, 1: Resolution of States, October 14, 1624, 34; and van Laer, 1924 [55].

11. Wieder, 1925, Doc. C, 126, 127, 112. For the Netherlanders' awareness of being in the Indies only on sufferance (*precario*), see Alexandrowicz, 1967, 46.

12. Governor-General de Carpentier to VOC Dirs., February 3, 1626, Blussé, 1995, 158. For negative reports from North America, see van Laer, 1924, [55], Jameson, 1909b, 45, and 48, and Muller, 1909, LXVIII and LIII. For failure to mention violence, Nijhoff, 1909, Bijlage Q, extract uit J. de Laet's *Nieuwe Werelt* (1625), 111–14, and Bijlage N, extract uit van Meteren's *Belgische Oorlogen* (1611), 107–8. Artwork produced in Brazil appeared to aim at making the Dutch presence there seem natural and, by that, justify their exploitation of the indigenes (Westermann, 1996, 115).

13. Instructions quoted in van Laer, 1924, Doc. C [55] and Doc. D [109]; for Grotius's caveat against coercion, see Scott, 1916, 68. For an example of the same caveat regarding the Bandanese on Bali, see von Saher, 1986, 7.

14. Andrew Marvell (1651), quoted in Schama, 1987, 263. Schama treats this subject with charm and fairness, 235–57, 261, 262.

15. For reflections on the notable insularity and remoteness of the Dutch from the native people of New Netherland, see Starna, 1991, 25, and see Rothschild, 2003, 31.

16. *CHSNY*, 1: Schagen to States, November 5, 1626, 37–38; Jameson, 1909j, under November 1626, 85, 87, and under February 1624, 71.

17. Jonas Michaëlius to Johannes de Foreest, August 8, 1628, quoted in Wieder, 1925, 50.

18. Jameson, 1909j, under October 1628, 88; Jameson, 1909h, Jonas Michaëlius to Adrianus Smoutius (1628), 127.

19. Trelease, 1960, ix.

Part III. Staying Alongshore

1. Thomas, 1991, 8.

Chapter 5. Sovereign People

1. [De la Court], 1702, 30.

2. *CHSNY*, 1: Schagen to States, November 5, 1626, 38, and see Jameson, 1909j under November, 1625, 82 n. 2. For the auction, see Stokes, 1915–28, 4: December, 1626, 67, quoting Wassenaer, *Historisch Verhael*, pt. XII, fol. 58.

3. Quoting Zandvliet, 1988, 75. For merchant houses preferring trade and quick profits to the uncertain returns from colonization, see Boxer, 1973, 258.

4. Alexandrowicz, 1967, 46.

5. Ceci, 1977, 228; *CHSNY*, 1: New Project of Freedoms and Exemptions, Point 5 (1635), 96.

6. *CHSNY*, 1: New Project of Freedoms and Exemptions, Point 5 (1635), 96, and for greater detail, 13: Patents to Pauw, July 12, 1630, 1, 2; Boxer, 1965, 212.

7. Meilink-Roelofsz, 1962, 232, 238.

8. New Project of Freedoms and Exemptions (1635), 100. For Eelkins, see Trelease, 1960, 55, and Salisbury, 1982, 148. For resentment of individual traders, see *CHSNY*, 1: Patroons to States, June 16, 1634, 85.

9. Van Klaveren, 1953, 58.

10. *CHSNY*, 1: Patent to Godijn and Blommaert, July 15, 1630, 43. Minuit was not altogether wrong in writing of village decisions taken in common. For councils in Algonquian villages and tribes, see Grumet, 1980, 47.

11. Jameson, 1909c, 104. For a manuscript sketch of the bay, see Colenbrander, 1911, opp. 154.

12. *CHSNY*, 1: Patent to Godijn and Blommaert, July 15, 1630, 43; for "property, command or jurisdiction" again used, Patent to Kiliaen van Rensselaer, August 13, 1630, 44.

13. *CHSNY*, 1: Patent to Godijn and Blommaert, July 15, 1630, 43.

14. Coen to VOC, November 16, 1621, Colenbrander, 1934, 212; Van der Woude, 1948, 336.

15. *CHSNY*, 1: Patroons to States, June 16, 1634, 84. For fierce shareholder criticism of the VOC in 1623, see Klooster, 2000, 4.

16. For Dutch clarification of non-Christian peoples' sovereignty, see Alexandrowicz, 1967, quoting Thomas de Cajetan, often cited by Grotius: "theirs are legitimate rulers, whether the people live under a monarchical or a democratic regime; they are not to be deprived of sovereignty over their possessions because of their belief," 59 n. C.

17. *CHSNY*, 1: Patroons to States, June 16, 1634, 84–85, 86 (emphasis added). Grotius makes this point in *De Jure Praedae Commentarius* and repeats one related to American Indians made in *De Indies* by Franciscus de Vitoria (Alexandrowicz, 1967, 59 n. B). For an enlightening study of the plural nature of early European legal systems, see Benton, 1999.

18. Biggs, 1999, 385–87.

19. Jameson, 1909d, under December 1, 1640, 210.

20. *CHSNY*, 1: Ass. of XIX to States, October 25, 1634, 94; Vitoria quoted in Jennings, 1984, 4; van Laer, 1908, Kiliaen van Rensselaer to Bastiaen Janse Krol, January 12, 1630, 159. For parallels with the "petty regencies" on whose sufferance the Dutch knew they remained in places such as Batavia and Ceylon, see Furnivall, 1939, 34.

21. Van den Vondel, *Op het Twaalfjarige Bestand der Vereinigde Nederlanden* (1609), in Rens, 1969, 32, line 11; quoting Rowen, 1986, 65; *CHSNY*, 1: Patroons to States, June 16, 1634, 86.

22. The unified territorial state of the eighteenth century was not the dominant ideal of medieval or early modern Europe (Biggs, 1999, 390).

23. Borschberg, 1994, citing *Commentarius in Theses XI*, 38, 58, 71, 225–27.

24. For *De Inquirio* (1636–37) taking up the same problems, see Borschberg, 1994, 123, and see van Gelderen, 1992, 207.

25. Schama, 1987, 61.

26. Van den Vondel, *Toneelschild* (1661), Rens, 1969, 101; Anon., 1615, n.p.

27. For "leagues," see Stokes, 1915–28, 4: 49; *CHSNY*, 1: WIC to States, May 5, 1632, 52.

28. Presser, 1948, quoting Vondel, *Het Gulde Veen* (1658), 180; de Vries and van der Woude, 1997, 179.

29. *CHSNY*, 1: Patroons to States, June 16, 1634, 87. For wampum, see Richter, 1992, 84, 85, and Kupperman, 1995b, 102–4.

30. See *CHSNY*, 1: Patroons to States, June 16, 1634, 86. For Franciscus de Vitoria's argument that foreigners could claim only lands of natives having no established ruler and that Indians had sovereignty if men among them "were true princes and masters of the others," see Lepore, 1998, 164. See also Stokes, 1915–28, 4: Wouter van Twiller to Massachusetts Bay, October 4, 1633, 79.

31. *CHSNY*, 1: Remonstrance of Ambassadors to Charles I, rec'd by States, June 11, 1633, 56.

Chapter 6. Masters of Their Lands

1. For identifications of Plymouth, see Colenbrander, 1911, under October 5, 1618, 5, and Cannenburg, 1964, entry of May 16, 1623, 9; van Laer, 1908, Log of Jan Tiepkesz, entries of October 8 and November 12, 1636, 355, 362.

2. Colenbrander, 1911, entries of October 5, 1618, August 18, 1619, and June 10–18,

1620, 5, 19, 23, de Vries quoted at November 26, 1629, 132, and for fortifications, entry of June 5–9, 1630, 140. See also Porter, 1994, 4.

3. Rink, 1986, 81; Cannenburg, 1964, entries of May 16, 1623, June 16, 1626, and May 17, 1623, 9, LX, 104.

4. For *Eendracht*'s seizure on May 3, 1632, see *CHSNY*, 1: WIC to States, exhibited May 5, 1632, 51, and States to Ambassadors, April 7, 1632, 46; for depositions before the admiralty court in early November 1633, Depositions, November 1–7, 1633, 72–81, and see Ass. of XIX to States, exhibited October 25, 1634, 94.

5. Colenbrander, 1911, entry of June 10, 1630, 141. For John Seldon's *Mare Clausum* (1635), see Rowen, 1972, 150, and see Scott, 1916, viii–x.

6. For the earlier incident, see Stokes, 1915–28, 4: under July 6, 1626, 66. For careless use of "Virginia," see *CHSNY*, 1: Resolution of States Respecting New Virginia, September 4, 1621, 26; WIC to States, May 5, 1632, 52.

7. *CHSNY*, 1: Albert Joachimi and Govert Brasser to States, April 10, 1632, and May 23, 1632, 49, 54.

8. *CHSNY*, 1: States to Ambassadors, April 7, 1632, 47.

9. *CHSNY*, 1: G. van Arnhem to States, April 5, 1632, 45; Ass. of XIX to States, exhibited October 25, 1634, 94, and see WIC to States, May 5, 1632, 50–52.

10. *CHSNY*, 1: Remonstrance of Ambassadors to Charles I, June 11, 1633, 56. Perhaps to legitimate their claim in English eyes, they referred to planting colonies, Joachimi and Brasser to States, April 10, 1632, 48 (emphasis added); Ass. of XIX to States, exhibited October 25, 1634, 94; see Alexandrowicz, 1967, 46, 235.

11. Alexandrowicz, 1967, 46, 47. In chapter 2 of *JBP*, Grotius inscribed but then excised this phrase. Perhaps he was either slightly uncertain or aware that his role was as adviser on the status of the East Indies, 46.

12. Stokes, 1915–28, 4: Wouter van Twiller to governor of Massachusetts Bay, October 4, 1633, 79.

13. *CHSNY*, 1: WIC to States, May 5, 1632, 52 (emphasis added). For the Grotius-Freitas controversy over the East Indies, see Alexandrowicz, 1967, 45. These phrases repeat the exact words of Grotius in chapter 10 of *JBP* regarding the East Indies (Alexandrowicz, 1967, 47). Kingsbury and Roberts, 1990: Grotius was explicit on the property rights of aborigines. Infidels and heathens held property according to their own systems of law. "Discovery was no basis to claim what is already held by another, even though the occupants may be wicked, hold wrong views about God, or be dull of wit," 47, quoting *JBP*, book 2, chapter 20, no. 9.

14. *CHSNY*, 1: Answer to Remonstrance of Dutch Ambassadors, April [?], 1632, 58.

15. *CHSNY*, 1: Answer to Remonstrance of Dutch Ambassadors, April [?], 1632, 58, 59. The United Provinces gave the WIC no original land charter, and land cessions were to be voluntarily offered by native peoples (Trelease, 1960, 40).

16. *CHSNY*, 1: Answer to Remonstrance of Dutch Ambassadors, April [?], 1632, 58. For a general awareness of this and other claims disputes, see Petition of Eight Men [with Additional Observations . . . [July 26], 1649: The New Englanders admit that the country is justly ours "but their pretense [is] the richness of the land and that it lies waste," 268 n. 8.

17. *CHSNY*, 1: Answer to Remonstrance of Dutch Ambassadors, April [?], 1632, 58, 59. For Grotius's insistence (against Portuguese claims) that the lands of the East Indies were not *terra nullius* or (a term also used) *vacuum domicilii*, see Alexandrowicz, 1967, 46. For feudal fantasies, see Hinderaker, 1997, 79.

18. Schiltkamp, 1964, 32.

19. Dyson, 1985, 51, 129, 130. For a people not worth annexing, see Whittaker, 1994, 17.

Chapter 7. Inland Drownings

1. Pynchon, 1997, 59 (emphasis added).

2. Hooft, 1999, 28; Egmond, 1996. For the colonists' plea for help, see *CHSNY*, 13: Dutch Inhabitants of Gravesend to Dir. & Council, September 8, 1655, 40, and 1: Commonalty to Adriaen vander Donck, September 6, 1650, 446.

3. Furnivall, 1939, 34. See also van Gelderen, 1992: the VOC and WIC settlements were only on the margins of places about which the companies "had further not the slightest concern," 101.

4. Wertheim, n.d., 6.

5. Day, 1904, 44, and, in agreement, van der Woude, 1948: territorial expansion in Java was involuntary, at least on the directors' part, 346, passim.

6. Quoting Masselman, 1963, 225, and quoting Furnivall, 1939, 34. For dominion, see de Klerck, I, 1938, 327, and van der Heijden, 1971a, 58.

7. Furnivall, 1939, 35. For Quilon, see Boxer, 1965, 209; van Balen, 1942, 113.

8. Van der Woude, 1948, 341, 340; Winius and Vink, 1991, 5, 2. For the Dutch failure to use their language as a political tool for at least three centuries of their colonial presence in the Indies, see Beekman, 1988, 64; Blussé, 1995, 158–60; quoting Hooft, 1999, 16, and see 15.

9. Jennings, 1984, 125; O'Brien, 1981, 54, 53, and for New Jersey, 54.

10. See Merwick, 1990, 6–67.

11. O'Brien, 1981, 67; Boxer, 1973, quoting Gaspar Dias Ferreira, 144.

12. Geyl, 1946, 7, 13. For a more elaborated version of his argument, see Geyl, 1961, 94–108, 254–62; Schama, 1987, 56.

13. Rens, 1969, 29; Geyl, 1946, 14. For Geyl quoting the synod, 1961, 92; Grotius quoted in Remec, 1960, 101.

14. De Vries and van der Woude, 1997, 175. For de la Court, see Rowen, 1972, 201.

15. De Vries and van der Woude, 1997, 175.

16. [De la Court], 1702, 7.

17. Ibid., 73.

18. Ibid., 85. For John Stuart Mill's opinion that "the establishment even of trading posts by a commercial company" burdened it with "unnecessary expenses," see Day, 1904, 44.

19. [De la Court], 1702, 343, 345. De Vries and van der Woude, 1997, put the cost as 1.5 million guilders, 175.

20. Jameson, 1909c, 105.

21. Le Petit, 1609, 37.

22. For the claims of Cornelius Auretius (Cornelius of Gouda) that archaeological evidence established the south of Holland as the home of the Batavii, see Tilmans, 1993, 35, and see 37. For Holland as Venice, see de Vries and van der Woude, 1997, 175.

23. De Vries, 1986, 85.

24. For Prince Lodewyck's reference to land towns, see Evans, 1972, 85; van Loo, 1997, 185, and see 169.

25. I am accepting Johan Huizinga's conviction that land war was repellent to the

Dutch national character but see Zwitzer, 1997, 53. For the army as internal threat, see Rowen, 1986, 76. For contemporaries' expressions of hatred of soldiers, see Evans, 1972, 108. For Vondel's paired opposites, see Rens, 1969, 24. Rens writes that his republican-ism echoed majority opinion, 17.

26. Rowen, 1972, 212, 213. For another allegory, see Anon., 1615, n.p. The author's characters are lion (Holland), leopard (Spain), water fowl (Holland's sailors), grasshop-pers (Holland's soldiers/marines).

27. Van Balen, 1942, 32.

28. Rowen, 1972, 213.

29. Scott, 1916, vii; Masselman, 1963: in 1602 the VOC failed to realize that "protect-ing and extending its trade would require vast sums to maintain armed forts and fleets able to repel envious competitors," 148. Its treaty-making powers opened the door for empire and territorial acquisitions, "something that had never been contemplated," 151.

30. Seraphim de Freitas, *De Justo Imperio Lusitanorum Asiatico* (Valladolid, 1625), quoted in Alexandrowicz, 1967, 51.

31. *CHSNY*, 1: Resolution of States, October 25, 1634, 95. For Wouter van Twiller's feline letter to Massachusetts Bay, October 4, 1633, see Stokes, 1915–28, 4: 79.

Chapter 8. Bells of War

1. Underhill, 1638, 36. For Lion Gardiner's later memoir entry recording that some Pequots were "flayed alive . . . and some roasted alive," see Hirsch, 1987, 1196.

2. Jameson, 1909j, under November, 1626, 83, 84.

3. *CHSNY*, 1: Considerations regarding a Truce with Spain, November 16, 1629, 42, and Effects of WIC, September 4, 1626, 35, 36. For Hendricksz, see Israel, 1986, 132; Boxer, 1973, 27.

4. Van den Vondel, *Verovering van Grol* (1627), van der Heijden, 1970f. The Dutch is *"Ick sing den legertraght den Princen van Oranjen,/ Die 't heyr Spinola, en all 'de maght van Spanjen/ Met sijn slaghorders tarte, in het bestorven velt/En Dulken de stadt Grol deed ruymen met gewelt"* (259, lines 1–4). For the *Aeneid*'s opening lines as a familiar way of beginning an epic poem, see Helgerson, 1992, referring to Luis de Camões's *The Lusiads* (published 1572), 28.

5. Van den Vondel, *Verovering van Grol* (1627), van der Heijden, 1970f, 293, line 747; 293, line 738; 293, line 746; 294, line 753; 293, lines 739 and 750: 294, line 751. Vondel uses *barrento*, an obsolete word translated by van der Heijden as *brandschatting*, 294.

6. Israel, 1986, 9.

7. *CHSNY*, 1: Ass. of XIX to States, October 24, 1634, 92; Anon., 1615, n.p.

8. *CHSNY*, 1: Extract, Dirs. to States regarding the Truce with Spain, November 16, 1629, 42, and Remonstrance of WIC against Peace with Spain [n.d., ca. March 1634], 64.

9. *CHSNY*, 1: Resolution of States on Report of WIC, October 14, 1624, 34; van der Woude, 1948, 359; Remonstrance of WIC against Peace with Spain [n.d., ca. March 1634], 67.

10. *CHSNY*, 1: Effects of the WIC, 1626, 35, 36; the directors quoted, Considera-tions regarding the Truce with Spain, November 16, 1629, 41; van Hoboken, 1982b refer-ring to de Laet's *Jaerlijck Verhael* and a Resume, *Kort Verhael . . . tot het eynde van den jaere 1636*, 195.

11. *CHSNY*, 1: Effects of the WIC, 1626, 37.

12. Anon., 1626, 3.

13. *CHSNY*, 1: Ass. of XIX to States, October 23, 1629, 39, and see Considerations regarding the Truce with Spain, November 16, 1629, 40–42. The directors undoubtedly had Willem Usselincx's visions of colonization in mind (see van Dillen, 1982, 150, and Schmidt, 2001, 176–84).

14. *CHSNY*, 1: Ass. of XIX to States, October 23, 1629, 39, 40.

15. *CHSNY*, 1: WIC to States of Holland and Westfriesland [1634], 67, 68; van der Woude, 1948, 336. See Colenbrander, 1934, for VOC shareholders' priorities: "the ideal of land settlement remained foreign to them," 9.

16. *CHSNY*, 1: WIC to States of Holland and West Friesland [1634], 67.

17. Redlich, 1965, 271, and 1964, 210.

18. Stokes, 1915–28, 4: under May 10, 1635, 81; *CHSNY*, 13: Council Minute, March 28, 1643, 12; Jameson 1909d, under June 16, 1640, 205.

19. Parker, 1988, 13; t' Hart, 1993, 43–45. The evidence for Underhill's service to Frederick Hendrik at Groenlo is circumstantial but not trivial, see (the frequently unreliable) Shelley, 1932, 102–4, and, in New Netherland, 296–324 (Schulte Nordholt, 1966, 73).

20. Wieder, 1925, Doc. D, *Naerdere Instructie voor Willem Verhulst*, April 25, 1625, 142; Stokes, 1915–28, 4: Wouter van Twiller to Massachusetts Bay, October 4, 1633, 79.

Chapter 9. "Only This and Nothing More"

1. *CHSNY*, 1: Subject of Ass. of XIX, March 23, 1633, 61, and Jameson, 1909d, under April 16, 1633, September 28, 1643, and June 25, 1635, 186, 233, 198, and 1909j, under April 24, 1624, 76.

2. Jameson, 1909j, under February 1624, 73, and 1909d, under May 17, 1635, and April 28, 1636, 192, 196. For the West Indies as a hunting ground, see van Loo, 1997, 181—90. For Stuyvesant, see van der Zee and van der Zee, 1978, 152; *CHSNY*, 1: Report and Advice on the Condition of New Netherland, December 15, 1644, 152; and Petition of Twelve Men, January 21, 1642, 202.

3. O'Donnell, 1968, 124–26. For evidence of natives probably on the alert, see Jameson, 1909d, under June 1, 1635, 193.

4. Stokes, 1915–28, 4: Isaack de Rasieres to Samuel Blommaert, 1628[?], 75.

5. For Raritans, see *CHSNY*, 13: Council Minute, July 16, 1640, 7; Stokes, 1915–28, 4: Deposition of Tymen Jansen, under March 22, 1633, 79, and depositions under March 28, 1638, 87. For his somewhat inflated estimate that in 1641 there were fifteen hundred people in New Netherland, one-half on Manhattan Island, see O'Donnell, 1968, xvi.

6. Jameson, 1909d, under May 17, 1635, 193, and May 8, 16, and 25, 1636, 197. For colonists, see *CHSNY*, 1: Proposed Articles of Colonization and Trade in New Netherland, August 30, 1638, 112.

7. O'Donnell, 1968, 130; *CHSNY*, 1: Proposed Articles of Colonization and Trade in New Netherland, August 30, 1638, 112. Orders of WIC to Minuit quoted in Wieder, 1925, Doc. C, 124. Resident director Wouter van Twiller acquired considerable land in the 1630s. The directors, however, accused him not of engrossing land but acquiring a scattering of potential beachheads (most of them islands) for privately trading with the natives; they vacated a number of his purchases. For data on van Twiller, see inter alia,

Stokes, 1915–28, 2: The Manatus Maps, 195, 200–201; 4: under June 16 and July 16, 1637, 86, and 14: Return of Wouter van Twiller's Property in New Netherland, March 22, 1639, 18, 19.

8. Stokes, 1915–28, 4: Wouter van Twiller to Dirs., August 14, 1636, 84.

9. *CHSNY*, 1: Remonstrance against a Peace with Spain [n.d., ca. March 1634], 63.

10. See van Overeem, 1982, 208; Anon., 1615, n.p. For soldiers and marines, see Rink, 1986, 118.

11. Helgerson, 1997, 56. For soldiers signed on with the VOC for seven years in 1698, see Parmentier and Laarhoven, 1994, 12; van Overeem, 1982, 208, 211. For soldiers as transients and mistreated by the WIC, see Boxer, 1973, 128, 129.

12. Feister, 1973, 35; Feld, 1975, 433; Boxer, 1965, 245.

13. Salisbury, 1982, 203. For wages earned in 1636, see Stokes, 1915–28, 4: November 3, 1636, 85; Jameson, 1909j, under November 1626, 87.

14. *CHSNY*, 1: Depositions, Jacob Jacobsz Eelkins, November 7, 1633, 81, and Subjects for Ass. of XIX's Consideration, July 18, 1634, 91. The figures of 150,000 and 160,000 are exaggerated. In 1635, the market price for mixed skins was eight guilders, bringing their profits closer to 128,000. In 1647, the value of sixteen thousand pelts would have been about 100,000 guilders (Groenveld, 2001, 25).

15. Jameson, 1909j, under February, 1624, where van Wassenaer lists mostly Mohawk words, not Algonquian, 73. Like others, Jennings, 1984, acknowledges the lack of written sources for Algonquian-speaking southern natives, 28.

16. Jameson, 1909c, 104.

17. For Plymouth, see Salisbury, 1982, 162. Regarding theft, see O'Donnell, 1968, 100. For VOC instructions to Abel Tasman, August 1642, see Eisler, 1995, 82.

18. Folkerts, 1996, 48–51.

19. Jesuit Relations, 1656–57, 43: 291 (regarding 1626), quoted in Jennings, 1984, 88. For the negative discursive effects of European efforts to spread the gospel, see Hulme, 1992, 3. For the indifferent efforts of the Dutch, see *CHSNY* I: Short Digest of Injurious Neglect, January 27, 1650, 334, and see Petition, July 26, 1649, 270; see also Hauptman and Knapp, 1977, 173, 174, and Rink, 1986, 77. Scholars (and many contemporaries) agree that the VOC was notably indifferent to evangelizing the native people. De Klerck, 1938: officials saw to it that "no mission work was done where it might damage trade. The inclination of the clergy to go and labor in the East was not too keen and, in general, the clerics were not held in high esteem in the Indies," 1:352; Masselman, 1963: the "propagation of Protestantism was of no concern to the United East India Company; nothing in the charter ever alluded to it. For years the fleets carried not a single clergyman," 225. For a balanced interpretation of religion in early New Netherland, see Jacobs, 2005, chapter 5.

20. For making migrants Netherlanders, see O'Donnell, 1968, 123; Wieder, 1925, Doc. E, 151, 152, and 30.

21. Stokes, 1915–28, 4: Jonas Michaëlius to Adrianus Smoutius, August 11, 1628, 74; Jameson, 1909d, under December 1, 1640, and June 1, 1635, 210, 193, 194. For a reference to "customary friendship" during this time, see *CHSNY*, 13: Declaration Respecting an Attack, July 17, 1647, 22.

22. Kingsbury and Roberts, 1990, 47, quoting Grotius, *JBP*, book 2, chap. 20, no. 41; *CHSNY*, 1: Remonstrance against Peace with Spain [ca. March 1634], 66 (NB: editor's pagination error).

23. *CHSNY*, 13: Extract, Stuyvesant & Council to Dirs., September 4, 1659, 108; Wertheim, n.d., 7, and van de Woude, 1948: during Coen's time, "the interests of the natives played altogether no role," 342.

24. Nijhoff, 1909, Juet's entry of September 11, 1609, 62; Jameson, 1909j, under April 1625, 80, and see 79 n. 1. Jameson, 1909g, 173, 179; O'Donnell, 1968, 38, 39.

25. See O'Donnell, 1968, 20, 46, and quoting vander Donck, 94, 85.

26. For natives in darkness and as barbarous but well-fashioned, see Jameson, 1909j, under February 24, 1624, 69, 72; as changeable, see Nijhoff, 1909, using de Laet's *New World*, 150 [for the original, Doc. R, in Dutch, 132–36]; as stupid, see Jameson, 1909g, 172.

27. Jameson, 1909g, 177; Stokes, 1915–28, 4: Jonas Michaëlius to Adrianus Smoutius, August 11, 1628, 74; O'Donnell, 1968, 107. For Michaëlius's revulsion for the natives, see Hauptman and Knapp, 1977, 174. Algonquians wanted a trading pidgin in order to protect their own languages and communicate with one another "without being understood by the newcomers" (Kupperman, 2000, 86).

28. Jameson, 1909h, and 1909g, 128, 173.

29. Day, 1904, quoting Ryckloff van Goens (1656), 47; *CHSNY*, 13: Propositions of the Natives at Fort Amsterdam, July 19, 1649, 25; for Megapolensis's admission that no Christian thoroughly understood the Mohawk language, see Jameson, 1909g, 172; Dirs. to Stuyvesant, April 4, 1652, 33.

30. O'Donnell, 1968, 74, 94; Eisler, 1995, Van Diemen's Instructions to Abel Tasman, 1642–44 [sailed in August 1642], 82 (referring to the exploits of the Englishman Francis Fletcher in Tierra del Fuego).

31. For the illegality of obliging the natives to trade, see *CHSNY*, 1: Remonstrance against a Peace with Spain [ca. March 1634], 67. For ridicule of Greek merchants, see Rowen, 1972, 160. For native business acumen, see Stokes, 1915–28, 4: Michaëlius to Smoutius, August 11, 1628, 74, and see Jameson, 1909i, under December 22, 1634, and January 3 and 8, 1635, 145, 151, 153. Starna, 1991, cites the trading practices of the Delawares and Susquehannocks, 23; Trelease quoted in Richter, 1992, 90.

32. Jameson, 1909j, under February, 1624, and 1909i, under December 11, 1634, 72, 139.

33. Stokes, 1915–28, 4: Michaëlius to Dominee Joannes de Foreest, August 8, 1628, 72; for no orders for occupation, see Jameson, 1909h, 131.

34. For Wassenaer's stress on the atrocities, see Jameson, 1909j, under November 1626, 84, 85.

35. Dyson, 1985, 130; de Klerck, 1938, 1:331; Wieder, 1925, 142. Van der Woude, 1948, asks the same question of the East India Company (338–42).

36. See Jameson, 1909j, under November 1626, 85, and Trelease, 1960, 47.

37. Jameson, 1909d, under November 2, 1641, 211.

38. *CHSNY*, 1: Assembly of XIX to States, October 25, 1634, 94.

39. Quoted in Schulte Nordholt, 1966, 69.

Chapter 10. The Connecticut Valley

1. Stokes, 1915–28, 4: 69; *CHSNY*, 13: Council Minute, July 16, 1640, 7; Trelease, 1960, 45–46; 1: Remonstrance of New Netherland, July 28, 1649, 290–91. For de Vries's account of the Delaware incident, see Colenbrander, 1911 under December 6, 7, 8, 1632, 154–56 and XXX.

2. See Richter, 1992, 90, and Jennings, 1984, 52; *CHSNY*, l: Deposition, Jacob Eelkins, November 7, 1633, 80.

3. Hosmer, 1908, 219.

4. Chakrabarty, 2002, 140–48. For at least two thousand English settled in Connecticut by 1642, see *CHSNY*, 1: Appendix rec'd from Lord Saye, read August 9, 1642, 128.

5. Pagdan, 1993, citing the work of James Boon, 13.

6. For his valuable reminder that "though recognized by no system of poetics, commerce, like conquest, has its genres," see Helgerson, 1992, 44, and see 45–48.

7. The best source for narratives of the Pequot war are the collections of the Massachusetts Historical Society. For skillful use of them and other accounts, see Kupperman, 2000. For Reverend William Hubbard's comparison of himself to Isaac and as a plagiarist, see Shelley, 1932, 297, 296; Vincent, 1637, is valuable and available as a 1974 reprint.

8. Arber, 1897, 282.

9. Vincent, 1637, n.p.; Shelley, 1932, 176, using Lion Gardiner, *Pequot Wars*, Mass. Hist. Soc. Coll., 3rd ser. III, 144, and 197, citing Proceedings of the Mass. Hist. Soc., LI, 285.

10. Underhill, 1638, 18, 2, 23. For another tract urging emigration and describing the Pequot war, see Vincent, 1637.

11. For the war's two years being "by the sword of the Lord," see Underhill, 1638, 40. Underhill's is a reference to 1 Chron. 20:3. It would have been common knowledge that a harrow was a farm instrument with particularly vicious teeth used after the plow to completely pulverize the soil; see Shelley, 1932, 194, quoting Captain John Mason, *History of the Pequot War,* Mass. Hist. Soc. Coll., 2nd ser. VIII, 140. For the Pequots pursued "to what the English thought was their extinction," see Kupperman, 2000, 108. Underhill, 1638, puts the number slain at the Mystic River fort at four hundred, but see n. 14 below.

12. Underhill, 1638, 15, 44, and see Shelley, 1932, 178, 198. For storm money, see Parker, 1972, 198. For mockery, see Underhill, 1638, 15, 16, 42.

13. For Emmanuel Downing's calculation in 1645 that one captive Indian was worth twenty African slaves, see Lepore, 1998, 162.

14. Underhill, 1638, 39, and see 8, 15. For William Bradford's account here, see Salisbury, 1982, 224. For Winthrop's figure of three hundred slain, see Hosmer, 1908, entry of May 25, 1657, 22. For three to four hundred, see Vincent, 1637, 12. For seven hundred dead, see Captain John Mason cited in Clark, 1914, 44.

15. Underhill, 1638, 9. See *OED*, cran: "an iron instrument laid across the fire reaching from the ribs of the grate to the hinder past of it, for the purpose of supporting a pot or kettle"; Scottish form of crane. For Lion Gardiner cited, see Kupperman, 2000, 229, and quoting Roger Williams, 230.

16. Underhill, 1638, 8, 16, and see 37, 39, 40–41. For the agreement of John Mason, Underhill's co-commander, that native warfare was primitive and relatively innocence, see Malone, 1991, 23. For the English discovery that native opponents failed to prepare for or intend the "slaughter" with which the continental wars had made some of them familiar, and English colonists who wanted the Indians to fight one another "with a greater willingness to suffer and inflict grievous loss," 22 and 23. For Roger Williams's estimate of their wars as "farre lesse bloudy and devouring then [sic] the Cruell Warres of Europe; and seldome twenty slaine in a pitcht field," see Kupperman, 2000, 107–8.

17. See Salisbury, 1982, 207. For de Vries's description in 1639 of the commander

at Fort Good Hope having only fourteen or fifteen soldiers and protesting against the English who had planted themselves nearby, see Colenbrander, 1911, under June 9, 1639, 233.

18. Underhill, 1638, 19. For House of Good Hope in 1643, see van der Zee and van der Zee, 1978, 146. For a specific identification of Dutch disinterest in missionizing and colonizing written by a seventeenth-century New Englander, see William Hubbard (1677) quoted in Edney and Cimburek, 2004, 347.

19. Murphy, 1857, 249, and Jameson, 1909f, 274.

20. Underhill, 1638, 26–28; for the date of May 24, see Hosmer, 1908, entry of May 24, 1637, 218.

21. Underhill, 1638, 25, 42, 36, and see Hosmer, 1908, entries of May 17 and May 25, 1637, 218, 220.

22. For Underhill's pursuit of Pequots to within thirty-six miles of Manhattan Island, see Vincent, 1637, 16. Narragansett-produced wampum reached the Dutch, French, English, and other Americans in a system "that ranged over six hundred miles" (Kupperman, 2000, 213).

23. Melvoin, 1989, 35. There is no evidence that the tribute was paid, 36. For the Pequot war as a point after which local tribes previously protected by the Pequots were obligated to accept protection from Connecticut and New Haven, see Salisbury, 1982, 225, 226. For natives accustomed to paying tribute to dominant tribes, see Kupperman, 2000, 97, 98. For fire money, see *CHSNY*, 14: Trial of the Case between Southampton and Southold, November 1, 1667, 602.

Part V. Deadly Encounter

1. Wesseling, 1978, 3.

Chapter 11. The Indian War Seen

1. Romein, 1975, 110. For the early modern wars' excesses as causing a sense of political ineffectualness, which in turn brought in centralized governments, see Raab, 1975. The wars were so obscene that they were "pornographic" (Carlton, 1992, 4). Pieter Cornelisz Hooft's *Historiën* (1628) presented one gruesome aspect of the wars in the Low Countries after another obviously trying to comprehend their grotesqueness for himself (Nieuwenhuys, 1971, 25).

2. Fishman, 1979, 3; Adair, 1986, 71, 138, 139.

3. Ceci, 1977, 264; for his account of the control of wampum as a decisive factor in the wars conducted by natives, Dutch, and English during this period, 214–64. For European practices, see Parker, 1972, 130, 131, 135. For historians who regard English practice in nearby colonies as inciting Kieft to collect taxes, see Ceci, 1977, 214 n. 5, 215, 219, 221; Jennings, 1984, 52; Melvoin, 1989, 35; and Schulte Nordholt, 1966, 59.

4. Mulder, 1862, cxvii, cxv. For extortion, see Adair, 1986, xiv, 42, 187, 207, 213, 331, 353; Fishman, 1979, 6–10; Gutmann, 1976, 75–78, 87; Parker, 1972, 17, 18; Redlich, 1956, 9, 63, 67; and Redlich, 1964, 338, 435, 471. For tribulation troops, see Mann, 1976, 313. For the torture of peasants, see Adair, 1986, 42.

5. Trelease, 1960, 65, 66. For official sources, see *CHSNY*, 13: Resolution, September

15, 1639, 6, and Council Minute, July 16, 1640, 7. De Vries writes that he got the account from the raid's leader, Cornelis van Tienhoven (Colenbrander, 1911, under July 16, 1640, 246). For torture, see Jameson, 1909d, under July 16, 1640, 208, and February 24, 1643, 227.

6. *CHSNY*, 1: Interrogatories [1644–47], Doc. M, Interrogatories to be proposed to Dr. Johannes de la Montaigne [sic], Article 2, 197.

7. Brandt, 1993, 357, and see 339.

8. *CHSNY*, 13: Resolution, September 15 (1639), 6.

9. *CHSNY*, 1: Remonstrance of New Netherland, July 28, 1649, 297.

10. *CHSNY*, 1: Report on Affairs of New Netherland [ca. 1650], 388. Schulte Nordholt (1966, 48) found it amazing that the war could dominate after 1640 given the company's earlier "trade meant peace" policy.

11. *CHSNY*, 1: Report of Board of Accounts, Points 3 and 4, [December 15, 1644], 150.

12. O'Callaghan, 1851, 101, 102 (emphasis added).

13. *CHSNY*, 1: Journal of New Netherland written in 1641–46, 183 (hereafter, [Kieft's] Journal). For the journal in Dutch, see Schulte Nordholt, 1966, 78–94.

14. For the raid, see Colenbrander, 1911, under July 16, 1640, 246. For rewards for heads, see *CHSNY*, 13: Ordinance, July 4, 1641, 7. For voluntary killings, see 1: [Kieft's] Journal, 184.

15. For Cornelis Melijn's testimony that exactions were demanded from more than ten nations, including the Tappans, see Murphy, 1857, 254. For Dutch activities around May 13–19, 1640, and Kieft sending soldiers to exact "obedience and contribution" from Long Island natives, see *CHSNY*, 14: Instructions to Proceed against the English on Long Island, under May 13, 14, 15, 1640, 28–30, Resolution to Release Englishmen, May 19, 1640, 30, 31, and Resolution to Send Soldiers, August 9, 1640, 32. For de Vries's ethnographic notes on the Tappans, see Jameson, 1909d, under Anno. 1642, 220–23.

16. Colenbrander, 1911, under October 20, 1640, 246, 247, and May 15, 1640, 245; for tribute paid to other tribes, under February 22, 1643, 262.

17. *CHSNY*, 1: [Kieft's] Journal, 183.

18. *CHSNY*, 1: Petition of Commonalty, October 13, 1649, 263 n. 3; Jameson, 1909d, under March 4, 1643, 232.

19. Melijn, 1649, n.p.; Murphy, 1857, 255–56.

20. Jameson, 1909d, under March 4, 1643, 232, and Anno. 1643, 228. For Kieft's explanation of the events, *CHSNY*, 13: Council Minute, February 27, 1643, 11, 12; Colenbrander, 1911, description of February 25 and February 26, 1643, 265.

21. *CHSNY*, 1: Short Digest of the Excesses and Highly Injurious Neglect . . . exhibited January 27, 1650, 337, and see Eight Men to Amsterdam Chamber of WIC, October 28, 1644, 213.

22. *CHSNY*, 13: Deposition, May 18, 1643, 14; Colenbrander, 1911, under September 1, 1641, 248; 1: Papers Relating to New Netherland, 1643–47, Doc. H, March 27, 1643, 194.

23. *CHSNY*, 13: Council Minute, March 28, 1643, 12. For freebooters, see Parker, 1972, 48, and Adair, 1986, 331. For roving mercenaries taking terrifying names, see Redlich, 1964, 117. For *moescoppen*, see Mulder, 1862, cxvii.

24. *CHSNY*, 13: Council Minute, March 28, 1643, 12, 13, and see 1: Papers Relating to New Netherland, 1643–47, Docs. E and G, 193, 194.

25. Roger Williams quoted in 1643 (van der Zee and van der Zee, 1978, 109).

26. *CHSNY*, 1: Memorial of Eight Men, November 3, 1643, 139, 140, and see Points relating to Affairs in New Netherland, February 2, 1643, 136.

27. *CHSNY*, 1: Board of Accounts, 1644, 152, and see 150. For the land's productivity again related to maritime needs, see Kuyter and Melijn to Stuyvesant, June 22, 1647, 206. For the warships, see Jameson, 1909e, 260. For plans, after the conquest of Brazil, to centralize Dutch operations in the Atlantic at Recife, see Klooster, 2000, 6.

28. *CHSNY*, 1: [Kieft's] Journal, 187. For the final pages of the journal as especially garbled, see the statement that here 120 English and Dutch combined forces and killed exactly 120 male natives.

29. *CHSNY*, 1: [Kieft's] Journal, 186, 187; for disputes regarding English soldiers and criticism of Kieft, Eight Men to Amsterdam Chamber of WIC, October 28, 1644, 212, 213; Jameson, 1909d, under Anno. 1642, 214. For Underhill's aggressions, see Schulte Nordholt, 1966, 73, and see Haefeli, 1999, 17: John Underhill brought the tactics of surrounding and destroying an enemy village, first used against the Pequots, to Kieft's War."

30. *CHSNY*, 1: [Kieft's] Journal, 185. Van der Zee and van der Zee carry the account and quote Kieft, dating this debate as June–July, 1644, 132–34; for the men's signatures, see Papers Relation to New Netherland, 1643–47, Doc. E, 193.

For the English mercenaries, [Kieft's] Journal, 184, 185; note that the number of natives killed mounts dramatically once the war is carried to Long Island under Underhill's command; see figure of five hundred to seven hundred slain, 187. For the commonalty's agreement to pay fifty of the English mercenaries, see Report of Board of Accounts, December 15, 1644, 151, and see Shelley 1932, 314. The commonalty's direct involvement in the killings is still debated; while denouncing Kieft, the whole community eventually stood behind him but wanted to avoid hostilities. Once involved, they were bitterly set against the natives (Schulte Nordholt, 1966, 62).

31. *CHSNY*, 1: [Kieft's] Journal, 187. For Underhill and Van Dyck moving out from Stamford to Greenwich (Connecticut) and for Underhill shortening the battle by firing the native huts, see van der Zee and van der Zee, 1978, 130, 129. Booth, 1880, places this massacre on Strickland's Plain, three miles inland from Greenwich, 122. For *vernietigingsmethod*, see Schulte Nordholt, 1966, 73.

32. *CHSNY*, 1: [Kieft's] Journal, 187.

33. *CHSNY*, 1: Interrogatories, Papers Relating to New Netherland, 1643–47, Doc. M, 195–201. For Stuyvesant's cover letter, Resolution of the States, January 7, 1648, 188.

34. Brandt, 1993, 362, 363, fig. 275 on 363; *CHSNY*, 1: Report of Board of Accounts [December 15, 1644], in which board accepts the figure of a thousand dead, 151; Melijn estimates sixteenth hundred slain (Murphy, 1857, 257).

35. *CHSNY*, 13: Articles of Peace, August 30, 1645, 18.

36. *CHSNY*, 14: Resolution to Employ a Long Island Sachem against Hostile Natives, May 29, 1645, 60.

37. *CHSNY*, 13: Resolution, August 31, 1645, 19.

38. *CHSNY*, 13: Extract, Dirs. to Stuyvesant, April 7, 1648, 23.

39. *CHSNY*, 13: Propositions Made at Fort Amsterdam, July 19, 1649, 25; Colenbrander, 1911, under April 25, 1640, 235–36, and see Deed of Land to Stuyvesant, July 14, 1649, 24.

40. *CHSNY*, 13: Extract, Dirs. to Stuyvesant, March 21, 1651, 28; Colenbrander, 1911, under July 16, 1640, 246; 1: Answer of WIC to Remonstrance of New Netherland, Point 64, January 27, 1650, 345.

41. Frijhoff, 1998, 34.

Chapter 12. The Indian War Given Words

1. Merwin, 2001, 65.

2. For his cautious acceptance of Melijn's authorship, see Murphy, Introductory Note, 1857, n.p. For reproducing some of the tract (uncited author) and translation of the title as used here, see O'Callaghan, 1851, 100, opp. 101. For accepting Melijn as author because of the authentic description of his and Kuyter's shipwreck, see van der Zee and van der Zee, 1978, 191. Frijhoff, 1998, suggests Jochem Pietersz Kuyter as author, 34 n. 30; Schmidt, 2001, considers the matter undecidable, 395 n. 88.

3. Van der Zee and van der Zee, 1978, 177.

4. For a discussion of literary devices in pamphlet literature, see Harline, 1987, 31, and Simoni, 1993, 131. As a best seller, see van der Zee and van der Zee, 1978, 191.

5. For speaking pictures, see Meijer, 1971, 126. For other qualities of popular literature and plays, see van der Heijden, 1972a, 28; Grimmelshausen's aside to readers in Adair, 1986, 27, and Scholz-Heerspinck, 1993, 42, 43. For New Testament citation, see Melijn, 1649, n.p. [final page]; these lines are omitted by Murphy, 1857.

6. Romein, 1975, 110, 111.

7. Zwitzer, 1997, 52. For Snaeyers, see Parker, 1995, 151.

8. The best account is Fishman, 1979. For Callot, see Griffiths, Willett, and Wilson-Bareau, 1998, 16.

9. Many Dutch commentators have analyzed the historiography of the Eighty Years' War: inter alia, see Romein, 1975, 137–40, and Zwitzer, 1997, 52. For the place of America in seventeenth-century histories, see Schmidt, 2001, 234–43.

10. Parker, 1995, 147, and 1972, 227, 11. For Solms refugees, see *CHSNY*, 1: Resolution of States, May 31, 1640, 118. For Vondel, see Schenkeveld-van der Dussen, 1986, 77, and van den Vondel, "*The Monsters of Our Age*" [1650], Rens, 1969, 97, lines 17–21; Westra, 1998, 14.

11. Alden and Landis, 1982, 500–10. Relevant to the style of *Breeden-Raedt* are, inter alia, *Amsterdams dam-praetje* (Amsterdam, J. van Soest, 39 pages) and *Amsterdams tafel-praetje* (Gouda, J. Corneliszoon, Amsterdam, J. van Hilten, 31 pages). See also *Haerlems schuyt-praetjen* (sometimes attributed to Cornelis Melijn). For *Breeden-Raedt*, see 502. For the bitter anti-WIC pamphleteering begun in the 1640s, see Schmidt, 2001, 282–88.

12. Murphy, 1857, 248, 250. The metaphor of the kettle also appears in *CHSNY*, 1: Remonstrance of New Netherland, July 28, 1649, 285.

13. Murphy, 1857, 251, 249; Meijer Drees, 1993, 284. The play appeared in 1668, 281; Murphy, 1857, 248.

14. Murphy, 1857, 259.

15. *CHSNY*, 1: Report of Board of Accounts, ca. December 15, 1644, 150; Jameson, 1909f, 280–82, 280.

16. Murphy, 1857, 259.

17. Murphy, 1857, 256 (Alba in the original).

18. Van den Vondel, "The Monsters of Our Age" [1650], Rens, 1969, 97; Vrancx's Maypole Series commemorates Hendrik's campaign (Fishman, 1979, 28, and figs. 8 and 9 following 77); Mann, 1976, 307.

19. *CHSNY*, 1: [Kieft's] Journal, 182; Jameson, 1909f, 274 and Eight Men to Amsterdam chamber of WIC, October 28, 1644, 213.

20. Jameson, 1909d, under Anno 1642, 215, 216; Colenbrander, 1911, under March 4, 1643, 266, 267; Murphy, 1857, 253. See also *CHSYN*, 1: Report of Board of Accounts, December 15, 1644, 151

21. Murphy, 1857, 259.

22. For Overijssel, see Fishman, 1979, 14. Trelease, 1960, accepts 8,000 Delawares, 3,000 Mahicans, 6,000 Long Island natives, 3,000 Wappings (one-half living in New York), 5. Rayback, 1966, argues for 20,000 Algonquian, 115. Starna, 1991, estimates a native population in and around New Netherland dropped from about 90,000 in 1600 to fewer than 14,000 in 1630–40, 22.

23. Parker, 1972, 135; Gutmann, 1976, 104; Donagan, 1994, 1152.

24. Van den Vondel, *Begroetenis aan Vorst Frederick Henrick* [1625], Rens, 1969, 42; Zwitzer, 1997, 44.

25. Mulder, 1862, 45; *CHSNY*, 1: [Kieft's] Journal, 184, and Jameson, 1909d, under October 1, 1643, 234.

26. See, inter alia, Jameson, 1909f, 280–83.

27. For Overijssel, see Fishman, 1979, 10, 11. For peasant uprisings in Germany, Bohemia, and the Holy Roman Empire, see Redlich, 1964, 515–32, and Parker, 1972, 48. For the American natives, see Murphy, 1857, 256, and Jameson, 1909d, under July 16, 1639, Anno 1642, and February 25, 26, 1643, 208, 213, 228, and 1909f, 282–84. Some of the same data are in *CHSNY*, 1: Report of Board of Accounts, ca. December 15, 1644, 151.

28. Nieuwenhuys, 1971, 26. For flight from the Dutch and vacant lands, see *CHSNY*, 1: Papers Relative to Condition of New Netherland, 1643–47: Eight Men to Ass. of XIX, October 24, 1643, 190, and for Martinhoeck, Information Relative to Taking up Land in New Netherland, March 4, 1650, 366.

29. For Malcontents, see Parker, 1972, 46, and in New Netherland, Colenbrander, 1911, under July 20, 1643, 269. For military brutalization of rebels, see Donagan, 1994, 1166.

30. For Miles Standish displaying a severed head in Plymouth as a warning to other natives, see Karr, 1998, 889. For trophies brought to Boston, see Jameson, 1910, 171; *CHSNY*, 13: Council Minute, September 15, 1643, carries some of Kieft's payments, 16. For the head of the Connecticut chief, see Jameson, 1909f, 281; 1: Interrogatories for van Tienhoven . . . Exhibited July 21, 1650, 412. For atrocities during the English Civil War, see Carlton, 1992, 2.

31. Van der Zee and van der Zee, 1978, 121; Mann, 1976, 167; Karr, 1998, referring to the orders of Sir Humphrey Gilbert, 887.

32. Carlton, 1992, citing *A True Representation of the Miserable Estate of Germany* (1638), 18; Adair, 1986, 38, 37; Griffiths, Willett, and Wilson-Bareau, 1998, 13; and Murphy, 1857, 247.

33. Steen, 1989, 114; Albrecht von Wallenstein to Karl Leonhart von Harroch [autumn, 1623], in Mann, 1976, 207.

34. For Montaigne, see Lestringant, 1990, 109. For Montaigne's essay on cannibalism, see Cohen, 1958, 105–19; Huygens, *"Een Boer, [1630],"* van der Heijden, 1968a, 243, lines 22, 23. For an illustration of Alva about to cannibalize a child, see Fishman, 1979, fig. 5 following 77.

35. Anon., *News from New England* (1676), quoted in Lapore, 1998, 281 n. 75, and Benjamin Tompson, *New Englands Crisis* (1676), quoted, 89.

36. Colenbrander, 1911, see following Dedication: *Lof-Dight op 't Journael van*

David Pietersz De Vries, Artillery-Meester van West-Vrieslandt ende 't Noorder-Quartier, door P. I. Offeringa, [5]; de Vries, using some of Megapolensis's material, presents the ethnographic detail of a chief eating a victim's head, see under April 30, 1640, 238. For Dutch interest in extreme torture, see Schama, 1987, 91.

37. Colenbrander, 1911, under March 4 and July 20, 1643, 267, 269.

38. Murphy, 1857, 254, 260; for soldiers' wanton killing of a child, 257.

39. Murphy, 1857, 257, 258. For cruelties as sport against defenseless persons, see Redlich, 1964, 465, 466. Donagan, 1994, would find here the classic form of the atrocity narrative: a massacre and its cold-blooded execution; circumstantial phenomena clustered around this core; and aggravated individual horrors, 1154, 1155.

40. Murphy, 1857, 258. For the English governor's gift, see *CHSNY*, 1: Eight Men to Amsterdam Chamber of WIC, October 28, 1644, 210.

41. Murphy, 1857, 257, 259, 258.

42. Murphy, 1857, 257, 258; for the soldier from Utrecht, 271. See van der Zee and van der Zee, 1978, 129.

43. *CHSNY*, 1: Interrogations to be Proposed to Cornelis van Tienhoven, Exhibited, July 21, 1650, 413. He was never actually questioned (Jacobs, 1998b, 5).

44. On de Bry, see Schmidt, 2001, 339 n. 108.

45. For Wenceslaus Hollar's identification of the "Virginia" native as Unus Americanus ex Virginia (Antwerp, 1645), see Doggett et al., 1992, 62. For Titicaca, see Adair, 1986, 424.

46. Schulte Nordholt, 1966, 68. For Bredero's poems as captions to illustrations in de Bry's publication of a Las Casas text, see Klooster, 1997, 42. For Las Casas's influence on the Dutch imagination, see Schmidt, 2001, 95–99, 115–21.

47. Lestringant, 1990, 15.

48. *CHSNY*, 1: Petition of Commonalty of New Netherland to States, October 13, 1649, 259.

49. Murphy, 1857, 256; O'Callaghan, 1851, also translates Melijn's *openbaren* as "declared," 104.

50. See *Waerschouwinghe* (1568) in van der Heijden, 1970a, 33.

51. For provincial contributions, see de Vries and van der Woude, 1997, 173; O'Callaghan, 1851, 4: 101.

52. Murphy, 1857, 278. For Grotius's judgment that a ruler destroying one of his peoples in order to "colonize the territory thus made vacant" is "not in his right mind," see Remec, 1960, 211.

53. For waiting for others to make war, see Rowen, 1972, 212.

54. O'Callaghan, 1851, 103. For "murder," see Murphy, 1857, 255, 259, and for "unjust" war, 278.

55. In his defense, Kieft's financial position was an impossible one. Both the company and burghers denied him essentially needed funds; see, inter alia, *CHSNY*, 1: Proposed Articles for Colonization and Trade to New Netherland, Exhibited August 30, 1638, 111.

56. *CHSNY*, 1: Kuyter and Melijn to Stuyvesant, June 22, 1647, 208.

57. *CHSNY*, 1: Commonalty of New Netherland, Further Explanations of . . . the Petition to the . . . States, July 26, 1649, 262, and for eleven signatures, see 270.

58. Murphy, 1857, 256, 246.

Chapter 13. The War's Haunting

1. Blussé, 1995, using *"Instructie voor de Luitenant Johan Jurriaensz ende vordere Raetspersonen waer naer hun in't aentasten van het Goude Leeuws eylandt ende . . . bij veroveringe desselfs sullen hebben te reguleren,"* April 19, 1636, VOC 1170, fol. 628, and *Dagregisters van het Kastreel Zeelandia*, May 7, 1636, 174–77. For Junius's career in Formosa, see Campbell, 1967.

2. Blussé, 1995 citing, *Of the Conversion of five thousand nine hundred EAST INDIANS In the Isle Formosa neere China . . . By Meanes of M. Ro. Junius, a minister lately in Delph in HOLLAND . . . Translated . . . by H. Jessei, a Servant of JESUS CHRIST* (London, 1650), 153.

3. Gentlemen Seventeen to Governor General, March 28, 1648, and October 14, 1651 (Blussé, 1995, 177).

4. Colenbrander, 1911, under February 25 and 26, 1643, 264, 265.

5. Van Gelderen, 1992, 101; and see Grotius quoted in Rowen, 1972, 154. Gouda, 1995, encounters the moralistic language of culpability and indictment in Dutch Indonesia, 242. The broader the Dutch presence in America, the greater the moral outcry against it (Schmidt, 2001, 275).

6. *CHSNY*, 1: Extract of Report of Henrick van der Capellen, December 28, 1644, 148; I: Mandamus, Kuyter, and Melijn, April 28, 1648, 250, 251; Schmidt, 2001, citing *Verheerlickte Nederland door d'herstelde zeevaert . . .* (1659), 291; Adriaen vander Donck to Johannes de la Montangne [sic], April 15, 1650, reproduced in Jacobs, 1998b, 6.

7. Quoting van den Vondel, *Begroetenis aan Vorst Frederik Henrik* [1625], Rens, 1969, 42, lines 227, 234. For war weariness, see Carlton, 1992, 294; Maland, 1980, 189; Raab, 1975, chap. 9 and passim; and 't Hart, 1993, 24.

8. Van den Vondel, "The Monsters of Our Age" [1650], Rens, 1969, 97, 98; van den Vondel, *De Getemde Mars* [1647], van der Heijden, 1970a, 297, and 300, lines 71, 72.

9. For Hooft's *Nederlandsche Historiën, sedert de ooverdraght der Heerschappije van Kaizar Karel den Vijfden op Kooning Philips zijnen zoon* (Amsterdam, 1642) *eerst boek*, 2–3, see Romein, 1975, 139, 140. For good and evil, see Presser, 1948, 24.

10. Van den Vondel, *De Getemde Mars* [1647], van der Heijden, 1970a, 305, line 196. Kieft quoted in *CHSNY*, 1: Postil to Petition of Inhabitants of Long Island, February 27, 1643, 417 and in 13: Resolution, February 25, 1643, 10, 11.

11. Draper, 1990, 197. Grotius's irenicism was particularly in vogue after 1631 (Rens, 1969, 26). For probable influence of Grotius on vander Donck, see Shorto, 2004, 99–101.

12. *CHSNY*, 1: Report of Committee of States on Melyn's Papers, n.d. [July/August?] 1650, 417–18, and see Short Digest, January 27, 1650, 332, and Interrogatories for Johannes de la Montaigne (sic) in Papers Relating to Condition of New Netherland, 1643–47, 197.

13. Schulte Nordholt, 1966, 56.

14. *CHSNY*, 1: Remonstrance of New Netherland, July 28, 1649, 294, 295 (emphasis added); Murphy, 1857, 267.

15. *CHSNY*, 1: Extract of Report of Hendrick van der Capellen exhibited December 28, 1644, 148; Remonstrance of New Netherland, July 28, 1649, 314 and 297; see also 332 and Short Digest of the Excesses and Highly Injurious Neglect which New Netherland . . .

Exhibited January 27, 1650, 337. For the charge of incompetence summarily dismissed, Answer of WIC to Remonstrance, January 27, 1650, 338 and see point 65, 345.

16. *CHSNY*, 1: Report of Board of Accounts, December 15, 1644, 150.

17. See Furnivall, 1939, 31, 39; Day, 1904, 36, 63, 6; de Klerck, 1938, 1:229, 230, 332; and van Klaveren, 1953, 42, 43. For the shares, see *CHSNY*, 1: Report of the States on Proceedings of the WIC, July 2/12, 1645, 158. For the relatively valueless shares of the WIC as against those of the VOC, see Boxer, 1973, 149. For abandoning New Netherland and small profits, see Report of Board of Accounts, December 15, 1644, 153; 1: Pretension and Claim of Patroons, June 16, 1634, 88.

18. Directors quoted, *CHSNY*, 13: Extract, Dirs. to Amsterdam Burgomasters and Regents, February 13, 1652, 30, and see 1: Provisional Orders in Report of Committee of States on Affairs in New Netherland, ca. April 11, 1650, 388; for kindness, 13: Extract, Dirs. to Stuyvesant, April 7, 1648, 23.

19. *CHSNY*, 1: Report of Board of Accounts, December 15, 1644, 140–56; for the natives' extermination as unchristian, 153.

20. Quoted in Lestringant, 1997, 109.

21. Prudon, 1968, 59, lines 274, 275; Day, 1904, citing M. van Ossenberch (1765), 47 n. 4; Meilink-Roelofsz, 1962, quoting unnamed author, marginal notation, 232.

22. De Klerck, 1938, 1:230; Masselman, 1963, quoting Aert Gysels regarding Coen, his former superior, 420.

23. Masselman, 1963, 420, 421, quoting J. A. van der Chrijs, *De vestiging van het Nederlandsche Gezag over de Banda eilanden, 1599–1621* (Batavia, 1886), 159, P. A. Tiele, *Bouwstroffen voor de Geschiedenis der Nederlanders in den Maleischen Archipel* (The Hague, 1886), 1:xlii–xlvii, l, and J. de Jonge, *Opkomst*, 4: lxi. He also cites six other historians, 421.

24. Masselman, 1963, 421, summarizing and quoting Petrus Johannes Blok, *Geschiedenis van het Nederlandsche Volk*, 4: 245, and H. F. M. Huybers, *Jan Pieterszoon Coen* (Utrecht, 1914), 104f.

25. Schulte Nordholt, 1966, 77, 57, 60, 68.

26. Ibid., 73.

Chapter 14. Watchful Waiting

1. *CHSNY*, 13: Stuyvesant's Journal under May 31, 1658, 84.

2. *CHSNY*, 13: Opinion of Stuyvesant and Council, November 10–27, 1655, 53, and Propositions Made by Natives of Long Island, November 27, 1655, 58.

3. *CHSNY*, 14: Declarations Concerning Destruction of Kuyter's House, March 9, 1644, and March 9, 1645, 53, 54; see Ehrlich, 1974, 78.

4. For analysis of natives and strangers bound together, see Dening, 2004.

5. *CHSNY*, 13: Orders Regarding a House at Hoboken, March 28, 1656, 67; Johannes de Decker to Stuyvesant, June 26, 1663, 261; Propositions Made at Fort Amsterdam, July 19, 1649, 25; Mohawk Treaty Propositions, September 6, 1659, quoted in Jennings, 1984, 47; 1: Report, Board of Accounts, December 15, 1644, 153.

6. Gehring, 1983, Stuyvesant and Council, August 28, 1654, 173, and for resale of lands, Response of Stuyvesant and Council to Remonstrance, December 13, 1653, 97. For the legal status of natives as witnesses, see Jacobs, 2005, 389–92, and Chiodo, 1974, 179.

For natives chiding the director and lacking confidence in him, see *CHSNY*, 13: Propositions Made at Fort Amsterdam, July 19, 1649, 25 and 1: Jacob van Couwenhoven and Dirck van Schelluyne to Adriaen vander Donck, October 6, 1650, 447.

7. O'Donnell, 1968, 4; Weise, 1884, 114; O'Donnell, 1968, 126; *CHSNY*, 13: Proposals Made by Long Island Natives, November 27, 1655, 58; Extract, Dirs. to Stuyvesant, April 7, 1648, 23. For memories of Wouter van Twiller, see 1: Report of Board of Accounts, December 15, 1644, 151.

8. For appearing awe-inspiring, see *CHSNY*, 13: Dirs. to Stuyvesant, September 20, 1660, 187. WIC to Amsterdam Burgomasters, February 13, 1652, 30; and Answer of van Tienhoven to Propositions of Stuyvesant, November 14, 1655, 56.

9. *CHSNY*, 13: WIC to Amsterdam Burgomasters, February 13, 1652, 30; Extract, Dirs. to Stuyvesant, April 4, 1652, 33; Resolution of Council, July 1, 1656, 69.

10. For natives' charge of military impotency, see *CHSNY*, 1: [Kieft's] Journal, 182; Petition of Commonalty, October 13, 1649, 259, 263 n. 3.

11. *CHSNY*, 1: [Kieft's] Journal, 183; 13: Answer of van Tienhoven to Propositions of Stuyvesant, November 14, 1655, 56.

12. *CHSNY*, 1: Remonstrance of New Netherland, July 28, 1649, 297.

13. Bolton, 1975, 2, 127.

14. Jameson, 1909d, under July 20, 1643, 233; *CHSNY*, 13: Message of Natives and Answer, October 21, 1655, 48.

15. O'Donnell, 1968, 72, 66. For depopulation, see Crosby, 1986, 202; Ehrlich, 1974, 8; Grumet, 1980, 45; Rayback, 1966, 119; and Starna, 1991, 22. For Mohawks, see Rothschild, 2003, 127. In the seventeenth century, the Mahican population alone dropped from four thousand to five hundred (Taylor, 1996, 438). For native knowledge of smallpox, see Newcomb, 1956, 11; for "fire money," *CHSNY*, 14: Trial of Case between Southampton and Southold, November 1, 1667, 602; quoting 1: Petition of Commonalty, October 13, 1649, 269 n. 10.

16. For the ten alleged killings, see *CHSNY*, 13: Remonstrance of Stuyvesant and Council to States, October 31, 1655, 49; natives' boast, 14: Declarations Concerning Destruction of Kuyter's House, March 9, 1645, 54; Stokes, 1915–28, 4: Jonas Michaëlius to Adrianus Smoutius, August 11, 1628, 74.

17. Jameson, 1909i, under December 14, 1634, 142.

18. O'Donnell, 1968, 106; Jennings, 1984, 89, referring to Paul Le Jeune, Relation of 1640–41, Jesuit Relations, 21: 33. The alleged sorcerer was Melijn (Gehring, 1983, Answer to Remonstrance, December 13, 1653, 97); Lepore, 1998, 98, quoting Anon., *True Account* (1676), 2 and 104, 105, quoting Nathaniel Saltonstall, *New and Further Narrative* (1676), 85, 86.

19. Arber, 1897, 27; Jameson, 1910, 165; Bradford quoted in Arber, 316.

20. *CHSNY*, 1: [Kieft's] Journal, 180, and for the Father of Hate and occasional reference to God, 187, 182, 184.

21. Lepore, 1998, 96, quoting Anon., *Further Brief and True Relation* (1675), 3–4.

22. For his insistence that the WIC and private individuals were buying coastal wampum-producing lands and not farming properties, see Ceci, 1977, 232, 233; quoting Vincent, 1637, 20.

23. *CHSNY*, 1: Remonstrance of New Netherland, July 28, 1649, 292, 293.

24. For New Jersey natives, see Newcomb, 1956, 7; quoted in *CHSNY*, 1: Petition of Commonalty to Stuyvesant from Colonies and Villages, December 11, 1653, 551; 13:

Opinion of Stuyvesant on Propositions, no date [shortly after November 10], 1655, 53. The Dutch weren't quite sure "what to do with their influence according to any general plan. They dealt with each tribe separately, and each situation pragmatically, as it arose" (Jennings, 1984, 123).

25. *CHSNY*, 13: Extract, Dirs. to Stuyvesant, April 15, 1650, 27; Schama, 1987, 249.

26. Quoting O'Donnell, 1968, 129; Kieft to Minuit, May 6, 1638, cited in van der Zee and van der Zee, 1978, 82; Gehring, 1983, Proposals of Stuyvesant to Council, May 30, 1654, 139; *CHSNY*, 13: Stuyvesant and Council to States, October 31, 1655, 49.

27. *CHSNY*, 1: Remonstrance of New Netherland, July 28, 1649, 287, 288.

28. *CHSNY*, 2: Deduction, November 5, 1660, 134 (Sloop's Bay is the westerly part of Narragansett Bay); quoting 1: Proposed Articles of Colonization and Trade of New Netherland, August 30, 1638, 111; 13: Extract, Dirs. to Stuyvesant, April 15, 1650, 27.

29. Murphy, 1857, 250.

30. For Stuyvesant's title, Ordinance against Selling Liquor, May 31, 1647, quoted in Scott and Stryker-Rodda, 1974, 366; *CHSNY*, 1: Commission to Stuyvesant, July 28, 1646, 178; Murphy quoting Melijn, 1857, 274. See also Remonstrance of New Netherland, July 28, 1649, 307, 310, 311–12.

31. *CHSNY*, 13: Extract, Stuyvesant to Dirs., April 21, 1660, 162; Stuyvesant to Dirs., December 9, 1660, 190.

32. For the log, see van der Heijden, 1971a. For an English translation, see Beekman, 1988.

33. De Vries quoted in [Dedication], *Aende Edele Mog: Heere Gecommitteerde Raden, van Staten van West-Vrieslandt en 't Noorder-Quartier*, Colenbrander, 1911, [4].

34. Colenbrander, 1911, 229, 187.

35. Masselman, 1963, Decision of VOC on October 23, 1623, 437, 438. For a brief but balanced analysis of Stuyvesant, see Jacobs, 1998a, 56, 57.

36. Alexandrowicz, 1967, 40; *CHSNY*, 13: Extract, Stuyvesant to Governor John Winthrop, April 3, 1648, 23.

37. *CHSNY*, 13: Extract. Dirs. to Stuyvesant and Council, December 22, 1657, 75, and for kind treatment, April 7, 1648, 23; Stuyvesant's Journal under May 30, 1658, 82.

38. *CHSNY*, 13: Propositions Made at Fort Amsterdam, July 19, 1649, 25; Minute of Return of Prisoners, October 18, 1655, 46; Instructions for Capt. Adrian Post, October 18, 1655, 47; Stuyvesant and Council, November 10–27, 1655, 51–57.

39. *CHSNY*, 13: Stuyvesant to Magistrates of Fort Orange, July 12, 1663, 278, and also Johannes la Montagne and Jeremias van Rensselaer to Stuyvesant, July 28, 1663, 283; Jeremias van Rensselaer to Oloff Stevensz van Cortlandt, August 27, 1663 (van Laer, 1932, 327); for broken promises to Esopus, 13: Instructions for Claes de Ruyter, June 3, 1660, 173, and for unfulfilled promises to Long Island natives, 1: Instruction of the Commissioners at Ass. of XIX, July 7, 1645, and verified in New Netherland in 1652, 498.

40. *CHSNY*, 13: Resolution not to Pay Ransom, October 13, 1655, 45; 1: Remonstrance of New Netherland, July 28, 1649, 311. For Long Island, see Gehring, 1983, Council Minute, December 3, 1653, 89; 13: Stuyvesant's Journal under May 30, 1658, 82.

Chapter 15. Alongshore Compromised

1. *CHSNY*, 13: Dirs. to Amsterdam Burgomasters, February 13, 1652, 29–30; Dirs. to Stuyvesant, April 4, 1652, 33. For population growth, see Hauptman and Knapp, 1977,

171; Jameson, 1909e, 259; and Rink, 1986, 142–71. For exports to New Netherland of 500,000 to 800,000 guilders annually from 1654 to 1659 (and higher thereafter), see Jacobs, 2005, 255.

2. Guha, 1997, 482.

3. *CHSNY*, 1: Permit to Sail to New Netherland [1656], 625, 626.

4. *CHSNY*, 1: Conditions Offered to Emigrants, [July?] 1656, 621, 620. For the WIC's erasure of indebtedness to Amsterdam by transferring ownership of Fort Casimir, see Weslager, 1967, 152, and van der Zee and van der Zee, 1978, 301, 302.

5. *CHSNY*, 1: Conditions Offered to Emigrants, [July?] 1656, 619, 620, and Burke, 1956, 65. For population data, see de Vries & van der Woude, 1997, 298, 286.

6. *CHSNY*, 1: Conditions Offered to Emigrants, [July?] 1656, 624.

7. *CHSNY*, 1: Resolution of Council of Amsterdam on a Plan to Colonize New Netherland, July 4, 1656, 618; For identifying New Amstel as a city-colony, see Jacobs, 2005, 131, but see 135.

8. For Romulus, see Barend-van Haeften, 1996, 13, and Arber, 1897, 145. The VOC urged its personnel and burghers to marry indigenous women "after the Roman and Portuguese precedents" (Boxer, 1965, 242). For the WIC's similar preference in Brazil, see Boxer, 1973, 130.

9. *CHSNY*, 1: Pretensions and Claims of Patroons, June 16, 1634, Points 6, 8, and 11, 87. For Wassenaer's identification of the average colonist as a tenant farmer, *zetboer*, see Wieder, 1925, 50 n. 1.

10. Stokes, 1915–28, 4: Symon Dircksz Pos to Kiliaen van Rensselaer, September 16, 1630, 77; quoting van Rensselaer to Willem Kieft, May 12, 1639 (van Laer, 1908, 428), and van Rensselaer to Megapolensis, March 13, 1643, 647.

11. *CHSNY*, 1: Observations on Duties, March 7, 1650 [to States from Delegates from New Netherland], 373, 374; Remonstrance of New Netherland, July 28, 1649, 301; directors quoted, 13: Dirs. to Stuyvesant, March 21, 1651, 28. For insisting that prosperity in the seventeenth-century Low Countries could be overblown, see Wilson and Parker, 1977, 112.

12. Scott and Stryker-Rodda, 1974, Council Minute, July 6, 1647, 393; "pioneers" used by Stokes, 1915–28, 2: 105.

13. *CHSNY*, 1: [Kieft's] Journal, 181.

14. Quoting Westermann, 1996, 81; Lepore, 1998, citing Francisco de Vitoria, 110. For Martin Luther, see Greenblatt, 1983, 10. For Steen, see Westermann, 1996, 82. Evidence for the Netherlanders' estimate of farmers is often ambiguous because the men whom *boer* referenced ranged from landless peasants to farmers of considerable financial substance. At one extreme, *boer,* rather like *colonier,* could mean a tenant belonging to the numerically limited Dutch feudal peasantry. At the other extreme, he might be categorized as a *boer* yet be notably prosperous, leasing his agricultural land but owning property near another town or in another province. In one of the maritime provinces, he might engage in commercial or specialized farming. Country folk and the sixteenth- and seventeenth-century Dutch rural economy generally have attracted a sizable and vibrant scholarship. I have found useful the work of Jan de Vries, Herman Arend Enno van Gelder, B. H. Slicher van Bath, A. T. van Deursen, and J. L. van Zanden.

15. Harline, 1987, quoting *Münster Chat* [1646], 213.

16. For ridicule, see Brandt, 1993, 390, and van der Heijden, 1967b, 8, and, for his warning to city burghers that where *boers* feast together there is blood and violence, G. A. Bredero's *Boeren Geselschap* in his *Lied-Boeck,* 15, lines 5–55. For landscapists, see Brown, 1986, 29. For farmers as animalistic and oversexed, see de Bièvre, 1988, 315, 324.

For staffage and rural scenes, see Gibson, 2000, 117, 128, 175. For rural workers in the colonies, see Westermann, 1996, 114.

17. For farmers as seamen, see Lambert, 1971, 172; *CHSNY*, 1: Remonstrance of New Netherland, July 28, 1649, 298.

18. Gehring, 1983, Proposals of Stuyvesant to Council, May 30, 1654, 139.

19. Gehring, 1983, Proposals of Stuyvesant to Council, May 30, 1654, 138; Stuyvesant and Council to Mayor and Schepenen of New Amsterdam, June 13, 1654, 144.

20. Gehring, 1983, Proposals of Stuyvesant to Council, May 30, 1654, 138.

21. Gehring, 1983, Response to Remonstrance, December 13, 1653, 97.

22. Gehring, 1983, Response to Remonstrance, December 13, 1653, 95, 96; Stuyvesant and Council to Petitioners, December 12, 1653, 94.

23. Gehring, 1983, Stuyvesant to Council, June 17, 1652, 28, 29; Response of Stuyvesant and Council to Remonstrance, December 13, 1653, 97, 96.

24. Gehring, 1983, Considerations of Stuyvesant and Council on Petition of Mayor and Schepenen, December 3, 1653, 87; Remonstrance, December 11, 1653, 92.

25. Gehring, 1983, Stuyvesant to Council, February 26, 1654, 119.

26. Jan Janse Oosterhout had emigrated from a village in North Brabant; Jan Teunisse van Tilberg left an agricultural village about fifteen to twenty kilometers south and farther east; Claes Lourensz arrived from Amersfoort in Utrecht, which shared an eastern border with Gelderland; Guysbert Teunisse came from the farming community of "Barevelt" (Barneveld), fifteen kilometers farther east into Gelderland; Lambert Janse arrived from Ootmarsz (Ootmarsum), an agricultural village about five kilometers from the German border; Jan Jacobsz van Gietere (Gieteren) came from a Drents farming community about twenty-five kilometers from Germany. For questioning of the men, see Gehring, 1983, 117, 118. For farmers arriving mainly from the eastern provinces, see Jacobs, 2005, 92.

27. Quoted in Keur and Keur, 1955, 35, and see 95, 119, 164; Stoett, 1967, *S. Costers Boere-Klucht van Teeuwis de Boer, en men Juffer van Grevelinckhuysen . . .* (t'Amstelredam, Cornelis Lodowijcksz, 1627), 29.

28. Quoted in Gehring, 1983, Minutes, June 13, 1654, 146. Even throughout the northern Netherlands, agriculture was the largest labor sector in the economy but never absorbed more than about half the labor force—by mid-seventeenth-century, it was only about one million (de Vries and van der Woude, 1997, 195 and see 208). In New Netherland, the exact extent of agriculture is still "unknown"; see Jacobs, 2005, 216, 214.

29. *CHSNY*, 13: Entry by Cornelis van Werckhoven for Two Colonies, November 7, 1651, 29; Hendrick van der Capellen to Cornelis van Werckhoven [February 1652?], 32. Van der Capellen's interest may have arisen from the partnership in a Staten Island property between his brother Frederick and David Pietersz de Vries, and a property bought there (perhaps without the company's knowledge) from Melijn, Extract, Stuyvesant to Dirs., July 21, 1661, 205, and Extract, Dirs. to Stuyvesant, October 9, 1659, 121.

30. *CHSNY*, 13: Extract, Dirs. to Stuyvesant, April 4, 1652, 33, 34.

31. *CHSNY*, 13: Extract, Dirs. to Stuyvesant, December 13, 1652, 34.

32. *CHSNY*, 13: List of Farmers, November 14/4 [sic], 1657, 74, 75; Fishman, 1979, 14.

33. Gehring, 1983, Council Minutes, April 8, 1654, 126; Council Minutes, November 24, 1653, 79; Considerations of Stuyvesant and Council on Proposals of Mayor and Schepenen, December 3, 1653, 73; and Considerations on the Petition, December 3, 1653, 88.

34. For fishing permits, see Bolton, 1975, 127; quoted in Ceci, 1977, 265–66; *CHSNY*, 13: Stuyvesant's Journal under June 1, 1658, 13: 85.

35. Stokes, 1915–28, 2: 349–51 and C. Plates 83, 84, and 4: under February 20, 1664, 233, the city's eminence is cited in Merwick, 1999, 121. For her estimate of 1,875 residents in New Amsterdam in 1664, see Goodfriend, 1992, 39.

36. Biggs, 1999, 386.

37. Rowen, 1972, 145.

38. Kern, 1910, 155.

Chapter 16. Considerations on a Just War

1. Jameson, 1909a, 383–86; see also *CHSNY*, 12:89–111. Fort Casimir was at New Castle, Delaware, and Fort Christina at Wilmington.

2. *CHSNY*, 13: Proposals Made by Long Island Natives, November 27, 1655, 58. For one version of the happenings, see 12: Councillors to Stuyvesant, September 12, [12/22?], 1655, 98, 99. In this account, the Susquehannocks play a leading and retaliatory role against the Dutch officials who had ended their valuable trading relationship with the Swedes on the Delaware (Kupperman, 1995, 105 and 111 n. 78). For Stuyvesant's and Council's Account, see 13: Remonstrance, October 31, 1655, 49, 50.

3. For Beverwijck, see Merwick, 1990, 77, and van Laer, 1928, 2: Court Minutes of August 6, 1677, 257. For efforts to control liquor and gun sales, see Gehring, 1983, Ordinance, August 28, 1654, 173; *CHSNY*, 1: Extract, Protest of van Dinglage, February 28, 1651, 455; woman selling liquor, 13: Indictment for Selling Liquor to Natives, April 2, 1656, 68, and see Meeting of Stuyvesant, Council, and Burgomasters, July 1, 1656, 69.

4. Gehring, 1983, Council Minutes, September 8, 1654, 182, and see 195.

5. Van der Zee and van der Zee, 1978, 273, and see *CHSNY*, 13: Opinion of van Tienhoven on Stuyvesant's Propositions, November 14, 1655, 57.

6. *CHSNY*, 13: Opinion of Stuyvesant, November 10, 1655, 52.

7. *CHSNY*, 13: Questions Submitted by Stuyvesant to Council, January 18, 1656, 58, 59; for van Tienhoven's estimate of natives' numbers as seven hundred, Opinion on Stuyvesant's Propositions, November 14, 1655, 56, and la Montagne's estimate of nineteen hundred of whom "800 were already here," Opinion of la Montagne, November 10, 1655, 55.

8. *CHSNY*, 13: Orders to Captain Adrian Post, October 16, 1655, 45, 46.

9. *CHSNY*, 13: Resolution Not to Pay Ransom, October 13, 1655, 45; see Gehring, 1983, Ordinance, August 28, 1654, 173.

10. *CHSNY*, 13: Residents of Gravesend to Stuyvesant and Council, September 28/ October 8, 1655, 39, 40; Dutch Residents of Gravesend to Stuyvesant, October 20, 1655, 47.

11. See *CHSNY*, 13: Thomas Wieler [Wheeler/Weyls] to Dutch of Gravesend, September 27, 1655, 40.

12. *CHSNY*, 13: Stuyvesant to Council, January 26, 1656, 60. For Stuyvesant's use of "massacre," see 12: Stuyvesant to Councillors, September 24, 1655, 103.

13. *CHSNY*, 13: Meeting of Stuyvesant, Council and Burgomasters, July 1, 1656, 69; Ordinance Forbidding All Persons Crossing the River, October 18, 1655, 46, and Instructions to Captain Adrian Post, October 18, 1655, 47.

14. *CHSNY*, 13: Propositions Made at Fort Amsterdam, July 19, 1649, 25, and see Articles of Peace, August 30, 1645, 18.

15. Bolton, 1975, 47.

16. *CHSNY*, 13: Propositions Made at Fort Amsterdam, July 19, 1649, 25.

17. Bolton, 1975, 131; *CHSNY*, 13: Minute, Return of Prisoners, October 18, 1655, 46.

For Stuyvesant's pressure on the Mohawks to control the River Indians as early as September 24, 1655, see 12: Stuyvesant to Councillors, September 24, 1655, 103.

18. *CHSNY*, 13: Instructions for Captain Adrian Post, October 18, 1655, 47, and Answers of Natives, October 26, 1655, 48; for twenty children held, Order to Remove a Hoboken House, March 28, 1656, 67. For differing communication modes, see Santos, 2005, 5. For the later Mohawk designation of the Delawares as women, see Trexler, 1995, 77, and Miller, 1974, 507–11. For no retaliation by Stuyvesant, see Chiodo, 1974, 193.

19. *CHSNY*, 13: Proposals of Stuyvesant Respecting Esopus Natives, February 9, 1660, 136.

20. *CHSNY*, 13: Remonstrance of Stuyvesant and Council to States, October 31, 1655, 50, 49; for general agreement on the innocent intentions of the River Indians, Opinion of Stuyvesant, November 10, 1655, 51.

21. *CHSNY*, 13: Remonstrance of Stuyvesant and Council to States [with Addenda], October 31, 1655, 51; for insufficient troops, 1: Committee of Ass. of XIX to States, November 16, 1627, 38. For Fort Christina, see van der Zee and van der Zee, 1978, 82.

22. *CHSNY*, 13: Order Regarding Hoboken House, March 28, 1656, 67.

23. *CHSNY*, 13: Extract, Dirs. to Stuyvesant and Council, March 13, 1656, 63, 64.

24. *CHSNY*, 13: Extract, Dirs. to Stuyvesant and Council [ca. mid- to late 1656] and December 22, 1657, 70, 75.

25. Chiodo, 1974, 69, 71, 78–82, 122–25. For an alliance proposed to Governor William Berkeley of Virginia, see 158, 159. For rejecting an "aggressive" war, see *CHSNY*, 13: Extract, Dirs. to Burgomasters and Council of Amsterdam, February 13, 1652, 30, and Extract, Dirs. to Stuyvesant, April 4, 1652, 33.

26. *CHSNY*, 13: Extract, Dirs. to Stuyvesant and Council [ca. late 1656], 71; see Gehring, 1983, Considerations of Stuyvesant and Council on Petition of Burgomasters and Schepenen, December 3, 1653, 87, and Council Minutes, December 13, 1653, 100, and April 8, 1654, 129. New Netherland's administrators had "an attitude toward war that subverted militia organization." It was in contrast to early Virginians' "almost continual raids into Indian country" (Shy, 1976, 27, 25).

27. Gehring, 1983, Council Minutes, July 2, 1654, 153, 154. For Connecticut's call for an offensive war against the Dutch in 1653, see Lepore, 1998, 287 n. 49.

28. Stokes, 1915–28, 4: under November 25, 1638, 88.

29. *CHSNY*, 13: Extract, Stuyvesant to Dirs., July 15, 1662, 223, 224; for one of several references to Stuyvesant's awareness of the more aggressive English ways of subduing natives, see [Tienhoven's] Opinion submitted to Stuyvesant, November 10, 1655, 57, and identification of aggressive war in the field with the English, Dirs. to Burgomasters and Regents, February 13, 1652, 30.

30. Chinua Achebe, quoted in Durix, 1987, 19; *CHSNY*, 13: Dirs. to Stuyvesant and Council, September 15, 1657, 74.

31. *CHSNY*, 13: Opinions of the Director-General and Council, November 10–29, 1655, 53–57.

Chapter 17. Cultural Entanglement

1. Stokes, 1915–28, 2: Second Period of Dutch Surveys, C Pl. 39, "Copy Made in c. 1660 of a Map of Minuit's Time, c. 1630," following 120. For Atkarkarton, see Schoonmaker, 1888, 2. For Atharhacton, see Fried, 1975, 180.

2. *CHSNY*, 13: Captain Martin Cregier's Journal, under July 30, 1663, 330. For yield estimates, see Ceci, 1977, 101.

3. *CHSNY*, 13: Extract, Stuyvesant to Dirs., July 21, 1661, 205. Copious documentation on Esopus and the wars of 1659–64 includes the Kingston (earlier, Wiltwijck) court records and notarial papers of Beverwijck (Albany), military officers' reports, and Stuyvesant's journal and correspondence.

4. *CHSNY*, 13: Declaration of Catskill Natives regarding Violence at Esopus [ca. mid-October 1659], 120.

5. *CHSNY*, Extract, Stuyvesant to Dirs. [ca. mid-October 1659], 125; Ensign Dirck Smit to Johannes la Montagne, September 29, 1659, 118. For the thirteen captives, see van Laer, 1932, Jeremias van Rensselaer to Jan Baptist van Rensselaer [June 3–6, 1660], 220.

6. *CHSNY*, 13: Proclamation for Fasting and Prayer, February 23, 1660, 145; Ordinance of Stuyvesant and Council [ca. November, 1655], 53.

7. *CHSNY*, 13: Instructions for Ensign Dirck Smit, October 18, 1658, 96, and see Smit to la Montagne, September 29, 1659, 118.

8. *CHSNY*, 13: Smit to Stuyvesant, September 29, 1659, 115. For de Vries quoting Kieft, see Colenbrander, 1911, under February 24, 1643, 263.

9. *CHSNY*, 13: for "mischief" caused by fellow villagers and the sergeant as well as exoneration of Smit, Cornelis Barentsz Slecht and Other Inhabitants to Stuyvesant [ca. mid-October 1659], 118, 119, and see Declaration of Inhabitants [ca. early October 1659], 117.

10. *CHSNY*, 13: Jan Jacob Stoll and Others to Stuyvesant, September 29, 1659, 116.

11. *CHSNY*, 13: Opinion of Cornelis van Ruyven, February 12, 1660, 140. For an excellent study of a single colonial event recorded in contesting local and provincial narratives and archives, see Stoler, 1992a.

12. *CHSNY*, 13: Extract, Stuyvesant to Dirs. [ca. mid-October 1659], 124. By summer 1660, it seems to have been common knowledge that the Esopus war began in a "very irregular way" and was "largely the fault of the Dutch" (van Laer, 1932, Jeremias van Rensselaer to Jan Baptist van Rensselaer [June 3–6, 1660], 220).

13. Schoonmaker, 1888, 13.

14. *CHSNY*, 13: Extract, Stuyvesant to Dirs., July 21, 1661, 205.

15. *CHSNY*, 13: Extract, Stuyvesant to Dirs. [ca. mid-October 1659], 124, and see for free plundering, Minute of Stuyvesant's Visit to Hempstead, June 23, 1663, 259, 260; Proclamation Calling for Volunteers, June 25, 1663, 260. For enticement money, see Mann, 1976, 273.

16. *CHSNY*, 13: Proclamation Calling for Volunteers, June 25, 1663, 260; taking captives, Extract, Stuyvesant to Dirs. [ca. mid-October 1659], 125, and Instructions for Magistrates at Wiltwijck, June 14, 1663, 249.

17. *CHSNY*, 13: Extract, Stuyvesant to Dirs. [ca. mid-October 1659], 124, 125.

18. *CHSNY*, 13: Declaration of Katskill Natives regarding Violence at Esopus [ca. mid-October 1659], 119, 120; Stuyvesant's Journal under June 4, 1658, 83; for soldiers beating natives, Proposals Made to Esopus Natives, October 15, 1658, 95; for the sachems' statement about the young men, Proposals Made by Esopus Natives, September 4, 1659, 106.

19. *CHSNY*, 13: Andries Laurensz to Stuyvesant, September 1, 1659, 106.

20. *CHSNY*, 13: Stuyvesant's Journal under May 31 and June 1, 1658, 84, 85; Laurensz to Stuyvesant, August 8, 1658, 88; Proposal Made by Esopus Natives, September 4, 1659, 106.

21. *CHSNY*, 13: Ordinance against Making Openings in the Palisades, November 27, 1662, 232; Proposals Made by Esopus Natives, September 4, 1659, 107; Proposals, October 15, 1658, 95, and for tricks played, Roeloff Swartwout to Stuyvesant, June 14, 1661, 201; Affidavit of Jan Gillisen Kock, November 7, 1657, 74. For liquor's spiritual and perception-altering qualities, see Mancall, 1995, 75–77.

22. *CHSNY*, 13: Council Rejection of Keeping a Tavern at Esopus, June 15, 1662, 222, and for retaining one house, Abraham Staats to Stuyvesant, January 16, 1660, 132. See van der Zee and van der Zee, 1978, 198, and Complaint against Christoffel Davidsz, September 3, 1658, 90. For native memories of 1655, see Proposals Made by Esopus Natives, September 4, 1659, 106. For Davidsz's and Chambers's lawless houses and Stuyvesant's concerns, Stuyvesant to Smit, December 11, 1659, 128, and Conference between Stuyvesant and Hackensacks and Haverstraws, June 3, 1660, 171, Smit to Stuyvesant, May 30, 1660, 171.

23. For hybridity, see Loomba, 1998, 173, and Werbner, 1995, 5. For cross-cultural exchange, see Gibson, 1996, 3, and Thomas, 1991, 1996, 1999.

24. *CHSNY*, 13: Thomas Chambers to Stuyvesant, May 2, 1658, 77, 78, and Certificate, July 11, 1658, 88.

25. For Grotius on total war, see Remec, 1960, 105, and 106 n. 2. For *soetelaers* in Esopus, see Christoph, Scott, and Stryker-Rodda, 1976, 1: Ord. Sess., May 22, 1663, 69, and see *CHSNY*, 13: Ordinance Against Receiving in Pawn Arms, Clothing, Etc. Belonging to Soldiers at Wiltwijck, November 27, 1662, 232. For *soetelaers* in literature, see inter alia, Stoett, 1967, *Coster's Teeuwis de Boer*, 51; and Redlich, 1956, 5, quoting Cornelis van Bynkershoek, *Questionium Juris Publici . . .* (1737). For a contemporary's illustration, *Die Plaetse der Suetelaers* at the 1594 siege of Groningen, see Muller, 1, 1908, following 24.

26. *CHSNY*, 13: Resolution, May 28, 1658, 80; Stuyvesant's Journal under May 30, 1658, 83, and see 82.

Chapter 18. No Closure

1. *CHSNY*, 13: Proposals of Stuyvesant respecting Esopus, February 9, 1660, 136, 137. For prosecution of war and court cases, see Vincent, 1990, 244, and see Remec, 1960, quoting *De Jure Belli ac Pacis*, 67 n. 1. For Stuyvesant's knowledge of Dutch-Roman law, see Merwick, 1999, 211.

2. *CHSNY*, 13: Proposals of Stuyvesant respecting Esopus, February 9, 1660, 137, and Treaty of Peace, March 6, 1660, 147–49.

3. See *CHSNY*, 13: Proposals of Stuyvesant respecting Esopus, February 9, 1660, 137, 138, and see Stuyvesant to Dirs., September 17, 1659, 111. For Netherlands patrols, see Egmond, 1993, 33.

4. Kingsbury and Roberts, 1990, 5.

5. *CHSNY*, 13: Proposals of Stuyvesant respecting Esopus, Opinion of Cornelis van Ruyven, February 12, 1660, 142, and see Resolution to Declare War, February 12, 1660, 142; van Laer, 1932, quoting Jeremias van Rensselaer to Jan Baptist van Rensselaer [June 3–6, 1660], 220. For English colonists' debates on the just war, see Lepore, 1998, 335, 340.

Papers compiled by Fernow and O'Callaghan in volume 13 are best for estimating the growth of the Dutch Esopus villages. For example, they reveal that by 1663 Wiltwijck was drawing tax revenues on 1,050 acres of land in addition to house lots and, together with Nieuw Dorp, numbered 200–300 settlers. For the investments of major fur traders from Beverwijck, see van Laer, 1918, *inter alia,* 54, 154, 158, 159, 189, 208, 209, 306, and see Petition of Philip Pietersz Schuyler et al., April 6, 1662, 219, 220.

6. *CHSNY,* 13: 142–96, and Extract, Stuyvesant to Court of Fort Orange and Rensselaerswijck, January 21, 1664, 356.

7. *CHSNY,* 13: Treaty of Peace with Hackensacks and Others, March 6, 1660, 147–49; for Esopus on the warpath, Table of Contents at June 27, 1663.

8. *CHSNY,* 13: Extract, Stuyvesant and Council to Dirs., September 4, 1659, 108, and Extract, Stuyvesant to Dirs., September 17, 1659, 111; for preventing future colonies, Extract, Dirs. to Stuyvesant, October 9, 1659, 121.

9. *CHSNY,* 13: Coetheos of the Wappings Makes Peace, March 15, 1660, 150, and see Stuyvesant to van Ruyven, March 18, 1660, 151.

10. *CHSNY,* 13: Stuyvesant's Journal under May 31, 1658, 85, and see Propositions Made by Chiefs of Katskills on behalf of Esopus Chiefs, April 21, 1660, 162. For banishment, see van Laer, 1932, Stuyvesant to Jeremias van Rensselaer, November 5, 1659, 186. For the Esopus Kil as reparation, Extract, Council to Dirs., July 26, 1660, 181.

11. *CHSNY,* 13: Dirck Smit to Stuyvesant and Council, June 12, 1660, 174; for diminished numbers of natives, Martin Cregier to Stuyvesant, July 5, 1663, 272, and Stuyvesant to Vice-Director at Curaçao, September 24, 1663, 297. For vagrancy and spying, see Extraordinary Sess., Court & Burgher Council of War, July 7, 1665, in Christoph, Scott, and Stryker-Rodda, 1976, 1: 242.

12. *CHSNY,* 13: Information of English Intrigues, August 27, 1664, 392. For Stuyvesant's report that the last of the captives taken in 1663 had been released, see Proclamation of Thanksgiving, May 31, 1664, 384.

13. For the treaties, see *CHSNY,* 13: Articles of Peace, May 16, 1664, 376, and Agreement Made between Richard Nicolls and Sapes Indyans, October 7, 1665, 400.

14. For Stuyvesant's report to the States and answer to charges of the WIC as well as other 1665 papers, see *CHSNY:* 2. For "investigative modalities" of Bernard S. Cohn, see Dirks, 1996, xiii, and see Dirks, 1992, 3.

15. Heesterman, 1978, 53. "The Dutch maritime empire . . . never developed the territorial commitment associated with the empires of Holland's chief rivals for imperial splendor" (Rink, 1986, 18).

16. Stoler, 1992b, Dening, 2004, and see Thomas, 1991, 3. For the French empire in Oceania as a "haphazard creation," see Matsuda, 2005, 6, 7, 16.

17. Cohn, 1996, 4. For fragmentation in British India, see Heesterman, 1978, 32; for "sly civility" and "cunning David," see Bhabha, 1985, and Gouda, 1995, 39; for the Dutch seaborne empire as mercantile experiments, see Schöffer, 1978, 80.

18. Wesseling, 1978, 4, quoting J. C. van Leur, *Indonesian Trade and Society: Essays in Social and Economic History* (The Hague, 1955), 289; Winius, 1996, 119, 111, 112, and see Verlinden, 1996, 91.

19. Stoler, 1992b, 321.

20. Weslager, 1967, 62. For the Dutch nation-state, see Gouda, 1995, 3.

21. Keyes, 1990, 50, 69. For a similar example of the disappearance of empire after its use as a title, see Postma, 1998, and Boxer, 1973, 258. Clearly, the date chosen to begin one's examination matters; e.g. Klooster, 1997, quite properly refers to "the Dutch empire . . . before ca. 1800," xiii.

22. Goslinga, 1985, 28.

23. Hulme, 1992, 2. For a study of empires of commerce in the early Ohio Valley, see Hinderaker, 1997.

24. Helgerson, 1992, 29, 30; Boxer, 1965, 66. For medieval colonizing projects settling Flemish agriculturalists in middle Europe, see Bartlett, 1993, 123f.

25. Jennings, 1984, 71, and see Jacobs, 2005: "no attempt was made to subdue the Indians in such a way that attempts to proselytize were feasible," 322.

26. Shomette and Haslach, 1988, 317, 191, 175.

27. Goslinga, 1985, 272, and Postma, 1998, 108–11.

28. Van der Zee and van der Zee, 1978, 481, and see Murphy, 1865, Selijns, *Epitaph for Petrus Stuyvesant, General of New York,* 161.

Weighing Up

1. Chakrabarty, 2002, 72.

2. Frost, 2003, quoting Dalrymple to Lord George Germain, March 1, 1780, 99.

3. Gouda, 1995, 242. For his hypothesis that the respect of Dutch colonials for existing indigenous customs and traditions in Indonesia until well into the twentieth century caused the "relatively weak and haphazard reactions" to their rule, see Schöffer, 1978, 81.

4. *CHSNY,* 2: Alrich to Commissioners, August 13, 1657, to Burgomaster de Graaff, August 16, 1659, and to Burgomasters of Amsterdam, May 7, 1657, 20, 69, 9.

Bibliography

Anon. 1615. *A Description of the Prosperitie of the United Provinces of the Netherlands.* London (a Walter J. Johnson facsimile publication [Norwood, N.J.: Theatrum Orbis Terrarum, 1979]). Original: *A Description of the Prosperitie, Strength & Wise Government of the United Provinces of the Netherlands. Signified by the Batavian Virgin, in her seat of unitie. Wherein Is Related the Whole State of those countries at this present time.* London, imprinted by Felix Kyngston, for Edward Marchant, 1615.

Anon. 1626. *An Excellent & Material Discourse . . . Those of Germanie should be subdued.* (The English Experience: Its Record in Early Printed Books Published in Facsimile [Amsterdam: Theatrum Orbis Terrarum, 1973]). Original: *An Excellent & Materiaal Discourse, Proving by Many & Forceable Reasons what great danger will hang over our heads of England and France, and also divers other Kingdomes and Provinces of Europe, if it shall happen that those of Germanie which are our friends be subdued, and the King of Denmarke vanquished. And therefore how neerely it concerneth them all to put to their helping hands without any further delay, for the ayding of the King of Denmarke, and other of our Confederates in Germany, who at this time abide the brunt and shocke of the Warre,* 1626.

Adair, Monte. 1986. *An Unabridged Translation of Simplicius Simplicissimus by Johann Jakob Christoffel Von Grimmelshausen, with an Introduction and Notes by Monte Adair.* New York: University Press of America.

Alden, John, and Dennis C. Landis, eds. 1982. *European Americana: A Chronological Guide to Works Printed in Europe Relating to the Americas, 1493–1776,* Vol. 2, *1601–1650.* New York: Readex.

Alexandrowicz, C. H. 1967. *An Introduction to the History of the Law of Nations in the East Indies (16th, 17th and 18th Centuries).* London: Oxford University Press.

Arber, Edward. 1897. *The Story of the Pilgrim Fathers, 1606–1623 A. D.; As Told by Themselves, Their Friends, and Their Enemies.* London: Ward and Downey.

Baker, Emerson W., and John G. Reid. 2004. "Amerindian Power in the Early Modern Northeast: A Reappraisal." *William and Mary Quarterly,* 3rd ser., 61: 77–106.

Barend-van Haeften, M. L., with assistance of E. S. Van Eyck van Heslinga. 1996. *Op reis met de VOC: De openhartige dag boeken van de zusters Lammers en Swellengrebel.* Zutphen: Walberg Pers.

Bartlett, Robert. 1993. *The Making of Europe: Conquest, Colonization and Cultural Change, 950–1350.* Princeton, N.J.: Princeton University Press.

Beekman, E. M. 1988. *Fugitive Dreams: An Anthology of Dutch Colonial Literature.* Amherst: University of Massachusetts Press.

Benton, Lauren. 1999. "Colonial Law and Cultural Difference: Jurisdictional Politics and the Formation of the Colonial State." *Comparative Studies in Society and History* 41: 563–96.

Bergman, R. A. M. 1933. "Jan Pieterszoon Coen: Een psychographie Bijdrage tot de leer der constitutielypen." *Tijdschrift voor Indische Taal-Land-en Volkenkunde* 73: 1–56.

Bhabha, Homi K. 1985. "Sly Civility." *October* 34: 71–80.

Biggs, Michael. 1999. "Putting the State on the Map: Cartography, Territory, and European State Formation." *Comparative Studies in Society and History* 41: 374–405.

Blussé, Leonard. 1995. "Retribution and Remorse: The Interaction between the Administration and the Protestant Mission in Early Colonial Formosa." In *After Colonialism: Imperial Histories and Postcolonial Displacements*, ed. Gyan Prakash, 153–82. Princeton, N.J.: Princeton University Press.

Bolton, Reginald Pelham. 1975. *New York City in Indian Possession.* 2nd ed. New York: Museum of the American Indian, Heye Foundation.

Booth, Mary L. 1880. *History of the City of New York.* New York: E. P. Dutton.

Borschberg, Peter. 1994. *Hugo Grotius: "Commentarius in Theses XI": An Early Treatise on Sovereignty, the Just War, and the Legitimacy of the Dutch Revolt.* Berne: Peter Lang.

Boxer, Charles R. 1965. *The Dutch Seaborne Empire, 1600–1800.* London: Hutchinson, Penguin Books.

———. 1973. *The Dutch in Brazil, 1624–1654.* Oxford: Clarendon.

Brandt, George W., ed. 1993. *German and Dutch Theatre, 1600–1848.* Compiled by George W. Brandt and Wiebe Hogendoorn. Cambridge: Cambridge University Press.

Brown, Christopher, ed. 1986. *Dutch Landscape: The Early Years, Haarlem and Amsterdam, 1590–1650. An Exhibition at the National Gallery, London, September 3 to November 23, 1986.* London: National Gallery.

Brugmans, H. 1973. *Geschiedenis van Amsterdam.* Vol. 3, *Bloeitijd, 1621–1697.* Utrecht: Spectrum.

Bull, Hedley. 1990. "The Importance of Grotius in the Study of International Relations." In *Hugo Grotius and International Relations*, ed. Hedley Bull, Benedict Kingsbury, and Adam Roberts, 65–93. Oxford: Clarendon.

Burke, Gerald L. 1956. *The Making of Dutch Towns: A Study in Urban Development from the Tenth to the Seventeenth Centuries.* London: Cleaver-Hume.

Campbell, Reverend William. 1967. *Formosa under the Dutch Described from Contemporary Records, with Explanatory Notes and a Bibliography of the Island* [Campbell's preface, 1903]. Taipei: Ch'eng-Wen.

Cannenburg, W. Voorbeijtel, ed. 1964. *De Reis om de Wereld van de Nassausche Vloot, 1623–1626.* 's-Gravenhage: Martinus Nijhoff.

Carlton, Charles. 1992. *Going to the Wars: The Experience of the British Civil Wars, 1638–1651.* London: Routledge.

Ceci, Lynn. 1977. "The Effect of European Contact and Trade on the Settlement Pattern of Indians in Coastal New York, 1524–1665: The Archeological and Documentary Evidence." Ph.D. diss., City University of New York.

Chakrabarty, Dipesh. 2002. *Habitations of Modernity: Essays in the Wake of Subaltern Studies.* Chicago: University of Chicago Press.

Chiodo, John Joseph. 1974. "The Foreign Policy of Peter Stuyvesant: Dutch Diplomacy in North America, 1647 to 1664." Ph.D. diss., University of Iowa.

Christoph, Peter R., Kenneth Scott, and Kenn Stryker-Rodda, eds. 1976. *New York Historical Manuscripts: Dutch, Kingston Papers.* Trans. Dingman Versteeg (with Revision of Pages 1–171 by Samuel Oppenheim). Vol. 1, *Kingston Court Records, 1661–1667.* Baltimore: Genealogical Publishing.

Clark, George L. 1914. *A History of Connecticut: Its People and Institutions.* New York: G. P. Putnam's Sons.

Cohen, J. M. 1958. "On Cannibals." In *Michel de Montaigne: Essays*, ed. J. M. Cohen, 105–19. London: Penguin Books.

Cohn, Bernard S. 1996. *Colonialism and Its Forms of Knowledge: The British in India.* Princeton, N.J.: Princeton University Press.

Colenbrander, H. T. 1911. *Korte Historiael ende Journaels Aenteyckeninge van Verscheyden Voyagiens in de Vier Deelen des Wereldts-Ronde als Europa, Africa, Asia, ende Amerika Gedaen door David Pietersz. De Vries.* 's-Gravenhage: Martinus Nijhoff.

———. 1934. *Jan Pietersz. Coen: Levensbeschrijving.* 's-Gravenhage: Martinus Nijhoff.

Condon, Thomas J. 1968. *New York Beginnings: The Commercial Origins of New York.* New York: New York University Press.

Cooper, Frederick, and Ann Laura Stoler, eds. 1997. *Tensions of Empire: Colonial Cultures in a Bourgeois World.* Berkeley: University of California Press.

Crosby, Alfred W. 1986. *Ecological Imperialism: The Biological Expansion of Europe, 900–1900.* Cambridge: Cambridge University Press.

Dathorne, O. R. 1996. *Asian Voyages: Two Thousand Years of Constructing the Other.* Westport, Conn.: Bergin and Garvey.

Davies, D. W. 1961. *A Primer of Dutch Seventeenth-Century Overseas Trade.* The Hague: Martinus Nijhoff.

Day, Clive. 1904. *The Dutch in Java.* London: Oxford University Press. 1966 reprint of *The Policy and Administration of the Dutch in Java.* New York: Macmillan.

de Bièvre, Elizabeth. 1988. "Violence and Virtue: History and Art in the City of Haarlem." *Art History* 11: 303–34.

———. 1993. "The Art of History and the History of Art: Cause and Effect in Historiography and Art in the Commonwealth of the Low Countries around 1600." In *From Revolt to Riches: Culture and History of the Low Countries, 1500–1700: International and Interdisciplinary Perspectives*, ed. Theo Hermans and Reinier Salverda, 163–81. London: Center for Low Countries Studies.

de Klerck, E. S. 1938. *History of the Netherlands East Indies.* Vol. 1. Rotterdam: W. L. and J. Brusse.

de Koning, Joep M. J. 1999. "Dating the Visscher, or Prototype, View of New Amsterdam." *De halve maen* 72: 47–56.

De la Court, Pieter. 1702. *The True Interest and Political Maxims of the Republick of Holland and West-Friesland. In Three Parts. The First Treating of Liberty in General. Of Manufactures. Fisheries. Traffick. Navigation. Toleration of Religion. A General Naturalization. Freedom from Imports. Impartial Justice; and Settling of Colonies.*

Part 2 and 3. *Of a Free Navigation, and Clearing the Seas. Of War and Peace. Of Treatys of Peace. Of Treatys of Peace and Alliances, particularly with England, France and Spain. Of the natural Strength and Fortifications of Holland. And, Of its Interest in all Respects as to the Government of a Single Person. Written by John De Witt, and other Great Men in Holland. Published by the Authority of the States.* London: Printed in the Year MDCCII; [no publisher].

Dening, Greg. 2004. *Beach Crossings: Voyaging Across Times, Cultures and Self.* Melbourne: Miegunyah Press of Melbourne University.

De Smidt, J. Th. 1984. "The Expansion of Dutch Private Law outside Europe in the Seventeenth and Eighteenth Centuries." In *The World of Hugo Grotius (1583–1645): Proceedings of the International Colloquium Organized by the Grotius Committee of* the Royal Netherlands Academy of Arts and Sciences, Rotterdam, 6–9 April 1983, 179–93. Amsterdam: Holland University Press.

De Veer, Gerrit. 1978. *Overwintering in Nova Zembla*. Utrecht: Spectrum.

De Vries, Jan. 1974. *The Dutch Rural Economy in the Golden Age, 1500–1700*. New Haven, Conn.: Yale University Press.

———. 1986. "The Dutch Rural Economy and the Landscape, 1590–1650." In *Dutch Landscape: The Early Years, Haarlem and Amsterdam, 1590–1650. An Exhibition at the National Gallery, London, September 3 to November 23, 1986*, ed. Christopher Brown, 79–86. London: National Gallery.

———. 1991. "Art History." In *Art in History, History in Art*, ed. David Freedberg and Jan de Vries, 249–84. Santa Monica, Calif.: Getty Center for the History of Art and the Humanities.

———, and Ad van der Woude. 1997. *The First Modern Economy: Success, Failure and Perseverance of the Dutch Economy, 1500–1815*. Cambridge: Cambridge University Press.

Dirks, Nicholas B. 1992. "Introduction." In *Colonialism and Culture*, ed. Nicholas B. Dirks, 1–25. Ann Arbor: University of Michigan Press.

———. 1996. "Foreword." In *Colonialism and Its Forms of Knowledge: The British in India*, Bernard S. Cohn, ix–xvii. Princeton, N.J.: Princeton University Press.

Doggett, Rachel, with Monique Hulvey and Julie Ainsworth, eds. 1992. *New World of Wonders: European Images of the Americas, 1492–1700*. Washington, D.C.: Folger Shakespeare Library.

Donagan, Barbara. 1994. "Atrocity, War Crimes, and Treason in the English Civil War." *American Historical Review* 99: 1137–66.

Draper, G. I. A. D. 1990. "Grotius' Place in the Development of Legal Ideas about War." In *Hugo Grotius and International Relations*, ed. Hedley Bull, Benedict Kingsbury, and Adam Roberts, 177–207. Oxford: Clarendon.

Durix, Jean-Pierre. 1987. *The Writer Written: The Artist and Creation in the New Literatures in English*. New York: Greenwood.

Duro, Paul, ed. 1996. *The Rhetoric of the Frame: Essays on the Boundaries of the Artwork*. New York: Cambridge University Press.

Dyson, Stephen L. 1985. *The Creation of the Roman Frontier*. Princeton, N.J.: Princeton University Press.

Edney, Matthew H. and Susan Cimburek. 2004. "Telling the Traumatic Truth: William Hubbard's *Narrative* of King Philip's War and His 'Map of New England.'" *William and Mary Quarterly*, 3rd ser., 61: 317–48.

Egmond, Florike. 1996. "De 'straf met de zak' of *Paena cullei*. De longue durée van een rituele strafvoltrekking." *Tijdschrift voor Geschiedenis* 109: 3–44.

———. 1993 *Underworlds: Organized Crime in the Netherlands, 1650–1800*. Cambridge: Polity.

Ehrlich, Jessica Kross. 1974. "A Town Study in Colonial New York: Newtown, Queens County (1642–1790)." Ph.D. diss., University of Michigan.

Eisler, William. 1995. *The Furthest Shore: Images of Terra Australis from the Middle Ages to Captain Cook*. New York: Cambridge University Press.

Enno van Gelder, Herman Arend. 1953. *Nederlandse Dorpen in de 16e Eeuw*. Amsterdam: Noord-Hollandsche Uitgevers Maatschappij.

Evans, John X., ed. 1972. *The Works of Sir Roger Williams*. Oxford: Clarendon.

Feister, Lois M. 1973. "Linguistic Communication between the Dutch and Indians in New Netherland, 1609–1664." *Ethnohistory* 20: 25–38.

Feld, M. D. 1975. "Middle-Class Society and the Rise of Military Professionalism: The Dutch Army, 1589–1609." *Armed Forces and Society* 1: 419–42.

Fernow, Berthold, and E. B. O'Callaghan, eds. 1853–87. *Documents Relative to the Colonial History of the State of New-York.* 15 vols. Albany, N.Y.: Weed, Parsons.

Fishman, Jane Susannah. 1979. *Boerenverdriet: Violence between Peasants and Soldiers in Early Modern Netherlands Art.* Ann Arbor: University of Michigan Research Press.

Folkerts, Jan. 1996. "The Failure of West India Company Farming on the Island of Manhattan." *De halve maen* 69: 47–52.

Fried, Marc B. 1975. *The Early History of Kingston and Ulster County, New York.* Marbletown, N.Y.: Ulster County Historical Society.

Frijhoff, Willem. 1998. "New Views on the Dutch Period of New York." *De halve maen* 71: 23–34.

Frost, Alan. 2003. *The Global Reach of Empire: Britain's Maritime Expansion in the Indian and Pacific Oceans, 1764–1815.* Melbourne: Miegunyah Press of Melbourne University.

Furnivall, J. S. 1939. *Netherlands India: A Study of Plural Economy.* Cambridge: Cambridge University Press.

Gehring, Charles T., trans. and ed. 1983. *New York Historical Manuscripts: Dutch, V: Council Minutes, 1652–1654.* Baltimore: Genealogical Publishing.

Gerretson, C. 1944. *Coens Eerherstel.* Amsterdam: P. N. van Kampan & Zoon.

Geyl, Pieter. 1946. *Eenheid en Tweeheid in de Nederlanden.* Lochem: De Tijdstroom.

———. 1961. *The Netherlands in the Seventeenth Century.* Part 1, *1609–1648.* London: Ernest Benn. [First published in 1936 as *The Netherlands Divided.*]

Gibson, Ross. 1996. "Introduction." In *Exchanges: Cross-Cultural Encounters in Australia and the Pacific,* ed. Ross Gibson, 3–5. Sydney: Museum of Sydney.

Gibson, Walter S. 2000. *Pleasant Places: The Rustic Landscape from Bruegel to Ruisdael.* Berkeley: University of California Press.

Gillis, John. 2004. *Islands of the Mind: How the Human Imagination Created the Atlantic World.* New York: Palgrave Macmillan.

Goedde, Lawrence Otto. 1989. *Tempest and Shipwreck in Dutch and Flemish Art: Convention, Rhetoric, and Interpretation.* University Park: Pennsylvania State University Press.

Goodfriend, Joyce. 1992. *Before the Melting Pot: Society and Culture in Colonial New York City, 1664–1730.* Princeton, N.J.: Princeton University Press.

Goslinga, Cornelis Ch. 1985. *The Dutch in the Caribbean and in the Guianas, 1680–1719.* Ed. Maria J. L. van Yperen. Assen: Van Gorcum.

Gouda, Frances. 1995. *Dutch Culture Overseas: Colonial Practice in the Netherlands Indies, 1900–1942.* Amsterdam: Amsterdam University Press.

Greenblatt, Stephen. 1983. "Murdering Peasants: Status, Genre and The Representation of Rebellion," *Representations* 1: 1–30.

Griffiths, Anthony, John Willett, and Juliet Wilson-Bareau. 1998. *Disasters of War: Collot, Goya, Dix.* Manchester: Hayward Gallery and Arts Council.

Groenveld, S. 1978. "Pieter Corneliszoon Hooft en de geschiedenis van zijn eigen tijd." *Bijdragen en Mededelingen* 93: 43–68.

Groenveld, Simon. 2001. "New Light on a Drowned Princess." *De halve maen* 74: 23–28.

Grumet, Robert S. 1980. "Sunksquaws, Shamans and Tradeswomen: Middle Atlantic Coastal Algonkian Women During the 17th and 18th Centuries." In *Women and Colonization: Anthropological Perspectives,* ed. Mona Etienne and Eleanor Leacock, 43–62. New York: Praeger.

Guha, Ranajit. 1997. "Not at Home in Empire." *Critical Inquiry* 23: 482–93.

Guicciardini, Ludovico. 1593. *The Description of the Low Countries.* [A Walter J. Johnson facsimile publication. Amsterdam and Norwood, N.J.: Theatrum Orbis Terrarum, 1976.] Original: *The Description of the Low Countreys and of the Provinces thereof, gathered into an Epitome out of the Historie of Ludovico Guicchardini* (London, Peter Short for Thomas Chard, 1593).

Gutmann, Myron Peter. 1976. "War and Rural Life in the Seventeenth Century: The Case of the Basse-Meuse." Ph.D. diss., Princeton University.

Haefeli, Evan. 1999. "Kieft's War and the Cultures of Violence in Colonial America." In *Lethal Imagination: Violence and Brutality in American History,* ed. Michael A. Bellesides, 17–40. New York: New York University Press.

Harline, Craig E. 1987. *Pamphlets, Printing and Political Culture in the Early Dutch Republic.* Dordrecht: Martinus Nijhoff.

Hauptman, Laurence M., and Ronald G. Knapp. 1977. "Dutch-Aboriginal Interaction in New Netherland and Formosa: An Historical Geography of Empire." *Proceedings of the American Philosophical Society* 121: 166–82.

Heesterman, J. C. 1978. "Was There an Indian Reaction? Western Expansion in Indian Perspective." In *Expansion and Reaction: Essays on European Expansion and Reactions in Asia and Africa,* ed. H. L. Wesseling, 31–58. Leiden: Leiden University Press.

Helgerson, Richard. 1992. "Camões, Hackluyt, and the Voyages of the Two Nations." In *Colonialism and Culture,* ed. Nicholas B. Dirks, 27–63. Ann Arbor: University of Michigan.

———. 1997. "Soldiers and Enigmatic Girls: The Politics of Dutch Domestic Realism, 1650–1672." *Representations* 58: 49–87.

Hermans, Theo, and Reinier Salverda, eds. 1993. *From Revolt to Riches: Culture and History of the Low Countries, 1500–1700: International and Interdisciplinary Perspectives.* London: Center for Low Countries Studies.

Hinderaker, Eric. 1997. *Elusive Empires: Constructing Colonialism in the Ohio Valley, 1673–1800.* New York: Cambridge University Press.

Hirsch, Adam J. 1987. "The Collision of Military Cultures in Seventeenth-Century New England." *Journal of American History* 74: 1187–1212.

Hooft, Hendrik. 1999. *Patriot and Patrician: To Holland and Ceylon in the Steps of Henrik Hooft and Pieter Ondaatje, Champions of Dutch Democracy.* Canton, Mass.: Science History Publications.

Hoogenberk, Hendrik. 1940. *De Rechtsvoorschriften voor de Vaart op Oost-Indië, 1595–1620.* Utrecht: Kemink en Zoon.

Hosmer, James Kendell, ed. 1908. *Winthrop's Journal, "History of New England," 1630–1649.* New York: Barnes and Noble.

Hulme, Peter. 1992. *Colonial Encounters: Europe and the Native Caribbean, 1492–1897.* London: Routledge.

Huygens, Constantijn. ca. 1630. "Een Boer." In *Profitelijk Vermaak: Moraliteit en Satire uit de 16e en 17e Eeuw,* ed. M. C. A. van der Heijden, 1968, 242–50. Utrecht: Speculum.

———. ca. 1630. "Een Ghemeen Soldaet." In *Profitelijk Vermaak: Moraliteit en Satire uit de 16e en 17e Eeuw,* ed. M. C. A. van der Heijden, 1968, 220–22. Utrecht: Speculum.

Ijzerman, J. W. 1926. *De Reis om de Wereld door Olivier van Noort, 1598–1601*. Vols. 1 and 2. 's-Gravenhage: Martinus Nijhoff.

Israel, Jonathan I. 1986. *The Dutch Republic and the Hispanic World, 1606–1661*. Oxford: Clarendon.

Jacobs, Jaap. 1998a. "Between Repression and Approval: Connivance and Tolerance in the Dutch Republic and in New Netherland." *De halve maen* 71: 51–58.

———. 1998b. "A Hitherto Unknown Letter of Adriaen van der Donck." *De halve maen* 71:1–6.

———. 2005. *New Netherland: A Dutch Colony in Seventeenth-Century America*. Leiden: Brill.

Jameson, J. Franklin, ed. 1909a. "Letter of Johannes Bogaert to Hans Bontemantel, 1655." In *Narratives of New Netherland, 1609–1664*, 379–86. New York: Charles Scribner's Sons.

———, ed. 1909b. "From the 'New World,' by Johan de Laet, 1625, 1630, 1633, 1640." In *Narratives of New Netherland, 1609–1664*, 29–60. New York: Charles Scribner's Sons.

———, ed. 1909c. "Letter of Isaack de Rasieres to Samuel Blommaert, [1628?]" In *Narratives of New Netherland, 1609–1664*, 97–115. New York: Charles Scribner's Sons.

———, ed. 1909d. "From the Korte Historiael ende Journaels Aenteyckeninge, by David Pietersz. de Vries, 1633–1643 (1655)." In *Narratives of New Netherland 1609–1664*, 181–234. New York: Charles Scribner's Sons.

———, ed. 1909e. "Letter and Narrative of Father Isaac Jogues, 1643, 1645, and *Novum Belgium* by Father Issac Jogues, 1646." In *Narratives of New Netherland, 1609–1664*, 235–54, 259–63. New York: Charles Scribner's Sons.

———, ed. 1909f. "Journal of New Netherland, 1647." In *Narratives of New Netherland, 1609–1664*, 265–84. [Ascribed to Willem Kieft or one of his supporters] New York: Charles Scribner's Sons.

———, ed. 1909g. "A Short Account of the Mohawk Indians, by Reverend Johannes Megapolensis, Jr, 1644." In *Narratives of New Netherland, 1609–1664*, 163–80. New York: Charles Scribner's Sons.

———, ed. 1909h. "Letter of Reverend Jonas Michaëlius, 1628." In *Narratives of New Netherland, 1609–1664*, 117–33. New York: Charles Scribner's Sons.

———, ed. 1909i. "Narrative of a Journey into the Mohawk and Oneida Country, 1634–1635." In *Narratives of New Netherland, 1609–1664*, 135–62. [Ascribed to Harmen Myndertsz van de Bogaert.] New York: Charles Scribner's Sons.

———, ed. 1909j. "From the 'Historisch Verhael' by Nicolaes van Wassenaer, 1624–1630." In *Narratives of New Netherland, 1609–1664*, 61–96. New York: Charles Scribner's Sons.

———, ed. 1910. *Johnson's Wonder-Working Providence, 1628–1651*. New York: Charles Scribner's Sons.

Jarvis, Michael, and Jeroen van Driel. 1997. "The Vinckboons Chart of the James River, Virginia, Circa 1617." *William and Mary Quarterly*, 3rd ser., 54: 377–94.

Jennings, Francis. 1984. *The Ambiguous Iroquois Empire: The Covenant Chain Confederation of Indian Tribes with English Colonies from Its Beginnings to the Lancaster Treaty of 1744*. New York: W. W. Norton.

Karr, Ronald Dale. 1998. " 'Why Should You Be So Furious?': The Violence of the Pequot War." *Journal of American History* 85: 876–909.

Kern, H., ed. 1910. *Itinerario: Voyage ofte Schipvaert van Jan Huygen [sic] van Linschoten naer Oost ofte Portugaels Indien, 1579–1592*. Vol. 1. 's-Gravenhage: Martinus Nijhoff.

Keur, John Y., and Dorothy L. Keur. 1955. *The Deeply Rooted: A Study of a Drenthe Community in the Netherlands.* Assen: Van Gorcum.

Keyes, George S. 1990. *Mirror of Empire: Dutch Marine Art of the Seventeenth Century.* New York: Cambridge University Press, with the Minneapolis Institute of Arts.

Kingsbury, Benedict, and Adam Roberts. 1990. "Introduction: Grotian Thought in International Relations." In *Grotius and International Relations,* ed. Hedley Bull, Benedict Kingsbury, and Adam Roberts, 1–64. Oxford: Clarendon.

Klooster, Wim. 1997. *The Dutch in the Americas, 1600–1800: A Narrative History with the Catalogue of an Exhibition of Rare Prints, Maps, and Illustrated Books from the John Carter Brown Library.* Providence, R.I.: John Carter Brown Library.

———. 2000. "Failing to Square the Circle: The West India Company's Volte-Face in 1638–1639." *De halve maen* 73: 3–9.

Kupperman, Karen Ordahl, ed. 1995a. *America in European Consciousness, 1493–1750.* Chapel Hill: University of North Carolina Press.

———. 1995b. "Scandanavian Colonists Confront the New World." In *New Sweden in America,* ed. Carol E. Hoffecker, et al., 89–111. Newark: University of Delaware Press.

———. 2000. *Indians and English: Facing Off in Early America.* Ithaca, N.Y.: Cornell University Press.

Lambert, Audrey M. 1971. *The Making of the Dutch Landscape: An Historical Geography of the Netherlands.* New York: Seminar.

Le Petit, Jean François. 1609. *The Low Country Commonwealth.* [Da Capo Press facsimile publication. Theatrum Orbis Terrarum. Amsterdam: 1969] Original: *The Low Country Commonwealth Contayninge An exact discription (sic) of the Eight United Provinces Now Made free. Translated out of French by Ed. Grimeston. Published by G. Eld, 1609.*

Lepore, Jill. 1998. *The Name of War: King Philip's War and the Origins of American Identity.* New York: Alfred A. Knopf.

Lestringant, Frank. 1990. *Le Huguenot et le Sauvage: L'Amerique et la controverse coloniale, en France, au temps des Guerres de Religion (1555–1589).* Paris: Aux Amateurs de Livres.

———. 1997. *Cannibals: The Discovery and Representation of the Cannibal from Columbus to Jules Verne,* trans. Rosemary Morris. Berkeley: University of California Press.

Loomba, Ania. 1998. "Hybridity." In *Colonialism-Postcolonialism.* London: Routledge.

Maland, David. 1980. *Europe at War: 1600–1650.* London: Macmillan.

Malone, Patrick M. 1991. *The Skulking Way of War: Technology and Tactics among the New England Indians.* London: Madison.

Mancall, Peter C. 1995. *Deadly Medicine: Indians and Alcohol in Early America.* Ithaca, N.Y.: Cornell University Press.

Mann, Golo. 1976. *Wallenstein: His Life Narrated.* Trans. Charles Kessler. London: Andre Deutsch.

Massarella, Derek. 1990. *A World Elsewhere: Europe's Encounter with Japan in the Sixteenth and Seventeenth Centuries.* New Haven, Conn.: Yale University Press.

Masselman, George. 1963. *The Cradle of Colonialism.* New Haven, Conn.: Yale University Press.

Matsuda, Matt K. 2005. *Empire of Love: Histories of France and the Pacific.* New York: Oxford University Press.

Megapolensis, Johannes. 1644. *A Short Sketch of the Mohawk Indians in New Netherland,*

Their Land, Stature, Dress, Manners and Magistrates, Written in the Year 1644, by Johannes Megapolensis, Jr. Minister There. Revised from the Translation of Hazard's Historical Collections, with an Introduction and Notes by John Romeyn Brodhead. In *Collections of the New-York Historical Society,* 3, ser. 2: 137–60.

Meier, Reinder P. 1971. *Literature of the Low Countries: A Short History of Dutch Literature in the Netherlands and Belgium.* Assen: Van Gorcum.

Meijer Drees, Marijke. 1993. "The Revolt of Masaniello on Stage: An International Perspective." In *From Revolt to Riches: Culture and History of the Low Countries, 1500–1700: International and Interdisciplinary Perspectives,* ed. Theo Hermans and Reinier Salverda, 281–91. London: Center for Low Countries Studies.

Meilink-Roelofsz, Marie Antoinette Petronilla. 1962. *Asian Trade and European Influence in the Indonesian Archipelago between 1500 and about 1630.* 's-Gravenhage: Martinus Nijhoff.

———. 1976. "Een vergelijkend onderzaek van bestuur en handel der Nederlandse en Engelse handelscompanieën Azie in de eerste helft van de seventeinde eeuw," *Bijdragen en Mededelingen* 91: 196–217.

Melijn, Cornelis. 1649. *Breeden-Raedt aende Vereenichde Nederlandsche Provintien. Gelreland. Holland. Zeeland. Wtrecht. Vriesland. Over-ijssel. Groeningen. Gemackt ende gestelt uyt diverse ware en waerachtige memorien. Door I. A. G. W. C. Tot Antwerpen. Ghedruct by Francoys van Duynen, Boeckverkooper by de Beurs in Erasmus.*

Melvoin, Richard I. 1989. *New England Outpost: War and Society in Colonial Deerfield.* New York: W. W. Norton.

Merwick, Donna. 1990. *Possessing Albany, 1630–1710: The Dutch and English Experiences.* New York: Cambridge University Press.

———. 1994. "The Work of the Trickster in the Dutch Possession of New York." In *Dangerous Liaisons: Essays in Honour of Greg Dening,* ed. Donna Merwick. Melbourne: University of Melbourne.

———. 1999. *Death of a Notary: Conquest and Change in Colonial New York.* Ithaca, N.Y.: Cornell University Press.

Merwin, W. S. 2001. "To the Words." *The New Yorker,* October 8, 65.

Miller, Jay. 1974. "The Delaware as Women: A Symbolic Solution." *American Ethnologist* 1: 507–14.

Morison, Samuel Eliot. 1952. *Of Plymouth Plantation, 1620–1647 by William Bradford Sometime Governor Thereof.* New ed. New York: Alfred A. Knopf.

Motley, John Lothrop. 1904. *Life and Death of John of Barneveld, Advocate of Holland, with a View of the Primary Causes and Movements of the Thirty Years' War.* Vols. 1 and 2. London: John Murray.

Mulder, Lodewijk, ed. 1862. *Journaal van Anthonis Duyck, Advokaat-Fiskall van den Raad van State (1591–1602).* Vol. 1. 's-Gravenhage: Martinus Nijhoff.

Mullaney, Steven. 1992. "The New World on Display: European Pageantry and the Ritual Incorporation of the Americas." In *New World of Wonders: European Images of the Americas, 1492–1700,* ed. Rachel Doggett with Monique Helvey and Julie Ainsworth, 105–13. Washington, D.C.: Folger Shakespeare Library.

Muller, P. L. 1908. *Onze Gouden Eeuw: De Republiek der Vereenigde Nederlanden in Haar Bloetijd.* Vols. 1 and 2. 2nd ed. Leiden: A. W. Sijthoff.

Muller, S. 1909. *De Reis van Jan Cornelisz. May naar de Ijzsee en de Amerikaansche Kust, 1611–1612.* 's-Gravenhage: Martinus Nijhoff.

Murphy, Henry C., ed and trans. 1857. [Melijn, Cornelis]. *Broad Advice to the United Netherland Provinces: Gelreland, Holland, Zeeland, Utrecht, Vriesland, Over-Ijssel, Groeningen. Made and Arranged, from Divers True and Trusty Memoirs, by I. A. G. W. C.* In Collections of the New-York Historical Society, 2nd ser., Vol. III-Part I, 237–81. New York: D. Appleton.

———. 1865. *Anthology of New Netherland, or Translations from the Early Poets of New York.* New York: Bradford Club. Friedman reprint, Port Washington, N.Y., 1969.

Naber, S. P. L'Honore, ed. 1921. *Henry Hudson's Reize Onder Nederlandsche Vlag van Amsterdam naar Nova Zembla, Amerika en terug naar Dartmouth in Engeland, 1609, volgens het Journaal van Robert Juet.* 's-Gravenhage: Martinus Nijhoff.

Newcomb, William W. Jr. 1956. *The Culture and Acculturation of the Delaware Indians.* Ann Arbor: University of Michigan Press.

Nieuwenhuys, R., ed. 1971. "Pieter Cornelisz. Hooft." In *Ziet, de Dag Komt Aan,* 7–30. Amsterdam: Salamander.

Nijhoff, Wouter, ed. 1909. Hen[ry] C. Murphy, *Henry Hudson in Holland: An Inquiry into the Origin and Objects of the Voyage which Led to the Discovery of the Hudson River.* Reprint of an 1859 booklet, with notes, documents, and a bibliography by Wouter Nijhoff. The Hague: Martinus Nijhoff.

Nooter, Eric. 1994. "Between Heaven and Earth: Church and Society in Pre-Revolutionary Flatbush, New York." Ph.D. diss., Vrije Universitiet van Amsterdam.

O'Brien, Raymond J. 1981. *American Sublime: Landscape and Scenery of the Lower Hudson Valley.* New York: Columbia University Press.

O'Callaghan, E. B. 1846, 1848. *History of New Netherland: Or, New York under the Dutch.* Vols. 1 and 2. New York: D. Appleton.

O'Callaghan, Edmund B., ed. 1851. "Extracts from a Work Called *Breeden Raedt aen de Vereenighde Nederlandsche Provincien.* Printed in Antwerp in 1649. Translated from the Dutch Original by Mr. C., Amsterdam, 1851: Fr. Muller." In *The Documentary History of the State of New York,* 4:99–112. Albany, N.Y.: Charles van Benthuysen.

———, ed. and trans. 1863. *A Brief and True Narrative of the Hostile Conduct of the Barbarous Natives toward the Dutch Nation* [1655]. Albany, N.Y.: Joel Munsell.

O'Donnell, Thomas F., ed. 1968. *A Description of the New Netherlands: Adriaen Van Der Donck.* Syracuse, N.Y.: Syracuse University Press.

Padrón, Ricardo. 2002. "Mapping Plus Ultra: Cartography, Space, and Hispanic Modernity." *Representations* 79: 28–60.

Pagden, Anthony. 1993. *European Encounters with the New World: From Renaissance to Romanticism.* New Haven, Conn.: Yale University Press.

Parker, Geoffrey. 1972. *The Army of Flanders and the Spanish Road, 1567–1659: The Logistics of Spanish Victory and Defeat in the Low Countries' Wars.* Cambridge: Cambridge University Press.

———. 1988. *The Military Revolution: Military Innovation and the Rise of the West, 1500–1800.* New York: Cambridge University Press.

———. 1995. "Dynastic War." In *The Cambridge Illustrated History of Warfare: The Triumph of the West,* ed. Geoffrey Parker, 146–63. Cambridge: Cambridge University Press.

Parmentier, Jan, and Ruurdje Laarhoven, eds. 1994. *De avontuur van een VOC- soldaat: Het Dagboek van Carolus Van der Haeghe, 1699–1705.* Zutphen: Walburg Pers.

Porter, Stephen. 1994. *Destruction in the English Civil Wars.* Dover, N.H.: Alan Sutton.

Postma, Johannes. 1998. "Breaking the Mercantile Barriers of the Dutch Colonial Empire: North American Trade with Surinam during the Eighteenth Century." In *Merchant Organization and Maritime Trade in the North Atlantic, 1660–1815*, ed. Olaf Uwe Janzen, 107–32. St. John's, Newfoundland: International Maritime Economic History Association.

Presser, J., ed. 1948. *De Tachtigjarige Oorlog*. 3rd ed. Amsterdam: Elsevier.

Prudon, H., S. J., ed. 1968. *G. A. Brederoods Spaanschen Brabander Jerolimo*, ed. H. Prudon, S. J. Assen: Van Gorcum.

Pynchon, Thomas. 1997. *Mason and Dixon*. London: Jonathan Cape.

Raab, Theodore K. 1975. *The Struggle for Stability in Early Modern Europe*. New York: Oxford University Press.

Rayback, Robert J. 1966. "The Indian." In *Geography of New York State*, ed. John H. Thompson, 113–20. Syracuse, N.Y.: Syracuse University Press.

Redlich, Fritz. 1956. *De Praeda Militari: Looting and Booty, 1500–1815*. Wiesbaden: Franz Steiner.

———. 1964, 1965. *The German Military Enterpriser and His Work Force: A Study in European Economic and Social History*. Vols. 1 and 2. Wiesbaden: Franz Steiner.

Remec, Peter Pavel. 1960. *The Position of the Individual in International Law According to Grotius and Vattal*. The Hague: Nijhoff.

Rens, L. 1969. *O Zoete Vrijheid!: Vondel Als Strijder voor Vrijheid en Vrede*. Leiden: A. W. Sijthoff.

Richter, Daniel K. 1992. *The Ordeal of the Longhouse: The Peoples of the Iroquois League in the Era of European Colonization*. Chapel Hill: University of North Carolina Press.

Rink, Oliver. 1986. *Holland on the Hudson: An Economic and Social History of Dutch New York*. Ithaca, N.Y.: Cornell University Press.

Rinkes, D. A. N. van Zalinge, and J. W. de Roever. 1927. *Het Indische Boek der Zee*. Leiden: G. Kolff.

Roelofsen, C. G. 1990. "Grotius and the International Politics of the Seventeenth Century." In *Hugo Grotius and International Relations*, ed. Hedley Bull, Benedict Kingsbury, and Adam Roberts, 95–131. Oxford: Clarendon.

Romein, Jan M. 1975. "Spieghel Historiael van de Tachtigjarige Oorlog." In *Vaderlands Verleden in Veelvoud: 31 Opstellen over de Nederlandse Geschiedenis na 1500*, ed. G. A. M. Beekelaar et al., 105–40. The Hague: Martinus Nijhoff.

Rothschild, Nan A. 2003. *Colonial Encounters in a Native American Landscape: The Spanish and Dutch in North America*. Washington, D.C.: Smithsonian Books.

Rowen, Herbert H., ed. 1972. *The Low Countries in Early Modern Times*. New York: Walker.

———. 1986. *John De Witt: Statesman of the "True Freedom."* Cambridge: Cambridge University Press.

Russell, Margarita. 1986. "Seascape into Landscape." In *Dutch Landscape: The Early Years, Haarlem and Amsterdam, 1590–1650: An Exhibition at the National Gallery, London, September 3 to November 23, 1986*, ed. Christopher Brown, 63–71. London: National Gallery.

Salisbury, Neal. 1982. *Manitou and Providence: Indians, Europeans, and the Making of New England, 1500–1643*. New York: Oxford University Press.

Santos, Sherod. 2005. "Poems from the Greek Anthology." *Raritan* 24: 1–17.

Schama, Simon. 1987. *The Embarrassment of Riches: An Interpretation of Dutch Culture in the Golden Age.* New York: Knopf.

Schenkeveld-van der Dussen, M. A. 1986. "Nature and Landscape in Dutch Literature of the Golden Age." In *Dutch Landscape: The Early Years, Haarlem and Amsterdam, 1590–1650: An Exhibition at the National Gallery, London, September 3 to November 23, 1986*, ed. Christopher Brown, 72–78. London: National Gallery.

Schilder, Gunter, ed. 1985. *Voyage to the Great South Land, Willem de Vlamingh, 1696–1697.* trans. C. de Herr. Sydney: Royal Australian Historical Society.

Schiltkamp, Jacob Adriaan. 1964. *De Geschiedenis van het Notariaat in het Octrooigebied van de West-Indische Compagnie.* The Hague: L. Smits.

Schmidt, Benjamin. 1999. "Exotic Allies: The Dutch-Chilean Encounter and the (Failed) Conquest of America." *Renaissance Quarterly* 52: 441–73.

———. 2001. *Innocence Abroad: The Dutch Imagination and the New World, 1570–1670.* New York: Cambridge University Press.

Schöffer, I. 1978. "Dutch 'Expansion' and Indonesian Reactions: Some Dilemmas of Modern Colonial Rule (1900–1942)." In *Expansion and Reaction: Essays on European Expansion and Reactions in Asia and Africa*, ed. H. L. Wesseling, 78–99. Leiden: Leiden University Press.

Scholz-Heerspink. 1993. "The Play of Language in the Flemish Chapbook, Frederick van Jennen (1517–1531)." In *From Revolt to Riches: Culture and History of the Low Countries, 1500–1700: International and Interdisciplinary Perspectives*, ed. Theo Hermans and Reinier Salverda, 40–48. London: Center for Low Countries Studies.

Schoonmaker, Marius. 1888. *The History of Kingston, New York. From Its Early Settlement to the Year 1820.* New York: Burr.

Schulte Nordholt, J. W. 1966. "Nederlanders in Nieuw Nederland, de oorlog van Kieft." *Bijdragen en Mededelingen van het Historisch Genootschap* 80: 38–95.

Scott, James Brown, ed. 1916. *The Freedom of the Seas or the Right which Belongs to the Dutch to Take Part in the East Indian Trade, a Dissertation by Hugo Grotius, Translated with a Revision of the Latin Text of 1633 by Ralph Van Deman Magoffin.* New York: Oxford University Press.

Scott, Kenneth, and Kenn Stryker-Rodda, eds. 1974. *New York Historical Manuscripts: Dutch*, trans. and annotated by Arnold J. F. van Laer. Vol. 1, *Register of the Provincial Secretary, 1638–1642.* Baltimore: Genealogical Publishing.

Seed, Patricia. 1995a. *Ceremonies of Possession in Europe's Conquest of the New World, 1492–1640.* Cambridge: Cambridge University Press.

———. 1995b. "The Conquest of the Americas, 1492–1650." In *The Cambridge Illustrated History of Warfare: The Triumph of the West*, ed. Geoffrey Parker, 132–45. Cambridge: Cambridge University Press.

Shelley, Henry C. 1932. *John Underhill: Captain of New England and New Netherland.* New York: D. Appleton.

Shomette, Donald G., and Robert D. Haslach. 1988. *Raid on America: The Dutch Naval Campaign of 1672–1674.* Columbia: University of South Carolina Press.

Shorto, Russell. 2004. *The Island at the Center of the World: The Epic Story of Dutch Manhattan and the Forgotten Colony That Shaped America.* New York: Doubleday.

Shy, John. 1976. *A People Numerous and Armed: Reflections on the Military Struggle for American Independence.* New York: Oxford University Press.

Simoni, Anna E. 1993. "1598: An Exchange of Dutch Pamphlets and Their Repercussions in England." In *From Revolt to Riches: Culture and History of the Low Countries, 1500–1700: International and Interdisciplinary Perspectives*, ed. Theo Hermans and Reinier Salverda, 129–62. London: Center for Low Countries Studies.

Slicher van Bath, B. H. 1963. *Agrarian History of Western Europe, 500–1850*, trans. Olive Ordish. London: Edward Arnold.

———. 1968. "Historical Demography and the Social and Economic Development of the Netherlands." *Daedalus* 97: 604–21.

Spolsky, Ellen. 1996. "Ordinary Dutch Landscapes." *Common Knowledge* 5: 166–79.

Starna, William A. 1991. "Indian-Dutch Frontiers." *De halve maen* 64: 21–25.

Steen, Charlie R. 1989. *The Time of Troubles in the Low Countries: The Chronicles and Memoirs of Pasquier de la Barre of Tournais, 1559–1567*. New York: Peter Lang.

Stilgoe, John R. 1994. *Alongshore*. New Haven, Conn.: Yale University Press.

Stoett, F. A., ed. 1967. *S. Costers Boere-Klucht van Teeuwis de Boer, en men Juffer van Grevelinckhuysen, revised here by N. C. H. Wijngaards*. Zutphen: W. J. Thieme. [Original: *S. Costers Boere-Klucht van Teeuwis de Boer, en men Juffer van Grevelinckhuysen: Op het Woordt, 't Krom hout brandt soo vuel alst reckt, alst by de vyer ken komen.* t'Amstelredam: Cornelis Lodowijcksz, 1627.] Reprinted in 1633, 1642, 1665.

Stokes, I[saac] N[ewton] Phelps. 1915–28. *The Iconography of Manhattan Island: 1498–1909*. 6 vols. New York: Robert H. Dodd.

Stoler, Ann Laura. 1992a. " 'In Cold Blood': Hierarchies of Credibility and the Politics of Colonial Narratives." *Representations* 37: 151–89.

———. 1992b. "Rethinking Colonial Categories: European Communities and the Boundaries of Rule." In *Colonialism and Culture*, ed. Nicholas B. Dirks, 319–52. Ann Arbor: University of Michigan Press.

Taylor, Alan. 1996. "Captain Hendrick Aupaumut: The Dilemmas of an Intercultural Broker." *Ethnohistory* 43: 431–57.

't Hart, Marjolein C. 1993. *The Making of a Bourgeois State: War, Politics and Finance during the Dutch Revolt*. Manchester: Manchester University Press.

Thomas, Nicholas. 1991. *Entangled Objects: Exchange, Material Culture and Colonialism in the Pacific*. Cambridge, Mass.: Harvard University Press.

———. 1996. "Tabooed Ground: Augustus Earle in Australia and New Zealand." In *Exchanges: Cross-Cultural Encounters in Australia and the Pacific*, ed. Ross Gibson, 143–61. Sydney: Museum of Sydney.

———. 1999a. "Liberty and License: The Forsters' Accounts of New Zealand Sociality." In *Voyages and Beaches: Pacific Encounters, 1769–1840*, ed. Alex Calder, Jonathan Lamb, and Bridget Orr, 132–55. Honolulu: University of Hawaii Press.

———, and Diane Losche, eds. 1999b. *Double Vision: Art Histories and Colonial Histories in the Pacific*. Cambridge: Cambridge University Press.

Tilmans, Karin. 1993. "Dutch National Consciousness in Early Humanist Historiography: The Italian Influence on Cornelius Aurelius (ca. 1460–1513) and His Contemporaries." In *From Revolt to Riches: Culture and History of the Low Countries, 1500–1700: International and Interdisciplinary Perspectives*, ed. Theo Hermans and Reinier Salverda, 30–39. London: Center for Low Countries Studies.

Trelease, Allen W. 1960. *Indian Affairs in Colonial New York: The Seventeenth Century*. Ithaca, N.Y.: Cornell University Press.

Trexler, Richard C. 1995. *Sex and Conquest: Gendered Violence, Political Order, and the European Conquest of the Americas*. Cambridge: Polity.

Underhill, John. 1638. *Newes from America. London, 1638.* Amsterdam: Da Capo Press; 1971 reprint, Theatrum Orbis Terrarum.

Unger, Richard W. 1971. "The Rise of the Dutch Shipbuilding Industry, ca. 1400–ca. 1600." Ph.D. diss., Yale University.

Van Balen, W. J. 1942. *Naar de Indische Wonderwereld Met Jan Huygens van Linschoten.* Amsterdam: N. V. Amsterdamsche Boek-en Courantmaatschappij.

Van den Vondel, Joost. 1625. "Begroetenis aan Vorst Frederick Henrik." In *O Zoete Vrieheid! Vondel Als Strijder voor Vrijheid en Vrede,* ed. L. Rens, 42, 43. Leiden: A. W. Sijthoff, 1969.

———. 1627. "Verovering van Grol, Door Frederick Henrick, Prince van Oranje." In *Die Tyrannie Verdrijven: Godsdienst-en Onafhaakelijkheidsstrijd in de 16e en 17e Eeuw,* ed. M. C. A. van der Heijden, 1970f, 259–95. Utrecht: Prisma Boeken, Speculum Series.

———. 1647. "De Getemde Mars." In *Die Tyrannie Verdrijven: Godsdienst-en Onafhaakelijkheidsstrijd in de 16e en 17e Eeuw,* ed. M. C. A. van der Heijden, 1970, 297–305. Utrecht: Prisma Boeken, Speculum Series.

———. 1650. "The Monsters of Our Age." In *O Zoete Vrijheid! Vondel Als Strijder voor Vrijheid en Vrede,* ed. L. Rens, 97, 98. Leiden: A. W. Sijthoff, 1969.

Van der Heijden, M. C. A., ed. 1967a. *De Ziel van den Poëet Vertoont Zich in Zijn Dichten: Lyriek van Vier Amsterdamse Dichters uit de 17e Eeuw.* Utrecht: Speculum.

———, ed. 1967b. "G. A. Bredero: *Boeren Geselschap* in *Lied-Boeck.*" In *De Ziel van den Poëet Vertoont Zich in Zijn Dichten: Lyriek van Vier Amsterdamse Dichters uit de 17e Eeuw,* 13–15. Utrecht: Speculum.

———, ed. 1968a. *Het Profijtelijk Vermaak: Moralitiet en Satire uit de 16e en 17e Eeuw.* Utrecht: Speculum.

———, ed. 1968b. "Roemer Visscher, Het Derde Schock van de Sinnepoppen." In *Het Profijtelijk Vermaak: Moralitiet en Satire uit de 16e en 17e Eeuw,* 83–176. Utrecht: Speculum [Original published 1614 by Willem Janse Blaeu, Amsterdam].

———, ed. 1970a. *Die Tyrannie Verdrijven: Godsdienst-en Onafhaakelijkheidsstrijd in de 16e en 17e Eeuw.* Utrecht: Prisma-Boeken, Speculum Series.

———, ed. 1970b. "Introduction," and [Anon] " '*De Waerschowinghe*' van Willem van Oranje." [Original: *Waerschouwinghe des Princen van Oraengien aan de Ingheseten ende Ondersaten van den Nederlanden . . .* Pamphlet: September 1568.] In *Die Tyrannie Verdrijven: Godsdienst-en Onafhaakelijkheidsstrijd in de 16e en 17e Eeuw,* 29–33, 35–53. Utrecht: Prisma-Boeken; Speculum Series.

———, ed. 1970c. "Jacob Revius en de Strijd Tegen Spanje." In *Die Tyrannie Verdrijven: Godsdienst-en Onafhaakelijkheidsstrijd in de 16e en 17e Eeuw,* 127–59. Utrecht: Prisma-Boeken, Speculum Series.

———. 1970d. "Joost van den Vondel en de 80 Jarige Oorlog." In *Die Tyrannie Verdrijven: Godsdienst-en Onafhaakelijkheidsstrijd in de 16e en 17e Eeuw,* 253–58. Utrecht: Prisma Boeken, Speculum Series.

———, ed. 1970e. "Nederlandsche Historien van P. C. Hooft." In *Die Tyrannie Verdrijven: Godsdienst-en Onafhaakelijkheidsstrijd in de 16e en 17e Eeuw,* 179–83. Utrecht: Prisma-Boeken, Speculum Series.

———, ed. 1971a. "Journael ofte Gedenckwaerdige Beschrijvinghe van de Oost-Indische Reyse van Willem Ysbrantsz Bontekoe van Hoorn. Begrijpende veel Wonderijcke en Gevaerlijcke Saecken Hem Daer Wedervaren. Begonnen Den 18 December, 1618 en Vol-eynt Den 16 November, 1625." In *Wonderlijk Geschiedenissen: Enkele Proze-geschriften uit de 17e Eeuw*, 73–207. Utrecht: Prisma Boeken, Spectrum Series.

———, ed. 1971b. "Berckhout, I. B. 1625. 'Sonnet op de Beschrijvinghe van de Gedenck-weerdighe Oost-Indische Reyse van den Vermaerden Schipper Willem Ysbrantsz Bontekoe' in Journael ofte Gedenckwaerdige Beschrijvinghe van de Oost-Indische Reyse van Willem Bontekoe van Hoorn . . . 1625." In *Wonderlijke Geschiedenissen: Enkele Prozegeschriften uit de 17e Eeuw*, 70. Utrecht: Prisma-Boeken, Speculum Series.

———, ed. 1972a. *Al Ziet Men de Lui . . . : Blijspel uit de 16e en de 17e Eeuw*. Utrecht: Prisma-Boeken, Speculum Series.

———, ed. 1972b. "G. A. Bredero's Spaanschen Brabander Jerolimo." In *Al Ziet Men de Lui . . . : Blijspel uit de 16e en de 17e Eeuw*, 91–256. Utrecht: Prisma-Boeken, Spectrum.

Van der Woude, Johan. 1948. *Coen, Koopman van Heeren Zeventien: Geschiedenis van den Hollandschen Handel in Indië (1598–1614)*. Amsterdam: C. de Boer, Jr.

Van der Zee, Henri, and Barbara Van der Zee. 1978. *A Sweet and Alien Land: The Story of Dutch New York*. New York: Viking.

Van Deursen, A. Th. 1978, 1979. *Het Kopergeld van de Gouden Eeuw*, 1–3. Assen: Van Gorcum.

Van Dillen, J. G. 1982. "The West India Company, Calvinism and Politics." In *Dutch Authors on West Indian History: A Historiographical Selection*, ed. Maria Antoinette Petronilla Meilink-Roelofsz, trans. Maria J. L. Yperen, 146–80. The Hague: Martinus Nijhoff.

Van Gelderen, Martin. 1992. *The Political Thought of the Dutch Revolt, 1555–1590*. Cambridge: Cambridge University Press.

Van Hoboken, W. J. 1982a. "The Dutch West India Company: The Political Background of Its Rise and Decline." In *Dutch Authors on West Indian History: A Historiographical Selection*, ed. Maria Antoinette Petronilla Meilink-Roelofsz, trans. Maria J. L. van Yperen, 129–45. The Hague: Martinus Nijhoff.

———. 1982b. "The West India Company and the Peace of Münster." In *Dutch Authors on West Indian History: A Historiographical Selection*, ed. Maria Antoinette Petronilla Meilink-Roelofsz, trans. Maria J. L. Yperen, 192–202. The Hague: Martinus Nijhoff.

Van Klaveren, J. J. 1953. *The Dutch Colonial System in the East Indies*. The Hague: Martinus Nijhoff.

Van Laer, Arnold J. F., ed. 1908. *The Van-Rensselaer-Bowier Manuscripts, Being the Letters of Kiliaen van Rensselaer, 1630–1643, and Other Documents Relating to the Colony of Rensselaerswyck*. Albany: State University of New York.

———, ed. 1918. *Early Records of the City and County of Albany and Colony of Rensselaerswyck*. Vol. 3, *Notarial Papers 1 and 2, 1660–1696*, trans Jonathan Pearson. Albany: State University of New York.

———, ed. 1924. *Documents Relating to New Netherland, 1624–1626 in The Henry E. Huntington Library*. San Marino: Henry E. Huntington Library and Art Gallery.

———. 1928. *Minutes of the Court of Albany, Rensselaerswyck and Schenectady, 1675–1680*. Albany: State University of New York.

———. 1932. *Correspondence of Jeremias van Rensselaer, 1651–1674*. Albany: State University of New York.

Van Loo, Ivo. 1997. "For Freedom and Fortune: The Rise of Dutch Privateering in the First Half of the Dutch Revolt, 1568–1609." In *Exercise of Arms: Warfare in the Netherlands, 1568–1648*, ed. Marco van der Hoeven, 173–95. Leiden: Brill.

Van Overeem, J. B. 1982. "The Westward Voyages of Cornelis Cornelisz. Jol, alias Captain Houtebeen, 1626–1640." In *Dutch Authors on West Indian History: A Historiographical Selection,* ed. M. A. P. Meilink-Roelofsz, trans. Maria J. L. van Yperen, 204–37. The Hague: Martinus Nijhoff.

Van Rijnback, A. A., ed. 1971. *Groot Lied-Boek van G. A. Brederode, naar de oorspronkelijke uitgave van 1622.* Rotterdam: Ad. Donker Reprint, 1971.

Van Strien, Kees. 1998. *Touring the Low Countries: Accounts of British Travellers, 1660–1720.* Amsterdam: Amsterdam University Press.

Van Troostenburg de Bruyn, C. A. L. 1884. *De Hervormde Kerk in Nederlandsch Oost-Indië onder de Oost-Indische Compagnie (1602–1795).* Arnhem: H. A. Tjeenk Willink.

Van Zanden, J. L. 1988. "De landbouw op de zandgronded van Oost-Nederland." *Tijdschrift voor Geschiedenis* 101: 190–205.

Vaughan, Alden T. 1992. "People of Wonder: England Encounters the New World's Natives." In *New World of Wonders: European Images of the Americas, 1492–1700,* ed. Rachel Doggett with Monique Hulvey and Julie Ainsworth, 11–23. Washington, D.C.: Folger Shakespeare Library.

Verlinden, Charles. 1996. "Spices or Empire in Africa, Asia and Brazil." In *Maritime History.* Vol. 1: *The Age of Discovery,* ed. John B. Hattendorf, 85–98. Malabar, Fla.: Krieger.

Vincent, Philip. 1637. *A True Relation of the Late Battell Fought in New England, between the English and the Salvages (London, 1637).* A Walter J. Johnson 1974 facsimile reprint, Theatrum Orbis Terrarum. Norwood, N.J. [Original: *A True Relation of the Late Battell fought in New England, between the English, and the Salvages: With the Present State of Things There. London: Printed by M. P. for Nathanael Butter and John Bellamie, 1637.*]

Vincent, R. J. 1990. "Grotius, Human Rights, and Intervention." In *Hugo Grotius and International Relations,* ed. Hedley Bull, Benedict Kingsbury, and Adam Roberts, 241–56. Oxford: Clarendon.

Von Saher, Herbert. 1986. *Emanuel Rodenburg, of wat er op het eiland Bali geschiedde toen de eerste Nederlanders daar in 1597 voet ann wal setten.* Zutphen: De Walburg Pers.

Weise, Arthur James. 1884. *The History of the City of Albany, New York, from the Discovery of the Great River in 1524, by Verrazzano to the Present Time.* Albany: E. H. Bender.

Werbner, Pnina. 1995. "The Politics of Literary Postcoloniality." *Race and Class* 36: 1–20.

Wertheim, Arthur Frank. n.d. *Nederlandse Cultuurinvloeden in Indonesië.* Amsterdam: Ploegsma.

Weslager, C. A. 1967. *The English on the Delaware, 1610–1682.* New Brunswick, N.J.: Rutgers University Press.

Wesseling, H. L. 1978. "Expansion and Reaction: Some Reflections on a Symposium and a Theme." In *Expansion and Reaction: Essays on European Expansion and Reactions in Asia and Africa,* ed. H. L. Wesseling, 1–14. Leiden: Leiden University Press.

Westermann, Mariët. 1996. *A Worldly Art: The Dutch Republic, 1585–1718.* New York: Perspectives/Abrams.

Westra, Frans. 1998. "Lost and Found: Crijn Fredericx—A New York Founder." *De halve maen* 71: 7–16.

Whittaker, C. R. 1994. *Frontiers of the Roman Empire: A Social and Economic Study.* Baltimore: Johns Hopkins University Press.

Wieder, F. C. 1925. *De Stichting van New York in Juli, 1625. Reconstructies en Nieuwe*

Gegevens Ontleend aan de van Rappard Documenten. 's-Gravenhage: Martinus Nijhoff.

Wilson, Charles, and Geoffrey Parker, eds. 1977. *An Introduction to the Sources of European Economic History, 1500–1800.* Vol. 1: *Western Europe.* London: Weidenfeld and Nicholson.

Winius, George, and Marcus P. M. Vink. 1991. *The Merchant-Warrior Pacified: The VOC (The Dutch East India Company) and Its Changing Political Economy in India.* Delhi: Oxford University Press.

Winius, George. 1996. "The Maritime 'Empire' of Portugal Strikes Root in Asia." In *Maritime History.* Vol. 1: *The Age of Discovery,* ed. John B. Hattendorf, 111–20. Malabar, Fla.: Krieger.

Zandvliet, Kees. 1988. "Golden Opportunities in Geopolitics: Cartography and the Dutch East India Company during the Lifetime of Abel Tasman." In *Terra Australis: The Furthest Shore,* ed. William Eisler and Bernard Smith, 67–82. Sydney: International Cultural Corporation of Australia.

Zwitzer, H. L. 1997. "The Eighty Years War." In *Exercise of Arms: Warfare in the Netherlands, 1568–1648,* ed. Marco der Hoeven, 33–55. Leiden: Brill.

Index

Page numbers in italics indicate an illustration.

Acknowledgments

Acknowledgments are one of the pleasurable protocols of publishing. The paragraphs celebrate how truly collaborative an effort a book is. They document the writer's reflective conversation with the written and voiced reflections of other scholars. They record the years that are a reading and postreading time when colleagues, critics, and the imagined audience for whom she is trying to faithfully reconstruct a moment in the past give the author greater clarity on her writing.

I owe special thanks to scholars in New York and Australia. I am grateful to Karen Kupperman, Dan Richter, David Voorhees, and Pat Bonimi for the high standards of scholarship to which their work has always urged me to aspire, and I thank Karen and Lauren Benton for the pleasure of speaking in 2004 at the Atlantic History Seminar at New York University. Charles Gehring and other scholars at the New Netherland Project uphold the same standards of excellence, and I am, as I have been for years, in their debt. Though not miners of New York's archives, John Gillis, Eric Hinderaker, Stan Katz, Stan Kutler, Ken Lockridge, and Michael Zuckerman have made me think about writing history, especially its ethical demands. Scholars in Honolulu, especially young men and women such as Katarina Teaiwa and J. Kehaulani Kauanui, have shared with me their excitement of writing (performing!) history creatively.

My debts in Australia travel outward from Canberra, north to Sydney, and south to Melbourne. My many years as a visiting fellow in the Humanities Research Centre and the Centre for Cross-Cultural Research at the Australian National University in Canberra have enlarged my notions about ways of interpreting the past. Seminars, conferences, colloquia, workshops, and conversations there inspired and gave shape to *The Shame and the Sorrow*. Participation in Greg Dening's annual Visiting Scholars Programme, Challenges to Perform: The Creative Imagination in the Production of Knowledge, allowed me, over the years, to learn from more than two hundred graduate students. As students will do, intellectually they changed my life. I gained confidence in the present work from Ros Dalziel, Penny Edwards, Debjani Ganguly, Mino Hokari, Sylvia Kleinert, Iain McCalman, and Judith and David MacDougall. Debbie Bird, Bill Gammage, Tom Griffiths, Howard Morphy, Peter Reid, Rebe Taylor, and Nicholas Thomas are among the many historians and anthropologists unraveling cross-cultural encounters in early Australia, and I have gained immensely from their insights. Thinking about history invariably reached special levels of meaning when sharing ideas with my dear friend Dipesh Chakrabarty. I am grateful to the librarians at the Australian National Library and the archivists of the East India Company records at the Australian National University libraries. They gave me every assistance.

At the University of Sydney, Shane White was always ready for a conversation about early New York. Ross Gibson encouraged me, as he does his students at the University of Technology, Sydney, to be adventurous and to love the words that are our poetic tools as writers. In Melbourne, I owe debts to colleagues at the University of Melbourne, where I am a senior fellow, and at Latrobe University, where I have offered workshops touching on writing cross-cultural history. I cannot adequately express my thanks to, among others, Bill Breen, John Cashmere, Inga Clendinnen, Joy Damousi, Rhys Isaac, John Salmond, and Charles Zika.

I am grateful for the professionalism and friendship of Peter Agree, social sciences editor at the University of Pennsylvania Press. He strove for a book that would be properly researched and presented but also one that would take a step forward in the journey that history writing is always undertaking. Collaborating with him and Dan Richter, editor of the Early American Studies series for the press and the McNeil Center, has been a very great pleasure. Erica Ginsburg, associate managing editor, handled the manuscript of this book with patience, skill, and generosity. To Emily Brissenden, who constructed the maps and to the European and American curators and librarians who provided illustrations, my thanks also.

I could not be a writer, I could not want to be a writer, without the inspiration and love of my husband, Greg Dening.